CHINA: AN ANTHROPOLOGICAL PERSPECTIVE

Political units (30)

Peking*
Tientsin*
Hopeh†
Shansi†
Inner Mongolia‡

Liaoning†
Kirin†
Heilungkiang†
Shanghai*
Shantung†

Kiangsu†
Chekiang†
Anhwei†
Kiangsi†
Fukien†

Taiwan†
Shensi†
Ningsia‡
Kansu†
Tsinghai†

Sinkiang‡
Honan†
Hupeh†
Hunan†
Kwangtung†

Kwangsi‡
Szechwan†
Kweichow†
Yunnan†
Tibet‡

Total

30 =
*Cities (3). = Municipalities
†Provinces (22).
‡Autonomous Regions (5).
SOURCE: Data from *World Atlas* published by China Cartographic Institute, Peking. December 1971.

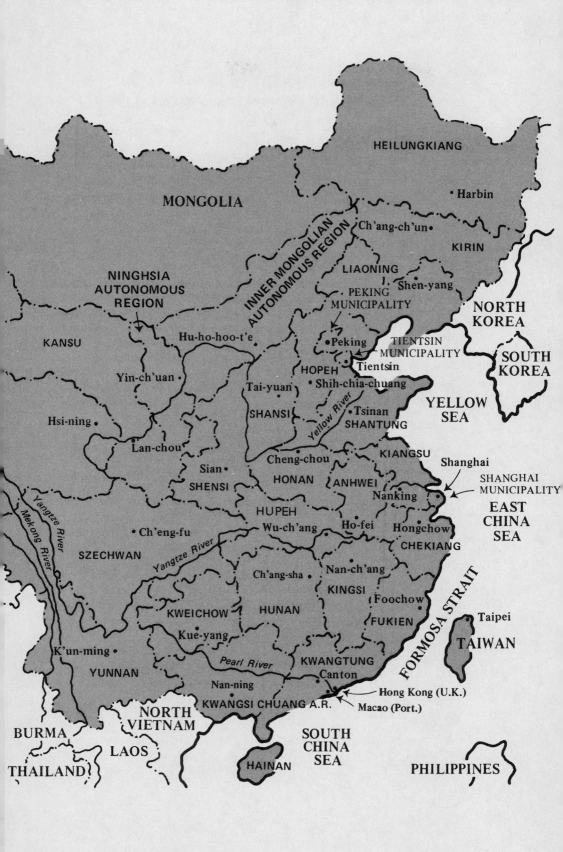

GOODYEAR REGIONAL ANTHROPOLOGY SERIES

Edward Norbeck, Editor

ANTHROPOLOGICAL PERSPECTIVES OF:

MODERN EUROPE
Robert T. Anderson

INDIA
Stephen A. Tyler

INDONESIA
James L. Peacock

CIRCUMPOLAR PEOPLES
Nelson H. Graburn and Barry S. Strong

NORTH AMERICAN INDIANS
William W. Newcomb, Jr.

MAINLAND SOUTHEAST ASIA
Ronald Provencher

CHINA
Leon E. Stover and Takeko Kawai Stover

Forthcoming:

Middle East

CHINA: AN ANTHROPOLOGICAL PERSPECTIVE

LEON E. STOVER
Illinois Institute of Technology

TAKEKO KAWAI STOVER
Roosevelt University

GOODYEAR PUBLISHING COMPANY, INC.
Pacific Palisades, California

to
NORMAN JACOBS

exemplar
of
detached observation
and
theoretical elegance

Library of Congress Cataloging in Publication Data

Stover, Leon E
    China: an anthropological perspective.

    (Goodyear regional anthropology series)
    Bibliography: p.
    1. China—Civilization.   I.   Stover, Takeko Kawai,
joint author.   II.   Title.
DS721.S778   951   75-7154
ISBN 0–87620–152–4
ISBN 0–87620–153–2 pbk.

Library of Congress Catalog Card Number: 75–7154

Current printing (last digit):
10 9 8 7 6 5 4 3 2 1

ISBN: 0–87620–153–2 (Paper)
          0–87620–152–4 (Cloth)

Y–1532–4 (P)
Y–1524–1 (C)

Production Editor: Janice Gallagher
Maps by: A. Marshall Licht

Printed in the United States of Ameria

CONTENTS

PART 2   INSTITUTIONAL DEVELOPMENT

ACKNOWLEDGMENTS

The authors thank the following publishers and copyright holders for permission to excerpt and reprint selections used in this book:

Leon E. Stover, "China—Last of the Agrarian States," *Technology and Human Affairs* 6, 1 (Spring 1974): 10–13. Reprinted with the permission of IIT Technology and Human Affairs, Illinois Institute of Technology.

Leon E. Stover, *The Cultural Ecology of Chinese Civilization: Peasants and Elites in the Last of the Agrarian States* (New York: Pica Press, 1974), pp. 69, 145 (maps). Reproduced with the permission of Universe Books.

George H. Cressy, "The Geographic Regions of China," *The Annals of the American Academy of Political and Social Science* 152 (1930): 3. Reprinted with the permission of the publisher.

R. M. MacIver, *The Modern State* (London: Oxford University Press, 1926), p. 344. Reprinted with the permission of the publisher.

George M. Foster, *Traditional Cultures and the Impact of Technological Change* (New York: Harper & Row, 1962), pp. 50, 53. Reprinted with the permission of the publisher.

Paul M. A. Linebarger, *The China of Chiang K'ai-Shek: A Political Study* (Boston: World Peace Foundation, 1943), p. 104. Reprinted with the permission of the World Peace Foundation, Boston; and Greenwood Press, Westport, Connecticut.

William Liu, "Chinese Society: Stratification, Minorities, and the Family," in Wu Yuan-li, ed., *China: A Handbook* (New York: Praeger Publishers, 1973), p. 672. Reprinted with the permission of Praeger Publishers, New York; and David & Charles, Ltd., England.

T. S. Eliot, *The Love Song of J. Alfred Prufrock: Collected Poems 1909–1962* (New York: Harcourt Brace Jovanovich, 1930), p. 12. Reprinted with the permission of Harcourt Brace Jovanovich, New York; and Faber & Faber, Ltd., London.

Hsiao-t'ung Fei, "Peasantry and Gentry: An Interpretation of Chinese Social Structure and its Changes," *The American Journal of Sociology* 52, 1 (1947): 7. Reprinted with the permission of the University of Chicago Press. Copyright 1947 by the University of Chicago Press.

C. Northcote Parkinson, *Parkinson's Law and Other Studies in Administration* (Boston: Houghton Mifflin, 1957), pp. 93–94. Reprinted with the permission of the publisher.

In addition, the authors thank William K. Carr for permission to quote from pages 24 and 28 of his unpublished manuscript, *Introducing Metalinguistic Instructional Material into Language and Area Study Programs*.

PREFACE

In our attempt to explain the rise of Chinese civilization and its modern transformation, we have not confined ourselves to the anthropology of folk culture. We have drawn also upon the sinology of high culture, unifying material from both fields in an effort to portray changes in the interaction between "little tradition" and "great tradition." These are the two cultural subsystems of peasantry and elite, named by Robert Redfield, whose working relationship contains the dynamics of the old agrarian state.

The introduction sets forth an overview of how this relationship evolved in China and how it is being transformed by the dynamics of modernization. China is the last of the agrarian states to survive into the twentieth century with its great and little traditions intact. The others have long since merged their aboriginal lines of evolution with the oekumene of world civilization under Western influence.

Part 1 treats the culture history of China with reference to the increasing size of the political unit and its emergent levels of organization. The chapter on prehistory establishes the formation of the folk village, the fundamental subunit that persisted to underpin all subsequent levels of political organization, from city-state, to territorial state, to empire. Other chapters show how the city-state and the territorial state also persisted in the form of subunits under empire, reclassified as counties and provinces. The political geography of empire, however, did not suddenly come to an end with the fall of the monarchy in 1911; a modernized spatial arrangement of powers is still in the making. Nor did the cultural arrangement between great and little tradition come to an end when its legal basis in the imperial code was abolished; the laws upholding differences of social class between elite and majority did not carry over from the terminal dynasty to the Republic of China (ROC), but the social values behind these differences did; and in a concealed way they continue to inform new methods of political control instituted by the People's Republic of China (PRC).

Part 2 treats the cultural continuities and discontinuities that mark the emergence of postimperial China, from the transitional period of the ROC to the advent of the PRC. Every chapter conforms to the same plan for each of seven institutional spheres: ecology, economy, politics, kinship, stratification, religion, and world view. Each institutional sphere is covered in the same sequence for (1) traditional high culture, (2) transitional folk culture, and (3) modern national culture.

The appendix is attached as a reminder that the first broad anthropological perspective on China was drawn in a museum collection gathered by the American lawyer and amateur ethnologist, Caleb Cushing, who first opened China to the diplomatic regulation of trade in 1844. The bibliography consists of works cited. Translations are our own except when credited. We strongly recommend that this text be read with maps at hand. *

The conceptual content and organization of this book were first tried out in 1958 at the start of our participation in the fifth semester of the Western Society sequence at Hobart and William Smith Colleges in Geneva, New York. We added China to a required series of courses in the history of Western civilization on the grounds that it offered a pattern contrast with the study of American society taken up in the sixth and final semester. We still think our approach contributes as much to thinking about China as it does to model making about civilizations in general, especially in contrasting modern with traditional ones.

In 1963, the senior author was invited at the suggestion of Taryō Ōbayashi to teach the course to undergraduates in the Department of Cultural Anthropology at Tokyo University. I did so under the founder and chairman of that department, Eiichiro Ishida. Upon Professor Ishida's retirement in 1964, his successor, Seiichi Izumi, asked me to stay on for another year, this time to adapt the course for the graduate school, the first time any non-Japanese ever taught there. He asked again in 1965, when I had to decline in order to take up my present position at Illinois Institute of Technology.

A tradebook version of my Tokyo University lectures, *The Cultural Ecology of Chinese Civilization* (Stover, 1974a), appeared some years later, but unhappily my delay outlasted the lives of the two chairmen who made the lectures possible.

The present work is by no means a textbook translation of the tradebook, but an extension and refinement of its leading ideas, especially as these have been filtered through the profound theoretical insights of Norman Jacobs, professor of sociology and Asian studies at the University of Illinois, Urbana. In concord with my wife and coauthor, Takeko Kawai Stover, this text is dedicated to Norman in appreciation of his highly original books and for his support and friendship.

Finally, we insist on thanking Edward Norbeck, editor of the Goodyear Regional Anthropology Series, for inviting us to write the book; David Grady for publishing it; and Janice Gallagher and Victoria Pasternack for their generous editorial improvements.

* For example, see Albert Herrmann, *An Historical Atlas of China*, new edition, 1966. Chicago: Aldine.

INTRODUCTION

The agrarian state is a type of civilization whose political center and high culture grew out of prehistoric roots. It is the oldest political state in history and the most archaic form of civilization known to archaeology. Archaic civilizations were not derived from, or affiliated with, other civilizations. They evolved from their own primitive agricultural beginnings, the Neolithic village cultures that preceded the rise of high culture and urban power centers, which continued to sustain high culture. As a result, the professional thinkers of these civilizations have always been preoccupied with the question of origins; they never gave thought to the future or to the problems of change and development. The task of high culture has been to rationalize the continuity between political power and its Neolithic foundations.

The Chinese agrarian state was the last of seven archaic civilizations: the Incan, Mayan, and Aztecan in the New World, and the Mesopotamian, Egyptian, Harappan, and Chinese in the Old World. All are dead civilizations. The pattern of Incan culture died under Spanish colonialism. The native order in Egypt declined with Hellenization of royalty and was decisively buried under the weight of Islamization. Although the fellah may be seen at his well sweep as he was three thousand years ago, Pharaonic Egypt was as dead at the time of the Arab conquest as it is today under Sadat. No one worships Osiris, no one can read hieroglyphics, no one mummifies the dead, no one is Pharaoh. Confucian China alone among the archaic civilizations survived into the twentieth century, after four millennia of indigenous history. The monarchy lasted until the revolution of 1911. After that, there were no more emperors.

In China today, people still eat steamed rice with chopsticks, a gastronomic custom dating back to the beginnings of Neolithic village culture in 5000 B.C. Chinese still read ideographs, a form of writing that originated with the rise of Bronze Age civilization in 1700 B.C. Traits such as these persist from long ago, but the old configuration of the agrarian state that once embraced them has indeed vanished. Under communism, in power since 1950, the government reaches into village life to exercise unprecedented controls over production, values, and beliefs. The downward flow of directives and propaganda from the ruling authorities in Peking has created a participant society mobilized to achieve profound developmental goals.

In the old days, only a tiny literate elite were politically active; the great masses of Neolithic peasant-producers who fed them were politically passive. The rulers of the great tradition were not sustained by peasant votes. The subjects of the little tradition, whose history originated in prehistoric villages, had simply been absorbed into civilization as its workhorses; they were regarded as an economic resource, not a political one.

China's Neolithic heritage is similar to the cultural heritage of all the village peoples of East Asia, Southeast Asia, South Asia, Africa, Latin America, and even backward parts of Europe. Some of these Neolithic villages exist today in isolation (for example, the tribal folk of the Amazon Basin or in the interior of New Guinea), others exist as part of a civilization (for example, the peasant folk of India).

The Neolithic village began as an alternative to the food-gathering, nomadic hunting economy that had sustained man for ninety-nine percent of human history. Shortly after the end of the Ice Age, about eight thousand years ago, people in West Asia learned to dwell in nucleated settlements within walking distance of their fields, and to pass their entire lives in a common effort to control the equally domesticated lives of their plants and animals. This was the food-producing revolution—the Neolithic revolution. By far the majority of the world's population still lives in a Neolithic state of culture.

America and Russia are the only great nations to have seriously upset the Neolithic way of life with large-scale, industrialized agriculture. The European migrants who settled North America found only nomadic hunting tribes in the wheat belt, easy to disperse. However, to imitate American machine agriculture, the Russians had first to destroy a Neolithic settlement pattern and remove its remaining inhabitants to collectivized tractor farms. The fundamental issue to be decided between the two nations in their competition for world resources is, Into whose orbit will the vast, remaining Neolithic peoples be drawn for conversion into industrial manpower? As Carleton Coon writes in his masterpiece of general anthropology, *The Story of Man:*

> *Although the Neolithic began three thousand years before writing, and five-and-a-half thousand years before the birth of Herodotus, the "father of history," Neolithic culture is much more than a subject of inquiry by prehistorians. Moving out of it may be the world's most difficult problem. (Coon, 1971:123)*

Alongside Russian and American competition to raise the developmental level of the Third World (in the interest of expanding their own workshops) is the Chinese bid to organize it politically at nearly the same level as now exists, without a great increment of new technology. From the Chinese point of view, the two great superpowers are overdeveloped, having deviated from the proper course of history, which is to return with sophistication to the Neolithic level of "classless primitive communes." In a land farmed with progressive intensification for forty centuries, accompanied by increased growth of population, which will reach one billion by 1980, the Chinese leadership is acutely aware of the finite limits of the environment. They perhaps rightly calculate that the entire world cannot afford to go the way of American capitalism or Russian state capitalism. What if all nations were to exert stress on the natural habitat with the force that these two industrial strategies do? The deposition of China's head of state, President Liu Shao-ch'i, followed a policy conflict with Party Chairman Mao Tse-tung over the increased human and industrial pollution that would result from economic growth and social modernization facilitated by Russian expertise. Mao realistically forbad the comprehensive industrial utilization of resources on the grounds that its progressive "glamour" would create more "garbage" than the already highly stressed land and rivers could endure, for human safety (Orleans and Suttmeir, 1970).

Nonetheless, the sophisticated development of Neolithic resources in China calls for more government on the part of the ruling elite and more political participation on the part of the majority. In traditional China, peasant folk were merely exploited, never administered. A tiny ruling class simply lived off the low surplus of a vast and inefficient Neolithic agriculture. The one-way movement of taxes and rents from the countryside to the town was paralleled by the movement of intellectual raw materials: Men of the great tradition did their job of cultural rationalization with folk materials derived from the little tradition. For example, the literati could write whole books about the myth of the kitchen god on the basis of unformulated peasant taboos and observances.

In Communist China, by contrast, the rulers reach into the countryside for more than ideas and taxes; they intervene for the sake of political organization and economic development. The modern state agitates and propagandizes. It trains people for literacy, by which medium (among others) it instructs them whom to hate, what to cheer, and why they must work hard. Under the lofty paternalism of the emperors it was said, "Heaven is high and the emperor is far away." Under communist rule, the people are asked to participate in national goals, to "work productively under Chairman Mao to make China a rich and strong socialist country." Confucius said of dynastic government that "The people are called to follow government policy but they are not required to understand it" (Lun Yu, VIII:9). Under communist rule, the people are required to understand government policy. This is a new and difficult task of government, since village folk were traditionally excluded from political communications of any kind. Messages about the justification for power, the ethics of ruling, and the theories of society and history circulated only among the ruling elite.

Today, production goals set by the ruling authorities in Peking are meant to be understood by everybody, not only by agents of the state. There is no paradox in Mao's claim that communism is more Chinese than Confucianism. Even though communism is an imported doctrine, news of its advocacy by the government is the main subject of propaganda, whereas the "famous teachings" of Confucius were made famous only among the ruling class.

Chinese civilization originated from a single line of development out of its Neolithic past; but its isolation has come to an end now that multiple influences impinge on its development. The aboriginal civilization carried forward, elaborated, and developed the cultural materials of its own folk base. A growing urbanism converted elements of folk culture into civilization. Traditional cities were centers of absorbed change, taking from the countryside the cultural raw materials needed by the literati to shape high culture. The cities of culture-contacted, modern China have become centers of imposed change; the backward-looking literati have become forward-looking intellectuals, directing change against the native folk culture on the grounds that it was diseased, on the basis of Western concepts of poverty, overpopulation and underproduction. The new intelligentsia's acceptance of foreign ideas about nation-building broke the bonds of common understanding once held between peasant folk and gentlemen of high culture on the basis of historical continuity. Cities now reverse the flow of cultural influence by imposing change on a rural society that before had been insulated from direct controls. So long as village society rendered its quota of revenue and labor, it remained free (at a subadministrative level) to pursue its own self-policing Neolithic round of life.

Today, control over folk culture takes place on three levels of formal organization that previously existed as informal ones. At the highest level is the commune, an administrative unit corresponding to the marketing community, the maximal unit of traditional community culture, which was an area of about eighteen or twenty villages centered on the market town. The production brigade is the modern counterpart of the minimal unit of traditional community culture, the village. Routine daily work is carried out by the production team, which corresponds to a neighborhood within the village of some twenty or thirty households, or to a hamlet of the same size.

The real social unit of agricultural labor is no longer the family but the production team. Family life among the Neolithic peasantry—now converted into a landless, rural proletariat—has been reduced to cost-accounting work-points earned by the household and to rearing children. Much of the time husband and wife share is occupied in service with a militarized group that works land collectivized on a village-wide basis. Inasmuch as collectivization, coupled with the primitive technology of Neolithic hand-gardening methods, must be a substitute for mechanization, the purpose of team organization cannot be to raise agricultural productivity. Rather, it is a governmental instrument of mobilization, a way of organizing people for doing other tasks during the traditional slack season. Commune controls also work to create forced savings for the benefit of the industrial sector, which amounts to a virtual defense economy. A defense industry is the one currency of nation-building that wins respect at home in the visible display of conventional arms, and abroad in the deployment of a sophisticated atomic arsenal and missile technology.

Chinese communist doctrine pictures the triumph of the People's Republic as the triumph of outraged peasants and workers who whistled themselves up like a hurricane and swept out the old order in their own interests. It is bootless to argue that the picture is false. The communist conquest was led from above, and its leaders, mostly elite persons of the republican regime, were moved by imported ideas of interclass struggle and national development. The myth of a self-transforming people, when propagated by mass communications, is itself an agency of change. The

Neolithic peasant, in the process of being manipulated, ceases to be a peasant. With the loss of his land, he has been made over into a rural proletarian. So endeth the Neolithic in the last of the agrarian states (Stover, 1974b).

Robert Redfield's method of dichotomizing the old agrarian states into great and little traditions* is useful in studying China, where a strict class analysis cannot bridge the subcultural differences between folk and elite (*see* Fried, 1952). They represent different parts of the same civilization, yet they are so dissimilar that a division of labor between sinology and anthropology has developed around them. But clearly, no anthropological perspective is complete if limited to village China alone.

After all, an ethnographic account of every one of the million villages of China would never add up to a picture of the civilization to which they belong. The measure of a civilization is not its common denominators as determined from a sample of its places. A village community is at once a place, where the behavioral norms of folk culture are located, and a unit of organization in the translocal aspects of civilization. S. M. Shirokogoroff (1939–40) criticized the village study of Kaihsienkung by his pupil, Fei Hsiao-t'ung, on the grounds that he had not referred his local data to an averaged-out abstraction, the "real" China. Shirokogoroff, a tribal ethnographer, expected the whole to be the sum of its parts, as in culture-area analysis. Culture-area analysis is not suitable for all problems dealing with the anthropology of Chinese civilization. If the village of Kaihsienkung is taken to be in addition a sample of the way localities belong to a higher-order unit of culture—village-and-city-and-national China—then the nature of the subunits also depends on the properties of the larger units they comprise.

To insist that the "real" China be explained as a sum-of-the-parts at the community level would hark back to anthropology's nostalgia for holistic simplicity. Thanks to Julian Steward (1950), the face-to-face orientation of community culture is no longer taken as the only valid archetype of culture. Under Steward's influence, even Redfield came to modify his general theory of folk society, which at first embraced tribal folk and peasant folk indifferently (Redfield, 1947; 1955b). He came to see, with Steward, that the isolated context of peasant folk make for a part-culture; because peasants are part of a civilization, they are not only the *subject* of their own folk culture at the community level, as are tribal peoples, but are also the *object* of integration at the national level (Redfield, 1955a; 1956).

Civilizations that contain peasant villages as subunits differ in integration from those that do not. This fact was not apparent at first to Western envoys, who hailed from political entities called "states" endowed with "sovereignty." Occidentals naturally read into the Chinese hierarchy of titled officials evidence of the same kind of highly organized state system. China looked like a sovereign nation-state but really was not one. Under the emperors, no all-embracing, controlling institution actually ex-

*This method was Redfield's contribution to *Comparative Studies in Culture and Civilization*, edited by himself and Milton Singer for the University of Chicago. Sinologists wrote about the great tradition of China in volume one, entitled *Studies in Chinese Thought* (Wright, 1953), and anthropologists wrote about the little tradition of rural India in volume six, entitled *Village India* (Marriott, 1955).

6   isted; the Chinese state turned out to be a "pseudomorph" (Linebarger, 1938:21). The problem of the communist revolution in China has been to convert the pseudomorph into the real thing.

What looked like a state (the Chinese bureaucratic apparatus) was merely the organized tip of an unorganized mass—the total body of gentlemen sharing the culture of the great tradition in all their home localities. In a realm founded on a Neolithic base, it was sufficient for the elite to rule formally in the bureaucracy or informally at home simply by holding themselves apart as literate carriers of an authoritative culture, *wen-hwa*, over and above commoners disadvantaged by *wen-man*, literary blindness. The men of the great tradition thereby viewed themselves as the exclusive embodiments of civilization, supported by so many energy slaves lacking culture altogether. The Chinese pseudomorph was therefore no nation-state exercising its sovereignty through the administration of civil law; its apparent shape derived from something less substantial: the translocal morality of high culture. The rule by an elite of the great tradition, with its monopoly on ideas about government, over the majority of the little tradition we call "culturalism."

Culture in the vocabulary of anthropology is a democratic extension of a word that has its counterpart in the Chinese word *wen-hwa*, in its original elitist meaning. The anthropological concept, first advanced more than a hundred years ago by Edward Tylor in his famous definition (1874:1), has now found its way into common usage, as recorded by *The American Heritage Dictionary:* "The totality of socially transmitted behavior patterns, arts, beliefs, institutions, and all other products of human work and thought characteristic of a community or population." This usage, pioneered by the social sciences, meets the current demand in liberal philosophy to find common ground between men in one society and another, or between social classes and ethnic groups within complex societies. Culture is thus anything the egalitarians want it to be. For Chinese of illiberal education in the Confucian classics, culture is, by definition, lacking among persons uneducated for government, formal or informal.

Culturalism, then, is our term reflecting the Chinese spirit of government as the arbitration by the literati, informed by Confucian ideology, of a status system divided between cultured and uncultured persons. The power of a cultured elite to exploit Neolithic peasants is said to derive from a moral superiority that pays its way by setting an example of right conduct rather than by providing administrative services. In reality, village folk take care of themselves without policing. To say they are guided by moral influence from above is a conceit the ruling class is able to express because the subadministrative regulation of the masses is a fact that does not contradict it. Culturalism names the largely self-governing power arrangement between elite and majority; its rationalization is the Confucian moral order.

The goals of culturalism were the only ones men of traditional high culture could accept as binding them in a single political community across the regional differences of a vast empire. If the Chinese pseudomorph ruled over territory of continental scope, it did so because its collective goals covered the ground insubstantially.

We may now restate the task of modern Chinese government by contrasting it with the culturalism of old. The task is to transform the pseudomorph into a sovereign entity capable of substantive administration. The problem of modernization is to remove the insulation that separated the little tradition from the great tradtion under the pseudomorphic state and to create a participant society joined with an authentic nation-state. In other words, the change from traditional to modern China can be described as the change from an orthogenetic state of culture to a heterogenetic one (Redfield and Singer, 1954). Chinese civilization originated as a single line of development (orthogenesis) out of its own Neolithic past, its isolation coming to an end with the press of multiple influences on its development (heterogenetic change), which occurred after its absorption into the world oekumene, thereby extending the unified range of man's civilization.

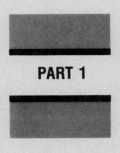

PART 1

CULTURE HISTORY

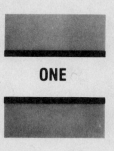

ONE

PREHISTORY

ORIGINS AND OUTCOME

In Figure 1, the anthropological approach to periodizing Chinese culture history (left-hand column) is set against the conventional breaks of written history and the horizons of prehistoric archaeology (right-hand column). The basis for our classification of culture eras is the political unit and the progressive enlargement of its boundaries, from tribal bands of food gatherers in the preagricultural era to the isolated folk societies of the first food producers in the era of Neolithic tribalism, through the eras of city-states and territorial states to the dynastic cycles of empire. Excepting the preagricultural era, the maximal political unit of each successive era incorporates the ones before it as subunits. The minimal subunit is the peasant village, derived from the Lung-shan culture of Neolithic tribalism. The city-state, the first supracommunal unit to subordinate the village, emerged as the district or county subunit under the territorial state or kingdom, which in turn emerged as the provincial subunit under empire. This pattern of emergent organization may be outlined as follows (the numbers refer to subunits in China proper during the terminal dynasty):

Empire (Ch'ing dynasty)
  18 provinces (territorial states)
    1,500 districts (city-states)
      1,000,000 nonisolated Neolithic villages

The persistence of earlier units in each newly emergent level of organization accounts for the nonadministrative qualities of the pseudomorphic Chinese state: each prior unit can more or less live without the later ones, but the reverse is not true. Peasants can do without emperors, governors, and district magistrates, but none of these can do without peasants. As Mencius says, "If there be no ruler, there is none to rule the peasant; if there be no peasant folk, there is none to feed the ruler" (*Meng Tze,* 3A:iii:14).

Theoretically, the village can revert to an isolated status in the absence of rulers, but the rulers cannot build state organization without villagers. In times of dynastic collapse or local rebellion, the top levels do in

Culture Eras	History and Archaeology	
——— Postimperial 1912 ———	——— ROC (to 1950); PRC* ———	
	Ch'ing	
	Ming	
[Mature Agrarian State]	Yuan	
		1279
	Second Partition	
Empire		907
(Cyclical Imperial Conquests)	T'ang	
	Sui	589
[Second Aristocracy]	First Partition	
		220
A.D.	Han	
B.C.	Ch'in	221
	Warring States	
Territorial States		Eastern Chou
770	Spring & Autumn 722	
(?) 1122	Western Chou	
City-States		
	Shang	Chou
(?) 1765		
	Lung-shan	
Neolithic Tribalism		
	Yang-shao	
c. 5000		
Preagricultural		

*ROC-Republic of China;
PRC-People's Republic of China.

FIGURE 1.   Chinese Culture History (to scale).

fact peel off like layers of onion skin, leaving the inner layers intact. If the monarchy falls, the provinces stand as kingdoms; if provincial government is inactive, local interests may invest the district and run its administrative city and supportive countryside like a city-state, and so on down to the marketing area and village level. As villages are not targets of administration but only of exploitation, they are more or less viable in the absence of government at any level of organization.

Contrast this with the genuine administrative integration of components making up the nation-state, in which nationwide governmental and private institutions of every sort penetrate the local level. There are towns and cities in the traditional Chinese pseudomorph, but no urbanization. That is, cities do not impress change on the countryside. In a nation-state such as the United States, in contrast, the rural places and small towns mirror national culture. The counterpart of federal government is local government, and the political parties have their local affiliations. Organized religion has its community churches. The labor union movement is expressed in union locals. The system of formal education is rooted in a nationwide distribution of public schools and upheld by federal guidelines on compulsory attendance. Hospitals and physicians follow minimum health measures set by the federal government. Citizens make a living by exchanging goods and services in a market system capitalized by a national web of banking services and protected by the legal defense of property rights at every level of justice within the court system—local, state, and federal—as guaranteed in the organic charter of nationhood. Finally, the financial rewards granted to the various occupations accord with popular beliefs about their value, from least to most respected, as conveyed by organs of public opinion that may reach national as well as regional and local audiences (*see* Steward, 1955: ch. 4).

No such institutional links between national and local culture as exist in the United States ever existed between the great and little traditions of China. Localities are so fully integrated within the body politic of the American nation-state that they can afford to highly specialize, including those sectors devoted to agriculture. One commercial farmer feeds fifty-one nonfood producers in the United States (a nation of 220 million) and still contributes to agricultural exports. In fact, of fifty-four million tons of wheat produced in the United States in 1973, thirty-two million tons were booked for export and only fourteen million allotted for domestic use, with the remaining eight million assigned for carry-over stock (Gardner, 1973:204–5). In China today, it still takes four to feed five in a nation of over 800 million, and additional grain is imported, in part from the United States.

Such is the ecological heritage of the Chinese past. With land acreage confined within fixed frontiers of arability, as limited by the Chinese technology of intensive cultivation, agricultural surplus has steadily declined with the growth of population. Over the centuries, the human crop has piled up faster than the food crop. The returns per man began falling long before the advent of the communist regime. It will take a large input of modern methods (such as chemical fertilizers) to make even the slightest gain in the returns per acre because traditional methods have pushed the output virtually to the limit. In the meantime, there is little labor to spare for industry because agriculture demands eighty percent of the labor force to keep itself fed; this is the basic problem any regime of whatever political complexion must face (see Chang, 1949).

Chinese intensive agriculture—hand gardening, horticulture—is the most productive method per unit of land ever devised in the Neolithic world, but in comparison with the high productivity per man-hour of capitalized agriculture, it is based on a make-work regimen barely able to support its own labor. In the end, Chinese farm labor became so redundant that its marginal productivity was reduced to practically zero. Sinologist Mark Elvin of Oxford refers to this outcome of Chinese culture history as "the high-level equilibrium trap in agriculture" (1973:313). It was long in the making.

The late Professor Ishida, founder of the Department of Cultural Anthropology at Tokyo University, insisted that "the lasting character of each people has its roots in the basic culture of the time when the people first came into being" (1964:279). He went so far as to specualte that perhaps the emphasis on cereal eating to the east of the Eurasian continent and on meat eating to the west could be traced to a geographical difference between graniferous and carnivorous populations of *Australopithecus*, the ape-like ancestors of man, known from late Pliocene to early Pleistocene times.

PREAGRICULTURAL ERA

Australopithecus is a transitional Lower Pleistocene form between the apelike *Ramapithecus* and the human genus *Homo*. Fossil remains of *Ramapithecus*, which date back to the Miocene/Pliocene boundary some fourteen million years ago, have been found in Africa, Europe, India, and China. The genus may have originated in India and spread east and west. Its australopithecine descendants are known from two widely separated areas, South and East Africa on the one hand, Java on the other. The type was first discovered in South Africa in 1924. The Indonesian representative, evidenced by two lower-jaw fragments, is known as *Meganthropus*, a robust precursor of *Pithecanthropus erectus*, or Java Man. *P. erectus*, the first fossil man to be recovered from Middle Pleistocene deposits, now has the company of similar remains discovered in Africa, Europe, and China. In the 1960s, these were lumped together as members of *Homo erectus*, dubbed by Coon (1971:32) the "half-brained men." But the species name *erectus* was retained in honor of Eugene Dubois, the Dutch physician who discovered and named *P. erectus* in 1891.

No australopithecine remains have as yet been unearthed by scientists in China, although Chinese pharmacists may have found some. In 1935, G. H. R. von Koenigswald, the Dutch paleontologist, bought some large hominid teeth in the drugstores of Canton and Hong Kong, where they were sold as dragon bones for grinding into Chinese medicinal preparations. The druggists said they found them in the limestone caves of Southwest China. Some of these drugstore teeth, von Koenigswald now believes, indicate the occupation of South China by Lower Pleistocene hominids resembling the australopithecines of Africa. He has named them *Hemanthropus peii* (Chang, 1973:382–3). Figure 2 places this name as the first entry for early man. Recent discoveries in Africa, however, indicate that the apemen may not have been ancestral to the human line but offshoots.

14

Geology	Climate	Man	Culture
RECENT	North: cool winter, hot summer. South: semi-tropical.	Modern *Homo sapiens*	Historical
			Shang
	Mild and moist		Lung-shan
			Neolithic
			Yang-shao
			Sheng-wen
			Mesolithic (Sha-yuan; microliths)
10,000 B.C.		Upper Cave Sjara-osso-gol Tzu-yang Liu-chiang	
PLEISTOCENE Late	Cool IV Glacial		Upper Paleolithic (Ordosian blade tools; burins)
	Warm	Early *Homo sapiens*	Middle Paleolithic (Shui-tung-kou; retouching)
	Cool III Glacial	Ting-Ts'un Ch'ang-yang Ma-pa Man	
200,000			Lower Paleolithic (Chopper-chopping core tools)
Middle	Warm	*Homo erectus*	
	Cool II Glacial	Peking Man Lantian Man	
600,000			
Early	Warm		
	Cool I Glacial	*Hemanthropus peii*	Precultural (Hsi-hou-tu; pebble tools)
3,000,000 B.C.	Preglacial		

FIGURE 2.   The Quaternary in China (not to scale).

Another finder traced a tooth from a Peking drugstore to the nearby limestone caves of Choukoutien, where an international team of paleontologists, geologists, and anatomists in the decade from 1927 to 1937 uncovered 14 skulls, 12 lower jaws, and 147 teeth belonging to the Chinese version of *Homo erectus*, which they classified as *Sinanthropus pekinensis*, popularly known as Peking Man. With the other erecti populations, Peking Man is a link between the apemen and our own species, *Homo sapiens*. From the neck down there is little (if any) difference between *erectus* and *sapiens*. The head of *erectus*, however, is intermediate in form as measured by the relationship between face and brain. The trend from the apemen to *sapiens* has been from large face and small brain in a thick skull toward small face and large brain in a thin skull, and with jaws light enough to no longer require heavy brow ridges to absorb the compressive force of mastication. The erecti in general are somewhat heavy jawed and beetle browed, and their cranial capacity falls short of that of *sapiens* by a third or more. Among several characteristic features of Peking Man are the congenital absence of the third molar in the lower jaw and a shovel-shaped depression on the backside of the incisor teeth. These traits persist with high frequency in modern Chinese and other Mongolid populations. Some authorities, however, doubt a genetic link between *erectus* and *sapiens* in China.

The occurrence of shovel-shaped incisors in the Mongolid subspecies of man must indicate the relative isolation of its homeland, remaining isolated long enough for the inbreeding of local peculiarities, both morphological and behavioral (on the genetics of both, *see* Baker, 1974). Indeed, during the Middle Pleistocene geological epoch, during which the East Asian erecti from Java to China flourished, an east/west difference in culture appeared on either side of Movius's Line—a geographical frontier running down the Tien-shan Mountains to the Pamirs, eastward along the southern slopes of the Himalayas, then south along the India/Burma frontier, into the Indian Ocean. To the west of this line evolved a distinctive Paleolithic tool, the pear-shaped handaxe; to the east, the disc-shaped chopper (Coon, 1965:48).

The fossilized bones of Peking Man are justifiably regarded as national treasures by the present regime. They disappeared, however, during the last confused days of World War II in China. Prehistoric archaeology has a patriotic significance for underdeveloped countries in their newly found nationalism, and so the new Chinese government soon resumed archaeological work at Choukoutien. In the same Lower Cave where the other bones of Peking Man had been found, a lower jaw turned up. In 1963, a second site was discovered in the Lantian district of Shensi province. It yielded another lower jaw and a fairly complete skull.

Formerly, Westerners conducted the excavations and reported their finds for Westerners in journals published by Westerners in China. The first reports on Peking Man appeared under conditions of intellectual colonialism (Black, 1933; Weidenreich, 1939). But like all forms of colonialism, it had its teaching effect on the native culture. The Ice Age replaced mythological concepts of remote antiquity, and the Chinese now do their own excavation and publishing, of which the reports on Lantian Man are but one small sample (*see* Woo, 1965). Moreover, the Chinese Academy of Sciences recently established a radiocarbon-dating laboratory (Pearson, 1973).

The chopper-chopping tools of *H. erectus* in China were chipped from cores of flint or quartzite in a consistent pattern, evidently from a mental blueprint transmitted down the generations by the symbolic means of human culture. This cannot be said for the pebble tools recovered from a Lower Pleistocene site found in 1959 in the southern Shansi village of Hsi-hou-tu. One authority associates these tools with the australopithecine occupation of China (Chang, 1968:41). The open-and-shut case for culture is the use of fire, never linked with remains of *Australopithecus* anywhere. Blackened hearth areas—those unmistakable spatial markers of a hunting band's encampment—have been found in the Lower Cave at Choukoutien, however.

Peking Man was a hunter, following the seasonal game trails. Like the hunting peoples of today, the men must have done the game hunting, the women the daily gathering of wild fruits, nuts, and grasses. This human division of labor by sex may be read into the food leavings at Choukoutien: charred animals bones indicating a heavy diet of venison, together with horse, elephant, rhinocerous, and beaver, in addition to pits of the cherrylike hagberry.

The continuous story of man is carried forward in Late Pleistocene times by Neanderthaloid forms of early *H. sapiens* known from northern, central, and southern China (Ting-ts'un, Ch'ang-yang, and Ma-pa Man, respectively). Their shovel-shaped incisors link *H. erectus* with the first populations of modern *H. sapiens* in China. Their butchering equipment still includes the old chopper-chopping core tools of Peking Man, but with retouching, plus some new flake tools—points and scrapers—reminiscent of the Mousterian tradition in Europe. Those from Shui-tung-kou in the Ordos may be taken to represent a Middle Paleolithic stage.

As in Europe, the first populations of *H. sapiens* in China appear during the fourth glacial advance and are known from a number of widely scattered sites. These include Upper Cave Man of Choukoutien, Ordos Man of Northwest China in Shensi province, Tzu-yang Man of Southwest China in Szechwan province, and Liu-chiang Man of South China in Kwangsi province. Their cultural relics are called Ordosian after the flake tools—blades, scrapers, and burins—of the Upper Paleolithic first discovered in the Ordos at Sjara-osso-gol (*see* Chang, 1963: map 2). In fact, these are the first Paleolithic tools of any stage known from China, discovered in the 1920s by the geologist and Jesuit priest, Pierre Teilhard de Chardin, who also participated in the Lower Cave finds at Choukoutien (Teilhard, 1941). A grassy scrubland continuous with Mongolia, the Ordos was once stocked with bison, wooly rhinocerous, antelope, and ostrich, which repaired for water to large, wooded oases. Here, Upper Paleolithic campers hunted the woods and fished the oases. Nothing remains today save vast, dry basins in the desert.

In Europe, the great geological event of Late Pleistocene times was the fourth glacial advance. Glacial action also took place in all the mountains of China, north and south, but the ice did not actually reach into the valley floors. Instead, the significant event for man there was a tremendous blow of dust, stripped by winds off the Gobi desert and deposited as loess, a powdery yellow soil, up to 350 feet deep over the uplands of North China. Loess covers the middle reaches of the Yellow valley where the river comes down out of the Ordos region, the Fen valley, the northern flanks of the Yellow River's major tributary (the Wei), and the length of the Kansu corridor. This loessial soil once supported the forested hunting preserves of Mesolithic men, but the trees were cut down with stone axes in Neolithic times to make way for the fields of China's first farmers. The widespread soil erosion caused by this denudation of the forest cover brought loess in suspension down the Yellow River, until the waters slowed on the flats of the North China plain. There, the yellow silt that gives the river its name continues to drop from suspension. Unless the river is diked and the dikes maintained, the river will overflow its own banks and meander, because the riverbed is constantly being built up higher than the surrounding plain. No great cities have ever been built along the lower reaches of the Yellow, due to periodic flooding and course changes. China's Sorrow, a permanent threat of flooding to the Yellow plain, is a consequence of the Neolithic axman who laid the foundations of Chinese civilization—a civilization that still suffers from a by-product of its prehistory.

The climate during fourth glacial times was cold and dry, the culmination of a series of fluctuations: glacial periods that got progressively colder, interglacial periods that were warm but that got progressively less warm. The climate following the Pleistocene was mild and moist. The vanishing ice sheets increased water distribution from melt waters flowing into streams, rivers, and lakes, and from marine transgressions flooding coastal regions. The significant result for man-the-hunter was thicker vegetation and an increased variety of plants and animals. The adaptation of Upper Paleolithic hunters to the changed conditions of the postglacial epoch may be gauged by the rise of a new state of hunting culture, the Mesolithic.

The original point of reference in the-*lithic* words is how stone tools were made, not how they were used. Thus, *Paleolithic* means core tools shaped by the hammering away of flakes from a solid nodule of flint or flint-like material. *Neolithic* means the grinding, pecking, or abrading into shape of pebbles or boulders of compact stone. *Mesolithic* is a later interpolation: tools knapped from flakes. Today the terms have sociological meaning as well. In this expanded vocabulary, *Paleolithic* means also a hunting state of culture dating from before the recent geological epoch. Paleolithic culture survived among the Tasmanians, who never acquired Mesolithic traits such as the dog as a hunting companion, the bow and arrow, spear thrower, harpoon, fishing spear, and microblades used in compound tools. *Mesolithic* means a skilled hunting culture whose upgraded technology was prompted by the disappearance of large cold-weather game and the appearance of a more variegated postglacial assortment, including aquatic species. *Neolithic* means settled village life and the domestication of plants and animals, including polished stone axes for clearing the land and adzes for working wood in the manufacture of dwellings and barnyard enclosures. This meaning may be applied to villagers who substitute metal blades (acquired by trade) for stone, as all the surviving Neolithic farming peoples have done, (*see* Coon, 1971).

The path to Neolithic hoeing and herding in China, as in West Asia, crossed through a Mesolithic state of culture. Eight thousand years ago the West Asian center of development, located in the uplands flanking the Tigris-Euphrates river (Braidwood, 1952), brought forth driable, storable crops in the form of wheat and barley grains. The Chinese center did likewise with local species of millet and soybean. Wheat, a West Asian cultigen, was imported later (*see* Chang, 1968:89, note 19). Chinese cattle, sheep, and goats are also of West Asian origin, but pigs and dogs originating in a Southeast Asian source of Neolithic culture came first.

Mesolithic people throughout the Old World preferred waterside hunting and gathering by sea, stream, and lake. In these places, hunting, fishing, and gathering were so productive that some residential stability was possible, thus paving the way for a settled, Neolithic life. In East Asia, the Mesolithic way of life flourished in the forests of Siberia, Manchuria, and northwestern China, and in the belt of wooded oases in Mongolia. No Mesolithic sites have been found in the treeless alluvial plains of eastern China. Transition to the Neolithic occurred somewhere between the two best-known Mesolithic sites of North China—at Sha-yuan on the edge of the loessial highlands to the west, and at Choukoutien (its Upper Cave locality) to the east. The south, after helping the north make this transition, was put in a conservative position relative to its dominating influence as a new source of innovation.

The Mesolithic of South China is continuous with that of Indo-China and is named Hoabinhian, after its type site in Vietnam. To be precise, the reference here is to late Hoabinhian, sometimes called Bacsonian. Not only did the Hoabinhian culture wait for upgrading upon Neolithic developments to the north, it also lacked the newer blade tools and retained a Paleolithic technology, still using chopper-chopping tools. The population was not even Mongolid (the incisors lack shoveling) but Australid, whose living representatives may be found among the so-called Negritos of the Philippine and Andaman islands and of the Malay Peninsula, and among the aborigines of Australia. The Negritos are remnants of a once widespread Australid population in South China, Southeast Asia, and Indonesia; the Australian aborigines are latecomers who arrived in their present home about twenty thousand years ago. The *Homo erectus* ancestor for the Australids is probably Java Man, although some authorities dispute this.

The Hoabinhians were Mesolithic hunter-fishers in practice, taking fish and molluscs from freshwater ponds and streams, small game from streamside forests, and wild plants from both woodland and aquatic sources. The importance of the Hoabinhian culture is its spatial location between the Southeast Asian center of Neolithic development in the Burma/India region (Sauer, 1969) and the North China center of development, and the coastal regions in South China and North Vietnam, from which migrations into the Pacific took place. To North China, the Hoabinhian culture transmitted the domesticated animals of the Southeast Asian Neolithic—dogs, pigs, chickens, ducks, and geese—and to the coastal emigrants it transmitted its agricultural crops, chiefly yams and taro.

The Hoabinhians also transmitted northward a remarkable musical instrument, the *pien ch'ing,* incorporated into Chinese court ritual and used in Confucian temples until the present century. The *ch'ing* is a lithophone, a set of sixteen rectangular plates made of jade or black calcareous stone and pitched to the Eastern pentatonic scale. Had not a complete set been recovered from a pond in 32 B.C. as a model for new ones, the *ch'ing* lithophone would have disappeared with ancient libraries burnt by the anti-Confucian founders of the Ch'in dynasty (Couling, 1917:387). The ritual significance of the *ch'ing* is "restrained order" (Watson, 1963:117) and is probably related to a story told about Confucius in the *Analects*. In these miscellaneous writings, Confucius is described as controlling his disappointment at not winning office yet again, this time in the state of Wei, by playing a lithophone with angry intensity.

> *The Master was playing the stone-chimes, during the time he was in Wei. A man carrying a basket where he and his disciple had established themselves. He said, How passionately he beats his chimes! When the tune was over, he said, How petty and small-minded!* (Lun Yu, *XIV:42*, tr. by Waley, 1938)

The prototype of the *pien ch'ing* was found two decades ago by a French archaeologist in a Bacsonian (late Hoabinhian) site in Darlac province of South Vietnam (*New York Times*, 1954:3). The surviving plates were made of the same schistic rock knapped by the Bacsonians for their stone tools and they sounded, at the slightest touch, in the notes of the complete Eastern scale. This ancient lithophone thus outbids the famous Sumerian lyre unearthed by Sir Leonard Woolley in Chaldean Ur as the oldest musical instrument in the world.

Like the North China Neolithic, the Southeast Asian Neolithic evolved directly out of a woodland Mesolithic economy favoring fishing in addition to hunting and gathering. In both instances, Neolithic planting resulted from intensified Mesolithic gathering. The crop differences depended on what the local ecologies had to offer for replanting. In the north, the millets were seasonally gathered and seasonally sown once a year. In Southeast Asia, bananas, yams, and taro potatoes were perennially gathered and perennially replanted by means of cuttings, not seeds. Unlike cereal crops, root, fruit, and tuber crops can be propagated immediately after being plucked down or pulled up merely by inserting a tuber, or stem, back into the ground or back in the water, in the case of kale and water spinach. But seed crops may be dried and stored, creating a cumulative supply essential to the property relations of civilization, its power controls over an immobilized farming population, and the disbursement of its surplus to nonfood-producing specialists. Moreover, root and fruit crops provide carbohydrates only, none of the fat and protein delivered by cereals, which otherwise must be supplied by fish and game. Civilizations are not built with a population of mobile hunters and fishermen, nor on the basis of nonstorable crops. Note that civilization—defined in terms of wheeled transport, metallurgy, and writing—arose from the grain complex of North China and not from the root-fruit-tuber complex of Southeast Asia.

In fact, the plant foods of the Southeast Asian Neolithic may have been cultivated as a sideline to an activity more central than agriculture: fishing. Perhaps the basic activity was the domestication of fiber crops such as jute and cotton for use as cordage in fishing nets and lines and as caulking in fishing boats. In addition, plants were cultivated for drugs such as tea and betel. The habit of chewing betel nut in Southeast Asia, South China, Indonesia, Melanesia, Micronesia, and Polynesia is as widespread as the planting of yams and taro potatoes—thanks to the intermediary role played by the Hoabinhian culture (*see* Chang, 1970).

The type of Mesolithic culture out of which the North China Neolithic emerged is represented by Sha-yuan. The Sha-yuan site is located on the eastern edge of the loessial highlands, along the Wei River near its juncture with the Yellow River. The area is semiarid now, but the arrowheads, bone tools, and the remains of fish, shellfish, and game animals show that the men who camped at Sha-yuan were woodland hunter-fishers of the sort who lived throughout Northeast Asia in early postglacial times, when the climate was mild and moist.

The Sha-yuan site is located in a small basin surrounded on three sides by mountains and plateaus but open to, and overlooking, the eastern plains on which Chinese civilization arose.

ERA OF NEOLITHIC TRIBALISM

In West Asia, the Neolithic evolved out of its own Mesolithic roots as one unitary package of new technologies: stone polishing, gardening, stock breeding, carpentry, weaving, and eventually pottery making. According to radiocarbon dating, the Neolithic came into being about 7000 B.C., in Jericho. In 8000 B.C., Jericho was still a Mesolithic campsite. Because the Neolithic in North China occurred several thousand years later, archaeologists are led to wonder how much that development owed, by way of cumulative diffusion, to West Asia. Until the advent of radiocarbon dating in China, the question was impossible to answer. The oldest radiocarbon dates for a Chinese Neolithic site come from Pan-p'o-ts'un, which show continuous occupation from 4500 to 3750 B.C. Pan-p'o-ts'un is located in the Wei River valley, not far west of the Mesolithic site of Sha-yuan, and thus is central to the Chinese Neolithic area of origin in the loessial highlands. Its beginnings can be dated at about 5000 B.C. (see Cheng, 1973:205). This would indicate a two-thousand-year lag behind the West Asian center. But the Chinese debt to the West Asian Neolithic is limited to a sampling of its grains and livestock, which were imported into an intensified Mesolithic economy that already possessed pottery, if indeed a Neolithic economy were not already under way.

It is now clear that pottery was a Mesolithic invention in East Asia before it was a Neolithic invention in West Asia. This is Grey Pottery, a coarse ware finished by beating with a cord-wrapped paddle or impressed with a wooden stamp carved to imitate this effect. It is known from the Hoabinhian culture of South China and Indo-China, the Jomon culture of Japan, and between these, from the Yang-shao culture of early Neolithic China. Mesolithic Jomon pottery from Japan has been dated by radiocarbon to about 9000 B.C. Japanese affinities with China go back to Upper Paleolithic times, when so much of the ocean waters were contained in the ice sheets of the fourth glacial period that the sea level dropped by hundreds of feet, exposing land between Japan and the mainland. A similar cord-marked ware is dated at about 8000 B.C. from Taiwan. Undated pottery of the same kind has been found in the Mesolithic sites of Mongolia and Soviet Siberia in the region of Lake Baikal. Wider still is the distribution of the Gobi microlithic culture—microliths, Grey Pottery, shells, and bones of fish and animals—in surface finds throughout the nonwooded areas of Manchuria, Mongolia, Sinkiang, and eastern Tibet. A Hoabinhian site with cord-marked pottery has been dated on the Thailand/Burma border at about 8000 B.C. (Chang, 1970; Cheng, 1973).

The same grey, cord-marked pottery of the Jomon and Hoabinhian cultures also figures as the basic utilitarian ware of the North China Neolithic, from its earliest manifestations in the Yang-shao culture to its latest in the Lung-shan. To this point, Grey Pottery found in early Neolithic sites in the North China core area has always been accompanied by the more elegant Painted Pottery, by which the Yang-shao culture was first discovered and named. Sites containing or ly Grey Pottery may eventually turn up in North China. Such sites would exemplify what Chang Kwang-chih, the first archaeologist to make a synthesis of Chinese prehistory, postulates as a Sheng-wen horizon contemporary with Hoabinhian and Jomon, at about 8000 B.C. By a Sheng-wen horizon, he means an early stage of Yang-shao culture lacking Painted Pottery. (The Chinese ideographs for *Sheng-wen* are read *Jomon* in Japanese). So far, evidence for such a horizon is known only from one site outside the core area, at Li-chia-ts'un, which is located (significantly) in a position geographically intermediate between the Chinese and the Southeast Asian centers of Neolithic development (Chang, 1968:112).

Apparently the residential pattern of the Mesolithic hunter-fishers almost everywhere in East Asia was so stabilized that they could afford to settle down with ceramic kitchenware and reap wild plants for cooking as regularly as Neolithic gardeners later did with cultivated plants. The transition took place in North China about 5000 B.C. and is known from more than a thousand sites of Yang-shao Painted Pottery, named after the village of Yang-shao-ts'un, near which the type specimens were unearthed in 1920.

Yang-Shao

Yang-shao pottery is hand-coiled, painted black and red on a yellow or white slip, and fired in an oxidizing atmosphere. Its true spatial range was not perceived at the time of discovery, due to the almost irresistible temptation of archaeologists to conclude that where their shovels first turn up a new type of artifact, there must be the center of its distribution. Yang-shao-ts'un in fact lies close to the eastern edge of the Painted Pottery area, on a river terrace alongside a small stream entering the lower Yellow River in the middle of the North China plain. The actual center must be somewhere on the western edge of the highlands of primary, wind-blown loess. From there, Yang-shao farmers probably cleared their riverside fields up and down the midcourse of the Yellow River—up into the primary loess and down into the lowlands of alluvial loess. Primary loess covers the Wei River valley and the Kansu corridor as far northwest as the tributaries of the upper Yellow River. This region was attractive, no doubt, for its capacity to hold water despite limited rainfall.

But the river terrace locales of the Yang-shao people indicate that they were hunter-fishers before they were farmers. They left behind a full inventory of Mesolithic equipment: arrowheads, spearheads, skin-scrapers, harpoons, fishhooks, and net sinkers. Yet hunting and fishing were only part-time activities, supplementary to food production. Yang-shao technology shows a decisive commitment to the Neolithic way of life, beyond the point of no return to food collecting. Neolithic equipment includes hoes, spades, digging sticks, weeding knives, mealing stones, kilns and pottery molds, spindle whorls, sewing needles, stone polishers, and three basic woodworking tools: axes, adzes, and chisels. The Yang-shao crops were native millets and soybeans, and later, wheat of western origin. Yang-shao domesticated animals were Southeast Asian pigs and dogs, to which were later added West Asian cattle, sheep, goats, and perhaps horses—as a food animal only. (New uses for these animals came with the beginnings of civilization. The Shang dynasty used dogs, cattle, sheep, and goats for sacrificial offerings, horses for pulling war chariots.) A ditch around the village kept the garden area free of domestic animals, which were left to forage in the forest. Space for the gardens was cleared by the axe.

The omnipresence of the stone axe in Yang-shao sites strongly indicates that the first farmers of North China practiced swidden agriculture. *Swidden* means deadening or felling trees, burning off the land, and then planting the ash-covered ground with seeds or stems. After a few plantings, when the fertilizing effect of the ash has worn off, the old garden is abandoned to long-term fallowing and a new site is cleared. Like swidden cultivators today in the forested hills of Southeast Asia and others recently nationalized in the mountains of South China, the settlements of Yang-shao farmers were as shifting as their fields; their residence was stabilized, however, insofar as they returned periodically to fallowed fields.

The Painted Pottery culture of the Yang-shao swidden farmers was first explored with an eye to the artistic value of the pottery itself, which is a fancy ware made only for ritual use as mortuary furniture. Art historians dismissed the crudely made, badly fired Grey Pottery of everyday use as too ugly and utilitarian to be worthy of museum display. Yet Grey Pottery belongs to China's oldest ceramic tradition, lasting until Bronze Age times, and is indigenous to the whole of East Asia. Painted Pottery has so many striking design parallels with the ceramics of Turkestan, the Caucasus, and the Ukraine that it may have been influenced by Neolithic cultures to the west, as Grey Pottery definitely was not.

Emblematic of Chinese civilization in the eyes of the natives themselves is a three-legged bronze vessel called a *li* tripod, on which early laws were cast. It first appeared as one type of Grey Pottery vessel in which water was boiled to steam food in an upper vessel that had a flat, perforated bottom. The two units combine to make a *hsien* steamer (Cheng, 1959: plate xxxiv). Chinese gastronomy thus has Neolithic origins, as do the chopsticks used for eating. Weaving silk from the cocoon windings of cultured silkworms is another tradition just as old.

Excavation in the Yang-shao horizon for other than art treasures was not conducted until 1953 and 1955, when the Chinese Academy of Sciences disclosed the settlement pattern of a site at Pan-p'o-ts'un, located on a loess terrace on the Ch'an River, a tributary of the Wei. The accumulated debris from about four successive occupations of Pan-p'o-ts'un contains evidence of almost fifty single-hearth dwellings of round or square plan, with semisubterranean foundations. Pit houses have Upper Paleolithic continuities with circumpolar hunters and are still used today by the Alaskan Eskimo. The typical Yang-shao pit house covered a floor space ten to sixteen feet in diameter; its walls above ground were constructed of wattle-and-daub screens; its thatched roof supported by one or more large center posts and a number of smaller peripheral posts (Chang, 1968:97–100; Cheng, 1959:75–86). Wattled walls, an application of weaving technology to house construction, are not structural members, which never were basic to Chinese architecture. Even today Western brickwork is sometimes used to build screens, not roof-supporting walls.

Any given occupational level at Pan-p'o-ts'un was inhabited by at least a dozen families. At its height, this site contained 200 houses, with a population of between 500 and 600, and 200 storage pits (Cheng, 1966:18). The living area with its kitchen gardens was set off from a specialized industrial space, where kilns were located, and from the cemetery. Yang-shao cemeteries frequently served more than one community. This arrangement foreshadows specialized communities—residential, agricultural, industrial, and funeral—comprising the dispersed layout of Shang urbanism.

A late occupation at Pan-p'o contains a rectangular, above-ground, multihearth dwelling whose partitioned floor plan measures roughly sixty-five by forty-one feet. The outer posts of its frame rested on a low foundation wall of pounded earth, an enduring method of Chinese construction used later in building city walls, temple platforms, and river dikes. Encircling the longhouse were the pit houses, their doorways all facing south. (The main entrance of all Chinese towns and cities and the Dragon Throne of the emperors always face south.) The longhouse was perhaps occupied by a lineage whose distinction was its religious leadership, undoubtedly shamanistic. From Upper Paleolithic times, man's first occupational specialist, according to Carleton Coon (1969:105–112), was the shaman. He was the magical equilibrium-maker when the little communities of early men were shaken by food shortages, illness, death, or snarled human relations. A picture painted on the inside of a ceramic basin from Pan-p'o is undoubtedly some kind of shamanistic headdress fitted out with fish emblems. Fish motifs, reflecting the Mesolithic heritage of the Neolithic, recur in Yang-shao pottery (*see* Watson, 1966: Fig. 17; Chang, 1968:93, 104; Cheng, 1966: Fig. 11).

The ecological importance of Yang-shao swidden farming, even considering its relatively low efficiency, was that it significantly raised the carrying capacity of the land over that of Mesolithic hunting and fishing. The effect of man's control over the lives of plants and animals through the technology of domestication is to increase their numbers and density and thus to increase his own numbers and density. The upshot of the Yang-shao way of life was more of it, and in fairly rapid order. As the population increased, it expanded outward from the center of Neolithic development, daughter villages budding off from established ones as the latter grew to capacity. New villages would have separated real daughters and sons, but kin ties would have remained alive to be celebrated at family reunions in cemeteries, following a death in the family. In the region of the westward expansion of Yang-shao culture, villages in neighboring valleys held a common burial ground on the hilltop between them. Officiating at the burial ground in a Neolithic cult of the dead must have been the shaman from the village longhouse (Chang, 1968:102–3).

The earliest Chinese words for shaman are inscribed on the Shang oracle bones—*hsi* for a male, *wu* for a female (although this distinction may be false). The word *shaman* itself is a Tungusic word meaning one "smitten," "inspired," or "excited," first recorded by Russian ethnographers among the Tungus of Siberia. Shamanism has been described by

Russian anthropologists as the native religion of Ural-Altaic peoples (including Eskimos) from the Bering Straits to Lapland. Other anthropologists have applied the name to analogous practices of medicine men among the American Indians and sorcerors among the Australian aborigines. The common belief is in demonistic nature worship, and the common practices are magical healing, divination, and spirit possession, as in communication with dead ancestors. The shaman's practical functions are accompanied, and perhaps legitimatized, by crowd-pleasing forms of entertainment such as dancing, ventriloquism, juggling, and tricks. The most common Chinese word for shaman, *wu,* means to dance or to posture; the ancient pictograph shows a dancer holding plumes or feathers in her (or his) two hands. Both male and female shamans belonged to the Shang and early Chou governments as state magicians. No doubt they carried over into this official role some of the practices they conducted out of their longhouse for the Neolithic folk of Yang-shao and Lung-shan times. The Shang oracle bones inscribed by shamans depict the magicians at work invoking the spirits of the king's ancestors, divining the future, and dancing for rain to the tune of drum and ocarina. Records from a later time depict shamans as mediums, impersonating the newly deceased ancestors of the Chou nobles, with whom the survivors feasted and drank. One may imagine similar drunken revels held in Neolithic cemeteries as well (Needham, 1956:127–35; Cheng, 1960:224–25; Rudd, 1928:97–99).

Lung-Shan

The expansion of Yang-shao shifting agriculture resulted in a more productive, permanently settled Neolithic agriculture associated with a new type of ceramic industry known as Lung-shan ware, or Black Pottery. Black Pottery is a wheel-turned ware made from natural black paste, fired in a reducing atmosphere, unpainted but burnished. It was turned up near the small marketing town of Lung-shan-chen in 1928 and recognized as evidence of a new culture following that of Yang-shao. Moreover, it was recognized not by art collectors but by a team of professional, Western-trained Chinese archaeologists. Like Painted Pottery, the vessels of Black Pottery were manufactured mainly for use in funerals and burials, and they provided models for many of the ritual vessels made of bronze in the Shang dynasty. Grey Pottery, refined by Shang craftsmen before the tradition finally came to an end, continued in production for domestic use during Lung-shan times. Also carried over from Yang-shao times were all of its domesticated plants and animals. The basic house type continued to be the Yang-shao pit house and, as the center of community attention, the longhouse.

Lung-shan agricultural productivity had been raised to the level that excess grain was reserved in large storage pits. Social differences based on the command of accumulated property are reflected in status burials. The material basis for this growth of social complexity lay with new agricultural techniques, chiefly fertilization with river silt and irrigation from wells, which made it possible to abandon the less productive swidden method of slash-and-burn cultivation. Farming had become efficient enough to support permanently settled village life.

At this point, units of settlement turned into units of fortification as well, such as that found at the site of Lung-shan-chen. Walls of pounded earth indicate that the peaceful propagation of the Neolithic complex had come to an end and that intercommunity raiding had started. In fact, raiding for booty and sacrificial victims was a matter of state policy in the Shang dynasty.

Yang-shao culture was homogeneous because it covered little territory. Lung-shan culture spread so far and wide as to gain regional diversity. Even the lustrous Black Pottery of the type site did not carry everywhere, although the absence of painted decoration did. More important, the art of making fine pottery had by this time been monopolized by specialized industrial communities, an economic feature of Shang urbanism.

The Lung-shan revolution in fully productive Neolithic agriculture spread all the way down the Yellow River to the sea, down the Hwai River, down the middle and lower Yangtze, and all along the Pacific seaboard. In the wet taro gardens of the Hoabinhian culture in the subtropical jungle valleys of South China, Lung-shan farmers discovered a weed which they transplanted into their own gardens and cultivated as rice. Soon rice cultivation spread to North China, even into some of the late Painted Pottery villages that persisted on the eastern margin of the Yang-shao area. To the west, in the loessial plateau, Yang-shao culture lingered on until Western Chou times. Elsewhere, Mesolithic cultures persisted even longer as sub-Neolithic cultural hybrids.

The Hoabinhian farmers cultivated the root, fruit, and tuber crops of the Southeast Asian Neolithic. This same complex was taken by Neolithic migrants from the region of South China and Indo-China to the Philippines and thence to Micronesia and Polynesia. A carbon-14 date of about 1500 B.C. from an early site on the Micronesian island of Saipan suggests that if a Neolithic people reached the Marianas by that time, the chain of migratory events beginning on the Asian mainland must have begun before rice was cultivated in the lowlands there. The suggestion is that if rice was first cultivated in the hills, then the ancestors of the Micronesian islanders must have departed before rice was brought into the lowlands for cultivation, thus accounting for the presence in the Pacific of root and fruit crops and the absence of rice. The reasoning is inadequate. Rice is a grass and as such it is a potential food only for those who know how to plant seed crops. For the Hoabinhians it was just a weed in their taro gardens; but for the Lung-shan pioneers in South China it appeared as another cereal crop, one well-adapted to wet conditions. Food habits are conservative and surrounded by tradition, so it is possible that Lung-shan farmers grew rice in the geographical proximity to, yet in cultural isolation from, their taro- and yam-growing neighbors. Emigrants headed for Indonesia and the Pacific probably departed from a coastal area that was familiar with rice, although it had been introduced by the Lung-shan newcomers. Then as now, South China and Southeast Asia must have consisted of a mosaic of cultural differences. The Pacific emigrants probably derived from only one component of the cultural mosaic. Racially, however, the islanders are a mixture of Mongolid and Australid elements (Chang, 1970; Coon, 1969:149).

The importance of Lung-shan is that it laid the technological foundations on which Bronze Age civilization in China was erected: plant and animal domestication at the level of full-time, Neolithic mixed farming and permanent settlement, carpentry, pounded-earth construction, and specialized industrial communities for pottery making and perhaps other crafts, such as weaving and bone working. The transition from the Neolithic to Bronze Age civilization was essentially sociological; the technological requirements began with the Neolithic revolution. In 1931, at the Hou-kang site in Honan province (which may be central to the emergence of Shang civilization), a Chinese archaeologist uncovered for the first time the archaeological sequence leading to that development: Shang over Lung-shan, and Lung-shan over Yang-shao (Li Chi, 1956:139–60).

TWO

ERA OF CITY-STATES

ANCIENT MYTHOLOGY

During the early years of empire, the learned men of the newly consolidated Chinese state applied themselves to digesting and mentally unifying the accumulated literary material belonging to the preceding centuries of political separatism. Political unity at the imperial level called for a new cultural identity. So prodigious was the scholarship of the Former Han dynasty mythologists in shaping this cultural identity that the Chinese are still known by the name of this imperial house: "men of Han" (*see* Karlgren, 1946). This name long remained ethnocentric, not nationalistic; a sign of cultural pride, not patriotism. Communist China still uses the term *Han* to distinguish ethnic from national Chinese, such as Mongolians, Uighurs, Tibetans, and other minorities.

By 91 B.C., the Grand Astrologer and Archivist, Ssu-ma Ch'ien, had finished the last pages of his great *Shih Chi*, or *Historical Records*. As court astrologer, he and others had put into effect a new calendar that remained in official use until A.D. 1927 (Goodrich, 1959:47). As grand historian, he had read nearly every book available in his day, from the texts of the oldest annalists to current government records, travelling widely to do so. These he summarized and compiled in the *Shih Chi*, a veritable encyclopedia of ancient literature. It opens with the mythical reign of the San Hwang, or Three Primordial Sovereigns *(hwang* means *sovereign)*, commencing in 2852 B.C., and closes with the reign of the author's own ruler, Han Wu-ti (140-87 B.C.).

Nothing in the *Shih Chi*, however, is known from independent texts earlier than the Western Chou dynasty. The later the actual texts, the earlier the legendary history they purport to recount; for only in an ever-more-remote past can the mythmakers find unoccupied time in which to fit accretions to the growing story. The creation, associated with the myth of P'an Ku and the emergence of order out of chaos, does not figure in the literature until as late as the third century A.D. The beginning of dynastic history found its myth in the person of Yu, who first appears in the early writings of the Western Chou (*see* Bodde, 1961).

No doubt all this tremendous legend collecting and fable making was stimulated by a rush of creative expression made possible with the invention of paper in early Han times, united with an epic subject to write about: the consolidation of imperial politics. No writings from before the Former Han dynasty have survived other than the terse inscriptions on oracle bones for the purpose of divination in the Shang dynasty and on bronze vessels for the purpose of presentation in the Shang and Chou courts.

For native Chinese intellectuals untutored in Western standards of evidence, legendary history with its fabulous prologue was real history, and real history was moral history. When they learned from Western geologists the real age of the world and from archaeologists the real age of civilization, they were able to identify false history for what it was (see Price, 1946). They were able also to verify legend where verifiable. Between 1928 and 1935, the Western-trained Chinese archaeologist Li Chi led fifteen seasons of excavations in the ruins of Yin and confirmed the king list of its twelve rulers. Until then, the rulers of Yin had been so many names recorded in the Shih Chi—names belonging to the final period of the Shang dynasty.

The Yin period of the Shang dynasty now stands as authentic history, its archival remains at An-yang verifying the genealogy recorded in the Shih Chi. Archaeology has unearthed other Shang cities whose identity with the dynasty's earlier capitals is all but certain, but no oracle bones inscribed with writing that would validate the pre-Yin king list have yet been found. Only the tradition of a moveable capital is confirmed. Preceding the Shang dynasty is the legendary Hsia, with its list of eighteen kings, beginning with Yu the Great. Archaeology is not likely to verify the Hsia, because under the remains of the Shang lie the remains of Lung-shan, a Neolithic culture lacking cities, state organization, and writing.

One sinologist (Creel, 1937:52–53) suggests that the genealogy of the Hsia kings preserved in the Shih Chi is a fiction devised by the founders of Western Chou and successors to the Shang house. Its purpose may have been to persuade Shang nobles that their dynasty was due to end the same way Heaven in the fiction ended the Hsia: by punishment of the "bad last" and installation of the "good first" (see Watson, 1962:29). As Chieh, the last sovereign of the Hsia dynasty, was said to have been overthrown for his wickedness by Prince T'ang, who then founded the Shang dynasty in righteousness, so Shou (a "bad last") was to be replaced by King Wu (a "good first"), a conqueror from the neighboring kingdom of Chou, whose dynastic name succeeded that of Shang. After the conquest, Western Chou annalists recorded the imaginary precedent. The fiction, however, has remained a fact in the logic of Chinese political morality up until the end of the dynastic cycle. Scholastic advisors to the Manchus, who replaced the Ming with the Ch'ing dynasty, knew all about the Mandate of Heaven from the original source of its exposition, the Shu Ching, or Book of History.

The Shu Ching is another compilation of the early Han dynasty. It purports to record documents spanning seventeen centuries, but in fact nothing in it is older than Western Chou. With the Shih Chi, the Shu Ching tells the story of Chieh's wickedness, the "bad last" king of Hsia. He is said to have oppressed his people with an iron despotism while indulging himself with a sexy consort, a lake filled with wine, and trees hung with meat delicacies. At length, indignation stirred Prince T'ang to take up arms against the tyrant and win a new dynasty amidst portents and convulsions of nature, as Heaven and Earth combined with men to show their displeasure with wickedness.

This is legendary history, of course, but the Han scholars who worked it out on the basis of preimperial documents were discovering for themselves the morality of imperial politics they were called on to teach their own rulers. Thereafter, the *Shu Ching* was essential to the sovereign's instruction by Confucian tutors. It provides the style by which the emperor refers to himself. He is a "Little Child"—that is, the emperor is to a higher power (Heaven) as a child is humble to his father. Similarly he is the "One Man" who holds his position by the Mandate of Heaven as the Son of Heaven. The emperor must serve Heaven as his officials must serve him; he stands as merely one link in a chain of command in some cosmic hierarchy, thereby disarming envy directed upward from below against royal privilege. The book also taught the emperor the signs of nature that presaged a possible loss of Mandate—eclipses, earthquakes, droughts, plagues—signs communicated to him by the court astrologer as indicators of court intrigues (Eberhard, 1957). Above all, the *Shu Ching* set the standard of Confucian political morality by which coups may be described as "rebellions." The distinction is erased between the actual historical nexus of the ruler's performance and his personal cultivation, that is, between his actions and his intentions (*see* Ch'en, 1972:196).

Han mythologists, filled with the newly won spirit of empire, projected emperors into the most distant past. The job of the San Hwang, or Three Primordial Sovereigns, was to teach uncultured men the arts of civilization and politics. The San Hwang, demigods descended on Earth from Heaven by way of miraculous births, exercised their sway over men who had not yet been taught politics. In this myth of beginnings, in which divine sovereigns act as culture heroes teaching mankind the culture of empire, reposes the sanctification of a lasting Chinese idea—that the principal function of government is not administration but education. The native Chinese model of government thus corresponds closely with the anthropological model of culturalism. In Han times, therefore, was fixed the cornerstone of Chinese political science, its method acquired in the homilies of the sort prepared by editors of the *Shu Ching*. The canon of Confucian classics (see Chapter 11) had not yet been established, but the body of ancient lore from which it was drawn was being shaped into a bibliography of unrefutable sacred texts for preachers of moral philosophy.

The first of the San Hwang is Fu-hsi, the Great Heavenly One, whose mission on Earth, starting in 2852 B.C. by traditional reckoning, was to instruct human animals in the ways of elementary human culture, the first step toward the civilized polity of empire. From his capital in present-day K'ai-feng, he instructed the people in hunting and fishing, making clothing from skins, cooking meat, avoiding incest, the laws of marriage and writing ideographs. The origins of human culture here are made synonymous with a Mesolithic, if not a Paleolithic, state of culture. The only incongruity is the art of writing, which Fu-hsi brought down from Heaven to replace knotted strings, or quipus. But even this can be rationalized anthropologically if the knotted-string records of ancient

China and of the Liu-ch'iu and Marquesan islands are traceable, as is the Mesolithic root-and-fruit complex, to a common source in the Hoabinhian culture. Indeed, one theory connects the origin of Chinese writing with the eight mystic trigrams and sixty-four hexagrams used in divination with the *I Ching*, or *Book of Changes*, which in turn are said to be derived from a type of quipu, or talley-stick (*see* Diringer, 1953:26, 101). Finally, Fu-hsi on his deathbed bequeathed his government to Shen-nung.

The reign of Shen-nung, the Divine Husbandman, began in 2737 B.C. He made wooden plows and taught the people husbandry. Except for the plow, a Neolithic state of culture is indicated. Consistant with this is the transition to the economics of commodity exchange between the specialized communities of an emergent civilization, for which Shen-nung instituted markets. Like Fu-hsi, Shen-nung passed on his government to a wise man of his own choice, Hwang-ti.

Hwang-ti, the Yellow Emperor (*hwang* means *yellow* as well as *sovereign*), took office in 2697 B.C. Yellow is the imperial color, the color of the northern loessland over which the kings of historical fact first presided. Hwang-ti inaugurated civilization proper by contributing wheel making, ceramics, and metallurgy. He built himself a palace—the first royal residence—and instituted a medium of exchange. Save for writing, precociously introduced by Fu-hsi, all the fundamentals of Bronze Age civilization are indicated here—wheels, metal, and palace architecture. Evidence for a medium of exchange, cowrie shells, appears in the archaeological record no earlier than the Shang dynasty. Shen-nung's wife introduced sericulture (raising silkworms for silk) but this, with pottery, was already part of the preceding Neolithic technology. Hwang-ti came to be worshipped in the imperial pantheon as the god of architecture.

The mythology of the San Hwang bears an uncanny resemblance to modern archaeological thought. Fu-hsi, Shen-nung, and Hwang-ti are culture heroes who taught the arts of Mesolithic, Neolithic, and civilized culture, respectively. The Han mythologers thus exhibit an intuitive sense of evolutionary change from the simple to the complex.

The predynastic rulers after the San Hwang number from two to six, depending on tradition. Ssu-ma Ch'ien recorded them all. The last two in all cases are Yao and Shun. They precede Yu the Great, who founded the Hsia dynasty in 2205 B.C. Yu is associated with the most important and oldest of all the ancient Chinese myths on record, the flood myth, dating from the earliest years of Western Chou. Thus it bears directly on memories of the preceding Shang dynasty, the first stage of Chinese civilization. Western Chou itself is a continuation of the Shang stage, the era of city-states.

Yao and Shun are the Erh Ti, the Two Emperors of Antiquity, who figure repeatedly in the Confucian canon as models of sagacity for hereditary rulers to follow. They were the last and best of the ancient sovereigns to appoint successors on the basis of merit, not blood, before Yu set the precedent for dynastic government. Tutors of the emperor from the Han dynasty onward have therefore justified their influence as a duty to instill in the emperor the wisdom of the truly meritorious sage kings of old. Again mythology backs up the importance of education in Chinese political science.

Yao found the territories of his empire flooded and he appointed Kun, the father of Yu, to recover them. Kun's method was to dam them up. This failed. Yao's successor, Shun, then appointed Yu. Yu's method was to channel the waters into the four seas. This worked. As a reward, Shun handed Yu the throne, which he subsequently turned into a dynastic possession.

Unlike the biblical flood myth, the Chinese waters were not called for by an act of divine retribution against sinful humanity. The floods were a fact of nature that had to be coped with by some means of hydraulic engineering. In fact, the Kun-Yu myth may embody a memory of policy conflict between two rival methods of water control in Western Chou irrigation, flood prevention and river navigation. The two methods are embankment of existing rivers (Kun's) versus deepening rivers and dredging new channels (Yu's). Kun (significantly) came to be the patron of dikes, embankments, and walls in the imperial pantheon, and Yu the culture hero of irrigation.

According to Joseph Needham (1971:249) in his monumental work on science and technology in China, these two methods were given mythological significance because they also gave symbolic force to opposing philosophies of government. Confucian jurists of the Eastern Chou dynasty argued the case for behavioral dikes against crime in their emphasis on *li*, or right conduct, carried to the point of ritualized perfection. In the *Li Chi*, the Classic of Ritual, it is said: "*Li* prevents the rise of disorder and confusion, and is like a dike which prevents the overflow of water" (*Ching Chieh*, 7). Against this the Taoists complained that the male principle of convex ridges alongside rivers violated nature; better to go along effortlessly *(wu wei)* with the feminine Valley Spirit of receptive concavities. The Confucianists want to dam up disorder by a vigilant education in exemplary behavior, while the Taoist position—as little government as possible—finds its analogy in the natural proclivity of water to find its own level: things will take care of themselves without excessive human interference. The flood myth thus combines into one cognitive whole two rival schools of civil engineering with two ideas about governing men.

It would be fruitless, no doubt, to examine the myth for any knowledge about the terrain of early civilization. The story of Yu, however, does contain some clues about the nature of Shang urbanism at the very start of civilization in China. Part of the *Shu Ching* purports to describe the political geography of the Hsia dynasty from contemporary records. Actually it describes that of the Shang dynasty as perceived by its inheritors, the Western Chou. This section of the *Shu Ching* embodies one of the oldest and most enduring of Chinese political concepts fundamental to the politics of culturalism—the symbolism of the Center.

Limiting the habitable earth are four seas enclosing a rectangle occupied by the Chinese dominion. Confucius harks back to this concept when he says in the *Analects:* "All within the four seas are brothers" (*Lun Yu*, XII:5). It figures in the title of Mao Tse-tung's favorite Chinese novel, the fourteenth-century *Shui Hu Chuan*, or *Story of the Water Margin*, translated by Pearl Buck as *All Men Are Brothers* (1937). Contrary to the expectations of Western humanists, this is no Chinese endorsement of their belief in world brotherhood. It is a statement of ethnocentrism, not egalitarianism. Its true meaning in paraphrase is: "All Chinese are Chinese by geographical definition, and anybody outside the four water margins is not a brother but a wild barbarian." The further from the Center, the more barbarian. *Chung Kwo*, or Middle Kingdom, is still part of China's self-designation on the world map.

One of the oldest documents in the *Shu Ching* thus establishes the centrality of the Chinese realm. Central to the realm itself is the capital city. It is central wherever it is located. The domains of Yu, from which the king receives tribute in accordance with local resources, are arranged in concentric squares around the capital, as shown in Figure 3. Within 500 *li* of the capital (one *li* is about one-third of a mile) are the agricultural fields. Beyond that in another zone of 500 *li* are the lands and cities of the state officers, who are also the kingdom's nobility. Beyond that is a buffer zone of barbarian principalities in the process of learning to be Chinese. In the next zone, barbarian acculturation to the Chinese center takes place under military pacification, and in the fifth and last zone, the barbarians run wild. The two outer domains are filled with barbarians whose tribal names are synonymous with the four directions: the *I* in the East, *Man* in the South, *Jung* in the West, and *Ti* in the North. But there is a fifth direction in Chinese cosmology, the topocosmic Center, pointing to the heart of civilization. The Wu Fang, or Five Directions, denote China at the *axis mundi* and the remainder of the world lying outside its four borders.

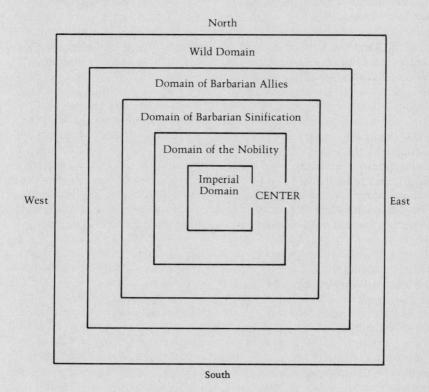

FIGURE 3.   The Five Domains.

Such is the world view of the Shang dynasty, as reported in legendary materials originating in Western Chou times and compiled by the myth-makers of Confucian politics in early Han times. In the Confucian mythology of government, the king's city is a topocosmic city aligned with the polestar, the celestial counterpart of the *axis mundi*, from which the ruler's *te*, or virtue, emanates in the four directions. Of Shun it was said that he had merely to sit on his throne, his back to the dark *yin* regions of the North and facing the bright *yang* regions of the South, and *te* came forth from him without need of activity on his part (Soothill, 1952:1–2, 114–15). The Confucian analects in particular are addressed to the doctine of government by virtue cultivated on the part of the royal person, using examples of the sage kings to insist that what happens at the Center determines all that happens around it. "The Master said, He who rules by moral force *(te)* is like the polestar, which remains in its place while all the lesser stars do homage to it" (*Lun Yu*, II:1, tr. by Waley, 1938). As the lesser stars—a celestial court—revolved around the polestar, so did the king's officers, noblemen, and distant tributaries revolve around the king. The myth also served to establish cultural distance between rulers and ruled, for Chinese officials were still called "stars in heaven" by peasants until the end of the monarchy.

The myth of the four quarters is common to many of the orthogenetic civilizations, in both the New and the Old Worlds (Perry, 1966; Wheatley, 1971). But only in China did the ethnocentrism of the myth remain so long uncontradicated by the opposing force of strong neighbors that it took contact with the steamboat powers of the West in the nineteenth century to disabuse Chinese rulers of it (Elisséeff, 1963). So it was still possible in 1796 for the Emperor Ch'ien Lung to write King George III of England, "My capital is the hub and center about which all quarters of the globe revolve" (in Backhouse and Bland, 1914:327).

SHANG

With wheel making, smelting, and writing, the Shang city-states of North China acquired the basic technologies of Bronze Age civilization, which had first appeared in ancient Sumer and Egypt between one and two thousand years previously. This lag is evidently the function of the distance travelled by knowledge and skills. But how much Chinese skill owes to West Asian knowledge is controversial. The controversy is irrelevant, however, because the further the diffusion, the greater the local influence on it.

To begin with, writing is strictly indigenous. No connections have been traced outside the Chinese realm. The idea of writing may have diffused from the West, but not the script itself. Some twenty percent of the Shang pictographs are part of today's Chinese lexicon of ideographs. The Shang lexicon of over 2000 characters is known mainly from 100,000 inscribed shells and bones—the shoulder blades of sheep and the plastrons of tortoises inscribed by diviners (Cheng, 1960:177–78). On behalf of the king, diviners consulted the spirits of his ancestors every ten days (the Chinese week) about weather and health for the next decade, and about the prospects of hunting and war. The questions were first brushed onto bone or shell, then inscribed. Brush-writing had its beginnings in a Yang-shao technique of pottery painting (Cheng, 1973:207). After it was inscribed, the oracle (bone or shell) was smeared with sacrificial blood, the catalyst for the meeting of the male forces *(yang)* of Heaven represented by fire, and the female forces *(yin)* of Earth represented by the turtle (Newberry, 1934: 52). Yin/yang dualism is as old as Yang-shao culture, whose spindle whorls are sometimes decorated with interlocking spirals of black (yin) and white (yang) (Cheng, 1966: fig. 23).

The oracle was consulted by reading yes/no answers from cracks produced in the bones by applying scorching heat from a point source. The outcome was recorded next to the prediction, then filed in storage pits —the state archives. The same means of divination with sheep and cattle bones but without the aid of writing was practiced during Lung-shan times, another example of continuity between Bronze Age civilization in China and its Neolithic foundations. Not recovered from the Shang archives nor from those of the Western Chou, thanks to decay, are historical annals written on bamboo slips; they were known to Han antiquarians, however, who claim to have transcribed some of them following the invention of rag paper in about A.D. 100 (Goodrich, 1959:52). Bamboo slips were the ordinary writing material until the advent of paper, and the Chinese ideograph for *book* derives from a pictographic representation of narrow bamboo slips tied together, to which format Chinese writing owes its typical vertical display.

Bronze metallurgy is an open question: Was it imported from the West, ultimately from Sumer where it evolved by 3000 B.C., or was it independently developed? One authority inclines to the latter opinion, believing that bronze may have appeared as early as Lung-shan times (Chang, 1968:238–39). The actual occurrence of bronze in China is dated from about 1700 or 1600 B.C. The case for an indigenous bronze industry is argued from the fact that Shang craftsmen used the new medium to carry forward traditional ceramic shapes and traditional design motifs carved in wooden and slate artifacts. But there is nothing to prevent an imported technology from being assimilated to local design restraints. In any case, the raw materials were easy to lay hands on. The usual formula for bronze is nine parts of copper to one of tin. Elemental copper was fairly abundant in the form of nuggets on the surface of the earth before man began using it in quantity, and was available as such in North China in Shang times. Tin occurs in chemical compounds, such as stannic oxide, but must be smelted out. Walnut-sized lumps of this compound, cassiterite, occurred on the surface of tin streams before exploitation led to underground mining. A tin stream is a dried stream bed into which cassiterite has accumulated. Shang craftsmen received tin from the present-day provinces of Szechwan and Yunnan from tin streams by way of trade, which had the effect of stimulating the regional cultures of Shu and Pa to approach a state level of organization.

The users of bronze were the power persons of the Shang city-states, kings and noblemen armed with metal weapons and glorified by metal luxury goods produced by a class of highly evolved, but captive, craftsmen. Everything relates either to war, hunting, or ancestor worship: dagger axes, knives, arrow- and spearheads, horse and chariot fittings, masks and helmets, bells and drums, and ritual vessels (*see* Cheng, 1960).

Wheel making, a technology associated with war chariots, is the most interesting trait because it suggests an Indo-European invasion. With the Indo-Europeans, the horse enters history. The Indo-Europeans were the first in a long series of warrior horsemen who emerged from the natural breeding grounds of the horse to dominate Neolithic settlements and scourge civilizations east and west from their center of origin in the Eurasian steppes. They were not horse riders as were the Scythians, Huns, Turks, and Mongols of later times. Their engine of war was a team of horses yoked to light, spoke-wheeled chariots. Wherever these chariots appear, among the Celts in the British Isles or among the Aryans in India, they are a sign of Indo-European conquest. It would be surprising if similar chariots found in the tombs of Shang kings did not signify the Indo-European conquest of Lung-shan China and an outside stimulus for the rise of civilization there, of which the Shang dynasty is the first stage. Certainly the Chinese royal dragon is nothing if not a mythic transformation of the horse. Even the ancient Chinese word for horse, *mar*, suggests comparison with the Irish *marc* and English *mare*. (Pulleyblank, 1966; Piggott, 1974; *see* also Fairservice, 1959;130–32).

Indo-European is a language family whose originators may be traced to the Ukrainian grasslands of southern Russia. Migrants in all directions from this area became the speakers of the Italic, Celtic, Germanic, Greek, Balto-Slavic, Indo-Iranian, and Tocharian languages. The Indo-European homeland, before the migrations began, was located on the northern fringes of the kingdoms of Sumer and Akkad, where a Neolithic people began domesticating the horse around 2500 B.C. It was the domesticated horse that liberated the Indo-European people from dependence on the agricultural half of Neolithic mixed farming and gave them freedom to move as pastoralists, first with the horse as a pack animal and later with the horse as a draft animal pulling war chariots.

The Indo-European chariot was modeled after the Sumerian battle car, drawn by onagers and rolling on solid wheels. The imitation was drawn by horses and rolled on spoked wheels, a combination that gave the chariot a speed and lightness that rapidly carried the Indo-Europeans, with the whole Bronze Age panoply of war, throughout the east/west corridor of the Eurasian steppes.

Surely the Indo-European charioteers continued on their way from the Iranian plateau in an eastward direction for several more generations, marrying locally and sending their warrior sons onward again, to hop from oasis to oasis across Chinese Turkestan (Sinkiang) and finally to settle in the densely populated Yellow River valley, there to dominate the Lung-shan farmers as Bronze Age overlords. The most eastern locus of an Indo-European language is in Sinkiang, where Tocharian was spoken until one thousand years ago and where in the southwestern corner, Tajiki and Sarikoli still are spoken, languages of the Iranic branch related to Baluchi, Kurdish, and Persian (Bessac, 1963:92). In the rest of China, the Sino-Tibetan family of languages is dominant. If the Indo-European hypothesis is correct, we must assume that a small number of invaders were, in time, absorbed by the native Chinese population.

Writing and the bronze industry in China show indigenous qualities by the time they appear in the archaeological record. The same is true for the horse-drawn chariot, which appears as mortuary furniture in the Shang tombs at An-yang but in none of the pre-Yin sites. Does that mean that chariots did not occur earlier or simply that they were not entombed earlier? The original overlords of the Lung-shan population would have behaved not like kings whose position was inherited but like Indo-European chiefs whose position was elective from among their fellow warriors. The royal tombs at An-yang already belong to a time when elective chieftainship (if it existed earlier) had been replaced by dynastic succession, complete with royal burials of the king's treasures and retainers. (The property of Indo-European chieftains at their death was distributed among their followers.)

The transition from the elective to the dynastic condition may be remembered from legendary material about the sage kings who appointed their successors up until the time of Yu. Shun appointed Yu, but Yu passed the throne on to his son. Another echo of Indo-European chieftainship, often phrased in the pastoral language of a shepherd caring for his flock or a cowchief his herd, is found in the *Shu Ching.* There Shun is said to have appointed five *mu,* or cowherds, to assist him. Another echo may be found in the speech in which Prince T'ang rouses the multitude to fight the "last bad" king of Hsia; the host spoken to may be interpreted as a tribal assembly of the sort Indo-European chieftains used to muster in planning their cattle raids and military adventures.

William H. McNeill, in his imposing work of culture history, *The Rise of the West* (1963:219), infers that the quadrilateral layout of Shang cities is the architectural heritage of the Indo-European charioteers' encampments, a form that in the west persisted in the campsites of the Roman army. But whether sources of outside influence may or may not be traced, the style of Shang civilization remains unique and indigenous.

At the height of Shang civilization, its core area covered little more than six thousand square miles in northern Honan. This is the area of high culture and city building. Beyond that lies a zone of developed Shang culture in everything but developed urbanism. And beyond that lies a wide peripheral zone in which Shang artifacts, or local artifacts with Shang motifs, occur in settings of Neolithic tribalism that may be classed as Lungshanoid. The archaeological record thus tends to confirm the political geography of the Shang dynasty as described in tradition as a cultured center and a less-cultured periphery. Ranged in concentric zones around the capital city were the homes of the nobility, and surrounding them were tribal peoples in all directions, some of them in the process of acculturation to Shang culture, others beyond the reach of its influence.

Shang urbanism is known from four sites. An-yang, the last capital (Yin), was the first to be excavated. This is the only site from which chariot burials, inscribed oracle bones, and a flourishing art have been revealed. Yin was the royal seat of the nineteenth through the twenty-ninth kings (styled *wang* in the oracle bones), who must have ruled from about 1400 to about 1100 B.C. Cheng-chou, almost certainly the next-to-the-last capital of Ao, was the royal seat of the tenth through the nineteenth kings. It was the nineteenth king, P'an Keng, who is said to have moved the capital from Ao to Yin. Cheng-chou is noteworthy as an archaeological site because excavations there have been carried all the way down to Neolithic levels. The other two sites, uncovered only recently, are located at Lo-yang and Hui-hsien. Lo-yang contains some twenty tombs equipped with human and animal sacrifices, as at An-yang, dating from all stages of Shang development. Cheng-chou occupies a strategic position for trade, where all routes across the North China plain funnel into the western uplands. At one time it may have been the capital city of Po, the third from the last of the Shang royal cities. The tombs at Hui-hsien seem to be contemporary with those of the last capital city of Yin at An-yang (Wheatley, 1971:96).

The earliest cities in the world originated in West Asia in 3000 B.C. and influenced urban development everywhere from Egypt to India. Chinese cities originated between 1700 and 1500 B.C., but not as copies of Mesopotamian ones. Early Chinese cities differ markedly in layout from those of Sumer, for example: the urban settlement pattern is not spatially compact but rather is dispersed among a variety of community types. The rural-urban relationship was expressed not in city as compared with countryside but instead as a network of specialized communities that included a number of farming villages, which supported everything. Other community types in this network were hamlets specializing in bronze metallurgy, bone work, jade, and ceramics. The organizational headquarters for all this was the royal community, with its palace buildings and temples surrounded by a wall. The royal necropolis (the ancient cemetery) was yet another center of activity.

At Cheng-chou (Ao), the palace complex was surrounded by a rectangular wall of pounded earth 1.3 miles in circumference, thirty feet high, and sixty feet across at the base. The labor required to construct this wall has been estimated, by experimenting on a small scale with the original technology of construction, at a minimum of 180,000 man-years (Chang, 1968:205). This same technology—the mass mobilization of men to excavate earth with shovels or hoes, to carry it in baskets or shirt bibs, and to compact it in thin layers within a wooden crib moved up for each new layer—has been used throughout Chinese history, including the building of the earth works enclosing the great water reservoirs constructed under the communist regime near the site of the Ming tombs.

No wall has yet been uncovered at An-yang (Yin). The most spectacular remains there are the eleven royal tombs for the twelve Shang kings of Yin (the twelfth died in a palace fire during the Chou conquest). These tombs are pits sixty-five feet square and forty-three feet deep, entered by either two or four stepped ramps. At the bottom, a twenty-three-foot square pit contains the body of the king in a double-walled wooden coffin. Placed on the shelf around this pit and on the ramps are the king's grave goods and slaughtered retainers. Here also were conducted compound animal sacrifices in a strikingly exact parallel with the Roman su-ove-taurilia: two pigs, three sheep, and five cows or oxen (Kroeber, 1948:736). Only at An-yang do the chariot burials, with horses, occur. It took about seven thousand working days to fill the big pits at An-yang with pounded earth.

Unlike the tombs of dead kings, the homes of living royalty were unimposing. In China, the monumental architecture associated with the early civilizations is concealed underground. The palace dwellings at An-yang were nothing more than Lung-shan longhouses mounted on pounded-earth platforms about six feet thick. Some were larger than their

Neolithic prototype—one rests on a platform nearly one hundred feet long—still they were nothing more than airy constructions of wooden posts and gables roofed over with thatch and walled in by nonsupportive screens of matting. The Chinese elite continued to inhabit the longhouse until the twentieth century; the Chinese compound housing the multigenerational great family is simply a series of longhouses set in parallel rows and enclosed on both sides by walls. Upper-class dwellings thus reflected in miniature the layout of the aristocratic center of the ancient city-states.

The transition to civilization can be followed through the changing settlement pattern. In Lung-shan times, the farming village existed in an isolated context of Neolithic tribalism. The pit houses of each village were disposed around their own ceremonial center, the longhouse of shamanistic leaders evidently in charge of a cult of the dead. These isolated villages later nucleated with one another to form multicommunity states centered on the longhouses of the royal complex.

Lung-shan villages, each with its own kiln, were modified in some instances to become specialized industrial villages for making not only high-quality pottery but also other luxury goods for royalty, ritual vessels for the priesthood, and military supplies for the nobility. Only the industrial village now contained a longhouse, doubtless the home of the family or lineage holding the craft secrets of the community's specialized technological skills, although this residence did not rest on an earthen platform, as did the shaman's longhouse that had once belonged to each farming village. The shaman's longhouse had been elevated to a religious center within the palace compound, under the king and his priesthood, serving all the communities of a small city-state. Still, the chief craftsmen of the industrial villages ranked higher than farmers and, like Bronze Age artisans elsewhere, must have worked under court supervision.

Significantly, the Shang political entity is associated with ceremonies of ancestor worship conducted in public, both in the royal compound and in the royal cemeteries. Each Shang king sacrificed to his own royal ancestors, seeking blessings and protection from their spirits. In addition, he sacrificed to Shang Ti, an anthropomorphic high god that figured as the Supreme Ancestor of all the people, high and low. It probably follows that the distance in social stratification between the hereditary ruling class and the people was calculated according to stratified kinship (see Fried, 1967:126), in which rank is determined by closeness to, or remove from, a given ancestor. In this way, ranking of individual family members may be calculated relative to the family head (as in the extended family of recent years), families relative to a lineage or clan head, and lineages or clans relative to each other by reference to an eponym—a fictive ancestor for whom the family or lineage is named. If the Shang king and the nobility belonged to higher-ranking lineages and the common people to lesser ones, then all were traceable to the eponymous First Ancestor, Shang Ti. The king may have reminded the people of their common ancestry with him by means of public ceremonies of ancestor worship, by which he laid claim to their labor and tribute.

Civilization, by definition, requires the political state to bring it into existence, and the state in turn requires social stratification, imposed by conquest or evolved internally. The organizing principle of the state in all the early civilizations has been the city-state, that is, a city and its supportive countryside. Until recently, the Chinese city never evolved beyond its Bronze Age function—the administration of the region in which it is set —to become a municipality with its own self-government (Eberhard, 1956:266–67).

In Shang dynasty China, the territory belonging to the city—palace center plus industrial hamlets plus Neolithic farming villages—coincided with the state. The Shang domain consisted of a set of such city-states of like political culture, each having its aristocratic center, whose kings, or *wang*, acknowledged a preeminent king in the lordly resident of the capital city. The title *wang* as written in the Shang script is derived from a pictograph meaning "territorial chieftain"—a man, legs apart, standing on his ground (Creel, 1937:343). The king of each city-state held liens on his own surrounding territory. Preeminence of the overking followed from his cultural leadership as the only person privileged to worship Shang Ti, the anthropomorphic First Ancestor of the Shang people, whose abstract representation was T'ien, or Heaven. Heaven was conceived as the gathering place for the spirits of all the high kings, from which vantage (if properly sacrificed to) they collectively bestowed blessings on the incumbent and his realm.

Like the ancient civilizations of Mesopotamia and Egypt, the politics of the Shang dynasty's state organization was clothed in ceremonies drawing in the participation of the ruled. The Shang ceremonies of state were those of ancestor worship. In later times, the Chinese Son of Heaven worshipped his father, Heaven, and his imperial ancestors in private, and no kinship with the people was imputed. But the Shang king worshipped in public, and the object of worship, Shang Ti, was said to be the ancestor of all the people—kings, nobles, and subjects. The mass of people is described in the oracle bones as *hsiao-jen* or *shu-jen*. *Shu-jen* remained throughout Chinese history a vernacular term for commoners; Confucius popularized *hsiao-jen* as a word for "little man" as opposed to gentleman.

Shang sacrifice used human victims, beheaded. They were captured during the autumn plundering campaigns—a mixture of war and hunting—which included that hallmark of Indo-European sport, cattle raiding. Slaves captured were put to chores of drudgery in the palace compound but not to the primary tasks of agriculture; a slave economy would cost more to supervise than it earned. Agriculture remained the task of Neolithic farmers, drawn to the spectacle of beheading, at which time they brought tribute for the First Ancestor. In the small communities of the Shang city-states, tax obligations were fulfilled in the course of government-led ceremonies that invited not mere spectators but participants—as in the pageantry associated with the labor of digging and filling the royal tombs. Mediating the participation of the *shu-jen* in the king's sacrificial rites were the officiating shamans, men or women of commoner origin; they were never drawn from the aristocracy (Eichhorn, 1969:31–42).

But as the political community grew from Neolithic villages to the proportion of territorial states and later to empire, hereditary rulers gradually amputated their houses from any real or fictive ties with the *shu-jen*. With the Chou enlargement of the Shang domain, the royal house no longer worshipped the First Ancestor, Shang Ti, but his impersonal abstraction, *T'ien*, or Heaven; and the nobility came to find conjuring and exorcism too unsophisticated for their tastes. The rationalism of Confucianism soon killed the appetite for magic altogether. By the fifth century A.D., shamans were excluded from state sacrifices, and their personal employment by emperors, even to evoke the spiritis of dead consorts, came to a stop by the end of the T'ang dynasty. In the Sung dynasty shamanism was proscribed by law, and provisions against it were retained in the penal code of the terminal dynasty. But by then, shamanism had long been driven back into the village sources of folk culture from which it sprang, there and in secret societies to work as a magical aspect of popular Taoism (Needham, 1956:137–38; Fitzgerald, 1950:46–47; Werner, 1919:187–91).

Ancestor worship, however, remained the dominant religion of China, even behind the rationalist disguise of Confucianism. The emperor conducted ancestor worship in public as a political act; heads of families conducted ancestor worship in private as an act of kinship solidarity. The Son of Heaven sacrificed to Heaven and to his imperial ancestors; household heads to their family ancestors. Shamans, as a professional class of priests, no longer figured in these rites. In the end, China produced priests but no priesthood. Perhaps this was inevitable. In ancestor worship, each individual has his own deity or deities to worship; and as no man has the motive, except as an act of treason against the state, to worship another's, the emperor as well as every family head must play the priest for himself (Werner, 1941). When elites of the realm came to quote with approval the words of Confucius, "For a man to sacrifice to ancestral spirits which do not belong to him is presumptuous" (*Lun Yu*, II:24), then was the idea of a universal church with an attendant class of hierophants long past the possibility of realization.

WESTERN CHOU

Little is known archaeologically of the Chou people whose armies took An-yang around 1122 B.C. Thenceforth, until the end of the era of city-states, Chinese political history is known as that of the Western Chou. This period was named by native historians after the fact, to distinguish it from the same regime moved to an eastern situation in Lo-yang after it was routed, but not defeated, by enemies to the west of its home capital of Hao in the Wei River valley. There, in the words of the *Book of Songs*, the Chou lived in "caverns shaped like pottery kilns before they built any houses" (*Shih Ching*, III:I:iii). The reference is to caves hollowed out of the loess deposits. Troglodytism, or cave dwelling, does not necessarily imply a low cultural level; well over ten million Chinese still live in loess caves in the provinces of Honan, Shansi, Shensi, and Kansu, as did Mao Tse-tung in his Yenan days (*see* Rudofsky, 1964: caption to fig. 16).

One long-held theory is that the Chou were a barbarian people on the western margins of Shang civilization (Creel, 1937; but for a reversal of opinion, *see* Creel, 1970). Evidence is growing, however, to indicate that Chou culture may be viewed as a local variant of Bronze Age civilization in China, one that developed out of regional differences in the same Lungshanoid horizon that produced Shang culture. Moreover, the relationship between Chou and Shang may be close enough to justify using the word *rebellion* in place of *conquest* on the part of Chou (Wheatley,

1971:111). The Chou conquest did not stop at the borders of the Shang domain. It carried far beyond into the unexploited Lungshanoid hinterland. Garrisoned there in a sea of sub-Neolithic and Neolithic natives, Chou colonists built fortified towns, but only the living quarters and temple buildings of the aristocracy were enclosed; craftsmen and the newly won peasantry still lived outside the walls in their own communities. Like the walls of Shang cities, the walls enclosing the aristocratic compound in the dispersed urbanism of Chou design were oriented for astronomical significance to the four cardinal directions, as calculated from the polestar of the time.

According to one tradition, the Chou conquerors took over fifty Shang city-states and founded close to seventy new ones (Wheatley, 1971:193, note 20). Not all members of the Shang nobility were extinguished, however. Some were allowed to continue in power in exchange for loyalty pledged to the first Chou sovereign, King Wu, leader of the conquest. Descendants of the defeated Shang kings were assigned feudal estates in Sung, in present-day Honan, said to be the home of Confucius's grandfather (Smith, 1973:41). Expert craftsmen were transferred to the industrial quarters of Lo-yang. Literate priests were retained in the Chou court as scribes.

Beyond the Shang domain, Chou noblemen took with them fully equipped parties of soldiers, peasants, and artisans capable of self-sufficient life. The peasant colonists in these parties practiced swidden agriculture under military supervision with military precision: eight units of forest land felled and tilled for themselves for every one devoted to their lord (Cheng, 1963:293).

Note that the Chou conquest was carried out by incorporating key elements from the entire class structure, not by advancing with military forces alone and subordinating all else before them. This is the distinction made by Max Weber (1922, 1951) between Chinese administrative feudalism and Western military feudalism. European feudal domains (fiefs) isolated military service as the basis for land granted by the sovereign; whereas Chinese feudal domains (prebends) of the Western Chou dynasty were granted on the basis of more broadly based community services. These prebendal endowments originated in the dispersed urbanism of the Shang dynasty. But even after the advent of compact urbanism (division of labor contained and repeated within each community) in Eastern Chou times, feudal holdings remained on a civilian footing. By that time, however, the nature of endowments began to change, and by imperial times prebends no longer were held as land grants but as bureaucratic posts. A prebend, according to Weber, denotes the rights of an office holder to income from either church or state lands. Weber thus notes a similarity between the medieval church in the West and Chinese feudalism, preimperial and imperial.*

In theory, the lands gained from the Chou conquest belonged to the Chou sovereign, who claimed the title *wang* exclusively for himself. But the Chou nobility eventually claimed kingship for themselves; they had,

*If we were to be consistent in the usage of Weber's vocabulary, the entire history of China from the preimperial dynasties to the last of the imperial ones would have to be characterized as feudal (prebendal). We will restrict the usage of the word *feudal* in the Chinese context, however, to preimperial times. For a technical discussion of prebendalism and other types of domain, see Wolf (1966:50–59).

after all, come to rule complete city-states, little kingdoms. In time they felt only vestigial loyalty for the royal domain from which they originally departed. But at first they had set out as kinsmen of the king, by blood or marriage, to colonize lands held by him as a partrimony to divide among his own. Of the sixty-eight new city-states, fifty were founded by members of the royal family. The states they founded they called the "older and younger brother states." The remaining eighteen were founded by affinal relatives (relatives by marriage). The city-states they founded they called the "soral nephew and uncle states" (Cheng, 1963:xxv). It is evident from the rituals of investiture that the lords of these states regarded themselves at the time as feudatories, sharing in a responsibility with their overlord to hold his real estate.

Myth recounted that the feudatories carried with them a clod of earth from the king's altar to *Sheh*, the god of the soil, to plant at the base of their own local altar. These altars were truncated pyramids of pounded earth, open to the air, located to the west of the palace gate at the royal center and at its patrimonial localities. The surfaces of the pyramids were faced with colored earths keyed to the numerology of the five elements and the five directions. On the sides were blue-green for east (spring, wood, bursting vegetation under the rising sun), red for south (summer, fire, yang), white for west (autumn, metal, weapons, war), and black for north (winter, water, damp, dark, yin). The top was surfaced with yellow for the center (midsummer, earth, the empyrean of Shang Ti). In addition, the king's noble descendants and affines were reputed in myth to have received from the king their territories, cities, and people, just as he himself received from Heaven his mandate to rule. His title, Son of Heaven, evidently is of Chou coinage, as is the word for Heaven itself, *T'ien*.

When appearing at the royal court, the feudatories were addressed as *kung, hou, po, tze,* and *nan,* usually translated in the language of European feudalism as duke, marquis, earl, viscount, and baron. Collectively they were the *chu-hou,* nobles who had received estates and titles from the king. These titles are known from Shang inscriptions, although nobody knows what they meant at that time. They were used in Western Chou times to indicate the size of territory a feudal lord developed under his rule (said to be the same as that received as patrimony from the king), but in his home state he was addressed as *kung,* or duke, whatever the size of his *kwo. Kwo* is a Shang word translated today as state, principality, or country. In writing it is derived from the Shang pictograph for city-state, a walled palace defended from within by a dagger-ax. The Chou king styled himself as the head of many clans, presiding over a *kwo-chia,* or nation-family. The rulers of empire used the same term as a conceit for empery (Kaizuka, 1956:17–22; Wheatley, 1971:119).

The language of European feudalism applies closely, but not exactly, to the Chou state. In medieval Europe, enfeoffment (investing with a fief) was a contractual agreement between king and individual noblemen; in China it validated preexisting ties between the sovereign and related families or branching clans. The European king invested nobility selected by him; the Chou king inducted an established aristocracy, the *chu-hou,* ranked by degrees of kinship distance with him as calculated in the male line of descent and by marriage into a community of patrimonial estate holders (Wheatley, 1971:197). The differences are not academic, although in both cases government was farmed out to a military aristocracy who practiced war as a game, and in both cases the limited sovereignty of the vassal states was only a temporary condition before their sovereignty was made complete (see Creel, 1970: ch. 11). Under Western military feudalism, however, the fact of local autonomy was in due time recognized by degrees, as in the Magna Charta. But the Chou kings never permitted this; they preferred usurpation to legalized autonomy. Guided by ideological claims to administrative universality, the Center kept its faith throughout the centuries, until under communism it acquired the technical means of control to infiltrate all localities in accord with an ancient, but impotent, ideal.

In time, the Chou nobility took the title of *wang* for themselves and asserted their independence as rulers of independent kingdoms, beginning to compete among themselves for the privilege of holding sovereignty over the whole. This may have repeated on a larger scale what happened when the Chou rebels annexed Shang. The high king of the Shang realm presided, from the vantage point of his capital city located at the *axis mundi*, over a number of like city-states headed by statesmen also styled *wang*. One king in his topocosmic city held superior prestige and religious importance in the eyes of the others and they over the lesser nobility. The Chou conquest apparently extended the Shang system. But while the imperial system finally put an end to Western Chou feudalism, Chinese emperors continued to rule as cultural leaders in the name of a unitary state divided not into principalities or kingdoms but into provinces, whose governors ruled like kings—if only for their term of office.

The state rulers of Western Chou began as feudatories in fact, even if no rules or ceremonies designated them as such. The momentum of the conquest took relatives, retainers, and officials of the king's great expedition beyond the Shang domain, where they simply pioneered their own claims in the uncivilized wilderness. Under these conditions they were not disposed to forget their civilized heritage nor soon launch their own campaigns to outdo the Center from which they spread outward. Creel summarizes the Western Chou by saying, "For a long time many Chinese states were little more than islands of Chinese culture and military control surrounded by people who were little if at all Sinicized, and potentially if not actually dangerous" (1970:70).

The four generations that conquered Shang and sat as the first kings of Western Chou were remarkable men whose abilities were compressed in so short a period of time—like that of Periclean Athens—that they created a resounding legend of historic consequence. Every king that sat on the throne, even after the royal domain had been reduced by the growing independence of its former vassals, sat as semidivine kings by anticipation. After death they would join *T'ien*, from which each successive Son of Heaven received his mandate (Creel, 1970:421). No higher standards of culture rooted in no greater epics of military and political success more effectively brought about a sense of local glory than did kinship with the king, reaffirmed by investiture for each new generation of an entrenched aristocracy.

The Chou regent actually had no power to refuse investiture, but he could scarcely dispute the authentication of natural heirs when the investiture ceremonies remained virtually the only commodity for which the *chu-hou* appealed to him, even after his military power had declined and his domain shrunk to almost nothing. In addition, the royal domain long continued as the headquarters for ancestral ceremonies conducted by the king on behalf of his clan and that of its branches, whose annual attendance at the court temple was not only required as a filial duty but welcomed as a chance to touch base with the center of high culture. The court ritual of the king influenced the court ritual of the *chu-hou,* with the result that the design of bronze vessels and other ceremonial goods carried a uniform artistic tradition throughout all *kwo* even when these states commenced internecine warfare. The boundaries of this tradition in fact defined the boundaries of China at the time, whose name, *Chung-kwo*—the central states—is still China's name.

The Chinese name for investiture, *feng,* harks back to the imaginary days of original enfeoffment. As a noun it means the local altar raised on a clod of earth carried from the royal altar to the god of the soil, and as a verb it means to raise a new altar, and thus is used as a translation for the phrase "to enfeoff" (Wheatley, 1971:197). But if the altar to the god of the soil, located on the west side of the palace gate, came to mark the cultural subordination of the Western Chou feudatory to the center, his political independence was marked by an altar to his ancestors located to the east of the palace gate. A cult of ancestors is divisive because its priesthood belongs to no universal church—a departure from European feudal society—but to the dominant male in each unit of worship, which is also a political unit, a *kwo.* Political unity under empire did not come to China until ancestor worship had been divorced from state business for all save the emperor, and was limited for others to the sanctification of private family business. The emperor, too, worshipped his own imperial ancestors in the interests of the royal clan; but worship of Heaven, in the interests of the realm, was his exclusive privilege.

Heaven worship, however, is only half of the equation. The Chinese emperor, like the Chou king, worshipped both Heaven *(T'ien)* and Earth *(Ti)* in his cosmic role as mediator between the two. The best place to locate the capital city in which to conduct the necessary rituals was the *axis mundi*—a place determined by geomancy where the axis of the cosmos turned with the axis of the realm; the realm itself was taken as the whole world under Heaven. As Mencius says, it is the job of the Son of Heaven "to stand in the center of the earth and stabilize the people within the four seas" (VIIA:xxi:2).

Ti, the Earth under Heaven, is not of the same earth built into local altars to the god of the soil. The former, Ti, is the nether counterpart of Heaven; the latter is *T'u,* the soil of which the earth is composed. Altars to the god of the soil existed at every level of the Chinese political hierarchy as a corresponding religious hierarchy, but Ti, the Sovereign Earth, remained a translocal concern of the emperor as it was of the Chou kings. Liu Pang, the founder of the Han dynasty, decreed that altars in the name of specific localities, once confined to the clan states, could be set up even by villagers. Chinese historians consider this the origin of neighborhood temples, seen in various parts of Chinese villages, devoted to the combined Earth-soil deities of T'u-ti. (Werner, 1932:412–16). It is more likely, however, that worship of the whole sovereign territory by kings and emperors was rather an aspect of high culture raised up from locality worship in folk culture.

The Ti of imperial worship is represented in the paired altars of Heaven and Earth which still stand today in the southern and northern suburbs of Peking. They were constructed of white marble built in terraces by the third and twelfth Ming emperors in 1420 and 1530 A.D. But in Chou times these altars were simple mounds of earth. Monumental palace and temple architecture came late in China. The relatively flimsy buildings within the aristocratic compound of the Shang high king at An-yang indicate that the capital city, as the material manifestation of the concentrated power of the state, depended for its cultural glamour from the very beginning more on the magical significance of location and layout than on imposing architecture. In time, palace buildings grew bigger and more substantial, but no change occurred in the overpowering symbolism of the topocosmic Center. Until the rise of the present nation-state, the strength of the Center remained a sign of weak governmental control over everything except moral commodities and cultural goods.

THREE

ERA OF TERRITORIAL STATES

In the archaeological record, the caesura between Western and Eastern Chou is evident in the change from dispersed to compact urbanism. Eastern Chou cities were built with a double wall. The inner one enclosed the aristocratic complex at the center, as in Shang and Western Chou cities, and the outer one, the city wall proper, embraced the formerly excluded workshops of the craftsmen and homes of the peasantry. The outer wall is a sign of interstate conflict that required the protection of sufficient numbers of commoners to provide essential services to the ruling class during times of siege. Ordinarily the immured peasantry would set out each day for their fields beyond the city walls, to return behind locked gates at night. Other peasants lived farther away in their Neolithic villages of old, but enough arable land was retained within the walls to feed the city population during enemy attacks.

During the era of city-states, warfare was the sport of self-equipped nobles who went raiding for slaves, cattle, and booty. The Shang king himself raided for victims to be decapitated in ceremonies of ancestor worship. Western Chou royalty repudiated human sacrifice, but Chou noblemen still enjoyed the game of war, which they elaborated in complicated rules of heroic combat. By Eastern Chou times, military campaigns had become more than bloody tournaments fought in war chariots for individual glory and the capture of moveable spoils; they had become political acts carried out with conscripted foot soldiers led by professional generals for the conquest of real estate and the enlargement of state territory. Thus were the many small states of the Western Chou reduced in number by the relentless annexations of powerful ones. With the addition of satellite states, city-states grew to the size of territorial states. Principalities declared themselves kingdoms bent on enlargement, which the Chou king was powerless to stop. Ties of kinship, originally relating the *chu-hou* to their sovereign and to each other, were abandoned to civil war. The growth of territorial states created administrative problems, to which Confucius proposed the solution of appointing nonhereditary stewards, which provided Chinese civilization with its enduring Confucian signature.

Chinese historians mark off two periods within the Eastern Chou: the Spring and Autumn *(Ch'un-ch'iu)* and the Warring States *(Chan-kwo).*

These are named after two books of the time. The *Ch'un-ch'iu (Spring and Autumn Annals)* is a local history for the state of Lu, the home of Confucius, for the years 722–479 B.C. At the opening of this period, about one hundred small states were posed in open conflict with each other; the period closed with forty larger states. The *Chan-kwo Ts'e (Intrigues of the Warring States)* covers military and diplomatic events between 463 and 221 B.C. The chan-kwo period opened with seven territorial states in conflict and closed with one unified state, Ch'in, which then proclaimed itself the first Chinese empire.

The administrative problems of Eastern Chou times followed from the fact that a defeated state meant the murder of its ruling house. The absorption of conquered territory placed on the victor the problem of finding loyal officers of state to govern it. The victor's own noble kinsmen, in being expanded to include cadet families set up to manage satellite states, broke the shared loyalties of a single community of blood interests. Cadet branches installed themselves in the duke's captured real estate for enfeoffment of their own blood lines. The aristocracy of the clan states thus began contending not only between state boundaries but also within them.

The Ch'un-ch'iu period saw feudalism destroyed as state boundaries were enlarged. Before that process began, a typical ruling house consisted of a single clan. *Lineage* would imply that the ancestor of the local descent group were a known historical figure; the word *clan* in the technical language of anthropology implies an eponymous ancestor—remote, mythical, even nonhuman (Winnick, 1958). The ruling clans of the Western Chou city-states took as their founding ancestors various figures of legendary history, later rationalized into a single, coherent history by the Han annalists.

During the Ch'un-ch'iu period, the ducal head of state ruled with the aid of his prime minister and close advisors, all brothers accorded the title *ch'ing.* Sons of the duke (except for his successor, the eldest son) filled lesser ministerial posts. Younger grandsons of the ruler were styled *tai-fu*, or great officers, acting as advisors to the ministers, whose sons in turn were styled *shih* (knight), except for the eldest who was a *tai-fu* of one grade or another. The *shih* were the lowest-ranking members of the ruling aristocracy who could attend court, which was held in the duke's combined ancestral hall and arsenal. All those privileged to attend court were by definition aristocratic members of the ruling clan. They were *chun-tze*, descendants of the ruler. Those who traced their descent beyond a certain point, sons of the lowest grade of knight, belonged to the nobility no longer but to the *hsiao-jen*, or little people, a term of Shang origin.

Ministers were in charge of interstate relations, making diplomatic alliances or military conquests. As a reward for success, the duke often enfeoffed them with districts of the vanquished states. Ministerial families in turn enfeoffed their own ministers and got away with it, because success bred further need by the ruler for their services. By *enfeoffment* we mean the old ducal practice of farming out administration to brothers and sons, in contrast with the newer practice of farming it out to professionals who were selected on the basis of ability, character, and experience. These officers were not given hereditary rights to the territory assigned them by the duke to administer, but they often took such rights upon themselves for the benefit of their own great families or clans. Deprived of privilege by cadet families, sons of the ruler no longer enjoyed official position by

reason of birth. Indeed, the ducal rulers themselves were sometimes reduced to mere figureheads. Some were assassinated, some driven into
exile; others were kept in nominal charge and were officially represented by
a prime minister chosen by an oligarchy of families that had broken the ruler's
power by branching off from his family, founding their own walled towns,
and taking the surrounding lands as hereditary possessions. (Hsu, 1965.)

CONFUCIUS

Confucius noted this turn of events with alarm. His own sovereign, the
twenty-fourth ruler of Lu, Duke Chao, was the plaything of the Three
Huan. The Three Huan were an oligarchy of three collateral families, descendants of ministerial families under an earlier ruler of Lu, Duke Huan.
Failing in their competitive struggle to unseat Duke Chao (succeeding
only in weakening him), they agreed to select and install a prime minister
in place of the duke's brother, who normally would have held the post.
Behind this façade of agreement stood the real power of Lu, Chi P'ing-tze,
the head of the dominant clan of the Three Huan. When Chi P'ing-tze felt
sufficiently dominant to emerge from behind the façade, he gathered eight
rows of sixty-four dancing girls in the forecourt of the Chi family temple,
the ritual prerogative of the Chou king (Tjan, 1949–52:394). The legal
sovereign of Lu no longer could afford even the four rows of sixteen
dancers allowed dukes. Confucius, in his thirty-sixth year, voiced his
alarm: "The Chi allow themselves eight rows by eight of pantomimi in
their ancestral hall! If they dare usurp the king's very own temple ritual,
what can't they get away with?" (Lun Yu, III:1). The answer is that Chi
P'ing-tze "got away with" usurping the ducal throne. Duke Chao subsequently departed Lu for the neighboring state of Ch'i, and Confucius,
always a strict legitimist, followed him.

While cadet families had taken control of many states, members of
the lower stratum of the feudal hierarchy, the shih, were also breaking
away from court ties. During the Ch'un-ch'iu period, the shih had become itinerant knights, looking to hire out their swords. Not only masterless knights roamed the countryside, but also masterless scholars, statesmen, artisans, and merchants, all seeking employment and enrichment for
their services under one ruler or another. In fact, by hiring such men from
the outside, a ruler was able to acquire talent for his cause and bypass the
local parvenue nobility.

Peasants, too, wandered about looking for an improved situation.
They no longer belonged to a noble family as its serfs. They now attached
to the great families as tenants. Instead of owing unrestricted labor service,
they paid a fixed amount of rent. This change was prompted by population
growth and the opportunity to open up and cultivate "wasteland," that is,
land not belonging to a state at the time it was established. State boundaries and the growth of a relatively free peasantry thus advanced in step
with newly cleared forests, irrigated lands, and drained marshes. Such
changes raised the demand for professional ministers, able to cope in dip-
lomacy or war with the heightening enmity of neighbors as they came to
touch upon each other across the vanquished wilderness.

Confucius himself became a masterless shih after the flight of his
duke. Being a legitimist, he certainly would never have considered working for the Three Huan. The skills he withheld from them, however, were

not those of the self-equipped knight. By his time, the hereditary class of *shih* came to include not only knights but also stewards and clerks to the houses of the nobility and their collateral branches. Confucius was this latter kind of *shih*, more in keeping with the original meaning of the term—a *priest-scribe*—as recorded on the oracle bones of the Shang archives. In Lu, he had been a young steward, clerking for his duke's stores and pastures. His father had been a *shih* of the knightly type, famed for his feats of battle, but impoverished. Chariot-riding heroes who could shoot and hack only their social equals in single combat were increasingly going out of demand in favor of massed infantry. The saving grace for the *shih* was a noncombative talent for literacy. Heads of state never learned to read and write because they regarded literacy as a more technical skill belonging to their servants.

In his travels, Confucius urged the sovereigns of various states to adopt a return to the peaceful pluralism of the Chou order, as it had been founded by those exemplars of political virtue, kings Wen and Wu, and by King Wu's brother, the duke of Chou, the founder of the state of Lu. Threatened by ambitious neighbors, the actual wielders of power could only deride Confucius for advocating the merits of a political system that everywhere lay in ruins. The royal domain was reduced to a defenseless plot with just enough room for the Chou king to stand his ground on the *axis mundi* and there exercise his ceremonial function of authenticating the claims to power of aggrandizing warlords. Clearly, Confucius ignored, and in no way contributed to, the gathering militarism leading to the conquest of empire (Fitzgerald, 1950:92).

Not finding a government post after a long quest throughout China, Confucius returned to Ch'i and there started a school to train ministers along the lines of his favorite ideal: a nonhereditary nobility, educated, not born, to serve their prince. For these superior men of educated merit he retained the name *chun-tze*, "descendants of the ruler," giving it a new meaning. But the new *chun-tze* were intended to be framers of policy, not merely its instruments. As Confucius put it, *"chun-tze* are not tools" *(Lun Yu*, II:12). In his curriculum, the names of kings Wen and Wu recurred in a veritable litany of praise because their success was ascribed by the duke of Chou in part to the wisdom of their advisors. The duke of Chou himself had acted as advisor to, if not regent for, the young King Ch'eng, the son and successor of King Wu. Confucius made the duke of Chou the patron saint of scholars just as the time when literate men were aspiring to become powerful ministers (Creel, 1970:76–78).

These aspirations were realistic owing to the rulers' need during the Spring and Autumn period to engage professionals whose morality would disassociate them from court politics, if possible. Quite a few students of Confucius won positions of high trust precisely because their moral training proved superior: they resisted the temptation to manipulate for their own advantage the lands assigned them to manage for the ruler. Ministers who so yielded were *hsiao-jen*, small men, whether of aristocratic birth or not. If Confucius redefined *chun-tze* to mean nonhereditary gentlemen of cultivated loyalty, he redefined also one of the old words for *commoner* to mean "a scoundrel lacking such cultivation."

But while Confucius upheld ducal succession, he inadvertently promoted a new brand of political loyalty to the ruler's cause at the expense of the old hereditary forms that he wanted restored. His managerial philosophy unintentionally helped destroy feudalism by undermining its religious support. Under the old feudal order Confucius admired, the ducal court was a place where services of ancestor worship were conducted in keeping with the fact that the business of statecraft was not separable from the business of running a local descent group, a clan having both real and mythical ancestors as its focus of collective representation. Ancestor worship functioned to rally kinsmen to the business of government, which was vested in them as inseparable shareholders related and ranked by blood ties. By offering loyalty to the task, the Confucian administrator ironically helped end the ducal power he was educated to serve.

Job loyalty removed the conduct of office from the procedures of ancestor worship. In advocating the separation of temple and court (or "church and state"), Confucius actually bent with a trend that he otherwise execrated in the struggles of the Three Huan. In contending for state power over the weakened authority of Lu's duke, these three families installed a prime minister of their choice, thus freeing the prime minister's office from the influence of any sanctions the dominant Chi family or the duke could exercise in either one of their ancestral halls. In defending the feudal nobility by training gentlemen of neutral ethics to serve it, Confucius helped end it (Hsu, 1965).

The market for the new managerial elite trained by Confucius was conditioned by the threat to nonliterate rulers posed by *hsiao-jen*, literate servants lacking ideals of service. Writing extended the ruler's administrative reach to include satellite states he could never have absorbed solely by means of oral communication with his kinsmen. But what the territorial states gained in extent they lost in solidity. More and more authority passed into the hands of ministerial families; and if the ruler bypassed his own nobility, his conquered territories fell into the hands of appointed ministers, whose literacy gave them control over information that could be kept secret. But the *chun-tze* of Confucian persuasion were trained not to use literacy as a means of keeping secrets, and therefore would neither enrich nor empower themselves at the ruler's expense.

In promising that the *chun-tze* is no mere tool, Confucius promises that the gentleman of cultivated loyalty is not just a medium. He is also a message about the *use* of that medium. And the message is: the *chun-tze* guarantees to use writing only as a means to contain the traditional word-of-mouth loyalties. (1) "The first thing is loyalty and keeping one's word" (*Lun Yu*, I:8). Being loyal, the *chun-tze* does not aspire to win some of the ducal real estate for himself. (2) "The *chun-tze* thinks of virtue; the *hsiao-jen* sets his heart on land. (*Lun Yu*, IV:11; *see* Hughes, 1954:21). But in the end, the stress on voluntary loyalty to the ducal cause was not sufficient to uphold it. The professional managers arose to become the scholar-officials of imperial times, when a state cult of Confucius, backed by the sovereign himself, guaranteed these officials their autonomy from hereditary concerns of the throne. The scholars who then prepared to enter the emperor's civil service called themselves *shih*, after the Chou stewards.

But Confucius was not the only personality associated with a school of ministerial philosophy. From the fifth through the third centures, six or seven of such schools flourished. It was a time, in the words of the *Shih Chi*, "a thousand flowers bloomed and a Hundred Schools contended." Among the most significant, in addition to Confucianism, were Taoism and Legalism (*see* Waley, 1939).

Of the Hundred Schools, the best known to Western readers is Taoism, actually a misnomer for Laoism. *Tao*, literally, "the way, " is Heaven's Way; to follow it means following the cosmic principle of least effort. The goodness policy advocated by each school consists in following the *tao* in accordance with its own brand of cultivated virtue *(te)*; this readies one to yield to least effort *(wu-wei)*. The concept of *tao* is evidently older than any of the Hundred Schools. Confucius certainly drew upon it. In the *Li Chi*, he is made to say: "I have yet to see the *ta tao*, the Great Way, flourish as it did under the eminent founders of the Hsia, Shang, and Chou dynasties, but I aim to restore it and make their way my way" *(Li Yun*, I:1).

The *tao* is any cosmically sanctioned plan of action undertaken as a matter of state policy, so long as the ruler sits at the *axis mundi* and is made perfect by right ritual. This doctrine doubtlessly grew out of the ceremonialism of the Shang kings. If so, then Confucius rationalizes Shang practice when he says: "To practice *wu-wei* and yet govern well—the divine sage-king Shun did it! How? By nothing more than sitting reverently on his royal seat and correctly adjusting his face southwards" (*Lun Yu*, XV:4). Herein lie the essentials of culturalism that carried over into imperial politics. The instructive influence of the supreme ruler stems from his personal virtue, as informed by the comic forces of Heaven, when his throne is properly oriented south. Let the sovereign follow the *tao*, says Confucius, and he will be like the polestar that keeps its position while all the others turn toward it.

Tao is the central concept of Laoism, however, not merely a background assumption. For Lao Tze, perhaps a contemporary of Confucius, least effort means no government at all: "Govern a big country as you would fry small fish." The assertion of authority through right ritual, such as laws and decrees, is as ruinous to the people as poking about at small fish ruins the cooking. It manifests a lapse from a primitive state of excellence, in which political control consists in doing nothing more than keeping the people ignorant and apathethic.

In the *Tao Te Ching*, Lao Tze explains what he would do were he king. He would not hire clever officers for they would set aspirations for power into motion. He would disallow all labor-saving devices in favor of strong backs and empty minds. His subjects would not dare travel by boat or carriage for fear of accidents. Nobody would be permitted to emigrate, and in addition, drilling with arms would be forbidden. No book learning or writing, only knotted strings would be used to aid the memory, as in the days of Fu-hsi. Everything else he would reverse to the days of Shennung and bring it about, quoting another Taoist, Chuang Tze, so that the people would be "contented with their food, pleased with their clothing, satisfied with their homes, should take pleasure in their rustic tasks. The next place might be so near at hand that one could hear the cocks crowing in it, the dogs barking; but the people would grow old and die without ever having been there" (*Tao Te Ching*, LXXX; tr. by Waley, 1934:241–42).

Thus only by nonaction is everything governed, a paradox. Lao Tze spurns the ritual regulations proposed by Confucius. It is not the duty of the ruler to interfere with the people by putting virtue on display but to meditate on the *tao*. We note, however, that the Laoist sage may afford to go into retreat only after he has used the powers of government to abolish government and restore things to a state of Neolithic tribalism. This would take an unremitting despotism to achieve, far beyond any regulations dreamed of by Confucius. There is no paradox, after all. The *tao* that does nothing yet accomplishes everything is a strong-arm principle that licenses government to impose a laissez-faire utopia by force (*see* Creel, 1929:99–100).

For Chinese readers, the freedom Lao Tze talks about is a freedom that transcends the political order, not one that functions within it. The Laoist program for returning to nature is appreciated rather as a course of action to be taken, by default, by the man disappointed in office. At the time of Confucius and Lao Tze, state rulers increasingly bypassed their hereditary ministers and appointed talented ones chosen from the lower aristocracy or from outside it altogether. Scholars, once stewards, could become ministers. But openings were limited. Confucius never held office, but he continued to nourish his ambition through his students. Lao Tze's response to a similar failure, one might suppose, was to cultivate a philosophy of failure that would make the unimportant drop-out important, so long as he followed the exacting course of Taoist nonaction. Doing nothing is not easy. The adept must dampen curiosity and desire; he must shun luxury and live simply and with humility. He must be equally charitable to the good and the bad, and must trust even the guileful with naive faith. He who wishes for nothing will not be disappointed; he who strives not, to him will it be given. Let him not seek understanding through study, like the Confucianist, for that awakens harmful notions. The proper thing is to meditate on the *tao*. By living like a recluse, mind emptied and ambitions enfeebled, the disappointed man will be vindicated; the *tao* will unite him with the cosmic stuff of the universe and grant him the glory of Heaven's prestige.

As a technique for overcoming the despair of the world, Laoism has had a lasting influence on Chinese intellectuals; it has served as consolation for all those who failed to win office or who lost it by offending unjust superiors or who resigned it in protest against the wrong turn of affairs. Men trained to govern but not appointed found in Confucius, the ideologue of the successful bureaucrat, only a stony reminder of failure (*see* Creel, 1929:91–100).

While the literature of Confucianism evolved as a set of sacred books informing the state religion, that of Taoism never became institutionalized in any form. As a system of ideas, Taoism was largely absorbed by Buddhism after the latter's entry in China during the first century A.D. The unappointed man could thereafter brood at his own expense in a Buddhist monastery. Authentic philosophical Taoism was nothing if it was not the hobby of a man rich enough to finance the leisure for contemplation. What has been called Taoism among the peasantry was simply the persistence of shamanism and divination under another name, filtered down from the great tradition.

LEGALISM

Alone among the Hundred Schools, only Legalism was propounded by hard-headed statesmen, not philosophers, who had served in high places. Legalist advisors to the prince of Ch'in prepared him to obtain mastery of the entire Chinese realm by means of a war policy that, in 221 B.C., successfully won the conquest of empire. During the fifteen years the Ch'in dynasty held the first empire, Legalism served as its official ideology, only to be declared heterodox under all subsequent dynasties—which were all Confucian. But the Legalists held no monopoly on intolerance. As Confucius says, "It is indeed harmful to come under the sway of exotic doctrines" (Lun Yu, II:16). So thoroughly was Leɂalism censored that many educated Chinese of traditional upbringing living today have never heard of it.

The first political thinker in the Legalist vein was Kuan I-wu (710–643 B.C.), better known as Kuan Chung. Kuan Chung had first been a merchant. The absolute increase in wealth generated by merchants freed of retainer status and employed in the service of rulers of their own choice had by this time begun to replace riches captured as booty by a warrior-nobility. Kuan Chung staked his fortune on the heir apparent of the elder duke of Ch'i, tutored him, then backed him in the war of succession following his father's death, and lost. The usual fate of a steward who served a losing family was to be extinguished along with his master. But the winner, Duke Huan, was so impressed with Kuan Chung's theory and practice of economics that he made him prime minister.

Kuan Chung's innovations in fiscal and military matters made Ch'i a great state. He collected facts about the state's resources in land, people, and stores, and then described these economic data with novel statistical formulas of his own devising. For the first time, economic statistics were recognized by a ruler of state as a source of power.

Kuan Chung's success is evidence, one hundred years before Confucius, of the growing independence of professional officeholders from the aristocracy. Kuan Chung may not have been the first member of this newly emerging class, but his principles of management were the first to appear in writing, in a book titled after his own name, the Kuan Tze. Authorship in ancient China, however, was not credited to a single writer. Rather, a book was the product of multiple contributions gathered over long periods of time and titled after the name of the most illustrious spokesman for, or practitioner of, the ideas contained in it. The Lun Yu, or Analects of Confucius, for example, was not written by Confucius. It represents an accumulation of sayings remembered by his disciples and added to by Confucianists of later generations.

The Kuan Tze did not surface until about 300 B.C., three-and-a-half centuries after the death of Master Kuan himself. Ssu-ma Ch'ien records in the Shih Chi that Kuan Chung's descendants held ministerial posts for more than ten successive generations. During that time, the evolving Kuan Tze would have been passed down as a recipe book containing the family secrets for handling government statistics. Most important in the Kuan Tze are the methods it relates for imposing a salt and iron monopoly. For salt, count the population, estimate the salt consumption per capita, and tax accordingly. A levy on iron would bring in a regular source of revenue because iron implements are as much everyday necessities as salt: every woman has her needle, knife, and cooking pan; every man has his plow, spade, and hatchet (see Hirth, 1908:103–105).

Moreover, political necessity requires the government to impose a monopoly on salt and iron. As both are commodities widely distributed from a few key centers of production, control of these by enemies of the state would enable them to finance rebellion. Since iron was not introduced into China until after 600 B.C., only a salt tax could have been proposed by Kuan Chung himself. The measures for imposing a monopoly on iron would have been added in due course by his descendants.

Kuan Chung (once a merchant himself) blamed merchants for undermining ducal authority by working not with the hereditary ruler for mutual profit but instead for cadet families. Branching, of course, was a symptom of culture change that finally transformed feudalism. The Legalist solution for the trouble caused by competition between ruler and branch families was to outlaw all economic alternatives to agriculture and all careers save the military. Kuang Chung estimated that the trouble lay with money. Get rid of a money economy and things would revert to the self-policing, primitive excellence of the Laoist utopia.

> An urgent task of the state is the suppression of secondary pursuits, the manufacture of luxury and art goods. If these are suppressed, the people will not find it possible to wander about and still get food. All will then necessarily engage in farming. When all the people work in agriculture, the waste lands will be brought under cultivation. When these added fields are cultivated, grain will be plenty. When grain is plenty, the state will be wealthy. With wealth, the state will have a strong army; with a strong army, it will be victorious in war; and with victory, its territories will be extended. (Kuan Tze, XLVIII; tr. by Maverick, 1954:93–94)

A dense population, abundant grain, a strong army, expanding territory were the Legalist desiderata, to be achieved by keeping the peasantry in a state of ignorance and apathy. In recommending this policy, however, the Legalists merely described the natural conditions of Neolithic backwardness in an archaic civilization.

The Legalists also expressed the inevitable currents of change sweeping the little city-states into ever-larger political units, as Confucius did not in his nostalgia for feudalism. Confucius harks back to small communities under the leadership of the Shang kings, whose public displays of ancestor worship directly engaged the participation of the *shu-jen*. The rituals of state were those of Neolithic tribalism elevated to royal dignity (*see* Newall, 1957:4–5). High culture had risen to the top by a process of orthogenesis, with a Bronze Age aristocracy emerging out of folk culture. But high culture had yet to become a great tradition codified by a class of culture-critics, the *shih*, whose technology of writing was developed by a class of Shang scribes of the same name. Confucius did this job of codification for a body of materials which were subjected to further rationalization by the Han exegetes and then by the Sung neo-Confucianists. Scholars of the Confucian great tradition, which included every man educated in ritual and literature for both formal and informal government, retained the name *shih* throughout the history of imperial China. Chinese high culture therefore remained continuous with its precivilized origins, even while the civilized business of government made for distance between literate gentlemen and peasants as nonliterate as their Neolithic forebears—or *nearly* as nonliterate. Scholars declared the difference absolute by asserting their absolute claim to moral superiority.

The Legalists, however, disvalued all written literature except the penal code. Their aim, after all, was organizational power over all of China, an area too big for strong centralization by liturgical means. Accordingly, the benefits of organization on such a huge scale were said to go to the ruler for his use in the exercise of unprecedented feats of power, not to the ruled on behalf of moral instruction. Bluntly put by one Legalist, "A weak people means a strong state and a strong people means a weak state" (*Shang Yang*, V:20:4a; tr. by Duyvendak, 1928:307).

Two Legalist statesmen, Wei Yang (d. 338 B.C.) and Han Fei Tze (d. 233 B.C.) shaped the conquest policy of Ch'in that finally won for it the hegemony of empire in 221 B.C. Flourishing some two centuries after Confucius, they had the opportunity to make of Confucianism a foil for their own doctrine. Writings of the Ch'in school of Legalism first appear under its founder's name as *The Book of Lord Shang*. Originally a subject of the state of Wei, Wei Yang received his aristocratic title, Lord Shang, under Duke Hsiao of Ch'in, following a ministerial appointment. Lord Shang's teachings actually repudiated the nobility as an obsolete ruling class that, save for the hereditary line of the ruler himself, should be replaced by a military hierarchy of soldiers whose merit was won on the battlefield. The duke of Ch'in, by opening government careers to meritorious soldiers drawn from a free peasantry, accelerated the destruction of feudalism in his state. All other careers in business and in culture—such as music, history, philosophy, or poetry—were taken as treasonable.

In place of the liturgical government advocated by Confucianists, the Legalists substituted fear of cruel penal law. In Confucian theory (rationalized out of the mythical past), rituals and ceremonies spread the virtue *(te)* of the ruler throughout the whole community. Such ritual did indeed once communicate its effect in the small-scale communities of the old city-states because it was visibly continuous with the folk culture of the *shu-jen*. One source for Confucian exegesis in this matter is the *Tso Chuan*, a set of annals that contains an entry for the reputed year of 710 B.C.:

> He who is a ruler of men makes it his object to manifest virtue and suppress what is wrong, that he may shed an enlightening influence on his officials, and is afraid lest he should fail to do this. Therefore he seeks to display excellent virtue to show an example to his posterity. Thus his ancestral temple is a roof of thatch; the mats in his grand chariot are only of grass; the grand soups (used in his sacrifices) are without condiments; and the millets are not finely cleaned. All this is to show his frugality. (tr. by Bodde, in Fung, 1952:36)

The Legalist approach to social control, in contrast, is discontinuous with folk culture. Let any subject so much as throw ashes in the street and his hands will be cut off. In the law of Shang Yang, even misdemeanors are punished severly on the theory that if small faults are checked, great crimes will never appear. This was called "punishment to end punishments" (Creel, 1953:128). The ruler had only to perfect the *te* particular to

Legalist theory (that is, have the intelligence to see that no crime escapes the sight of his officials), and he could sit back in his cushions, "listen to the sound of stringed and bamboo instruments," and thereby "cause the masses to have no possibility of not working" (*Shang Yang*, IV:18:10b; tr. by Duyvendak, 1928:291–92).

But while Confucianism and Legalism share a common Taoist belief in the principle of least effort, *wu-wei*, they differ fundamentally in their views of human nature. Confucianists must believe man is by nature good; how else may he be receptive to moral example? According to Mencius, the most famous Confucianist after Confucius, human psychology is in harmony with ethical instruction (Creel, 1953:77). Legalists, on the other hand, believed it was not. Han Fei Tze, the aristocratic envoy from the state of Han, who stayed in Ch'in to advise prince Cheng on the eve of his imperial conquest, summed up the Legalist position with the devastating words; "The most enlightened way of governing a state is to trust measures and not men" (*Han Fei Tze*, LV; tr. by Liao, 1959:II, 332). In other words, the Legalist ruler "does not count on people's doing him good but utilizes their inability to do him wrong" (*Han Fei Tze*, L; tr. by Liao, 1959:II, 306). To which the Confucian reply is "Try to keep order by means of legal regulations and people will evade punishments without conscience. Keep order by right ritual and people will volunteer to follow the example of your moral power" (*Lun Yu*, II:3). This idea is dismissed with the sharp Legalist observation that such practice requires "every lord of men to come up to the level of Confucius and all the common people of the world to act like his disciples. It won't work . . ." (*Han Fei*, XLIX; Liao, 1959:II, 282).

The difference is not that the Confucianists fail to recognize the place of law, but that the Legalists make law apply to everyone with the single exception of the hereditary autocrat himself, the supreme arbiter of Legalist doctrine. In contrast, Confucian policy would apply law selectively, leaving room for a voluntarily observed code of conduct, *li*, among gentlemen of moral cultivation. The *Li Chi*, or *Classic of Ritual*, says: "*Li* does not apply below among the common people, punishments *(hsing)* do not apply above them" (*Chu Li*, I:iv:10).

This policy, endorsed by the state cult of Confucius, remained in force throughout the entire imperial era—except for its first fifteen years. These were the years under Shih Huang Ti, the first emperor, formerly the prince of Ch'in, whose advisors were Han Fei Tze and other Legalists. Thus, the final outcome of the disputes of the Hundred Schools was that the Ch'in dynasty, the first and only triumph of Legalism, lasted for less than a generation; whereas the official ideology under every emperor thereafter was Confucianism.

Legalism failed because its totalitarian goals were too far in advance of the technical means for achieving a centralized administration. All subsequent imperial regimes acknowledged in fact, if not in propaganda, a large measure of autonomy at all levels of government beyond the limits of the metropolitan center. Because the capital city was essentially a self-sufficient state belonging to the emperor, the emperor was able to speak the language of an antique culturalism as if he still sat at the *axis mundi* of the Shang state, swaying a small political community by the personal example of his ritual perfection. Educated in Confucian doctrine, the emperor illuminated it in all of his officials, both in central and local government. It was a moral doctrine that honored learning above birth, wealth, or the penal code. The educated man's virtue was supposed to be contagious, and Chinese officials were recruited from men of letters, not aristocrats or lawyers. Indeed, no legal profession ever existed in traditional China, no persons who assisted plaintiffs or defendants in the conduct of cases brought before the tribunals of the land (Giles, 1911:50). Officials were expected to prevent rather than determine litigation. "What is necessary," said Confucius, "is to cause the people to have no litigations" (Lun Yu, XII:13).

But behind the benevolent façade of Confucian "instruction through personal example" lay a Legalist reality. Cruel and barbarous punishments awaited all commoners—whether innocent or guilty—whose fear of the law was insufficient to keep their troubles out of the magistrate's court. Terror was taken as an extension of instruction by one's betters. Mencius (IA:IV:5) describes the ruler of a state as "a parent to his people," a phrase that came to be applied to imperial magistrates—fu-mu kuan, or father-and-mother officials. How parental they were in laying on the bastinado is described by an early nineteenth-century traveler, John Barrow: "A Chinese, after receiving a certain number of strokes, falls down on his knees, as a matter of course, before him who ordered the punishment, thanking him, in the most humble manner, for the fatherly kindness he has testified toward his son, in thus putting him in mind of his errors" (Barrow, 1805:256).

In view of such exemplary punishment, it is small wonder that Westerners, coming from a less severely patriarchal tradition, desired to conduct trade in China out of their own extraterritorial enclaves, exempt from Chinese law and its practice of beating witnesses in court (Waley, 1958:62–63). Ironically, the Chinese feared to adopt the Western handshake because it recalled a form of judicial torture, the finger-squeezing punishment, by which the hand was crushed with sticks between the fingers.

Among Chinese litigants, however, few were elites of the realm. The elite solved their problems out of court by means of personal relations as guided by the gentleman's voluntary code of li. For the lowly and ignorant, however, law was the only way to deter crime. As the Emperor K'ang-hsi proclaimed, "I desire . . . that those who have recourse to the tribunals should be treated without any pity, and in such a manner that they will be disgusted with law, and tremble to appear before a magistrate. In this manner the evil will be cut out by the roots" (Huc, 1855:I, 125).

In theory, the Confucian school triumphed with its ideas of government based on benevolence and justice; but Legalist ideas persisted in practice. Benevolence was extended only to the elite, who were exempted from penal law because they were exemplars of self-control by definition. For commoners, however, justice was done by way of a Legalist terror policy that aimed to use punishment to end punishments.

FOUR

ERA OF CYCLICAL IMPERIAL CONQUESTS

Once brought into civilization as its workhorse, the Neolithic community changed little. Some authorities believe that the introduction of iron implements from about the end of the fifth century B.C. coupled with the use of ox-drawn plows in the fourth century led to the working of huge estates by gangs of slaves, serfs, or hired laborers. Evidence exists for the ownership of large estates in the Han dynasty (Ch'u, 1972), but if large-scale agriculture based on the iron-tipped traction plow was practiced (and this is a matter of dispute), it certainly had no lasting effect. There is nothing to contradict the assumption that Han manorial lords exploited their estates by letting plots to tenants who tilled the land much as independent peasant families tilled their own small grain fields.

It is unlikely that the coming of iron had the influence in China that it had in West Asia, where the Neolithic revolution in 7000 B.C. led to plow agriculture—a second agricultural revolution permitting a single man to cultivate a relatively large area—even before the advent of cities and civilization in 3000 B.C. The addition of iron-tipped plows made extensive field cultivation all the more efficient, as measured by output per man-hour. In China, a revolutionary change from gardening with hoe and spade to extensive agriculture with the traction plow never took place. The original Neolithic revolution had already committed small landholders to working with the intensive methods of horticulture before the arrival of the animal-drawn plow. The advent of iron somewhat earlier had done nothing to alter the efficiency of gardening, as measured by output per unit of land. Iron replaced flaked-stone sickles and polished-stone hoe and shovel blades or trimmed the edges of wooden ones, and that was that. Animal power was taken on merely as a useful auxiliary to be dispensed with when necessary. And the necessity was always pressing, given the competition of livestock with humans for plant life in a garden landscape. The agrarian foundation of civilization in China remained Neolithic, with iron substituting for stone (McNeill, 1963:218–19).

What changed more than Neolithic village life were the different ways by which the ruling class arranged to exploit it. To the peasant it made little difference if his surplus was delivered to a hereditary feudal lord, the owner of a manorial estate, a government official, or a gentleman landlord. By the Sung dynasty, a coolie proletariat of folk origin came to live in the cities, which enabled the state to replace seasonal corvée labor with a poll tax to pay a permanent labor force, a policy furthered in the Ming dynasty when the poll tax was merged with the agricultural tax (Loewe, 1965:145).

In the era of city-states, society was divided into a hereditary elite and a majority variously called *shu-jen* or *hsiao-jen*. The latter term, meaning "little people," occurs in the sayings of Confucius in apposition to *chun-tze*, or "superior men." Originally these two words distinguished commoners from a nobility, but Confucius reinterpreted them to mean a difference between plebeians and educated worthies. His reinterpretation fell in line with social changes that had taken place during the era of territorial states, when hereditary ministers were replaced by appointed ministers. A new class of scholar-officials came to power, determined to make their sovereign's native state the center of imperial hegemony. The old feudal pluralism with its exogamous states named *pai-hsing* (the "hundred clans") made way for the political unity of empire, when *pai-hsing* came to mean the "hundred names" of the peasantry into which the aristocracy had sunk. The exogamy of the clan states thus became the surname exogamy of all, at the same time commoners first acquired surnames.

During the era of cyclical imperial conquests, unification came more and more to depend on a civil bureaucracy whose officials were appointed to serve on the basis of Confucian learning, not birth or wealth. Following the short-lived military empire of the Ch'in dynasty, Chinese emperors drew their officials from great landed families. This second aristocracy, a manorial version of the feudal aristocracy destroyed by the Ch'in dynasty, did not survive the disorders of the First Partition, when the Han dynasty fell to the competition of regional courts. With the Sui and T'ang dynasties of the Second Imperial Unity, claims by a birth elite for membership in the ruling class were met by rivals who sought to qualify for office by educating themselves for the civil service examinations. The emperor brought forward the examination system out of earlier institutions as a means of checking hereditary power of any kind outside the imperial house. The monarch thereby acknowledged that he could not vanquish his noble rivals without paying the cost of sharing his regained power with a bureaucracy, as Ch'in had not shared it (Levenson and Schurmann, 1969:82–83). The examination system, with its ethical foundations in the Confucian job morality of detachment from court politics, brought about in the Ming and Ch'ing dynasties government by philosopher-statesmen, admired so much by Western intellectuals of the Enlightenment that they introduced into Europe a civil service on the Chinese model. The same model, however, gave rise to the lofty authoritarian connotations of the word *mandarin* in our language, from the Portuguese *mandar*, "to command" (Pulleyblank, 1954:61–64).

What follows is the history of imperial high culture, or rather, its geopolitical basis. The Ch'in unification was short-lived because its Legalist policy reached beyond the only possible norm of government for the time, that of culturalism. A modern Chinese political scientist has observed: "The only lasting unity is one based on homogeneity of ideas and culture, and not on a forced obedience to a common body of law" (Wu, 1928:234).

The Confucian state was necessarily a political pseudomorph lacking the power of legal sovereignty as we know the state to possess under the politics of nationalism. Instead the Chinese contrived the state as a world system, as a cosmological empire having a concentrated Center at the *axis mundi* and no outer physical boundaries. The emperor sat at the center of the world and attracted, on the basis of an expensive display of cultural glories, the voluntary adherence by the ruling class to his ceremonial leadership as regulated by the imperial calendar. Each dynasty drew up its own calendar regulating court ritual; loyalty by the elite of the realm was measured by conformity in domestic ritual at home, in the pageantry of administration in office.

A constant factor in the imperial model, however, was its standard of ritual deference to authority—prostration. Known as the *k'o-t'ou* in the Ch'ing and Yuan dynasties, and the *fu-fu* in the Ming, ritual abasement is as old as the Chinese political tradition. Ssu-ma Ch'ien describes it in the *Shih Chi* for a supplicant before the legendary Emperor Shun: "He bowed his head to the height of his hands, and prostrated himself before the Emperor with his face to the earth" (*see* Rockhill, 1905:5). The emperor in turn prostrated himself in the same act of subordination upon the altar to Heaven, as did an official before a written message received from the emperor, a supplicant on business before an official, the head of a joint family before the spirit tablets of his ancestors, and a daughter-in-law before her mother-in-law.

Upholding the hierarchy of court, official, and domestic ritual was in fact the whole substance of culturalism and the essential business of empire, not a peripheral attribute. When the empress dowager, regent for the last of the Ch'ing emperors, acquired a number of foreign cars, she was unable to ride in any of them. The board of rites could not solve the problem "how she might ride in an automobile in which there would also be, in sitting posture, one of her servants, the chauffeur" (Reinsch, 1922:109). Up to the time of the empress' death, the board had not yet found a way that the chauffeur could kneel while driving the imperial car. This was no trivial problem. To pass over it would be to dismiss the chief glory of imperial culturalism: the liturgical leadership of the throne in its ritual assertion of stable inequality and the unity of *t'ien-hsia*, "all under Heaven," under one system of moral authority, completed in the cosmic posture of stars around Polaris in Heaven.

According to Confucian theory, all that is required for government is right ritual and appropriate music, the signatures of each dynasty. Thereby is fixed the repose of superior men by reference to the heights of Heaven in music (yang), and the order of the people by reference to the depths of Earth in ceremonies (yin). The *Li Chi* says: "Heaven is high, Earth is low; all things are distributed between these two and differ in kind" (*Yo Chi*, I:28). As the Han exegetes of the White Tiger Lodge explain, "Rites are the meeting-corner of yin and yang, the link connecting the affairs of men, that wherewith Heaven and Earth are revered, the spirits are treated, the order among high and lowly is maintained, and the *tao* of man is kept straight" (Tjan, 1949–52:390).

The subject of this chapter is the geopolitical aspect of Chinese culturalism taken in historical perspective—that is, how the emperor made
use of regional geography to finance royal glory. His problem was to transport wealth in grain from some productive Neolithic source to a place of
sufficient concentration in the capital city. Sufficient meant financing
enough cultural glamour at court to attract the admiration of all other
persons of power living off the Neolithic landscape in their own less-
concentrated localities. From these places of informal landlord government, ambitious men invited themselves to win distinction as grandees of
formal government. The emperor was able to confer that distinction because he controlled unique resources of production and transportation.
Political unity obtained as long as elites of the realm found their local re-
pute enhanced by imitating ritual forms belonging to the ruling house, and
as long as they were not tempted to follow a rival center of high culture.

The history of empire may be divided into three imperial unities and
two partitions (see Figures 4–8). Note that the first three of the twenty-two
official dynasties are omitted because the Hsia, Shang, and Chou are
preimperial, the Hsia being mythical. Each diagram in Figures 4–8 illustrates in chronological sequence the name and number of the dynasty (beginning with the fourth) and its capital city. The diagrams are drawn to
scale to indicate the duration of each. On the left of each diagram are the
territories of South China; on the right those of North China; and on the
far right, the northern borderlands from which the rulers of the conquering
dynasties entered China.

In the view of Chinese historians, every partition was a time of chaos,
confusion, corruption, and immorality. Except for the Ch'in dynasty, unity
has been only a unity of cultural authority over elite persons, and centralization has been centralization only in political control over government
officials. Partition means nothing more than disunity in the realm of high
culture. But for men of the great tradition, this was disruptive enough. In
their opinion, more than one throne would as much violate the imperial
monopoly on ritual leadership as two suns in the sky would violate the
cosmic order. According to Mencius, "Just as there are not two suns in the
sky, so there cannot be two kings on earth" (*Meng Tze*, VA:iv:1). But under
one sun or two or under no sun at all, the Neolithic life of the men of the
little tradition remained intact.

FIRST IMPERIAL UNITY

The prince of Ch'in, restyled *wang*, accomplished the conquest of empire
in 221 B.C. (see Figure 4), at which time he called himself Shih Hwang Ti,
the First Emperor. Understanding full well that he had initiated a new
form of political unity by enlarging the scale of political control, he chose
his title accordingly. He united in himself the virtues of the San Hwang, or
Three Primordial Sovereigns, and the Wu Ti, or Five Emperors, and joined
their titles in the one of Hwang Ti. *Shih Hwang Ti* means "Hwang Ti the
Only First," as if to say only one man in all of history can be the First
Emperor of the first Chinese empire. His title proclaims: "History begins
with me." Indeed, all imperial rulers thereafter designated themselves
Hwang Ti, Emperor. Thenceforth, *wang* joined the other ranks of feudal

62   nobility as an honorary title emperors could bestow on favorites, in this
case limited to sons and close relatives of the emperor's.

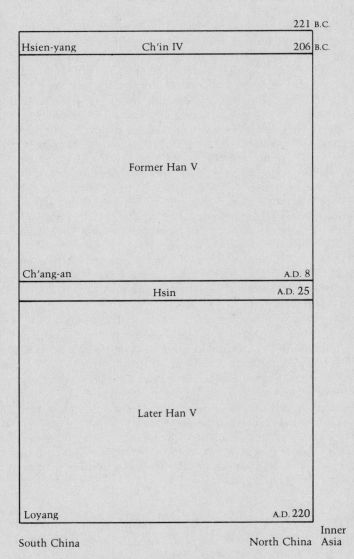

FIGURE 4.   First Unity (to scale).

Legalist advisors during two generations had prepared Ch'in for its
imperial triumph. They realized that human institutions do not stand still,
that everything changes with time, and that the sentimental hope of the
Confucianists for restoring the "good old days" of feudalism at its best was
a vain one. Han Fei tells the story of a farmer who once saw a hare knock
itself unconscious by running in blind panic into a tree, and who then

spent the rest of his life waiting beside the same tree in the hope that more hares would do the same thing. The return of antiquity, Han Fei says, is just as likely (Creel, 1953:123–24).

Legalist advisors in Ch'in proposed to hasten as a matter of policy those social changes that were undoing Chou feudalism. They hastened the superannuation of the old landed nobility by two dramatic measures. First, a new military nobility of eighteen degrees, rewarded with posts and pensions, was created on the basis of merit won on the battlefield and gauged by the number of enemy heads taken (Gernet, 1968:95; Loewe, 1965:134). Second, the economic relevance of the state's entire feudal holdings was voided by digging an irrigation canal one hundred miles long, the Cheng-kwo Canal, between the Lo and Ching tributaries of the Wei River. This opened to immigrants the alkalai "wastelands" of what has remained to this day the fertile heartland of Shensi province (Chi, 1936:76). Attracted by the life of a free peasantry unbound to feudal lords, immigrants provided the Ch'in ruler with his own supply of grain, farmers, and soldier-peasants, under a centralized regime that penalized all occupations other than farming while it encouraged military careers with rewards. Such rewards and punishments were, in Legalist jargon, the "two handles of government." This policy gave the ruler enough surplus to buy out and resettle the 1200 families of the nobility in the Ch'in capital, whose concentrated demand for luxury goods did much to stimulate trade.

In warfare, Ch'in borrowed the tactics, if not the actual troops, of their barbarian neighbors, the Hsiung-nu, of the northern steppelands. The Hsiung-nu, ancestors of the Huns, first appear in recorded history around 400 B.C., but they probably emerged as a distinct people by the eighth century B.C. They occupied the steppe zone of Central Asia, a belt of grassland stretching from southern Russia to Manchuria, similar to the American Great Plains (Watson, 1971:101). The Hsiung-nu fought from horseback, firing reflex bows, a tactic unknown to the majority of Ch'in's enemies, who lacked the experience of conflict with border peoples. Mounted troops, however, were always used by Chinese armies as auxiliary forces subordinate to foot soldiers drafted from the peasantry. Thus cavalry never amounted to an elite force, as it did among the knights of the European Iron Age.

Ch'in also learned from border warfare how to administer conquered barbarian territory with military commandaries, called *chün*. Extended after the conquest to the whole of the Ch'in empire and staffed by its new military nobility, *chün* served as the empire's ultimate outpost of administration, subordinate to the province, which in turn was subordinate to the capital city at Hsien-yang. Heading the provincial level of government were a civil and a military governor, plus an overseer responsible to the emperor directly (Bodde, 1938). This hierarchy of administrative functions, from district to province to metropolitan center, provided a model for all imperial regimes to come, save for the fact that personal representatives of the emperor no longer were appointed as overseers. The First Emperor tried to read all the important papers of state himself—his literacy was a novelty for a head of state—and to visit his overseers in periodic tours of all the provincial capitals to demonstrate his ideal of centralized bureaucratic control. The technologies of communication and transportation were not adequate for this feat at the time, however, and local governmental authorities could not be forced to relinquish for long the autonomous powers they felt it was their right to hold. The regime fell to a feudal reaction within fifteen years, overthrown by a combination of disaffected generals from the old aristocracy and big landowners armed with their own militia.

In its ambition to take the whole country by force, Ch'in swam with the currents of change, moving away from feudal pluralism toward imperial centralism. The actual change was toward a recasting of feudalism in the form of official posts—that is, the sovereign was enabled to grant prebends anew following loss of control over endowments in the form of land, which had been usurped by the statesmen who now contended for the privilege of authorizing this shift in emphasis to bureaucracy.

But in some respects Ch'in still looked back, while in others it looked too far ahead. It looked back to the early Bronze Age of the Shang dynasty insofar as it attached to the emperor's court and made captive the services of artisans, craftsmen, and merchants. The state monopolized the iron industry and horse breeding, another factor explaining why cavalry was not the free and noble thing it was in Europe (Gernet, 1968:99). Ch'in looked too far ahead insofar as it aimed to create totalitarian controls that had to await the use of radio and telephone by Adolf Hitler in the twentieth century to be realized. Albert Speer, Hitler's minister for armaments and war production, made this intelligent observation at the Nuremburg Trials: "Earlier dictators needed highly qualified assistants, even at the lowest level, men who could think and act independently. The totalitarian system in the period of modern technical development can dispense with them; the means of communication alone make it possible to mechanize the lower leadership" (quoted in Bullock, 1962:380).

Subsequent to the fall of Ch'in, all Chinese emperors had to compromise with political nationalism and settle for moral nationalism; recognizing the force of local autonomy ranged against autocracy, they yielded the Legalist theory of powerful government to the Confucian theory of exemplary government based on the precedent of the Chou court.

Even the Ch'in emperor dressed his forceful methods of government with a number of moralistic arcana, believing, for example, that his newly established dynasty ruled by virtue of the element water. Accordingly, the name of the Yellow River was changed to Te Shui, Powerful Water. Like all emperors after him, he signified the beginning of a new reigning house with a change in the calendar, starting the year from the first day of the tenth month, the same time congratulations were to be made at court. The official color of the dynasty was black (that of the Chou was red), to be worn for clothing and to be flown in pennons and flags. While the Ch'in emperor is credited with the rational policy of standardizing weights and measures, this cannot be separated from a numerological bent endemic to culturalism. Six is the number of the element water, so the First Emperor standardized contract tallies and official hats at six inches in length and cart axles at six feet. Six feet made one pace, and each equipage had six horses (Fung, 1952: vol. I, p. 163, n. 1).

But what the Ch'in empire gained by conquest in extent, it would soon give up in solidity. Empire is neither a territorial state nor a kingdom writ large. Kingdoms may be centralized by force, as the major states were during the warring-states period, but the lasting organization of kingdoms into empire called for unity fixed in something more insubstantial. This is remarked in a story about Liu Pang, the first Han emperor, who won the throne from the nobility after the fall of Ch'in only after years of fighting. His chamberlain habitually quoted from the *Shih Ching (Book of Songs)* and the *Shu Ching (Book of History)*, to Liu Pang's exasperation. At length he cried: "What good are the *Shih* and the *Shu*? I conquered the empire on horseback." The chamberlain replied: "True enough, but it is not on horse-back that you will be able to govern it" (*see* Needham, 1954:103). In other words, the monarch may vanquish his rivals in war, but the power thus regained from them cannot accrue to him alone. To share it, in step-ped a class of civilians educated to justify their influence by pronouncing incantations to the sacred names of kings Wen and Wu, whose greatness was the greatness of their advisors, and whose advice was based on none other than the philosophy of liturgical government preserved in Confucian learning.

The revolutionaries who overthrew Ch'in fought under the slogan, "Back to feudalism," that is, back to usurped holdings in landed prebends. Indeed, some of the old feudal states set up their administration again for a few years, but this was not to be the pattern of the future. Great manorial estates, headquarters of a second aristocracy, persisted for a longer time until the outset of the Third Unity, but with weakening influence. How-ever the feudal aristocracy of the era of territorial states was finished; and the second aristocracy of land-buying, land-consolidating manorial lords reappeared in strength only during times of imperial disunity. The politics of empire and bureaucratic prebends had come to stay (outlasting two par-titions of some four hundred years each), until the twentieth century.

The great landed families were students of Confucianism, a literature so thoroughly proscribed under Ch'in that legend says its books were burned and its scholars buried alive. But the influence of Confucius per-sisted because he expressed, in the language of Chou feudalism, the au-tonomy of a nonhereditary ruling class, so long as its members exalted the sovereignty of the hereditary ruler, the Son of Heaven. The Han emperors from the first extended their patronage to Confucianism. It succeeded as the lasting ideology of empire because, unlike Legalism, Confucianism ap-pealed to both sides of the imperial equation: to the emperor's monopoly of hereditary glory and to the local autonomy of the ruling class. For the emperor this meant limiting imperial power to the exercise of cultural influence. But to the emperor's advantage, Confucian ideology disallowed a hereditary nobility other than his own—an arrangement that more and more appealed to his bureaucratic officers, who could thus take the posi-tion of volunteering to serve royalty by working in the *name* of the em-peror but not *for* him.

Confucianism validated the status of scholar-officials on their own merits in advance of appointment to prebends by the royal house. In addi-tion, the emperor could find growing satisfaction in attracting voluntary adherents to the brightness of his cause. By the end of the Han dynasty, the number of officials and secretaries concentrated in the capital city and fed there on salary came to number over 130,000. The administrative needs of the court, swollen to truly imperial proportions, actually far outweighed those of the empire as a whole.

That learning and not the ownership or inheritance of great estates was the preferred route to a political career was signified by the founding of an imperial university in the capital city for the study of the Confucian classics. After examination its graduates were sometimes drawn into government service, although a fully developed system of examinations as a regular basis of recruitment did not take place until centuries later, in the Sung dynasty. Meanwhile, two political systems coexisted throughout the empire for purposes of administration: first, a bureaucratic domain of trained officials, and second, the manorial estates of the second aristocracy and the hereditary estates given by the emperor to members of the royal family. But the principle of recruitment to office on the basis of managerial merit had already been established during the first Imperial Unity; it had only to be enlarged in the future, to the greater cultural glory of the emperor (Li, 1971:104, 123; Meskill, 1973:43).

Contributing to the scholastic dimension of culturalism were the assemblies of Confucian experts invited by the Han emperors to discuss the meaning of the surviving historical writings of the Spring and Autumn period. The first of these assemblies, held in 51 B.C. in the Stone Canal Pavilion of the palace, has been compared in significance with the Council of Nicaea, the first ecumenical conference of church fathers convened under Constantine in A.D. 325 (Needham, 1954:105). The text of a second court conference, held in A.D. 79 in the White Tiger Lodge, has come down complete in the *Pai Hu T'ung Lu* (Tjan, 1949–52), in addition to the text of another conference, held in 81 B.C. to discuss the effects of the government's nationalization of iron and salt in 119 B.C.—that is, state control of commerce and industry—recorded in the well-known *Yen T'ieh Lun* (Gale, 1931–34). All three of these palace gatherings lent prestige to Confucianism, already instituted as a state cult in 136 B.C. by the great Han Wu-ti.

The royal house also augmented its prestige as it enlarged its territory; the conquests of the Han dynasty did not stop with the boundaries of the Ch'in empire. The military machine under Han Wu-ti continually annexed new lands for the glory of the imperium: Inner Mongolia at the expense of the Hsiung-nu in 127 B.C.; Outer Mongolia in 115; North Korea in 109; Kwangsi, Kwangtung, and North Vietnam in 112; and Kweichow and Yunnan in 111. Conquests in the semiarid steppelands north of the Great Wall, however, could not be consolidated with Chinese settlers (the soil being unsuitable for farming), so that conflict with the Hsiung-nu was not ended but merely delayed until the day the Chinese military machine relaxed its vigil. That day came with the disorder caused by the Hsin interregnum, but reinvigorated forces of the Later Han, allied with one faction of Hsiung-nu against another, weakened this particular breed of northern barbarians forever. Others would come to conquer later.

An important by-product of the campaigns against the Hsiung-nu was the opening of the Great Silk Route, beginning at Ch'ang-an and Loyang and stretching all the way to the Mediterranean for a distance of four thousand miles. Also new musical instruments from Central Asia—

the flutelike *heng-ch'ui*, the guitarlike *p'i-p'a*, and the violinlike *hu-chin*—enhanced the pageantry of imperial processions.

It would be unfair to overlook the significance for culturalism of the imperial beauty contests. Ladies were pushed into the emperor's harem by great families of the land, others were summoned after the emperor noticed them on his travels, and yet others were chosen for him in official beauty contests. The mother of the child chosen as heir apparent would, of course, become empress, and her family would thus rise to power and wealth (Wilbur, 1943:38). The significance for culturalism is the emperor's display of a great appetite for sexual beauty. Concubines did not always get into bed, however; many acted as mere serving maids waiting on the emperor, servants in all but rank.

The emperor's wealth to command all these pleasures underscored his dominance as a figure of attention, especially admired for his military prowess by his soldiers, whose loyalty he required for personal security. In this respect the Chinese emperors resembled the Indian rajahs and the Indianized leadership of Indonesia as late as President Sukarno. How else would one identify the most important man in the realm? By today's standards, wealth and pleasure as indicators of cultural leadership are associated with "backward" countries; in the industrialized nations, political leadership has replaced the trappings of conspicuous comforts and hedonistic pleasures with real and substantive powers. These days, one stripteaser in the life of a modern statesman is cause for scandal.

Whatever the glories of the Han court that fascinated both the aristocratic and the nonhereditary elite of the realm, they all had to be financed with revenue no other region than the imperial granary could match in scale. From the start of the Han dynasty, Liu Pang enclosed the area of Shensi province for himself and the Liu clan, giving regions of lesser productivity to his best generals. Emperor Wu made the capital city even more a center of concentrated wealth with the aid of a transport canal cut from Ch'ang-an, south of the Wei, to meet the Yellow River. The canal served also to irrigate thousands of acres in the vicinity of the capital. At this time, North China was still the most productive; the southern conquests, marked only by a few garrisons, had not yet been followed up with drainage and irrigation ditches. In fact, landscaping the southern frontier to make it suitable for Chinese peasant farmers did not proceed fast enough to absorb population growth, the inevitable result being that the second aristocracy lost ground in the subdivision of its patrimonial estates (Wilbur, 1943:20–27).

FIRST PARTITION

One measure of imperial glory is the intensity of rivalry to usurp it. The house of Han fell in A.D. 220 (see Figure 5) to a powerful general named Ts'ao Ts'ao. The moment that he deposed the last of the Han emperors (a mere child) and proclaimed a new dynasty, two rival generals also proclaimed themselves emperor in other parts of China.

The division of the country into three self-proclaimed imperiums shows the close relationship between dynastic power and regional geography. The ternary division of the Han empire into the San Kwo, or Three Kingdoms, follows the main lines of regional stress, as analyzed by Chi

Ch'ao-ting in his classic of Chinese geopolitics, *Key Economic Areas in Chinese History* (1936). According to Chi, imperial unity means control by the emperor of a region superior to any other in both agricultural productivity and transport facilities. Such a region he calls a Key Economic Area (KEA). There are four KEAs, two primary ones and two secondary ones (see Map 1).

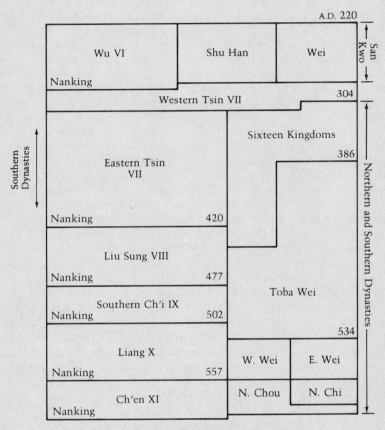

FIGURE 5.   First Partition (The Six Dynasties).

Primary

A. The Yellow River basin, including the Hwai River system
B. The lower Yangtze River basin

Secondary

C. The upper Yangtze River basin (the Red basin of Szechwan)
D. The Hsi, or West River, system (empties at Canton)

Unity exists when the emperor controls either area "A" or area "B," with or without areas "C" and "D." No imperial unity can stand on the resources of the latter two, either separately or together.

The Three Kingdoms of Shu, Wu, and Wei divided among them the four KEAs. Shu occupied secondary area "C," based on the irrigation system of the compact Chengtu plain installed by Ch'in governors, with its

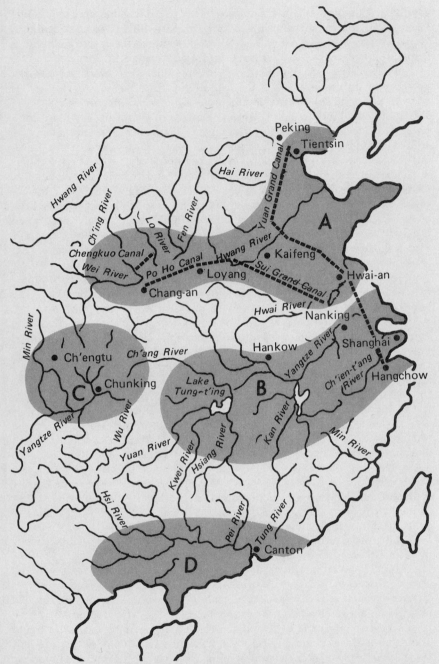

Map. 1. Rivers, canals, and Key Economic Areas during various periods of Chinese history. "A" is the KEA for the First Unity, "B" for the Second and Third Unities. "C" and "D" are secondary areas that make for important regional divisions. Adapted from Chi Ch'ao-ting (1936).

Map 1. Key Economic Areas (KEAs).
From Stover, 1974a.

capital at Chengtu. Wu based its power on the navigable and productive facilities of the middle and lower Yangtze (KEA "B"), with its capital at Nanking, and included also KEA "D." Wei occupied the traditional seat of imperial power, KEA "A," with its capital at Loyang.

In the three-way competition among Shu, Wu, and Wei for the privilege of shining imperial glory over all of China, Wei in area "A" to the north clearly had the advantage in population, natural resources, and political tradition. Wei's taxable subjects numbered about 29 million, compared to 11.7 million for Wu and a bare 7.5 million for Shu (Eberhard, 1950:111). In addition, Wei occupied the alluvial loessland of the lower Yellow River valley—the ancient and fertile home of Chinese civilization.

The kingdom of Shu was held by an independent ruler during the San Kwo period, the first of seven or eight times in Chinese history. This explains why KEA "C," the Red basin of Szechwan, is a secondary area. Like all KEAs, area "C" is able to stand alone with its own glorious court when the light of the imperial court fails to attract all China. But when the imperial throne attracts the cultural loyalties of powerful men *except* those in the Red basin, the idea of empire is not diminished.

The potentially richest area of all, the lower Yangtze River occupied by Wu, was not yet fully colonized by Chinese. Much of the population—Tai peoples who brought the sowing of wet rice into the swidden cycle of southern agriculture—still existed in a state of Neolithic tribalism reminiscent of the Yang-shao horizon. By the end of Han times, however, area "B" had begun to resemble the high nutritional density of the northern areas as it gradually absorbed Chinese migrants, both peasant farmers and aristocrats. Wu drew its power from this growing population. Its capital city at Chien-k'ang (renamed Nanking in the Ming dynasty) in the Hwai River basin supported over a million inhabitants—evidence of well-organized grain transportation over inland waterways in the most strategic region of China. This area is strategic because the Hwai basin dominated the lake country that, with a hundred miles of connective canals, eventually linked up the old, established north of KEA "A" with the newly developing south of KEA "B." The two areas had to be linked up by transport canal eventually because, while the lower Yangtze of area "B" evolved to become the richest of all the KEAs, the capital city and its concentrated military strength had to remain in area "A" in order to defend the great semicircular barbarian frontier, 2,500 miles long, from Tibet in the southwest to Manchuria in the northeast.

The first government to push a canal between the two areas was the episodic house of Tsin, which inherited only twenty-seven years of imperial glory from the victorious campaigns of Wei. It was an empire divided up in landed estates among the founder's relatives, who took up residence in the capital city of Loyang and there lived off their rents, as did many grandees of the second aristocracy under the Han dynasty. But a small force of Hsiung-nu soon swept down upon the city and murdered emperor, relatives, and the entire body of supportive officialdom, numbering some 30,000. The leader of this expedition proclaimed himself emperor, only to be extinguished by another ambitious Mongolian chieftain, and so on sixteen times within a hundred years, under a variety of Turkic, Mongol, and Hunnish peoples. The short-lived houses of the Sixteen Kingdoms were followed by a more durable and extensive Toba Wei dynasty, whose tribal rulers, originating in eastern Mongolia, were forced out by more invasions followed by further political fragmentation. Chinese historians call this mélange of barbarian statelets the Northern Dynasties.

The Northern Dynasties did not exploit the Chinese environment in the Chinese way. This accounts for their quick turnover and limited jurisdiction. To the west they sat astride the Great Silk Route and taxed the caravan trade. To the east they impressed grain with armed troops, who often indulged the nomad's contempt for civilization by killing the producers and burning their villages. The Northern Dynasties came to an end only after the northern landscape had been devastated and depopulated beyond its ability to repay the effort of plundering it. The ruin of the north is another explanation for the rising economic importance of the south, in addition to its own internal growth.

With no imperial cause to dignify officeholding, the Chinese elite abandoned the northern statelets in great numbers. With the capital city depopulated owing to a decline in the riverine transport of grain, Loyang fell into rubble. Forsaking urban security that no longer existed, the elite repaired to private citadels, miniature city-states, where peasants exchanged their vulnerability in the open countryside for immured roles as tenants and soldiers. For every ten of these self-sufficient estates (encompassing up to several thousand retainers), six or seven moved to South China and reestablished manors in the region of the lower Yangtze.

A general of Western Tsin, a member of the royal family serving in the south, founded the Eastern Tsin at Nanking after Loyang fell to the Hsiung-nu. His court was the rallying point for a mass migration from North China, one of the largest migrations recorded in history. The emigrants, who did much to sinicize the south, kept the second aristocracy going under a succession of Chinese houses: Eastern Tsin, Liu Sung, Southern Ch'i, Liang, and Ch'en. With Wu, these houses comprise the Southern Dynasties—the line of imperial succession from dynasties six through eleven. The whole of the First Partition is thus officially recorded as the period of the Liu Ch'ao, or Six Dynasties. The last five of them, along with the barbarian houses of the north, are known collectively as the Nan Pei Ch'ao, or Northern and Southern Dynasties.

SECOND IMPERIAL UNITY

When imperial unity was restored under the Sui dynasty (see Figure 6), its capital city, Ch'ang-an, was relocated in the political north, but its granary was located in the more productive south. The Sui Grand Canal linked the two. Like the Great Wall, the Grand Canal was constructed or rebuilt from older sections. The most strategic section, running north and south between Hwai-an and Yang-chou, connecting the Yangtze and the Hwai River, had been cut during Eastern Tsin times. The southern terminus of the Sui Canal began at Hangchow. From Hwai-an it turned northwest along a tributary of the Hwai, and beyond, to K'ai-feng. From there grain boats headed up the Yellow River for the remaining journey to the capital, Ch'ang-an. Adverse currents up the rapids of the Yellow River made the journey difficult, but easier and shorter water transport to the Yellow plain was blocked by its exposure to nomadic horsemen. Ch'ang-an was at least immune from raids, and as soon as the steppe nomads were controlled during the Third Unity, the capital city gravitated back to its uncompromised situation in the northeast.

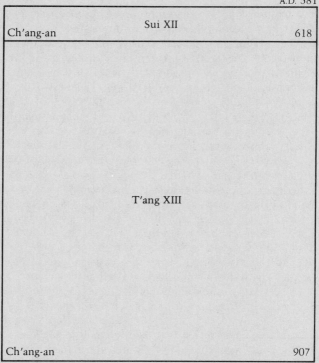

FIGURE 6.   Second Unity.

Again like the Great Wall, the Sui Grand Canal was built with corvée labor. On one stretch alone it is recorded that 3.6 million laborers were assembled from all able-bodied men between fifteen and twenty years of age. A child, old man, or woman from the same region was drafted to bear food and cook for each laborer. Including police and section chiefs, the total numbered 5.5 million. Earth-moving equipment was limited to hoes, baskets, and shirt bibs—a primitive technology that still gets the work done today when millions of men are organized to apply it. This work was carried on despite heavy losses from death and flight.

By the time of the Second Unity, the KEA of empire had shifted to area "B," but area "A" still retained its old political importance. For the Sui and T'ang dynasties of the Second Unity, the Grand Canal was both an economic and a military necessity. Economic because the productive rice regions of the Yangtze were located in the south, and military because the barbarian threat came from the north. The Sui Grand Canal prompted a dependence on the growth of area "B" that, from the T'ang dynasty onward, permanently settled the location of the imperial granary in the south and the imperial capital in the north.

SECOND PARTITION

Like the First Partition, the parts of the Second can be grouped in a north-south division (see Figure 7). Initially, the north carried the legitimate succession of states—the Wu-tai, or Five Dynasties—with capital cities located either at K'ai-feng (four times) or at Loyang (once). Both were supplied by the Yellow River. At about the same time, a decade of other states, the Ten Kingdoms, occupied various river valleys in the south. Eventually two Tartar tribes, the Liao and the Chin, successively occupied the north, while the Chinese held central and southern China with the native Sung dynasty.

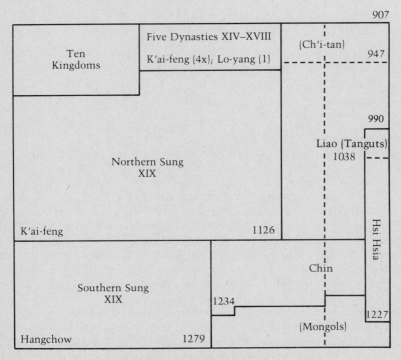

FIGURE 7.   Second Partition.

The Chinese have assigned dynastic succession to the north despite the fact that they detest the military dictatorships of the Wu-tai. Unitary control over KEA "A," the oldest and once the most productive center of the civilization, evidently carried more weight with Chinese historians than the peaceful and Confucian—but more fragmented—regional governments of the Ten Kingdoms in the south. The dissection of the Yangtze landscape by mountain and valley encouraged a greater persistence of local political cultures than was encouraged in the open country of the Yellow plain.

The Ten Kingdoms were founded by ambitious military governors who took over the southern provinces of the T'ang empire. They no longer cared to share the imperium with their emperor, but neither did they see any profit in contesting with each other. Each regional court was able to accumulate great wealth under peaceful conditions by setting up government monopolies and by working in association with great merchants for trading in tea, salt, and porcelain, whose foreign markets extended as far as India, Indonesia, Western Asia, and Japan. Of course, each kingdom provided ample rice and adequate river transportation to deliver food to its capital city.

The regions into which the Ten Kingdoms divided approximate those natural areas that belonged to imperial provinces, or combinations of these (Wang, 1963:1).

Kingdom	Modern Provincial Area
Wu	Kiangsu, Anhwei
Nant'ang	Kiangsi
Wu-Yueh	Chekiang
Min	Fukien
Nan Han	Kwangtung, Kwangsi
Ch'u	Hunan
Early Shu } Later Shu }	Szechwan
Nan P'ing	Hupeh
Pei Han	Shansi (after 950)

In all, six natural regions lay behind the power of the ten different states. Like the provinces of imperial government, they were centered on, not demarcated by, rivers—a continuing fact of economic geography emphasizing the importance of water transport in Chinese politics.

Regionalism was finally defeated with the end of the Sung dynasty and the beginning of the Third Unity. Sung culture marks the divide between the end of the second aristocracy and the beginning of the mature agrarian state. Thereafter, China never fell into disunity for long. Even barbarian conquests eventuated in imperial unities along Chinese lines.

During the Sui and T'ang dynasties, the Chinese military machine kept the northern frontiers guarded by a constant play of offensive and defensive action. The struggle was lost under the Five Dynasties, when a large portion of North China was infiltrated by a confederation of Tartar hordes named Ch'i-tan, or Khitan, from southeastern Mongolia. In 946, the Ch'i-tan ruler proclaimed overlordship of the Chinese in the dynastic name of Liao, even though he did not advance his military conquests any farther south than the northern part of the Yellow plain. From Peking, he rather demanded and got exhaustive payments of "protection money" from the Sung in the form of gold and silk. The Sung armies were at a disadvantage because the enemy occupied the borderlands where horses could be raised.

Of all the "protection money" extracted by the Ch'i-tan from the Chinese, none of it reached nomadic tribesmen to the rear of the frontier, in the region of the Amur river. These disadvantaged members of the confederation, the Jurchen Tartars (Tungusic forefathers of the Manchus), rose up against their rich-living brethren and captured Peking for themselves in 1125, ending the Liao dynasty. One prince fled to the west with a small band of followers and founded the Kara-Khitai state of the Western Liao among the Uighurs of Central Asia, in the oasis country in the vicinity of Kashgar and Samarkand.

The Jurchen set themselves up as the new rulers of China under the name Chin, meaning Golden. The Golden Hordes swept into K'ai-feng and captured the Sung emperor and his entire court, ending the Northern Sung dynasty. A new capital was set up at Hangchow for a Southern Sung dynasty, which the Chin were fighting to penetrate when they were swept away by the Mongols in 1234 under Genghis Khan, who also wiped out the Western Liao in 1211.

The conquests of Genghis Khan in Central Asia included destruction of the Tanguts in 1227. The Tanguts were a Tibetan pastoral people who had built a kingdom astride the old Silk Route along the upper reaches of the Yellow River. In 1038 the Tanguts stopped paying tribute to Northern Sung, from their tax on the caravan trade, and proclaimed their own empire, that of Hsi Hsia. Without sufficient horses for the Chinese armies, denied them by control over the steppeland on the part of the Liao and later by the Chin, Sung troops had no means of access to counter the Hsi Hsia threat to Chinese sovereignty. The geopolitical fact of the matter is that if the Chinese were to control for themselves their own agricultural economy in China proper within the Wall, they had to hold enough pastureland outside the Wall to supply their cavalry. Only then could they defend against the steppe peoples, who made up in the mobility of their striking forces what they lacked in numerical inferiority, one nomad to every forty Chinese. Hence the strategic importance of locating the imperial capital in the north, close to the barbarian frontier.

THIRD IMPERIAL UNITY

Grandsons of Genghis Khan extended his conquests in Central Asia with the force of sweeping plunder, to include four khanates that reached across the whole of Eurasia, from Hungary to Korea. With a simple bow-and-arrow technology, mounted nomads killed more people in a century of Mongol rapine than did all the guns and power machines of two world wars and Hitler's extermination camps combined (Drucker, 1967:32). After an initial play of destruction in China, however, Mongol troops settled there in garrisons. China fell within the khanate of the great Mongol, Kublai Khan, who learned to master the traditional Chinese methods of administering native officeholders. The Mongols held the supervisory posts jointly with Chinese, leaving the lesser posts and the life of the local gentry totally to the Chinese elite. Chinese peasants worked the land, Chinese officials and landlords taxed and rented it, and the Mongol emperors were glorified for it throughout the Yuan dynasty (see Figure 8). The same pattern was repeated under the conquering dynasty of the Manchus, the Ch'ing.

Sandwiched between the Yuan and the Ch'ing is the Ming, the one native dynasty of the Third Unity. Its political arrangements were taken over almost intact by the Manchus, including the Ming statutes. The Manchus adopted the existing provincial system, except for making a few subdivisions of the fifteen Ming provinces, for a new total of eighteen. The Manchus gave every support to Chinese institutions and Confucian scholarship. Indeed they posed as a legitimate native dynasty come to rescue the Chinese from bad government, as evidenced by rebellion. They justified their conquest in terms of the Chinese concept of dynastic succession: the passing of the mandate of Heaven from the "bad last" to the "good first." But the rebellion in question was none other than that of some Ming generals who found it profitable to aid the Manchu conquest in the first place. In the history of the Ch'ing dynasty, it is written: "Our government conquered Peking from the hands of the rebels, not from the

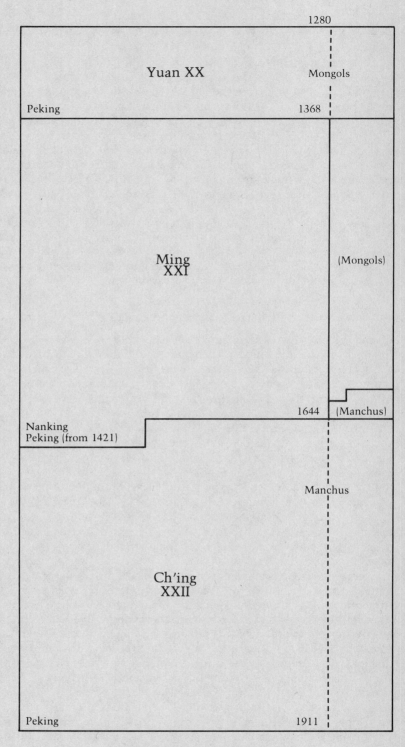

FIGURE 8.   Third Unity.

Ming dynasty. The rebels dethroned the Ming emperor. We revenged the wrong at the expense of our own treasure and blood" (Hsieh, 1925:19). So well did the Manchus learn the lessons of Confucian morality that they were able to describe their own barbarian invasion as a native Chinese rebellion.

All three dynasties of the Third Unity established capitals at Peking, the Ming doing so after it discovered it could not handle its border problems from Nanking. As shown on Map 1, for the supply of Peking from KEA area "B," a second Grand Canal was constructed under the Yuan and maintained by the last two dynasties. The Yuan Grand Canal repeated the course of the Sui Grand Canal, from Hangchow up to the Hwai River. But from there, instead of turning west toward Ch'ang-an, it continued northward to Tientsin, for a total length of 1,286 miles.

Steamship transportation in the latter half of the nineteenth century reduced the cost of hauling tribute grain by a factor of ten. But by this time, the economic areas began losing the controlling significance they exercised when agricultural productivity and water transport were the combined measure of the Dragon Throne's power to outshine rival courts set up on the basis of smaller natural regions. With the advent of industry, electric communications, railroads, steamships, and overseas commerce, the KEAs figured as but one factor among others in deciding the role of central government.

The turning point came with the Opium War of 1840. Through various treaties signed afterward, the steamboat powers of the West exacted rights of extraterritoriality from seventy-three coastal and riverine ports, treaties that were not abrogated until 1945. The strength of Western influence caused the Chinese gentry to lose interest in acquiring their wealth and power under the emperor's cultural umbrella, as agents of his glory. Furthermore, the xenophobia shown by the Chinese to the Western barbarians was transferred to the Ch'ing house. Once "Chinese" were opposed to "barbarians," the apposition of "Chinese" to "Manchu" was awakened. Significantly, this awakening first took place in the area of Canton, where trade with the West began—the same area from which Sun Yat-sen drew his support for his revolutionary party in the revolution of 1911 (Wakeman, 1966:58). The ethnic problem, however, was probably only a cover for the deeper problem of gentry demoralization. To this point, the gentry had never organized their own government. As a class, they accepted any monarch, native or foreign, who was able to seize power and who recognized the right of landowners to manage the affairs of informal government—and on the basis of that experience to enter formal government—if only temporarily for the purpose of gathering enough influence to protect or enhance their own interests (Fei, 1946:9). But now the cultural umbrella under which they held their educational honors and imperial prestige in the countryside was ripped to shreds; the throne was no longer able to assert the centrality of Chung kwo in a world that for the first time included truly dangerous neighbors.

The fall of the Ch'ing dynasty ended more than a dynasty. It ended the era of cyclical imperial conquests. With it ended the culturalism of the Chinese pseudomorph and began the nationalism of the Chinese nation-state.

FIVE

PERIODIZATION

MAO'S REVOLUTIONARY STAGES

A direct result of President Nixon's visit to China in 1972 is the current exchange of books between Chinese and American libraries. Among the books most desired by the Chinese are two works of Lewis Henry Morgan, the nineteenth-century American lawyer and amateur ethnologist. They are his *Ancient Society* (1878), a work of cultural evolution, and *The League of the Iroquois* (1851), a study of the government and social organization of the Iroquois Confederation of Senecas, Mohawks, Oneidas, Onondagas, and Cayugas. Librarians for the State University of New York at Stony Brook report that Chinese interest in the former work is high because Morgan "described the Marxist notion of how society evolved" and in the latter because he described "the type of social organization the Chinese are now attempting in their own country" (Andelman, 1973:1).

Karl Marx read *Ancient Society* (Morgan, 1878) and came to the conclusion that if communism existed in the past, as Morgan said it did, then it could exist again in the future, this time on an advanced technical basis. Chinese Marxists agree, but they allow that the second coming of communism will be achieved without the high technology insisted on by Russian Marxists. The Iroquois Indians, an example of Morgan's New Stone Age barbarians, evidently put Chinese Communist party theoreticians in mind of the "classless primitive communes" Mao Tse-tung (1965: II:306) has ascribed to the prehistoric past, to whose democratic foundations history must return.

Prehistory is thus drawn into an ideological dispute about the career of man, from human origins to human destiny. Morgan's ladder of evolutionary development runs from savagery (Old Stone Age), through barbarism (New Stone Age), to civilization (Iron Age). Morgan drew on a scale of ages devised by museum curator-archaeologist Christian Jurgensen Thomson from his guidebook of 1836, which reflected his exhibits of prehistoric tools in sequence from stone to bronze to iron. In 1865, Lord Avebury (John Lubbock) refined Thomson's three ages by lumping bronze and iron into one Metal Age—the outcome of two ages of stone—for which he coined the words *Paleolithic* (age of the ancient hunters) and *Neolithic* (age of the early farmers). The word *prehistory* was coined in 1851 (*see* Daniel, 1963).

Before Marx read Morgan, however, he allowed his baseline in primitive communism to generate a threefold development of societal types: the Asiatic, Graeco–Roman, and German–medieval. He characterized the Asiatic line as unprogressive, a dead-end case of stagnated underdevelopment. Later he discovered that his multilineal approach, however heuristic, would discourage practicing revolutionary parties in Asia (to make a socialist revolution they would have to appeal for intervention from a more advanced Western society), so he turned to the political advantage of a unilineal approach, clothing it with Morgan's scientific authority (see Wittfogel, 1957: ch. 7; Feuerwerker, 1968:225–26). Thanks to this switch, Mao has been able to assert his independence from the Soviet Union on theoretical grounds. His position from the start has been that "We Chinese can make our own revolution, thank you, because China's past is no different from any other civilization's." For Mao, as for Stalin, the three ages of man between the communism of the past and the communism of the future are those of slavery, feudalism, and capitalism. The difference is that Mao claims to have a keener appreciation of future history than the "revisionists" in Moscow: a restoration of primitive democracy, not mistaken progress toward a state-operated version of American industrial capitalism.

The striking anomaly in Mao's application of Marxian schematics to Asia is the insistence on a capitalist stage (see Figure 9). The vested interest Mao has in finding capitalism in China stems from the fear that if one of the intermediary stages is not really necessary, we may begin to doubt the inevitability of the final goal. This obligatory, if fleeting, stage Mao dates from 1840, the year of the Opium War with England, a war that signalled a serious business interest in China by the Western powers as a whole. The stage ends only 109 years later with the advent of the PRC, which initiated semisocialism and socialism, transitional phases on the way to communism. The capitalist stage Mao rewords as colonial, semicolonial, and semifeudal society. By colonial he means the outright colonial occupation of parts of China by the Japanese during the Sino-Japanese War and its merger with World War II. By semicolonial and semifeudal he means the mixed situation that resulted after 1840 from the impact of foreign capital on a feudal (landlord) economy. The upshot was neither complete domination of China from the outside by foreign enterprise nor complete transformation by example from the inside. Feudalism lasted for 2610 years in China, according to Mao, yet for all that time it carried within itself the latent seeds of capitalism.

Mao's statement that, "China would of herself have developed slowly into a capitalistic society even without the impact of foreign capitalism. Penetration of foreign capitalism accelerated this process," (Mao, 1965: II:309) is surely casuistic, but never mind. Mao is talking politics, not anthropology. Whatever plans Mao has for the communist future in China, moreover, he has said little or nothing about them. In the third chapter of Quotations from Chairman Mao Tse-tung (entitled "Socialism and Communism") there is not one line explaining what either socialism or communism means, but merely the repeated affirmation that communism is inevitable and will triumph. The rest is an appeal to live a simple life and work hard to build socialism, as if purposive poverty were in itself a source of reward and happiness (Schram, 1967:xxiii). Perhaps this is how he imagines, from a romanticized picture of the American Indians, what life among the Iroquois used to be. On the other hand, Mao may have used the centralized powers of state at their height to plan for their inevitable weakening and decentralization. In this light, according to one analyst of Asian developmental models, the communes may represent a "calculated devolution of responsibility toward self-reliance and local enterprise in finance, farming, small industry, education, and social service" (Lockwood, 1974:827).

In any case, the difference between the political and the anthropological periodization of culture history is that the former aims to justify policy and the latter aims to classify the events of the human story with the same detachment natural philosophers have brought to the study of the external world. It is the difference between history as sanctification and history as truth. The practice of finding purpose in the past is sheer divination in the service of national destiny, a deceitful practice that is all too prevalent in a world whose need is none other than one history of man and the end of competing national mythologies (Plumb, 1973).

Chinese communist historians evince an urgent need to show that China's history is no different in development from that of Western peoples. To have borrowed so much from the West, including the doctrine of communism itself, makes it impolitic to accept a history different in kind and separate from the West's. Especially to be combatted is the notion of a peculiar, Asiatic form of human society, innately stagnant and unprogressive. Given the assumption that human history everywhere has followed a common pattern of organic development, the problem of historiography in Communist China is limited to periodization. The scriptural authority for all intellectuals working in this field is Mao Tse-tung's article of 1939, "The Chinese Revolution and the Chinese Communist Party" (in Mao, 1965: II:305–34). His "revolutionary stages," as described in this article, are shown in Figure 9, alongside our own periodization. (On theoretical history, *see* Meskill, 1965; Steward *et al.* 1955; and Wittfogel, 1957).

The biggest single issue in communist historiography is the lengthy duration of the stage of feudalism, from the end of the Shang dynasty in 770 B.C. to the opening guns of "foreign aggression" against China with the Opium War of 1840 A.D. Here there is room to differentiate some historical movement. Mao presents feudalism as a time of unremitting serf labor. Recent Chinese historians have allowed some movement from feudal lords to landlords (Fitzgerald, 1968:127), a change that roughly corresponds to our distinction between the preimperial aristocracy and the second aristocracy. But on the whole, Chinese communist historians make too much of feudalism as a persistent and lethal contradiction between landlord and tenant, the resolution of which had to wait until collectivization. That communism was not the inevitable outcome of Chinese history is well attested by the alternative form of development now flourishing on the island of Formosa, to which the government of the Republic of China repaired after its military defeat on the mainland in 1949.

The period of classless primitive communes, which embraces the Paleolithic, Mesolithic, and Neolithic in China, may be accommodated in an all-inclusive period—prehistory. The period of slavery coincides with our era of city-states. While slavery was not in fact the economic basis of early civilization in China, Mao's period does cover an era clearly bracketed off from others, beginning with the rise of Bronze Age cities (dispersed urbanism) and closing when their inner wall was doubled by the addition of an outer wall (compact urbanism).

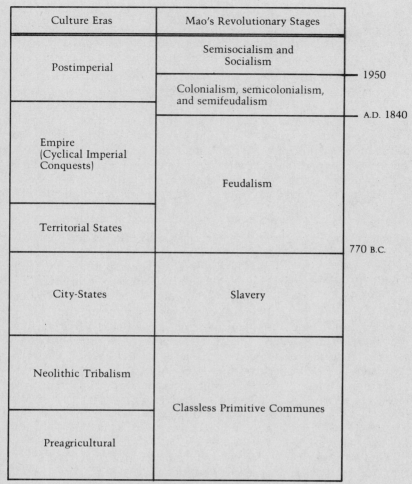

Culture Eras	Mao's Revolutionary Stages	
Postimperial	Semisocialism and Socialism	
	Colonialism, semicolonialism, and semifeudalism	— 1950
Empire (Cyclical Imperial Conquests)	Feudalism	— A.D. 1840
Territorial States		
City-States	Slavery	770 B.C.
Neolithic Tribalism	Classless Primitive Communes	
Preagricultural		

FIGURE 9.   Mao's Revolutionary Stages (not to scale).

Mao's feudalism covers our era of territorial states and almost all of our era of cyclical imperial conquests. But any common factor general enough to cover these two eras may be extended to cover the era of city states as well. Throughout all that great stretch of time, from the beginnings of the Bronze Age, Chinese civilization may be described as a low-energy, single-landscape civilization, powered only by the organic energy produced from the plants of a one-sided Neolithic economy (*see* Cottrell, 1955: ch. 2). This condition persisted until contact with the industrialized West brought about some diversification of the economic landscape. This same stretch of time is united politically by one form of prebendalism or the other.

All the other primitive civilizations were transformed at an earlier date by the rebounding influence of their own cultural protégés, the Iron Age civilizations. The archaic pattern of the Incan and Meso-American civilizations dissolved under the Spanish conquistadores; that of Egypt under the Arab conquest; Mesopotamia was absorbed into the Roman empire; India into the Muslim. China alone survived long enough in its aboriginal condition to develop its orthogenetic potential to the limit.

Consider what are the basic technologies of Bronze Age civilization as they are known from their earliest centers of development in Mesopotamia and Egypt? They are the wheel, writing, and smelting. These civilized technologies, in turn, were founded on the Neolithic technologies of plant and animal domestication, carpentry, pottery making, and weaving. All the orthogenetic civilizations except China were overwhelmed by Iron Age developments, which in their fullness included cheap iron for making tools and weapons, riding on horseback, writing (the alphabet), using money, organizing craftsmen into guilds, and organizing local kingdoms into an empire tied together by a system of posts, as in the Roman and Persian empires (Coon, 1969: chs. 7 and 8). China acquired all these Iron Age traits by diffusion, save for the alphabet, but used them in an archaic political context.

Horse breeding. The Chinese courier service used mounted riders, but not to any great extent. Breeding horses, like domesticating barnyard animals other than scavengers, such as pigs and chickens, was too competitive with horticulture. Consequently, pastureland was maintained only in the transitional ecological zone between steppe and sown, and at great military expense because the same zone was contested for by steppe nomads. Imperial dispatches most often went by river and canalboat. The capital city of Peking was supplied by the Grand Canal, a combination of natural and artificial waterways, not by horse-drawn carts. Inland water transport remained of strategic importance, as the Nile was to ancient Egypt and the Tigris-Euphrates to Mesopotamia.

Money. Coins of imperial mintage existed for penny transactions, but real commerce was conducted with silver ingots that varied by region in shape and purity. These ingots, with silver dollars of Western import, were treated as Bronze Age bullion, to be weighed in the steelyards of merchants and bankers.

Guilds. Merchants, artisans, and craftsmen were organized in guilds, as in the Iron Age societies of the West; and they were allowed to set their own price ceilings, unlike their counterparts who worked under royal overseers at Bronze Age courts. But the literati, the arbiters of social status, considered even the wealthiest merchant a member of the lower class. The literati continued to arbitrate a two-class, Bronze Age social structure—a consumption elite living off the fruits of the land (officials collecting taxes and gentlemen collecting rents), and a productive majority (peasant farmers and their appendages, petty merchants, and artisans). The men of high culture, pure in their physiocratic elegance, were able to depreciate the prestige of big merchants even though they held legal title to elite status. They were depreciated socially because they did not live directly off the land and because their economic interests were as localized as the regional forms of bullion they weighed in their steelyards.

Alphabet. The absence of the democratizing alphabet in China has traditionally been associated with the literati's power to arbitrate a two-class system. The restricted literacy of ideographic writing gave only the men of the great tradition a translocal culture and made them cosmopolitan agents of empire; nonliteracy kept the culture of the little tradition parochial and divisive. Small wonder that literate merchants strove to acquire the official badge of literacy—either through purchasing academic degrees from the government or by preparing their sons for the civil service examinations—to overcome scholastic snobbery. Absorbed in this struggle of definitions, merchants never emerged as an independent middle class, as they did in the late Iron Age cultures of Europe. The Chinese elite continued to monopolize a cultural tradition that cut across regions and provinces, thanks to the absence of a democratizing alphabet—a common denominator the nonliterate majority lacked by definition. Village and town folk had no means to align themselves with the civilization at large. They were reduced to, and divided by, their parochial cultures. Confucius is doctrinaire on this point: "The catholicity of the *chun-tze* is not comparable; the particularism of the little people is not catholic" (*Lun Yu*, II:14).

Universalism was the secret of cultural domination by the few of the great tradition over the Neolithic men of the little tradition, whose Bronze Age elitism was shared across an empire vast enough to be a product of Iron Age politics, but was not. It was the ascendancy of moral over political power.

Chinese society under the emperors did partake of an Iron Age technology that made iron available to everybody as a cheap metal for tools and implements but not for weapons. In Bronze Age fashion, the state still monopolized the arsenal as it did the chief means of transportation. As the Bronze Age kings of ancient Egypt and Mesopotamia held control over river navigation on the Nile and the Tigris-Euphrates, so did the emperors of China hold control over the empire's key transportation facility, the Grand Canal, built to supply the metropolitan center with tribute grain.

WEAPONS AND TRANSPORT

A number of qualifications complicate but do not contradict the preceding generalization. Take the arsenal first. In theory, the state held a monopoly on all military weapons, including firearms introduced from the West. Under the reign of Tao Kwang, the *Peking Gazette* reported:

> For the people to have firearms in their possession is contrary to law, and orders have already been issued to each provincial government to fix a period, within which all matchlocks belonging to individuals should be bought up at a valuation. (quoted in Davis, 1836: vol. 1, p. 321)

This order was of course impossible to enforce, and arms did come into the hands of rebellious elements organized in secret societies whose very names often reflected their violation of the government monopoly on weapons, such as the Big Sword Society or The Red Spears. Both the T'ai-p'ing Rebellion and Sun Yat-sen's revolutionary party had early connections with the same secret society, the Triad.

Secret societies in China were illegal by definition. The only permissible political organization was the state, and organizations opposed to it were underground bodies whose illicit aims were expressed merely by calling themselves *hui*, which in Chinese simply means "society" or "organization." They comprised a number of rebellious elements not content to settle for the low ceiling on ambition placed on them by the Confucian state with its essentially Taoist preference for Neolithic subjects ignorant and apathetic. Membership came from a number of discontented groups, including semiliterate drop-outs from the examination system, dismissed yamen runners, itinerant craftsmen, disbanded troops, smugglers, coolies, and street porters. The Boxer Rebellion drew largely on watermen thrown out of work when coastal shipping by steam vessels replaced their barges on the Grand Canal. The largest source of discontent came from rural vagrants squeezed off the land by overpopulation into banditry and beggardom.

In 1926, Mao Tze-tung estimated the revolutionary potential of this class of discontented groups at twenty million (Schram, 1963:176; this statistic is omitted from the official translation in Mao, 1965: vol. 1, p. 19). By making it the beneficiary of a land reform program, Mao was able to use the problems and aspirations of this class of marginal men to terrorize landlords in a shooting revolution that, under the guidance of trained agitators, led to millions of deaths. The secret societies of old drew on the same class of men, but they never accomplished anything like genuine revolution. Quite the reverse. The force of opposition to the imperial order by the *hui* was invariably redirected to its support. Once recruited into a *hui*, its membership of oppressed persons was invariably officered by local gentry, who absorbed it as a clientele for their own intrigues.

Elsewhere clans served the same purpose. In other words, the *hui* functioned as an aspect of the traditional Chinese state, with its balance of forces between the formal government of imperial officials and the informal government of squires, not as an alternative to it. (On this complex subject, *see* Chesneaux, 1971). But insofar as landed gentlemen actually extended the monarch's policy of culturalism into the countryside, their control over the swords, spears, and guns held by the arsenals of the *hui* also extended the state's control over weapons. The state, after all, embraced both formal and informal government within one sanctified order of stable inequality.

All men of the great tradition, in or out of office, upheld the idea of the state, and those out of office made up by far the larger portion of the Chinese ruling class. Note that the ruling class, the *shih*, is named after a class of self-equipped knights, one of whom was the father of Confucius. Chinese civilization, for all its Iron Age borrowings, simply did not evolve the democracy of violence that, by putting cheap swords into everybody's hands, weakened centralized government controls under the genuine Iron Age empires. The Chinese empire owed its weak centralization rather to a wide geographic extension of its liturgical controls over the landed gentry, who in turn exercised the same local monopoly on weapons as did Bronze Age nobles in their landed prebends. A universal business currency for everybody, alphabetic writing for everybody, self-defense with cheap metal weapons for everybody—these traits helped decentralize and democratize imperial politics in the Iron Age of the West, but their absence in China gave to its imperium a decentralization without a corresponding democratization.

Another factor associated with the persistence of Bronze Age politics in China was central government's control of the Grand Canal (known in Chinese, significantly, as *Yun-ho*, or Transport River). For a fee merchants were allowed to burden the state's grain barges with a supercargo of their own. This concession to business interests, however, was one the throne could afford without violating essentials of the physiocratic doctrine it upheld in the act of monopolizing primary access to the canal with as much of its military might as it could spare from frontier duty (see Hinton, 1956; Elvin, 1973: ch. 8). The emperor thereby asserted his most important function, that of financing the cultural glories of his capital city with more agricultural wealth than any rival could concentrate, short of overthrowing him.

Culturalism remained the chief business of state for the Chinese empire as it had for the Bronze Age city-states, because the real power in the countryside—the local gentry and earlier, the second aristocracy—upheld the prestige of the emperor in this leadership role and in no other. The emperor's power was derivative insofar as the ruling class coincided with an educated class literate in a political philosophy in which the emperor himself was tutored by members of the same class. The literati carried forward and codified in Confucianism an ancient practice of government that limited political leadership at the center to illuminating the moral authority of the ruling class in its surrounding localities. This was the most visible aspect of the Confucian state, as described by its own historians. It coexisted with a gathering trade and commerce that worked through an ever-more-complicated hierarchy of central places. If in the feudal West a duality obtained between the prebendal domains of the church and the fiefs belonging to the state, in China a duality obtained between a commercial domain and a prebendal domain identified with the state, actually a kind of church. Although the empire was undergoverned relative to its commercial development, a religious faith in this political pseudomorph allowed Confucian believers to assert the dominance of the state-idea as their guiding truth.

In Chapter One we showed that China's self-name—Chung-kwo, or Central Kingdom—is derived from the sacred geography of the Shang realm. An alternate term is *Chung-hwa*, or "Central Cultural Florescence." As explained by a Yuan dynasty historian:

> Central Cultural Florescence *is another term for* Central Kingdom. *When a people subjects itself to the Kingly Teachings and subordinates itself to the Central Kingdom; when, in its clothing it is dignified and decorous, and when its customs are marked by filial respect and brotherly submission, when conduct follows the accepted norms and the principle of righteousness, then one may call it* [a part of the] Central Cultural Florescence. (cited in Wright, 1963:39, n. 8)

The "Kingly Teachings," of course, are the Confucian classics. They stand in the van of a civilizing mission, as described by the Chinese historian above, to bring high culture to all of East Asia. But because political boundaries were indefinite in the past, the center was not the empire itself but its capital city, from which the ruler's cultural influence extended with diminishing force throughout the realm and beyond. They were elites of the realm by definition, who in their domestic ritual imitated the court ritual of the sovereign, as in the small community of ritual belonging to each Bronze Age *kwo*, and who verbalized this practice in the words of Kingly Teachings. Thus did the amalgamation of kingdoms into empire retain in China the archaic culturalism of its parts for the political expression of the whole.

Concealed behind the mythology of a strong state lay the strength of a thoroughly complex network of commerce whose reality was politically unacknowledged and therefore not elevated in a system of reflective thought. Great merchants reduced to estimating the parity of local forms of bullion were in no position to challenge the universal currency of moral ideas carried by men in government, formal and informal, across all China. With the leadership class alone did a translocal tradition of culture hold, by virtue of a restricted literacy consecrated to the sacred texts of political philosophy. An elitist concept of government formulated in doctrine prevailed over the fact of a participatory, but unrationalized, economy. Strange to say, had the Legalist doctrine with its straight talk about economics prevailed, the Chinese empire may have come to approximate the more liberal features of its Iron Age fellows in the Western world. Surely the Confucian hostility toward Legalism stemmed from a profound suspicion of its democratic implications, notably in its abolition of a privileged minority, self-governed by *li* and exempt from penal law.

Sanctified by the emperor's patronage, Confucian literature and ritual worked to the advantage of scholar-officials and scholar-landlords, animating their respective formal and informal governments with a single ruling idea expressive of an archaic, two-class system divided between a cultured elite and an uncultured majority. The marketplace, for all its translocalized network, remained parochial by default—witness the use of bullion of regional stamp and form in the manner of trade between Bronze Age kingdoms. Yet despite this technical handicap, trade flourished with all the vigor of an Iron Age economy belonging to the Roman or Persian Empires. Men of the great tradition, however, associated this reality in China with the voiceless interests of the little tradition, and that was that; they had the political power to define what belonged to high culture and what did not. Upward social mobility meant joining the ranks of the arbiters of social status; for others, mobility was directed in a horizontal plane, in gathering economic influence throughout the central-place hierarchies of trade and commerce. Achievement in this direction on the part of big merchants could be converted into something honorable only if they could obtain certificates of a higher morality from the state in the form of academic degrees issued by purchase or earned by examination.

It is astonishing to see how little moral power the economy had on its own, a substantial reality created by artisans and craftsmen and merchants big and small in an urban network of modern proportions. A sure sign of economic development in the eyes of economists is an urban pyramid so perfected by interconnections of trade that, when the size of its cities is multiplied against their rank, from the biggest one at the top to the many smaller ones at the bottom, the result is a numerical constant. Over time, the cities of imperial China came to be distributed in almost a perfect rank/size pyramid, as in the modern industrial nations.

The fact is that the world's premodern urban history has been chiefly a Chinese phenomenon. In 1800, the population of the world was about one billion, of which four percent lived in cities of over ten thousand residents. One-third, if not fully one-half, of these urban dwellers lived in China, a proportion that has obtained for two thousand years (*see* Rozman, 1973). Cities did not originate in China, but in China they most proliferated; at the same time they remained almost unchanged in political significance, even while changing in economic significance. The first Chinese cities, dating back to the aristocratic compounds of the Shang dynasty, were centers of Bronze Age fiefs, or prebends, and prebendal centers they remained. In observing this to be the case, allowing for the shift of emphasis from land to office, there is some justification for bracketing off Mao's period of feudalism as one cultural era, and even for extending it farther back in time to include his prior one, slavery.

For all that time, Chinese cities never lost their prebendal function, whatever their changing economic role. For example, the minimal political unit of the Bronze Age, the city-state, persisted into imperial times as the minimal unit of administration, the *hsien*, or county seat, plus its supportive countryside. Some *hsien* to this day retain the same names they bore as Shang dynasty *kwo* three thousand years ago (Bishop, 1922). At all times the township served as a unit of exploitation for the authorities in charge, be they feudal lords or magistrates. What was administered by an imperial officer was a local fiscus for his own expenses and profit. The metropolitan center had its own fiscus, but the empire as a whole, supplied mainly by the Grand Canal, did not. From there the emperor presided as a moral guardian of the bureaucracy, assuring officials that they could hold their posts as administrative fiefs for a turn of duty, so long as the incumbents acknowledged their autonomy as a concession granted by his majesty.

But while appointments to provincial capitals were the emperor's to make, governors were as empowered as kings to appoint prefects and magistrates to their own prebendary realms. Yet the whole game was played out using the language of strong centralism, which was the language whereby officials acknowledged the emperor's cultural sway. Giving force to this was his topocosmic Center at Peking, the largest city in the empire; it served as a resplendent and compelling model for independent fiscal units on a smaller scale, from provincial to *hsien* capitals. In fact, Peking was the largest city in the world from the fifteenth century until the time of the Industrial Revolution in England.

Below the *hsien* level were unofficial central places belonging to the commercial domain, the periodic markets and the intermediate market towns. These found higher levels of interconnection in the various administrative cities, whose official business—that of prebendal exploitation—merely coexisted with their economic centrality. In all, eight ranks may be drawn for the developed urbanism of late imperial times in the early Ch'ing dynasty, from the biggest city to the smallest town, as follows: 1 metropolitan center (Peking), 3 regional centers, 12 large provincial capitals, 30 small provincial capitals, 90 prefectural capitals, 600 *hsien* capitals, 2,500 intermediate market towns, and 12,000 periodic markets. The population figure for each of these eight ranks very nearly comes out to a constant one million when rank is multiplied by size, equalling the size of the largest city. This clearly demonstrates the close approximation of the urban pyramid in premodern China to the perfect rank/size pyramids found in modern countries, although the *amount* of urbanization was considerably less; only six or seven percent of the total population of 150 million was located within the pyramid (Rozman, 1973:283).

Although the shape of the Chinese urban pyramid is modern, its premodern basis is revealed in the periodic markets of the bottom level. The per-capita demand of the peasant householding units among villagers and urban plebes was simply too small to allow for permanent and continuous markets. This made the pyramid somewhat bottom-heavy. Furthermore, increased population before the advent of factory industrialism did nothing to change the ratio of rural to urban dwellers. The introduction of New World crops—maize and potatoes plantable on dry uplands—made for a population increase of 150 percent during the first two centuries of the Ch'ing dynasty, but the increase was distributed through the urban pyramid in the same porportions (Rozman, 1973:282). With the advent of factory industrialism, both the rural-urban ratio has changed in the direction of more urbanism and the shape of the pyramid has become somewhat top-heavy, at least in South China, where Shanghai has a population six times greater than Nanking, the next ranking city. In fact, Shanghai is now bigger than Peking. According to the 1953 census, 13 percent of the total population lived in an urban pyramid with 409 settlements of between 20,000 and 100,000 at the bottom, 93 settlements of between 100,000 and 1 million in the middle range, and capped by 9 great cities of from 1 to 10 million (calculated from Ullmann, 1961:15). The Communist regime has inherited a well-developed system of urban networks, which its leaders have been able to convert into a centralized political command structure from what was originally a trade structure coexisting with a primitive political system.

A similar urban pyramid developed in premodern Japan; its political significance kept pace with its economic significance, leading to a strong centralization of government, under whose authority plans for modernization were carried out after contact with the West. In China, this did not happen. Unlike the Japanese case, the urban pyramid in China was not used as a political instrument through which the orders of central government were sent down the hierarchy in order to direct tax receipts upward to a single imperial fiscus. Although the Chinese structure reflected a sophisticated centralization of commercial places, it did nothing to alter the functioning of an archaic political order.

Indeed the first products of Western technology—railroads and telegraphic communications—were absorbed wholly into the value system of Chinese political culture. Railway building, initiated by the throne and constructed with foreign loans contracted for by the central government, led to a major political issue from the start, beginning in about 1896. As a national system of railways would strengthen the hand of the center against the autonomy of the provinces, its construction was opposed by local officials and by local gentry (who incidentally phrased their political objection in terms of peasant taboos against disturbing the natural elements). The upshot of the railway issue was anti-Manchu agitation to protest the throne's invitation of foreign capital, and the formation of "railway protection clubs" in four provinces, which then proceeded to invest in, and build, their own local systems. Provincial opposition to a national system of telegraph lines was likewise resolved in favor of regional systems (Hsu, 1970:521–22, 554–55; Fairbank et al., 1965:629–31). Joining these issues contributed strongly to the overthrow of the monarchy in the revolution of 1911, after which Western technology continued to be applied in defending (if not overdefending) regional interests, this time in the form of civil war waged with modern weapons. Not until the Communist takeover of 1949 were civil and military technology mastered in the interests of central power, accompanied by liquidation of China's "feudal" ruling class.

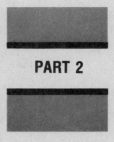

PART 2

INSTITUTIONAL DEVELOPMENT

SIX

ECOLOGY

POLITICAL GEOGRAPHY

Any landscape is the material expression of the culture exploiting it. And although the political culture of China has changed rapidly under communism, it is well to remember that the physical environment and the patterns of land use, in relation to variation in land forms, climate, inland waters, soils, vegetation, human occupancy, and resource utilization, are constant and slow-moving factors. Nonetheless, features of the landscape perceived one way under a policy of provincial autonomy united with nondevelopment are perceived differently under a new state-idea that calls for political integration and economic growth. In the course of nation building, the old pseudomorph is being recast as a sovereign political entity. This change is called modernization. But it is a difficult one (some would say impossibly so) given the momentous heritage of a low-energy civilization.

The past, dating from Neolithic times, has imposed man-made features on the natural habitat which live on in the form of deforestation, tilled fields, irrigation ditches, footpaths, and hillside terraces. These can be modified by planning insofar as labor can be mobilized to plant trees, amalgamate small individual plots into large collective farms, realign ditches and paths, and extend terraces upward. Not so easy to modify is the political ecology of these features. Villages and their surroundings of cultivated fields repeated themselves across the landscape in cellular units with about the frequency of spacing between individual farmsteads found in the midwestern United States (Dittmer, 1925). In China, this unit of repetition is the *hsien,* as old as the city-state that emerged with the beginnings of civilization. At the center of each unit (never larger than one thousand square miles) was its seat of government—a walled city always within a day's walk—as were its periodic markets located in unwalled towns, when these did not coincide with an administrative city.

These urban centers call attention to the fact that the ecosystem of Neolithic tribalism was extended by civilization far beyond the immediate village environment and biotic assemblage of men, plants, and animals. The local web of life was determined by the existence of the state no less than by local adjustments (*see* Steward, 1955:32). But the exploitative powers of the state were limited by the cellular pattern of the units exploited. An early nineteenth-century observer of the Chinese landscape clearly saw that, "the executive government must adapt its wants to the ordinary supplies, instead of calling on the people for extraordinary contributions" (Barrow, 1805:270). Certainly the facts of human geography are less easily revised under the new state-idea than is the revolutionary determination to do so for the purpose of national territorial organization.

The political geography of the Ta Ch'ing empire reveals much about the physical constraints on communist plans for spatial reconstruction. The great Ch'ing empire at its height covered somewhat less than 4.3 million square miles. Its boundaries unsurveyed, the imperial pseudomorph simply extended from its metropolitan center of high culture to increasingly uncivilized distances. Beyond the fuzzy edges of the realm lay the suzerainties of Nepal, Burma, Laos, Siam, Annam, the Liu Ch'iu Islands (Okinawa), and Korea, with which trade was conducted in the name of tribute. The realm, greater China, encompassed two grand areas of differing administration: the territories of outer China and the provinces of China proper (see Map 2). Outer China included the territories of Manchuria, Mongolia, Sinkiang and Tibet—more than half the realm but inhabited by less than four percent of the total population, all non-Chinese. China proper, the agricultural heartland, extended over 1.5 million square miles and was occupied in eighteen provinces by Han Chinese, except for a few tribal peoples living on the mountain slopes of South China.

Of the space contained within the provincial boundaries of China proper, perhaps less than fifteen percent was politically relevant, and all of that limited to one land form: the alluvium of river valleys, plains, deltas, and mountain basins. What appears to be an exception is the Red basin of Szechwan, a granary enclosed by a mountain fortress in which the cultivated land is still ninety-eight percent terraced. Terraces, however, are extensions of alluvial bottomland. So we may generalize and say that the empire drew on one specialized source of organic energy—the plants of a one-sided Neolithic economy located on one specialized soil type.

Diversified specialization of the economic landscape increases demand for transportation, as in the modern industrial nation-state, which lives in many environments at once. It extracts raw materials from a variety of special landscapes devoted to agriculture, ranching, sea fishing, lumbering, and mining. The raw materials are moved with power transport to manufacturing centers, there to be processed by power machinery and redistributed as finished commodities. Each landscape is not exploited separately but is pooled by means of a complex interplay between the institutions of factory industrialism, marketing and commerce, banking and finance, and advanced transportation (Chapple and Coon, 1942:249).

Specialization of the economic landscape in one direction does not create a similar demand for transportation, because it is repetitive and cellular. To live everywhere in one environment means exploiting it cell by cell. Imperial China was able to sustain considerable urbanization with premodern methods of transportation on inland waterways only because the Chinese method of intensive farming allowed for a compact umland —that is, the radius of exchange between city and cultivated area in which produce is traded against fertilizer in the form of night soil. Following the usage of geographers, we distinguish urban umland from rural hinterland.

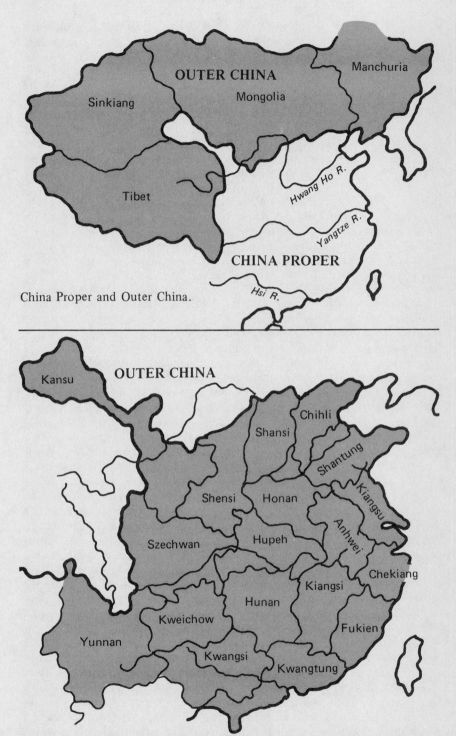

China Proper and Outer China.

Map 2. Greater China under the Manchus, showing the eighteen provinces of China proper and the dependencies of outer China.
From Stover, 1974a.

At the turn of the twentieth century, cities of over 100,000 in Kwang-tung province were supported by umlands no bigger than 33 square miles. Shanghai, a small town when it became a treaty port in 1842, had by 1954 grown to a city of 4 million, yet it could be supplied by junk and sampan from an umland within a radius of 100 miles. Adjusting for the fact that Shanghai is a port city, one side of it facing the sea, the radius may be calculated at no more than 62 miles (Whitney, 1970:60). In 1954, the ac-tual area of Shanghai's umland was 140,000 square miles, with a farm population of 1,700 persons per square mile.

The one city not living off its umland was the metropolitan center, which drew tribute grain along the Grand Canal from the Yangtze delta. But all major administrative cities were located along waterways, artificial or natural. In the areal division of powers, administrative cities and their supportive regions have been located along navigable rivers, not between them. As a result, provincial boundaries of China proper have been defined by watersheds rather than by the rivers themselves (Whitney, 1970:44). The exceptions, such as the Shensi/Shansi borders along the middle reaches of the Yellow River, and the Yunnan/Szechwan borders along the upper Yangtze, occur where rivers run in torrential gorges, not valley floors.

In China today, the urban map still follows the drainage map, which follows the population map. In other words, population density is still the best correlate of political relevance and therefore of administrative centers (see Whitney, 1970:117). Because the population is confined mainly to its nutritional base in the alluvial soils of the drainage system, the population also follows a dendritic pattern, branching out from the plains and basins of the great arterial systems—the Yellow, Yangtze, and West rivers—into their smaller tributaries (Trewartha, 1957). The watersheds of these sys-tems are compartmentalized into three zones by east-west folding trends in the mountain ranges. The Yellow system, draining into the Yellow Sea, is contained between the Yin Shan to the north and the central mountain belt to the south, which begins as the K'un-lun Shan rimming the south-ern curve of the Tarim basin and enters agricultural China as the Tsingling Shan with its offshoots the Ta-pa Shan and Ta-pieh Shan. This central mountain belt, which reaches almost to the Pacific, divides China proper into its two great geographic regions—Pei-yang, or North China, and Nan-yang, or South China. This mountain belt marks the southward limit of brown and dusty loess, cold winters, vast expanses of level land, and dry crops such as millet and kaoliang; it also marks the northward extent of hilly land green with abundant rainfall, water buffalo, tea, bamboo, and two or three annual crops of rice. The Yangtze system, draining into the South China Sea, is contained between the Tsingling mountains and the Nan Ling, the most southerly of the folding trends. To the south of these lies the Hsi, or West River system, which empties at Canton into the South China Sea.

In the native Chinese method of classifying regionalism, the provinces are arranged along the productive reaches of the rivers that bisect them (note also the designation of Key Economic Areas as shown in Map 1).

1. The upper Yellow River provinces: Kansu, Shensi, and Shansi
2. The lower Yellow River, or North China plain, provinces: Honan, Chihli, and Shantung (KEA "A")

3. The upper Yangtze River provinces: Szechwan (KEA "C"), Yunnan, and Kweichow
4. The middle Yangtze River provinces: Hupeh and Hunan (KEA "B," with region 5 below); Kiangsi
5. The lower Yangtze River provinces: Anhwei, Kiangsu, and Chekiang (KEA "B," with region 4 above)
6. The south coast provinces: Kwangtung and Kwangsi (KEA "D," drained by the West River); Fukien

To these must be added one important drainage area in outer China, the Manchurian plain, whose river system, the Liao, attracted great numbers of Chinese migrants toward the latter part of the nineteenth century, the Manchu government at last permitting it. This area is notable today as the most urbanized area of all China; its industries and railheads, built in the 1930s with Japanese incentive, attracted fully one-half of the country's investment capital.

The names of the provinces are combinations of names of prominent districts or indications of their relation to outstanding geographic features. In the first group, the upper Yellow River provinces, in whose valleys the Chinese Neolithic began, are Shensi ("pass-west") and Shansi ("mountain-west"). Kansu, a name formed by taking one syllable each from two older units in the area, may be translated to mean "sweet solitude," and it certainly is China's most sparsely populated province. Its loess plateau is contiguous with that of Shensi, but its border with Tibet is a forested, mountainous area paralleled along the panhandle by a high, arid strip producing grass for a short season.

The second group, or lower Yellow River, comprises the most populous, large region in China, excepting the so-called Peking grid in northern Chihli province, a Manchu incorporation of Mongolian steppe country whose streams gather and outfall at Tientsin. Coming down the Yellow River and turning toward the sea we cross Honan ("river-south"). North of Honan lies Chihli ("direct rule"), the metropolitan province in which Peking ("north capital") is located. The important seaport of the north, Tientsin, is also located in this province. Finally, on the seacoast is Shantung ("mountain-east"), whose mountainous parts, rising out of the Yellow delta, hold coal and iron ore.

The third, or upper Yangtze River, group begins with Szechwan ("four-streams"), whose irrigated plain about Chengtu, the capital, and its terraced lands to the northeast make it the second most densely populated area after the Yellow plain. To the south of Szechwan are Yunnan ("cloud-south") and Kweichow ("precious district"), both of which occupy a high tableland dissected by steep canyons and crossed by rugged mountains, making this region the least cultivated of all areas within China proper. Penetrated by a French railway during the period of foreign domination, it was for a time a commercial adjunct of French Indo-China. This railway followed the Red River, whose drainage of the plateau outfalls into the Tongking Gulf in North Vietnam.

The fourth, or middle Yangtze, group comprises the lake region of central China. Hupeh ("lake-north") and Hunan ("lake-south") are exceedingly rich rice-growing provinces. The lakes themselves serve as natural reservoirs that limit the flooding in the northern plain that has made the

Yellow River "China's Sorrow," despite the construction of artificial dikes. At a point 600 miles up the Yangtze, navigable by deep-sea vessels, is its juncture with the Han tributary from the northwest at Hankow ("Han-mouth"), where three great cities are located—Hankow, Wuchang, and Hanyang. These are grouped as the Wuhan cities, which under British influence have become a great steel-producing center. Farther down the river is Kiangsi, a province whose name ("river-west") obviously places it in relationship to the Yangtze delta, and which once was as important for tea and porcelain as for rice.

More important to the world of international trade are the lower Yangtze River provinces, the fifth group. These are Anhwei, Kiangsu, and Chekiang, where the business of raising, spinning, and weaving silk was located in its heyday. Anhwei ("peaceful and beautiful") is still a large rice-producer and densely populated but subject to frequent flooding by the Hwai River, whose bed was usurped by the Yellow River between 1194 and 1853, thereafter discharging its waters into the Grand Canal. Kiangsu has long been one great, canalized rice field. On the Yangtze delta, protruding into the Yellow Sea from this province, is Shanghai ("above-sea"), now the largest city in China and the center of every kind of industry known in the West since the twentieth century. Chekiang ("Che-river") is largely mountainous, but with more prosperous rice growers in its valleys than are found in the neighboring coastal province to the south, Fukien.

Fukien is drained by a short and narrow river system, the Min, flowing out of highlands scarce in arable land and isolated from the interior. The name is compounded from words for the capital city, Foochow, and another place name; the area formed a separate state named Min during the Five Dynasties period. From the start, the natural harbors of its coastline have given Fukien a character based not on agricultural wealth but on fishing and trade. The other two provinces of the southern coastal region, the sixth group, are the two Kwangs: Kwangtung ("plain-east") and Kwangsi ("plain-west"), both drained by the Hsi system with its outfall at Canton, China's first port of large-scale trade with the West, beginning in the seventeenth century. Hong Kong, originally an uninhabited island off the Canton estuary, has been developed by the British into an even greater world port. From the two Kwangs and Fukien have come Chinese immigrants to Formosa, Malaysia, the South Sea islands, the Philippines, and America, rather than to Manchuria and Central Asia, as did the emigrants from the northern provinces.

Provinces and groups of provinces (such as the two Kwangs) have long represented cultural differences, the minimal unit of such differences being the marketing area and the maximum unit being the contrasting divisions of Pei-yang and Nan-yang. In comparison, the PRC prescribes economic compliance in accord with communist theory and not provincial tradition. So far as the regime has replaced the laissez-faire policy of a self-regulating peasantry with commune management, it has scored a political success; but this rational form of administration has not yet met with the same economic success in all regions. Some local ecologies are more resistant to prescription than others.

Because no rice-growing communes are ever shown to foreign visitors, one must conclude that wet agriculture is less tolerant of communism than dry. Of thirteen model communes visited by a Pakistani delegation in

1965 (see Burki, 1969), two (the Evergreen and Red Star) produced vegetables and dairy products in Peking's umland; one (Leap Forward) raised sheep in Inner Mongolia; four (Kawkang, August First, Tsin Yah, and Hsin Lung San) produced dry crops, with some extensive tractor farming in the Manchurian lowlands; two (Peng Pu and Hsu Hang) produced vegetables for market in Shanghai's umland, one (Tung Chun) in Hangchow's, and one (Stonewall) in Canton's. Of the two remaining communes in the southern rice region (West Lake and People's Suburban), one raised tea and the other fished. Rice occurs only as a small fraction of the produce in six of the above. One of these, the Stonewall in Canton's umland, admittedly suffered a paradoxical combination of drought and flooding. There is no real paradox, however. Rice is very sensitive to skill and additional effort, which it may not get with collectivized labor. Any delay in getting a labor brigade to repair embankments damaged by a rainstorm will leave the paddy fields to drain, causing ruin of the rice by drought and of the surrounding dry crops by flooding (Chi, 1962).

It is difficult to mobilize a work brigade to undertake in huge collective fields the tedious labor that owner-operators or tenants used to apply out of self-interest in the work of diking, terracing, watering, planting, and transplanting even the smallest private field. Toward the end of the Ch'ing dynasty, one observer (Ross, 1911:77) counted exactly nineteen rice shoots planted at the standard distance of eight inches apart in a terraced plot no bigger than a tablecloth, duly embanked with mud walls and irrigated with its own trickle of water the width of a pencil. This was in Szechwan, where the same observer saw vertical terraces reach as high as one mile, with different crops for different altitudes: vegetables below, then corn, then wheat, and last rye at the apex. Today there are no model communes open for inspection in Szechwan, which also happens to be, with Kwangtung province, an important center for the cultivation of opium poppies.

MAN AND LAND

The economist who called China a "vegetable civilization" (Goodnow, 1927) has been scorned by sinologists for depreciating Chinese culture, especially its fine arts and spiritual values. Yet there is no contradicting the ecological fact that all human activity must be powered by an energy source, and that in premodern China this came from the soil of a one-sided Neolithic landscape, not from forests, pastures, coal mines, or hydroelectric plants. During the transitional period of the Chinese republic, a high degree of inanimate energy was used in modern arsenals, shipyards, railroads, mining, steel mills, and cotton-spinning and silk-reeling factories (Biggerstaff, 1966:611), but Chinese investment capital for all this was drawn largely from land rents—capital that never returned for reinvestment in agriculture. Like the monarchy, the republican government took no responsibility for the success or failure of agricultural production, and the growth of industrialization simply isolated cities from the countryside, creating a modern sector with no returns for the hinterland—not even the products of industry, which were manufactured for export with cheap native labor. A further drain on the countryside was the removal of its leadership to the treaty ports where the gentry found new opportunities to express their managerial talents. The resulting discontinuity, new to a civilization whose cities had always been commercial and governmental extensions of agriculture, led to the recapture of urban centers in the name of rural interests by the Communist revolution after twenty-two years of civil war—a civil war waged literally along rural/urban lines. The old continuities, evolved through orthogenesis from the very beginnings of Chinese civilization, were broken by modernization. This is what makes the republican era transitional between the two worlds of the imperial pseudomorph and the Communist nation-state. In the same interval, however, the technology and ecological fundamentals of Chinese farming remained unchanged.

According to one estimate made in 1928, the amount of land within the Republic of China suitable by climate and topography for crop production was put at 700 million acres, with only 180 million acres under cultivation. The difference between potential and actuality is a measure of the Chinese peasant's ancient specialization in a single land form. Realizing the full potential would require technology belonging to the Industrial Revolution with its power machinery, or to the much earlier second agricultural revolution with its traction plow. With a Neolithic technology, the average area of cultivated land per farm for agricultural China, including Manchuria (where the farms were still larger), was estimated at 3.1 acres. This was as large an area as the average farmer and his wife and son could spade up in time to put in the crop, and then cultivate using hand tools. The farmer who had a bullock or donkey could handle a somewhat larger area, but even this was considerably less than the small Negro tenant cotton farms that once were common in the southern United States. In the rice area of southern China, the average area per farm was only 1½ acres; in northern China, where wheat, millet, and the sorghums are dominant and only a part of the land will grow a second crop in the same season, somewhat less labor per acre was required, and the family farms were about twice as large, averaging 3⅓ acres of cultivated land per farm (Baker, 1928).

Restricting land utilization to about one-fourth of the potentially arable area was the small quantity of power available per man, particularly for plowing. Not being able to increase his acreage, the Chinese farmer instead had to increase his yield by intensive means of hand cultivation, that is, by gardening methods. For Chinese horticulture to yield one calorie of food, less than one calorie of human muscle power has to be invested. Contrast this with machine agriculture in the United States today, which expends about five calories in fossil fuels to obtain one calorie of food energy (Steinhart and Steinhart, 1974:312). China's low-energy heritage is still evident in today's communes, where 264 million acres are cultivated at the ratio of 0.4 acre per capita in contrast to 386 million acres cultivated in the United States at 2 acres per capita. That means four times the population in China concentrated on forty percent less cropland (Crook and Bernstein, 1974:v).

With statistics from 1926, the geographer George B. Cressey calculated the nutrition density in various regions of China. Nutrition density is a measure of the population per square mile of cultivated land, a more meaningful figure than population density per square mile in a country that specializes its agriculture in a landscape of premium fertility. A high degree of specialization is evident in the fact that nutrition density approximates population density the more fully the total area is cultivated. The following are a few regional comparisons, listed from high to low nutrition density (Cressey, 1930:3).

	Nutrition Density per Sq. Mi.	Percent of Total Area in Cultivated Land	Population Density per Sq. Mi.	Cultivated Land per Person (acres)
Southwestern Tableland	4189	4	157	0.15
Hills of the Two Kwangs	3495	8	285	0.18
Southeastern Coast	2684	15	417	0.23
Central Mountain Belt	1930	15	290	0.31
Red Basin of Szechwan	1468	39	581	0.43
Yangtze Plain	1277	71	897	0.37
Loess Highlands	1242	17	211	0.51
North China Plain	978	66	647	0.65
Manchurian Plain	802	15	89	1.07

The scarcer the preferred land form in any given region, the higher the nutrition density. As this often means compromising with soils of lesser fertility, it also means an increase in the size of cultivated land per person. The higher the percentage of the total area under cultivation, the more abundant the preferred land form, and the smaller the per-capita holdings. In other words, Chinese farmers have gravitated to areas where they can obtain the greatest reward on the least land. Hence the restriction on agricultural potential.

Regional differences apart, the ecological dynamics of Chinese horticulture may be described in the following general terms.

1. *Intensive application of labor to soils of high arability.* Hand gardening requires the sacrifice of labor's productivity for productivity of the land, the reverse of machine agriculture, which obtains high yields per man-hour at the expense of low yields per acre. Hand gardening is both a cause and an effect of high population density, a fact that has not changed with the advent of collective farms in China (Spencer, 1957). The work brigades (not families) in Chinese communes carry on intensive garden cultivation. Seeds are still planted in rows, not sown broadcast, to make each plant accessible to individual weeding, hoeing, and manuring (Wittfogel, 1956:158). Above all, no task is more labor intensive than transplanting rice sprouts. Each spear taken from the nursery is individually set out by hand, pinched between thumb and forefinger, and pushed into the mud several inches under water in a flooded paddy field—all the way down the line, row by row.

Proper care in spacing the rice is especially important to obtain the best grain-to-straw ratio. Straw has always been important for mat weaving and as a fuel. The guiding principle used to be conservation of seed. With the present method in communes, however, more grain per area is favored over more grain and less straw per plant. With the aim of increasing gross yields, the government prescribes close planting, something peasants never would have done on their own because the cost in seed grain is proportionally higher. The cost in effort is higher, too, so the effect of commune organization on farm labor has been to intensify labor even further. The yields of the two systems are compared below (Geddes, 1963:37). (A *mou* is 0.165 of an acre; a *catty* is 1⅓ pounds.)

Old System	Close Planting
9–10,000 shoots per *mou*	15–20,000 shoots per *mou*
500 catties of rice per *mou*	600–650 *catties* per *mou*
taller plants	shorter plants
more and larger panicles	less filled grain
less straw	more straw
maximum yield per plant	maximum yield per area

Close planting calls for twice the investment of seed for one-fifth the gain in yield. By contrast, the old system reflects the "make-do" practices of the unpoliced Neolithic peasant, who was geared to maximizing not a gross national product but to maximizing the farm population itself.

2. *Crowding of space and time.* F. H. King, an American agronomist, first analyzed those techniques of intensive farming that enabled the Chinese peasant to stretch his land resources by increasing his time assets (King, 1911: ch. 11). The first of these techniques is composting, a method that shortens the time required for the subsoil to restore its exhausted plant-food substances after each harvest. The farmer produces the necessary biochemical reactions for the next crop outside his fields while the previous one feeds. Composting is an advanced method of fertilization, raising the carrying capacity of the land to a very high level. The chief ingredient of the compost stack is night soil (human manure) and animal manure. A family of four and two pigs can produce about six tons of manure a year (Geddes, 1963:37–38). This is mixed with ash, loam, silt, uprooted weeds, and other decayed vegetable matter.

Another technique of intensive farming is combining intertillage with multiple cropping, as in sowing cotton seed among stalks of growing wheat ten to fifteen days before harvest. The work involved is beyond belief, for its calls for nothing less than spading and fertilizing the ground between furrows, inch by inch, in the midst of a stand of maturing grain. The results are thirty days saved in growing cotton. The effect of overlapping land usage of this sort is the same as if the growing season had been lengthened, or as if extra acreage had been added to the field. Space assets are also extended by the practice of setting out rice in nursery beds before the seedlings are transplanted and spaced out in fields. New technology to aid in this work has been limited to semimechanized, hand-operated rice planters and insecticide sprayers.

3. *Exclusion of livestock.* The most numerous barnyard animals in China proper today are chickens and pigs, both scavengers, whose numbers in 1945 were estimated at over 239 million and 59 million, respectively (Phillips, Johnson, and Moyer, 1945:15). In recent years, the pig population has grown markedly to about 260 million to increase manure for the rural economy and supply pork and hog bristles for export (Sprague, 1975:549; Spencer and Thomas, 1971:533). Cattle in the north and water buffalo in the south continue to be used for both draft power and meat, although a combined increase from about 34 million head to 76 million still supplies insufficient animals for either purpose. In Republican times, meat provided only two percent of the caloric intake of the Chinese (Trewartha, 1957:238), and this was largely reserved for the gentry. The water buffalo as a traction animal is not very strong, but the plow it pulls in the soft mud of waterfields has less drag than in dry soils. Not many farm holdings were ever large enough to justify using water buffalo, how-

ever, and even then they were supported not on pasture land at the expense of arable land but on garbage, fecal matter, and tropical grasses too coarse and tough for the tender mouths of cattle and horses (Huntington, 1927:94).

The scarcity of livestock accords with a "vegetable civilization" in which animal power competes with human labor and meat products compete with plant foods. An agricultural population that specializes in starchy cereals and vegetables for human consumption is so much denser than one practicing mixed farming that human labor is cheaper than animal power. This makes meat more expensive than vegetables; by the time cattle have turned grassland into beef, the caloric value of the plants has been reduced for the human consumer by nine-tenths. The Chinese have not been able to permit animals to eat plants that they themselves might eat directly; to permit land to be used to raise plants for animal fodder would limit the number of men who could be fed from the same land (Cottrell, 1950:15–20).

4. *Concentration on carbohydrate foods.* The influence of population density on food production in China has worked to select "energy-producing" carbohydrate foods over "protective foods." The native carbohydrate foods, originating during the Chinese Neolithic, are millet and rice, to which wheat from West Asia was added anciently and maize from America in the sixteenth century. These cereals yield more calories per acre than do the protective foods, such as leafy vegetables and fruits, richer in protein, minerals, and vitamins, in addition to meat, eggs, and dairy products. The protective foods of all sorts require more land than do the energy foods to yield the same number of calories (Chang, 1945:35). A special case must be reserved for the leafy vegetables of the umlands, which may be raised as cash crops only because the fertilizer required for everyday application is available in the form of garbage and night soil collected from the urban market (Yang, 1959a:31–35).

5. *Priority of the human crop over the farm crop.* Because horticulture is both a cause and an effect of high population density, the map of the rural population is necessarily a map of arable land of premium fertility. It takes just as much hand labor to cultivate mediocre soil as highly fertile soil. The Chinese peasantry has thus tended to maximize its population on the one land form, alluvial soil, that would best repay intensive labor. Were a farm family of four taken from a Republican farmstead of two acres on the Yellow plain and resettled on fifty acres of mediocre soil north of the Great Wall, it would starve to death if required to work with intensive methods. The growing season w~uld be over before even a fraction of the field could be fitted (Trewartha, 1957:238).

In the language of economics, labor in Chinese horticulture is "underemployed." But this says merely that the Chinese method is not the Western method of extensive farming with its high output per man-hour, accomplished with the expenditure of costly fuels burned in power machinery. In the West, a high standard of material living is the economic objective. The Chinese objective is a high output per unit of land, accomplished with spade and hoe. John Lossing Buck in his massive three-volume work, *Land Utilization in China* (1937), found that it took twenty-six man-days to produce sixteen bushels of wheat on one acre of land; by contrast, it took forty-five horsepower-hours to produce fifteen bushels of nonirrigated wheat in Idaho in 1949 (Cottrell, 1955:141). This amounts to about forty times more horsepower to produce just about the same amount of grain per acre. The Chinese objective is to support the most dense population with the least expenditure of energy. Again, this is incompatible with the Western objective—a high standard of material living. Therefore it is not that Chinese farm larbor is underemployed but rather that the farm population itself is the principal crop. When the human crop has priority over the food crop, the Western description of horticulture as a "make-work" method for redundant hands is ethnocentric. Chinese horticultural technology is better described in its own terms as capital-saving and labor-absorptive. By the year 1980, the Chinese population will reach over one billion, and only intensive agriculture will support it.

Superficial consideration of the communist impact on the Chinese countryside suggests that collectivization has changed the ecodynamics of traditional Chinese farming methods. For example, when Buck made his agricultural surveys in republican China (Buck, 1937), he found fifteen percent of the land in the northern wheat region irrigated, as against sixty-nine percent in the southern rice region. Irrigation projects carried out in North China under the present regime have now tended to blur this technological distinction (Buchanan, 1970:175). But this does not change the fact that the north gets less rain yet is more fertile by virtue of its loessial soils and calcareous alluvium; the south receives monsoon rainfall, but its higher temperature more readily leeches out the fertility of the soil unless amply fertilized. The fertilizer industry has high priority in China today.

The hardship put on southern soils by a warmer and rainier climate is nonetheless naturally compensated for by an extended growing season that allows double or triple cropping. One great difference between north and south is no longer visible now that all the fragmented, individual landholdings have been consolidated into collective farms. Northern holdings used to be larger on the average in order to accommodate limitations imposed by a shorter growing season; the smaller holdings in the south reflected the advantages of multiple cropping bestowed by a better climate. Yet the old differences of labor allocation persist. Northern communes have industrial tasks assigned to them by the state to occupy the slack season once filled with handicrafts. But southern communes are less diversified by industry because no slack season ever existed to be filled with nonagricultural labor. It is true that communes have changed farm owners and farm tenants into a landless proletariat and have modified the postharvest disposition of agricultural commodities, but the agricultural regimen remains what it has always been—a low-energy system of horticulture using simple tools and a large expenditure of human labor (Spencer and Thomas, 1971:533).

External Frontiers

The ecodynamics of Chinese horticulture have determined the direction in which Chinese civilization has spread outward from its heartland on the Yellow plain. The direction was south, not north. The northern frontiers of the Chinese sown land including the barbarian steppeland have remained relatively fixed, whereas those to the south have continually expanded.

The historic expansion of the Chinese landscape deep into the south and only part way toward the north has had different consequences for the non-Han peoples on the periphery. Owen Lattimore writes: "The geographical environment of the South favored a long survival of barbarians who remained, generally speaking simply 'pre-Chinese.' In the North the spread of the Chinese pushed the surviving barbarians toward a new environment in which they ceased to be 'pre-Chinese' and became 'non-Chinese'" (Lattimore, 1940:354–55). By "pre-Chinese," Lattimore means swidden farmers of the Yang-shao type. Because the hill tribes of southern China continued to practice swidden methods, he classifies them as pre-Chinese, a people whose generalized state of Neolithic culture had not yet specialized in one direction as had the Neolithic tribal peoples absorbed by early civilization. Because the last remaining strongholds of the pre-Chinese, such as the Miao tribe, were situated in mountainous areas of China proper, we may designate these locales as internal frontiers and the people occupying them as internal marginals (see Stover, 1974a: ch. 3 for the significance of internal marginals). Today, the Miao work coal mines under the hills they once moved about as itinerant farmers. Lattimore's "non-Chinese," on the other hand, are the steppe nomads located north of the Great Wall—external marginals located on an external frontier. These have been brought into the Chinese national economy in other ways.

The external frontiers of the north—Mongolia, Manchuria, Chinese Turkestan, and Tibet—presented, and still present, natural barriers to the expansion of Chinese horticulture but not to their political integration as economic landscapes complementary to the agricultural one within the new nation-state.

Mongolia. An arid steppeland with no possibilities for irrigation farming, Mongolia was never colonized by Chinese. The non-Chinese inhabitants have always depended on livestock herding. Outer Mongolia has been a Soviet satellite since 1921. The provinces of Chahar, Jehol, Suiyuan, and Ninghsia were incorporated into the Inner Mongolia Autonomous Region and Ninghsia Hui Autonomous Region by the Chinese People's Republic. Inner Mongolia's distinct ethnic, cultural, and geographical identity now serves as a specialized herding landscape linked with the Chinese national economy. The Leap Forward Commune is located here, in which 252 families of nomadic tribesmen work to sell live animals, wool, milk, sheepskins, kumiss, cottage cheese, and butter to the state trading corporations. Some of its income is earned by selling camel seats, leather belts, and embroidered cushions to the state (Burki, 1969:57).

Manchuria. Home of the Manchu rulers of China's terminal dynasty, Manchuria (known as the Eastern provinces) embraces steppeland to the west, forests to the east, and a riverine plateau along the lower Liao River. The Manchurian lowland is the only part of the Eastern provinces suitable for occupation by Chinese farmers, but the opportunity was not given by the Manchus until the turn of the twentieth century, when they were compelled to do so by Chinese population pressure. Here the growing season is shorter than in the wheat region of China proper, the population less dense, and the form of agriculture more extensive. The Manchus themselves were mixed farmers, unlike the Mongol conquerors of China, who were strictly herdsmen. The Eastern provinces—Liaoning, Kirin, and

Heilungkiang—are now incorporated directly within the provincial administrative system of the People's Republic. The Kawkang and August First Communes are located in the umland of Shenyang (Mukden) in Liaoning province. Kawkang specializes in the hand gardening of vegetables, the August First in the tractor farming of grain and also in small industrial enterprises for manufacturing bricks, soybean curd, noodles, and straw mats (Burki, 1959:60, 64).

Chinese Turkestan (now Sinkiang Uighur Autonomous Region). This territory contains the driest desert in the world, the Tarim basin. The oases around it are the homes of Islamic Uighurs whose discontinuous occupation, even with irrigation agriculture, proved unsuitable for traditional Chinese provincial administration. Traditionally the area was held under military subjugation and was never colonized by Chinese until recently, when the People's Republic chose this as one of the main regions for agricultural expansion and the absorption of millions of its growing population. The aim is to reclaim some twenty million acres between the oases by rechanneling some of the internal drainage now running into Lop Nor, a great salt lake, from the melt waters of snow and glacial ice in the Tien Shan mountains. The danger of shifting sands is evident in the ruins of dead villages and towns buried by sand after 1200 A.D. (Tregear, 1965:285–90). Sinkiang must be developed at all costs, however, because of its strategic importance in relation to the Soviet Union, which is in a position to agitate its anti-Chinese minor nationalities. The interior Tarim basin is China's testing ground for atomic bombs.

Tibet. The Tibetan plateau is today divided into two administrative provinces—the bleak heights of Tibet itself and at a much lower level Tsinghai, which contains the Tsaidam basin, another desert like the Tarim basin with another salt lake, the Koko Nor, but surrounded with rolling steppeland noted for its horsebreeding. Some degree of pastoral nomadism including yaks and mountain sheep is possible in the high plateau, but agriculture is impossible except for highland barley scratched out of the stony perimeter and in the valleys of the southeastern slopes where Lhasa, the capital, is located. For the control of Lhasa, Manchu forces entered Tibet in 1740 and installed their own candidate at the head of the Lama Buddhist church, the fountainhead of belief among Mongols as well as Tibetans. Acting as protector of the Lama Buddhist church, the Manchu army in Lhasa at the same time displaced Mongol control over trade routes across Central Asia.

China's interest in Tibet today lies in Tsinghai, which abounds with coal and oil fields, plus a crystallized salt lake thick with deposits of almost pure sodium chlorate, the center of an emerging chemical industry. The surrounding steppeland, with careful water conservation coupled with long summers, is open to some cultivation and promises to receive more of China's millions who are expected to develop pastoral farming on a large scale (Harrison, 1972:346; Tregear, 1965:298–301). Concern with Tibet proper is for military security.

SPATIAL RECONSTRUCTION

One of the key administrative problems in redesigning China's spatial economy is to strike the right balance between intraregional self-sufficiency and interregional specialization (Wu, 1967:200). Intraregional self-sufficiency prevailed at various levels—provincial, district, and marketing area—during imperial times and was not much altered during republican times. The first interregional railroad system in China had the effect of contracting space in a north-south axis against the east-west compartmentalization of geography dictated by folding trends and river flow. The railroad linked the great industrial heartland of the Manchurian lowlands with the Peking grid, the Yellow plain, the Yangtze delta, and the central lake region. But it was in operation no more than a decade before the Japanese occupation dismembered it and disarticulated the industrial heart from the Chinese body; the Eastern provinces, renamed *Manchukwo*, had become an overseas province of the Japanese empire. Disarticulation was the norm under the culturalism of dynastic government, an unsolved problem under the transitional modernism of the republic, and an opportunity for the economic integration of regional specialities under the accomplished nationalism of the People's Republic. At least one main rail line now connects every province except Tibet with a national grid of 25,000 miles. In addition, the system has eleven international rail connections: five with North Korea, two each with the U.S.S.R. and North Vietnam, and one each with Mongolia and Hong Kong. The mileage of inland waterways navigable by power boats has been doubled from that inherited from the republic, and its highway system extended six times to a total of 300,000 miles. A relatively dense network of domestic air routes had been developed by 1960 under the Chinese Civil Airways Administration.

The new areal division of powers divides the nation into a Western China of two regions (Tibet and Sinkiang-Mongolia) and an Eastern China of four regions (Northeast, North, South, and Southwest), as shown in Map 3. Western China includes all the territories of outer China under the empire, except for Manchuria; it represents over half the national real estate and five percent of the population. Eastern China contains forty-six percent of the land area and most of the population, which is still confined to the dendritic pattern of the drainage system.

1. *Northeast.* Here a dense network of railroads links coal and iron ore mines, hydroelectric power plants, and factories in support of China's oldest and foremost center of heavy industry. At the same time, extensive level land of medium fertility makes the Manchurian plain the most adaptable of all regions to mechanized agriculture; its surrounding mountains provide two-thirds of the nation's forest reserves.

2. *North.* The advantages of KEA "A" (see Map 1, p. 69) in the north have recently been reasserted, its primacy reinforced by terrain suitable for road and rail construction as pathways to mines of coal and iron ore on the perimeter of the Yellow plain. These are exploited for industrial districts located in a triangle formed by the cities of Peking, T'ang-shan, and Tientsin. Almost totally new to factory industrialism since 1949, the region is a major producer of steam locomotives, tractors, iron, steel, chemicals, textiles, electronics, and paper. Since 1955, the region's rich but flood-prone agriculture has been subject to the control measures of a comprehensive Yellow River plan, including reforestation of the eroded upper reaches and the building of dams, reservoirs, dikes, and irrigation canals. The north contains the most densely populated, culturally homogeneous, population of any region, uniformly Mandarin in language.

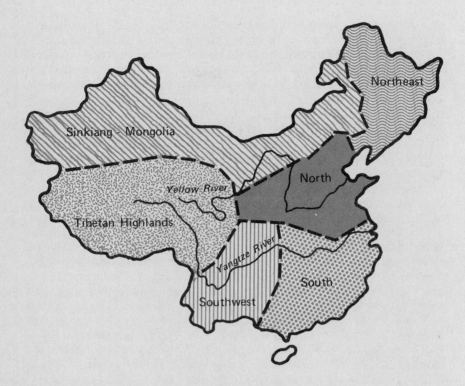

Map 3. Regional Divisions of the People's Republic of China.
From Crook and Bernstein, 1974

3. *South.* The ethnic and linguistic pattern of the south is a mosaic, the product of repeated migrations of Chinese and the progressive isolation of the pre-Chinese natives within the internal frontiers of hill and mountain, which occupy eighty percent of the land surface. This is now dotted with open-pit coal mines worked by the former hill tribes. The largest Chinese ethnolinguistic group is comprised of the Cantonese, a non-Mandarin-speaking people prevailing in Kwangtung and Kwangsi. Speakers of Min and Hakka occupy the small, seaward-facing basins of the southeastern uplands, traditionally given to deep-sea fishing and coastal trading. This is the most famous tea-growing area of China, which supplied the American clipper ships whose cargo was dumped during the Boston Tea Party. Failure of the tea trade through Indian competition prompted Chinese emigration to Malaya, Borneo, and Indonesia, from which remittances are allowed to return free from confiscation by the state, in order to permit capital investment in a region still so depressed it cannot meet the economic needs of its pressing population with its timber and fishing resources and certainly not with its restricted agriculture. The Yangtze plain, with its immense output of rice, is the area of supreme political relevance in the south, snaking 600 miles inward from the delta. Wuhan, consisting of the tri-city conurbation of Hankow, Wuchang, and Hanyang, is an important center of heavy industry, occupying a strategic location

controlling inland waterways, road, and railroad transport over the central lake basin. On the delta lies Shanghai, China's largest industrial and commercial metropolis, especially noted for textiles, iron and steel, and shipbuilding.

4. *Southwest.* This region combines the Red basin and the southwestern plateau, differing in their physical and demographic characteristics but alike in a common disadvantage—separation from eastern China by vast distances and difficult terrain. The southwest is fairly industrialized, however, thanks to the local coal and iron deposits which attracted relocation of the machine industry during the Japanese occupation. The key to the further development of the southwest has been the construction of rail links to the coast, which began in 1952.

The four economic regions just described were defined as administrative units up until 1954, by way of bringing their constituent provinces up to the national level of organization. They still function as military regions. But the first-order units of administration at present consist of twenty-one provinces, five autonomous regions, and three municipalities. The twenty-one provincial units closely correspond to the eighteen provinces of China proper inherited from the republic, minus Kwangsi (now an autonomous region) and including Tsinghai and the three provinces of Manchuria. The autonomous administrative regions are Inner Mongolia, Kwangsi, Sinkiang, Ninghsia, and Tibet, where non-Han ethnolinguistic groups predominate—Mongols, Chuang, Hui, and Tibetans, respectively. "Regional autonomy," however, is the opposite of what its name implies; it is more accurately described as the "regional detention" of nonassimilable and potentially rebellious peoples whose local economy or religion will not yield to forms of control exercised over Han Chinese (Moseley, 1966). The municipalities are Peking, Shanghai, and Tientsin.

At the lower levels, changes have been numerous and frequent, particularly in the wake of the administrative confusion caused by the creation of the People's Communes after 1958. Further modifications probably followed the Cultural Revolution in 1966–69 (on all of the above, *see* Central Intelligence Agency, 1971).

Since 1958, the basic administrative unit of the countryside has been the commune. G. William Skinner has traced the evolution of this unit and its changing role in the organization of space with great anthropological insight in a masterly series of articles appearing in the *Journal of Asian Studies* (Skinner, 1964–65; *see also* Johnson, 1970 for an economist's evaluation). In traditional China, formal government did not extend below the *hsien*, or district level. The village and the market town (when not coinciding with a political center) existed as natural communities at the subadministrative level. On the average, a market town served 19 to 20 villages within a marketing area that varied from fewer than 10 square miles in the fertile umlands to more than 50 square miles in mountainous or dry regions. At first, communist planners designed communes to be three times as large as the marketing area. Given about 74,000 marketing areas in China, this meant about 24,000 communes. These ranged in size from 77 square miles in agricultural China to much larger ones north of the Great Wall. In number of households per commune, the figure varied from 8,000 in areas of high nutrition density to fewer than 1,700 in areas of low density.

The commune represents a merging of several agricultural production cooperatives, which were formed in 1955 as an organizational stage on the way to the full collectivization of property rights. The peasant is paid a living wage for performing labor on a planned basis. This makes the commune not only an administrative organ but also a production unit, all products to be taken and marketed by the commune. Furthermore, the commune has been given the responsibility for maintaining a rural education system and a militia. It is also the agent of the state's trading and banking organizations. With complete control of economic resources, commune government is directed to undertake the building of small-scale industrial establishments and water conservation projects.

This highly centralized plan for mobilizing the rural population at first dispensed with the traditional periodic market system and replaced it with a single supply and marketing department within each commune. The planners had hoped to break down the parochialism of folk culture, which for peasants, petty merchants, and artisans had been confined mainly to the boundaries of their home marketing area. The new mechanism failed to replace the functions of the old marketing system, however, and the subdivision of communes into smaller units began in 1961. By 1964, the old pattern was reestablished and the market town once again fulfilled its old function. Here agents of production teams, brigades, and communes could make purchases and sales on behalf of their collectives, and other members could market the products of the small private plots allowed them. As Skinner notes, it was "infeasible to contain or constrain the interlocked network of natural marketing systems within the boundaries of discrete administrative units" (Skinner, 1964–65:374).

The reconstruction of the system was based on field studies of the actual flow patterns of rural trade, with the aim of rationalizing their natural tendencies. By 1963, the number of communes had increased through subdivision to 74,000, almost exactly the number of local marketing areas in Republican China. In the end, Communist ideology had to yield to the laws of distance and the market.

SEVEN

ECONOMICS

CONFISCATION

In his *Principles of Political Economy*, John Stuart Mill aimed to explain the principles of an expansive market economy. He did so by contrasting his subject matter with its exotic opposite, confiscatory appropriation —profiteering—in a stationary preindustrial economy. Mill described this mode of appropriation as:

> *Characteristic of the extensive monarchies which from a time beyond historical record have occupied the plains of Asia. . . .* [Wealth is] *torn from the producers, either by the government to which they are subject, or by individuals, who by superior force, or availing themselves of religious or traditional feelings of subordination, have established themselves as lords of the soil.* (Mill, 1901:I, 30)

No government, however, is ever a mere monarchy; the supreme ruler inevitably rests his power on the support of a ruling class. The Chinese emperor thus rules in the interest of the elite no less than with their cooperation. The "lords of the soil" belonging to a confiscatory regime include not only the monarch in whose name government taxes are collected, but also the families of landowners who collect rents under the emperor's cultural umbrella.

The psychology of profiteering is explained by the seminal American sociologist Robert MacIver. In his classic work, *The Modern State*, MacIver contrasts his subject matter with its premodern ancestor, the dynastic state:

> *In the dynastic state the aspect of power or coercion is necessarily dominant, though it may be obscured by the influence of tradition and a religion consonant with the subjection of the many to the few. Under dynastic conditions the state has a peculiar character, since it does not even ostensibly make the welfare of the whole its object. It requires therefore the support of all psychological influences which impress the mass of men with the sense of its own majesty and of their inferiority.* (MacIver, 1926:344)

Profiteering, then, means that taxes and rents are lifted for the enjoyment of the "lords of the soil," not for the payment of public services given in return. Ironically, the eighteenth-century Enlightenment, which brought a service-oriented government to Europe, was abetted by a mistaken perception of the Chinese civil service as an ideal machine for distributing administrative welfare. Little did the men of the European Enlightenment realize that in China, office itself was an emolument of privilege. However, profiteering is archaic, and it displaces investment in productive enterprise. Modernization and development are therefore opposed to it.

But the heritage of exploit and drudgery is immensely difficult to overcome. Politically it means reversing the centrifugal tendencies of the provinces, traditionally bound to central government by no adequate unifying principle. The areal division of powers under the Chinese monarchy, as we have seen, was defined by geographic and ethnographic regions to which the court was quite external—except for the emperor's cultural leadership in illuminating a doctrine of exploitation carried out by local officials for the glory of his name only, and not for making other than symbolic contributions to the metropolitan treasury. (The emperor supplied his treasury directly from his own resources.) Economically, the heritage of exploit means a small national income, however it is allocated. The contrast between an abundance of manpower located on a one-sided Neolithic landscape and the scarcity of capital is extreme. The costs of modernization, at least at the outset, must be paid for by the same method that once sustained the old ruling class: confiscatory taxation of peasant drudgery. If the distribution of capital was restricted in the bad old days to consumption by the "lords of the soil," now it must be concentrated for industrial investment. The peasant masses must still be kept at a low level of income, if not to fulfill the Taoist (and Confucianist!) utopia of ignorance and apathy, then to achieve forced savings for modernization.

The starting point of modernization is necessarily incompatible with rising expectations. Yet ignorance and apathy are to be deplored; indeed, knowledge and activism are desirable if agriculture is to be carried out to meet national production goals. Compliance, by definition, cannot take place among self-regulating Neolithic villages, but it can among landless communards if their drudgery is lightened by a sense of informed participation in the nation's economic growth. Still, as we shall see, this sense of participation requires rural ignorance of the higher salaries earned by the more favored industrial workers in the cities.

Of course, controlling envy among commoners was one problem the emperors never had to contend with. The problem took care of itself because no information about the wider civilization had to be communicated by a government from whose subjects no populist legitimacy was required. For almost all commoners, the imperial establishment that exploited them called forth no picture of government other than an imposing image of some far-away, vast mansion, the *kuan-fu* or house of officials. At most, ordinary peasants would see the local magistrate carried through the streets of the county seat in a closed sedan chair, only to disappear with his regulation pomp and parade behind the impenetrable walls of the district headquarters. By keeping his distance, the magistrate communicated all that needed to be said about government: that its foundations rested on the conquest, not the consent, of the governed. Directed against unlettered peasants, this message conveyed by bailiffs and tax collectors was sufficient to create those "religious or traditional feelings of subordination." So one-sided was the annual contest between payer and receiver that the magistrate's bailiffs were able to extract a surcharge of at least ten percent on the officially demanded tax to provide a personal income otherwise unpaid by the state (Morse, 1910–18: vol. 1, pp. 20–31).

In closer touch were those agents of informal government, the scholar-landlords, whose imperial credentials and social visits with the magistrate gave them a share in the mystique of the *kuan-fu*. But they also carried their own dignity. These gentlemen could always be seen in their long white gowns, some in their town offices where they collected rent or in villages where they owned property, others in teahouses where they adjudicated quarrels, but everywhere in the streets of the market town and in country lanes, never toiling, strolling about and nodding to all their tenants or prospective tenants and walking their characteristic feet-splayed walk.

The "lords of the soil," then, comprised officials raising taxes in the name of the emperor and gentlemen landlords lifting rents in the name of their families, both under the cultural auspices of the emperor. They viewed it as their right as members of a morally superior class to take their "meat and fish" from the toil of the common man; both belonged to the same political leadership class, men sharing in the culture of the great tradition. We must remember that from their point of view, they stood as men of culture over little people of no culture; their literacy and knowledge of the classics brought them closer to the cosmic Center of moral perfectability than anyone belonging to the little tradition could hope to approach.

What kept the little people in subordination, however, was less the coercive power of the state, as displayed by soldiers garrisoned in the administrative towns and cities, but quite simply the lack of alternatives (banditry apart). A single-landscape economy given to horticulture can support only so many parasitic "lords of the soil," and no more. For the 1880s, officials, gentlemen, and their dependents have been calculated at two percent of the population living off twenty-four percent of the land's substance (Chang, 1962). The carrying capacity of the ecosystem to feed the farming population was large, since it was labor-absorptive at the expense of the population's material standard of living; for the same reason, the capacity to support an elite emancipated from toil was very small.

Moreover, the natural means of birth control—infanticide, war, famine, and disease—failed to curb the population beyond the capacity of the land to absorb agricultural labor; calculated for Yunnan, the maximum is about 600 persons for every 150 acres of rice land (Fei and Chang, 1945:11). Population pressure beyond the carrying capacity of local conditions pushed the excess into beggardom, thievery, and landless labor—a class of persons who, in relation to essential resources, were expendable. In normal times, the expendable class reached five to ten percent of the total population, or as much as fifteen percent in other times (Lenski, 1966:281–83).

This constant imbalance in the ratio of population to resources necessarily invited a certain amount of tenancy. Herein lies the secret of

Chinese landlordism. Competition for a place on the land, even as a tenant or day laborer, gave the landlord who had land or jobs to hire out a commanding position without resorting to threats of coercion from the imperial garrisons. The limited effects of birth control resulted in more people than the dominant class was able to employ. In fact, landlords did not even have to supervise the work of their tenants, much less dirty their hands by doing the tillage themselves. Any tenant who did not regard his situation as a favor extended by the gentry would find himself replaced by another, chosen from a number of supplicants who did find it so, and who would be more than willing to pay for the privilege with forty to fifty percent of his harvest (the usual rate before the payment of rent was increasingly converted to money during republican times).

Contained in landlordism is the full round of the Taoist utopia: political apathy at the bottom, *wu-wei* at the top. The tenant toiled from a position of supplication, and the gentleman took in his rent without even putting forth the effort of supervision. The leisurely life of the landlord who profited from land hunger was, in fact, a sign that all was well in the land; things would be worse if it were wasted by famine, war, brigandage, or disease. The economy in normal times displayed its bounty in the opportunities for tenancy, opportunities regarded by farmers close to the margin of expendability as largesse handed down from above. The presence of gentleman landlords in the countryside was indeed a barometer of economic health. To them, in turn, redounded the gains of formal government when it displayed its own economic health in the expensive splendors of the court and in the pageantry of administration. That royalty and officialdom could be trusted to consume all its confiscated wealth in such extravagance was a reassurance to gentlemen and commoners alike (*see* Jacobs, 1971:134).

It was the force of this mystique that raised landlordism above the level of mere gangsterism, for it gave to the gentry a noblesse oblige by which the collection of rent could be considered a boon to the tenant. The parasitic metaphor, then, is not wholly apt. There is, after all, an exchange involved with profiteering. When the fruits of confiscation can be seen to be spent on the conspicuous pleasures of the court, on the pageantry of office, and on the leisure of gentlemen landlords, then all is well in the land. Thus the cultural splendors of the great tradition worked to engender those "religious or traditional feelings of subordination" of which the "lords of the soil" availed themselves.

The normal condition of economic health still called for a rate of expendability of about ten percent of the population. Land hunger, stemming from competition for limited amounts of the one land form that will yield results with a Neolithic technology, is the material force behind culturalism. However, the same population pressure that made sharecropping possible without supervision also worked against a certain number of gentry families. The elite gave birth to more children than they could maintain in elite status. The surplus sank downward to the peasant class, where the same pressures reduced another fraction to the class of expendables marked for malnutrition, deprivation, childlessness, and high mortality (Eberhard, 1966:180–81).

The economics of profiteering thus work only in the context of net downward mobility. All the same, this economic system belongs to a political system in which people exist for the good of the rulers, not the rulers for the good of the people. Those in a position to profiteer as "lords of the soil" are, by definition, members of a physiocratic ruling class, be they the scholar-officials of formal government or the scholar-landlords of informal government.

Formal government was by far the most profitable, although the salaries of the imperial civil service were negligible. The incumbents were expected to supply the deficiency through customary exactions known as "squeeze." The Chinese word for squeeze, *k'o-lo*, appears in a Ch'ing dynasty dictionary of administrative terms compiled by clerks for the use of clerks, with the following gloss: "To squeeze public funds and put them into one's own purse" (Sun, 1961:110). Another term in use was *lou-kwei*, "unrecorded leak," that is, a drip unrecorded by the water clock. A district magistrate, for example, a 7th rank official, averaged 30,000 Taels of squeeze per annum. The Tael was a measure of silver bullion differing by region anywhere from 540 to 583 grains of silver, but averaging 1⅓ ounces of pure silver. The magistrate's salary was only Tls. 45 per year, with an additional stipend for expenses amounting to about Tls. 1000 per year. His combined salary and stipend for a three-year term, however, would not even cover the cost of one set of his official robes, which amounted to at least Tls. 3400. A laboring man, by contrast, earned no more than 5 to 10 Taels or less than $0.50 per year, plus food (Chang, 1962:13, 16).

But squeeze itself was subject to squeeze by higher officials in a chain of confiscation reaching all the way up to the emperor himself. It was said that the Hoppo, or administrator of the Canton customs, had to pay in bribes the amount equalling the net profits of his first year in office in order to obtain it, the profits of his second year to keep it, and those of his third year to drop it and provide for himself (Morse, 1910–18: vol. 1, p. 34). This was the fattest post in the empire, taxing the shipping in the ports of the coast of Kwangtung and in the delta of the Canton River.

In addition to the maritime customs, there existed a series of customs stations for the taxation of goods in transit along rivers and on land after they had left their port of entry. Among the land stations was the Peking Gate, whose wardens levelled tolls even on the passage of mandarins on affairs of state. So did guardians of the palace and chamberlains who opened the way to the audience hall. All of these tolls, which were graded according to the rank of the official passing through, added significantly to the sovereign's treasury (Morse, 1910–18: vol. 1, p. 35).

What was a matter of venality and corruption from the Western viewpoint was merely the second track of a two-track system of financial transactions in China. One was the formal budget of ritual statistics in which officials made symbolic contributions to the imperial treasury, and the other was the series of customary exactions, or *lou-kwei*, that distributed real wealth throughout the system, not concentrating it at the center. *Lou-kwei* was permitted because there was not enough absolute wealth for the executive to concentrate and redistribute in salaries as a means of enforcing the dependency of officials on their superiors in the formal system. On the other hand, much of the state revenues diverted into private pockets actually reached Peking in the shape of customary gratuities and assessments (Morse, 1910–18: vol. 1, p. 550). Moreover, the competition to get in, get rich, and get out made for a high rate of turnover that precluded specialized experience (Metzger, 1973:155). Experts in all fields—whether in administration or in Western technology—were thus relegated to a class of nonranking advisors (Folsom, 1968).

Li Hung-chang, one of the greatest statesmen China ever produced, once said that "the value of any appointment was in direct proportion to the money that could be made from it," and from that frank statement we arrive at the underlying principles of Chinese dynastic government (Etherton, 1927:30). This is not a reflection of the venality of men but a reflection of the poverty of material resources in an underdeveloped vegetable civilization, unable to extract and direct revenue sufficient for the service of the state in the form of salaries to make officials attend to their professional duties as administrators. Aggrandizement was theirs by default under a central government whose military, civil, and court expenses were dispersed in the ratio of 25:1:7 (Barrow, 1805:63). The emperor's biggest expenses were military, for the security of his realm's inner Asian frontier and the security of his private pipeline to agricultural wealth, the Grand Canal, from which he financed the cultural glories of his court—the next biggest expense. This left very little for official salaries, but without the military and court expenditures there would have existed no imperial establishment to which the service of officials would have been attracted. Officials were therefore positively encouraged to practice squeeze by way of ensuring the political control of wealth outside the orbit of direct control.

Informal government under the local gentry included arbitration of peasant disputes, management of local irrigation works for peasant clients, and organization of local defense. Next in importance was landholding, then service fees for teaching and secretarial work, money lending, and investment in mercantile enterprise. These three sources of gentry income—informal government, land, and business—returned income during the late Ch'ing dynasty (1887) in the ratio of 3:2:1 (Chang, 1962. *See* Feuerwerker, 1969:2, for a revised estimate).

Wealthy merchants, but not petty ones, actually belonged to the ruling class, although the scholastic sector depreciated the merchants' membership in the elite because commercial profits were not considered as elegant, physiocratically, as those taken in rents and taxes. After all, it was the scholar-gentry, represented by officials and educated landlords, who arbitrated social status. The merchant-gentry occupied only 1 percent of the ruling gentry as a whole, which class and its dependents occupied no more than 1.9 percent of the total population. Commercial profits were so high, however, that the few who made them—there were not many lines of profit to follow across a single-landscape economy—earned the equal of all the income squeezed out of government service by all officials, or half the income earned on rentals by all landlords. This immense wealth invited officials to squeeze business by requiring large payments to purchase legal title to membership in the ruling class.

The classical community of interest between commerce and business revolved around salt, a state monopoly for which the great salt merchants produced, distributed, and collected royalties. Foreign trade was another state monopoly from which commercial agents could take their huge profits, so long as they handled a key diplomatic question for central government by controlling the behavior of the resident foreigners. By the time this problem got out of hand with the Opium War, the imperial form of government itself was in trouble.

Scholar-officials were almost equally small in number: only 23,000 men, or 1.6 percent of the ruling class, ever held office at one time. The bulk of income from government (about two-thirds of it) actually came from informal government. But as the total income from the informal government of the local gentry equalled that of formal government, we can see how profitable was office-holding for the few who managed to win appointments. Income from informal government was divided among much greater numbers in smaller per-capita amounts (Chang, 1962).

The bulk of the ruling class consisted of the at-home gentry. All of these men had either gone through the civil service exams or had purchased academic degrees, but only those who earned higher degrees were qualified to serve in the bureaucracy. The at-home gentry also included retired officials whose landholdings were purchased or increased from the profits of their posts. Total rents equalled total income from office. This again indicates a large gain from office for a select few, and a relatively low return on land if taxation is taken into account. But gentry status, which was a legally privileged status belonging to the "lords of the soil," carried with it immunity to the full force of taxation, thanks to an equation of interests between local government and local gentry. The main burden of taxation fell on the peasants. Lucky ones found it convenient to register land under the name of some patron. The patron collected a fee for this service amounting to less than his client would pay the district magistrate in taxes, and he pocketed the difference as clear profit (Jacobs, 1958:41-42). The pretended landlord was also in a preferred position to buy the land if it came up for sale, at which time he became the real owner with a policy of sharecropping at the rate of fifty percent. To the Westerner this is rack-renting, just as squeeze in office is viewed as corruption; but from the native Chinese viewpoint, which traditionally did not embrace the ethics of the Enlightenment, the "hunting and fishing of the people," either in the form of rents or taxes, was a right taken in exchange for moral leadership. For the ruling class this was not a hypocritical and self-serving rationalization but a deeply felt ethical component of culturalism.

SUBSISTENCE

Fifty years after Columbus, American food crops—maize, sweet potatoes, white potatoes, and peanuts—entered China by way of Portuguese traders. These new dryland crops had the effect of expanding by millions of acres the Chinese definition of arable soil since they could be cultivated with little effort by Neolithic peasants in sandy loams, dry hills, and lofty mountains. Very shortly, sweet potatoes replaced yams and taro in the rice-short region of the southeastern coast, and in time China, along with India, became the world's leading peanut-producing countries. By the eighteenth century, sweet potatoes were widely grown in the Yangtze valley and in the Red basin and even along the rocky shores of Shantung; by the nineteenth century they had even replaced cereal crops on the North China plain because they proved to be a dryland crop superior to millet, barley, and sorghum. With the white potato they were so extensively cultivated in the hills and mountains of the southwestern plateau, above the reach of maize, that the resulting deforestation and soil erosion caused silting of the Yangtze drainage system and consequent flooding in the central lake region. In the end, American food crops supplied twenty percent of the total food production (Ho, 1959:83–192).

Nonetheless, the effective increase in usable land did little to alter that imbalance between population and economic resources advantageous to landlords. If anything, the cultivated area did not increase in proportion to the population, which more than doubled by 1600 (after the initial introduction of American crops) from an estimated 65 million to 150 million. By 1850, the population had reached 430 million, although this was cut back so much by the catastrophe of war during the fourteen years of the T'ai-p'ing Rebellion (1850–64) that the area it ravaged, the lower Yangtze river provinces and Kiangsi, was still underpopulated in 1953 by fourteen percent. This is not counting the population rise in the delta city of Shanghai and its surrounding umland (Ho, 1959:277–78). In any event, the increased opportunities elsewhere for landlordism had little effect on employment because intensive methods of cultivation remained as efficient for tenants as for owner-operators.

Contrary to Communist propaganda, the significant problem in the countryside of Republican China was not the problem of tenancy but the problem of rural credit. Although the new crops had diversified agriculture, without the means of capitalizing production for the market, the farmer remained at a subsistence level, unable to replace food crops with cash crops to any great extent. His need for cash was still greater than the market's for his commodities (Ho, 1959:263; Meskill, 1973:294–95). Consequently, the industries that sprang up with foreign investment were not nearly self-supporting. The great textile mills of Shanghai, for example, imported most of their cotton by ship from India and the United States and exported most of the finished products in the same directions. The cotton fields of Yunnan (as yet unlinked by rail to the coast) produced entirely for the native handicraft industry, which in turn was not in the least displaced by factory products. In the treaty ports, both agricultural raw materials and factory goods were collected for export in small amounts from many producers, but at the insistence of foreign merchants who came to China seeking them, not Chinese salesmen who went abroad (Cressey, 1934:139, 145). This is the condition Mao has described for Republican China as semicolonial.

Colonialism means a group of people who leave their native country to form a settlement (colony) subject to the parent state. Chinese cities that contained colonial settlements were called treaty ports, and they came to number seventy-three along the maritime seacoast and the navigable length of the Yangtze before their extraterritorial status was abolished in 1943. (For a complete list of treaty ports, see Allen and Donithorne, 1954:265.) By that time the Chinese regarded extrality as derogating from their national sovereignty, but at first they were pleased to keep Westerners, another species of barbarian, at arms's length in their own enclaves. The first few treaty ports—Amoy, Canton, Foochow, Ningpo, and Shanghai—were opened following the Treaty of Nanking, signed with

England in 1842, following China's defeat in the Opium War. China thus signalled her inability to prevent the outgo of silver, taken in during centuries of exporting tea and silk to the West in exchange for opium.

The modern industrial sector of the Chinese economy first appeared in the treaty ports. But because the emergence of modern industry was assisted by Chinese businessmen and not dominated altogether by foreigners, China's political status was described by Mao as semicolonial rather than colonial. And although Mao has branded colonialism of any degree an unmitigated evil, it nonetheless served as a means of transferring to China not only the technology of industrialism but also the idea of national sovereignty, which took root only to stimulate a reappraisal of the treaty ports. In fact, one criticism leveled by intellectuals against the First Republic (1912–26) was that it did not reduce at a stroke the semicolonial status in which foreigners held the nation.

Such a stroke was impossible, of course, because the idea of nationhood, with its flag and constitution, was too far in advance of the fact. The modern sector of the economy did not grow in concert with the agricultural sector. Not that the rural economy did not grow. It did, but not in the modern way, with an increased output per capita. Rather its growth took place by way of population growth coupled with an expansion of acreage. As a result, the traditional sector of the economy was able to compete and coexist with the modern sector (Wang, 1973: ch. 1). The only interaction between the two sectors was a movement of the gentry to the cities, where they found new business opportunities, leaving a leadership vacuum in the countryside to be filled by the Chinese Communist party (CCP).

The CCP, in its initial attempt in 1930 to bring down the ruling Kwomintang (KMT) party, aimed to bring about an orthodox Marxist coup d'état by coming to power on the backs of an agitated industrial proletariat. Members of this class, however, were not numerous enough for the purpose. The same imbalance between population and landed resources that supplied rural gentlemen with tenant sharecroppers now supplied urban factories with cheap labor. Both peasantry and gentry found a new situation in the cities. Had the Communists succeeded in the cities, they would have commanded the disarticulated modern sector only. As it happened, they were driven to make a revolution in the countryside by default. Harassed by KMT troops, the Communists might have been defeated in the rural areas as well, had not the Japanese occupation displaced the Nationalists westward to occupy their wartime seat of government in Chungking. Mao Tse-tung's experience in organizing rural bases behind the Japanese lines for guerrilla warfare led him to eventual conquest of both rural and urban China (see Johnson, 1962).

In the process of leading a peasant war of national liberation against the Japanese, the Red Army replaced the gentry in the countryside. It was, after all, the landlords' traditional function to organize the militia, which they did with credit against the T'ai-p'ing rebels to their own gain in power. This power was fatally weakened when the gentry removed in numbers to the treaty ports. By this time, after the revolution of 1911, gentlemen had lost their legal standing as elite persons of the realm, but they survived as an advantaged class—we may call them the neogentry —seeking new advantages in the modern sector of the economy. This cut gentlemen off from their heritage of rural leadership, causing "social erosion" in the countryside (Fei, 1953: ch. 7).

The neogentry went into many fields: professional military service, party politics, modern business, the professions, and academe. Basic to the attraction of urban life, drawing the old rural gentry out of the countryside, was the presence of the treaty ports with their international settlements, where the power of modernity was evident not only in technological imports but also in the state-idea of national sovereignty, which gave force to the ability of foreigners to establish colonies and win the rights of extrality from a China weaker in both respects. Even clothing of foreigners was imitated for the mana their life-style conveyed, although this was often satirized by writers whose dissent, identifiable with the political Left, was informed with a streak of nativism. After all, the constituency of the ruling party of Republican China was limited to the commercial bourgeoisie and other elements of the modern sector divorced from the traditional economy.

In deserting the political leadership role of the old rural gentry for a new role of leadership in the cities, the neogentry did not altogether abandon landownership, although the kind of land owned and the manner of renting it out differed. In traditional times, rural gentlemen were resident landlords of the hinterland, commanding rents from sharecropping or fixed levies in kind by the force of their personal presence united with land hunger. The neogentry living in cities owned truck farms in the urban umlands on an absentee basis and collected a monetized rent through paid collection agents, a purely commercial arrangement enforced by the municipal police or soldiery.

In addition, opportunities for connection with the land through office-holding had expanded under the republic; the expansion of the agricultural economy in both size and diversity allowed for an expansion of government below the *hsien* level, where subdistrict units called *ch'u* were formed. To these offices of the republic were attracted officials still traditional in their confiscatory approach to taxation but modern in their approach to professional tenure. The traditional official was rotated into office from outside the province at a high rate of turnover, leaving the local gentry as the only permanent carriers of political culture in the countryside (Jacobs, 1958:28, 42).

Local officials under the republican government were elected by the local elite and were not forced to return to their landed estates elsewhere after a short term of office. Instead they were more-or-less permanent fixtures of formal government in their own localities. For these officials, the archaic practice of squeezing public funds behind the façade of elective government gave them relatively lasting access to land taxes independent of landowning.

The addition of all kinds of service-oriented departments, in keeping with the Western-inspired notion of government accountability (in rhetoric if not in practice), enormously increased the number of urban-based officials and civil servants living off the land but not as landlords. For example, when Communist troops entered the three provinces of Szechwan, Yunnan, and Kweichow in April of 1950, they counted 400,000 civil servants (Human Relations Area Files 1956: Southwest China, vol. II,

p. 444). Compare this with a total of 2,042 local officials for all of China proper toward the end of the Ch'ing dynasty. The difference is very large, even if we count the traditional official's private retinue (paid out of his own pocket) of about eight clerks and copyists, some ten degree-holding scholars brought with him from his home district to serve as private secretaries and business experts, and from ten to twenty trusted personal servants (Ch'u, 1962).

Land deserted by the urbanized gentry was taken over by peasants, some of whom earned the purchase price in factory labor (Fei, 1944). Since members of the ruling class no longer personally dominated the hinterland as resident landlords, the low ceiling on mobility was lifted somewhat. The economic striving of ambitious peasant families during the republican period is well described by Pearl Buck in *The Good Earth* (1931). The successful characters in her story are businessmen-farmers of the sort known in Russia as *kulaks* (Wong, 1973:53); they owned and operated land as peasants would but also rented some of it to tenants in the manner of the old rural gentry. However, they were rich peasants in their life-style, not gentlemen. Mao's father was a very prosperous Chinese kulak (who may represent what Mao had in mind when he described a Chinese capitalist stage). Both Russian and Chinese kulaks presented obstacles to collectivization of the land and were eliminated by the state in both countries. It is therefore puzzling to find Chinese Communist propaganda directed against landlords pictured not as kulaks but as rural gentry.

Decades before the Communist victory in 1950, the intellectual basis for justifying the revolution was prepared by Chinese economists, who found in the anticapitalist thinking of Marx a convenient vehicle for their traditional anti-Western feelings. They claimed that the countryside had been bankrupted by the commercialization of agriculture stimulated by the treaty ports and abetted by land concentration in the hands of the gentry, whose exclusive interests and not those of tenant farmers were protected by the nationalist government (see the Institute of Pacific Relations, 1939; Ch'en, 1936, 1939; see also Potter, 1968; and Myers, 1970 for a rebuttal of the Marxist approach).

It is now a settled point of Communist doctrine that the source of harm to the Chinese economy in causing land concentration was the existence of the treaty ports—that colonialism led to impoverishment of the peasantry and a bifurcation of the rural population into landless laborers and wealthy landlords. When President Nixon visited China in 1972, his hosts treated him to this official explanation as embodied in a "modern revolutionary dance drama" entitled, *Red Detachment of Women*. This was said to dramatize the victory of Mao Tse-tung's thought in "the fierce struggle between two classes, proletariat and bourgeoisie, and the two roads, socialism and capitalist" (Foreign Languages Press, 1971). The struggle centers on the refusal of a poor peasant girl to submit to the cruel oppression of her despotic landlord and her firm resolve to join the Red Army, which promises to redistribute land to the tiller. The landlord is portrayed in traditional garb, but he has connections with urban merchants dressed in Western business suits; his own costume is not that of the simple white gown belonging to the traditional rural gentry, however, but the heavy silk brocade of the dynastic official, and he wields a most unlikely whip against his tenants.

Significantly, *Red Detachment of Women* takes place on Hainan Island, the one truly tropical region in China, located off the Liuchow Peninsula of Kwangtung province. Here tropical agriculture was commercialized to an extent exceeding that of truck farms in the urban umlands of the mainland. In addition to producing three crops of rice a year, the island exported (and still exports) sugarcane, coffee, natural rubber, coconuts, and figs, in addition to timber cut from the slopes of its central mountain range (Shabad, 1972:185, 190). By contrast, the homeland of the Communist movement in the Yenan area of Shensi province had the lowest rate of tenancy in all of agricultural China.

The historical fact of the matter is that landlordism was a political issue in the rise of communism in China, but not a significant economic one. The official explanation is that the treaty ports, seats of colonialism, increased the rate of tenancy by stimulating the commercialization of agriculture, whose proceeds were drained from the countryside for investment in urban factories. Products from factories in turn redounded to the destruction of the native handicraft industry. The *Red Detachment of Women* is an artistic statement of the Marxist theory that communism was generated as a revolutionary force in the name of a "land to the tiller" movement aimed at sweeping away a destructive landlord class identified with foreign imperialism.

Unfortunately there were no land surveys carried out in Manchu China of the sort conducted by Buck in Republican China. The evidence strongly suggests, however, that no major discontinuity in the pattern of land utilization took place in the interval (Feuerwerker, 1969:3–16; Muramatsu, 1966). The pattern had been and remained one of small owner-operated farms; these predominated, with a mixture of part-owners and tenant farmers. Landlord holdings had not become concentrated in the hands of big owners but remained scattered as small holdings; many small landlords let out to farm families who tilled land in the same manner as did owner-operators. Owing to the unfavorable population/land ratio, which possibly even worsened over time, tenants were motivated to work as hard and efficiently in republican as in imperial times (Jacobs, 1958:28). Leaving out the Chinese differentiation of topsoil and subsoil rights, which complicates the concept of part-ownership (Tawney, 1932:36), the pattern of land utilization (Buck, 1937:193–96) for 1929–30 is as follows:

	Wheat Region	Rice Region	China North and South
Owner-Operators	73%	38%	54%
Part-Owners	18%	37%	29%
Full Tenants	6%	25%	17%

These figures relate to land that was ninety-three percent privately owned, a proportion that was probably no less during imperial times. No landed aristocracy of feudal vassals existed under the empire, so there was no pattern of large estate holdings concentrated in the hands of big landlords to carry over into republican times. Yet the Central Committee of the CCP in 1947 claimed that up to eighty percent of the arable land was owned by landlords (United Nations, 1951:55, n.1).

It is true that the urbanization of the rural gentry raised the level of tenancy in the umlands (as much as ninety percent around Canton), but these had always of necessity been areas of commercialized agriculture. In the hinterland, grain crops are storable, can be transported at leisure, and can be used for payment of rent in kind. Not so the nonstorable vegetables of the umland, which require short-time transport, quick sale for cash, and the use of cash to buy fertilizer from night soil collectors (see Eberhard, 1965:88). Monetized rent easily fits this picture. The difficulty was that truck farmers, being businessmen working for a profit, were not so ready to pay rent as were tenant farmers in the hinterland, who were willing to pay up to half their crop (even without any supervision) just for the chance to avoid being squeezed off the land altogether by the competitive crush of land hunger. As a result, collection agents in the umland did, on occasion, need to rely on threats of coercion from city police or by the soldiery. (Perhaps this is the source of the imagery for the whips held by landlords dressed in Mandarin costumes in Red Detachment of Women.)

But for Communist propaganda and art to populate the hinterland with landlords identified with the traditional gentry is anachronistic, and of course to give them whips is a distortion of the noncoercive force of their patriarchal influence as cultured men of the realm. The only gentlemen-landlords still living in the countryside in number were those isolated far from the treaty ports, such as in Yunnan province (see Osgood, 1963). Elsewhere the land deserted by the old rural gentry was taken up by rich peasants, or kulaks. In working that part of the land they did not rent out, they were not as leisured and cultured as the gentlemen they replaced, and perhaps in their role as landlords they were not as gentle. The Communist image of the wicked landlord whipping his tenants into submission is probably a composite picture drawn from uncultured kulaks of the hinterland (including Mao's own father, no doubt), the collection agents of the umland backed by police, and a garbled memory of the rural gentry.

The political leadership role of the gentry was assumed by the Red Army when it mobilized guerrilla warfare with peasant partisans during the Japanese occupation (Johnson, 1962). The CCP propelled itself into power by taking over leadership of the militia after it was deserted by the neogentry. The kulaks must then have been perceived as potential competitors in the countryside and therefore as enemies to be painted in the darkest political colors of despotism and tyranny, deepened by association with imperialism. This association, however, was indirect, existing only insofar as kulaks filled the vacuum left by rural gentry attracted to the treaty ports. Only in the umlands of the treaty ports was there a direct economic association between foreign-dominated industry and investment money derived from rents. This association, of course, was mediated by the neogentry, who had become absentee landlords there.

Certainly, landlords of whatever character cannot be blamed for bleeding the hinterland of capital for investment in the semicolonial enterprises of the treaty ports. (On the communist animus toward cities and treaty ports, see Murphey, 1970.) The problem from the beginning was a disarticulation between the traditional sector of the economy and the modern industrial sector. This difficulty was inherent in China's unfavorable man/land ratio. The basic problem inherited by the Communist regime was one of too many people trying to make a living off too little land —about 2.5 persons per acre. This made for subsistence living if not a subsistence economy. As a result, the growing industries of the treaty ports could not absorb enough labor from the hinterland to ease the dependency burden of its labor-intensive methods, a necessary first step toward the capitalization of agriculture. Industrialization and agrarian reconstruction are interconnected parts of one problem, in which farmers must feed enough factory workers to make the machinery and fertilizer necessary for more productive farming (see Chang, 1949:69, 206). Yet the circle is not yet closed, even though the Communist government transfers as a matter of policy more capital out of agriculture into industry than did the nationalist government, warlords, and landlords, combined (Yang, 1959a:158–59). But even in this case, the transfer is not primarily from the communes of the hinterland, which are organized for the maintenance of their own populations, but from communes of the umland, where agriculture had always been commercialized.

The difference is that the state now provides umland farmers with the organizational means to grow both food crops and industrial crops. In republican times, the only defense against market fluctuations was the economic organization of households, so that if cash crops such as tobacco for cigarette factories did not pay off, the loss was suffered at the expense of the farmer's own food crops (Boeke, 1953:103). Of course, no change in the political economy could reverse the disaster suffered by growers of mulberry leaves and silkworms for the silk-reeling industry, because the business as a whole had been lost during the world depression of the 1930s to an Asian competitor, Japan, as the tea business in late imperial times had been lost to India.

On balance, it seems that the old disarticulation between agriculture and industry still obtains. Agriculture everywhere is organized under the commune system, but in the hinterland it still serves a maintenance economy, and only in the umland does it serve industry, as before. In other words, China has acquired under the Communist regime more political than economic unity. Ironically the new controls are being used actually to enforce the old disjuncture between the traditional and modern sectors of the economy. No doubt this policy is all the easier to follow considering the ready source of foreign exchange gained from narcotic exports, which alone are sufficient to finance the nuclear arsenal. The quiet export of opium through Macao returns more than double China's official trade turnover by supplying seventy percent of the heroin consumed in the United States. This source of foreign exchange alone has sufficed to pay for China's nuclear weapons program (Wren, 1974). The most significant part of the modern sector is thus supported rather by American addiction than by Chinese peasant labor in the traditional sector, which is carried as a dependency burden. It's an interdependent world. By the end of the 1970s, however, it is calculated that China's main source of foreign exchange will derive from the exploitation of off-shore oil deposits in the Yellow Sea, whose reserves rival those of Saudi Arabia and Iran combined (Farnsworth, 1975:2).

DEVELOPMENT

The Communist conquest of China began as a civil war in which the rural population was mobilized against the urban strongholds, first of the

Japanese occupation and then of the nationalist government. Diagrammatically, radical forces in the countryside surrounded conservative ones in the cities. Contrast this pattern with the reverse arrangement of the same forces in the defeat of the T'ai-p'ing Rebellion, when a rival dynasty centered in the Yangtze delta attempted to move its armies northward against Peking between 1850 and 1864. The radical T'ai-p'ings were driven into the cities (notably Nanking) and there defeated by the surrounding conservative forces of empire, specifically by local militiamen gathered into the provincial army of Kiangsu under the leadership of its governor, Li Hung-chang (see Kuhn, 1970). This contrast is the measure of the postimperial urbanization of the rural gentry, those "lords of the soil" whose traditional role as agents of informal government and leaders of the militia made them more than mere landlords. With their desertion of the countryside followed its radicalization by the Communist movement, whose party members replaced the rural gentry.

Subsequent to the military defeat of the nationalist government in 1949, the Communists carried out a nationwide program of land reform. Their slogan of "land to the tiller" provided a necessarily rural slant to their chief article of Marxist doctrine—that reallocation of wealth is the key to the well-being of society. In theory this meant redistributing the holdings of big landlords, but in practice it meant the small holdings of kulaks, since the gentry had already vacated most rural areas of China. Besides, the holdings of gentlemen-landlords had never been very large to begin with, and the countryside remained occupied by owner-operators and part-owners of small family farms. Nonetheless, the method of land reform called for putting at least one landlord on trial in every village, and the cadres who carried out these instructions did so with a considerable amount of violence—an estimated thirty million executions (New York Times, 2 June 1959).

Every cadre was educated in a document drawn up in 1933, "How to Analyze Class Status in the Countryside" (in Wu, 1973:825–26), which taught them how to distinguish between big landlords, rich peasants, middle peasants, poor peasants, and workers. These distinctions, as a measure of exploit and drudgery, proved difficult to make. For one thing, some tenants had always chosen to rent land, preferring to invest their limited capital in equipment and thus to farm more land than they could afford to purchase. Busy and enterprising, many of these tenants enjoyed a higher standard of living than some of the traditional landlords, who had preferred to lower their standard of living for the sake of face—a gentleman did not work with his hands if he had the least bit of land to rent out. Other tenants simply could not handle the business responsibilities of land ownership in an economy dominated by peasant freeholders, and they willingly sought dependency on landlords. In other cases a man would rent the land of his absent brothers as a way of keeping it in trust for them until they returned, if ever. Given the rule of "homoyogeniture"—a word coined by A. L. Kroeber to name the customary norm of inheritance in China, which was equal division among all legitimate heirs, that is, the equal division of the father's land among his sons—heirs often received land holdings too small to sustain a family (Jacobs, 1958:149). The relentless pressure of the population invariably drove potential farmers off the land into towns and cities, where they sought marginal self-employment or apprenticeship in some craft or line of trade (U.S. Department of Agriculture, 1944).

Like unicorns, however, whip-cracking owners of great, landed estates were hard to find. More evident was the worsening population/land ratio. The idea that reallocation of landed wealth was the answer to China's most significant problem is now thoroughly and emphatically discredited in the regime's present efforts to limit population growth. The PRC is the only country in the world exhorting its people to limit families for the good of the state rather than for family welfare. The Chinese population is going to reach at least one billion by 1980, outracing the proportionate allocation of resources no matter what steps are taken now in the way of contraception, abortion, sterilization, or late marriage. Not only is the Marxist belief in reallocation dealt a telling blow here; so, too, is the economic-threshold idea that population in the Third World will subside once its countries have attained a measure of development similar to that of the industrial world. Population must be limited first, or it will lessen the amount of industrialization that can be purchased (Holden, 1974; Aird, 1972).

But this realization had not yet dawned during the period of land reform in China. Nonetheless, the psychology of land reform is not easily understood. A conspicuous leisure class on whom to pin the blame was difficult to find after working landlords—the kulaks—had replaced the rural gentry. Moreover, landlords' holdings were never very large in China. The amount actually redistributed was incredibly small—no more than from 0.15 to 0.45 of an acre per capita. In fact, the net result of equalizing with poor farmers and tenants was a smaller size for the average farm (Whitaker and Shinn, 1972:416–18). The landlords put on trial were more often than not pathetic figures possessing only a jot more land than their fellow villagers.

Apart from the terror tactics of the land reform cadres, an important factor is the attitude toward scarcity taken by peasants everywhere. This attitude, which is well documented in the comparative literature of anthropology, is that any open striving for material gain is a disturbance to the balance of social order (see Potter et al., 1967; Wolf, 1966). This is stated in the Chinese case to the effect that, "with only a limited supply of land available, any attempt to enlarge one's own farm holding will mean dispossessing others" (Fei and Chang, 1945:301). If someone gets more, someone else gets less, and the loss is visible to everyone. George M. Foster has expressed the position further: "Even if an individual cannot see that he is suffering as a consequence of another's progress, he knows that he must be; the logical premise on which his society is based tells him it *has* to be so." (Foster, 1962:53)

In relation to the Chinese, however, this attitude would apply only among commoners and not to their relationship with the rural gentry. The gentlemen of old were cultured enough to belong to another world governed by another set of rules, beyond peasant envy. As between peasant and gentry, landed wealth was the one party's disproportionate, but legitimate, share of a fixed supply; poverty was the consequence of the other party's having a larger proportion of the same supply. Margaret Mead has generalized for all premodern agrarian societies: "The distinction is not between richness and poverty but between privilege and the absence of privilege" (Mead, 1962:80). Poverty is associated with a sense of *under*privilege, differing from the sense of *non*privilege; the latter is experienced by peasant folk who lack any means of escape from toil and the watchful envy of fellow villagers.

Fei Hsiao-t'ung claims that a considerable number of peasants after a stint of factory work in the cities returned to the land not only with increased purchasing power but also with novel expectations of working for a higher standard of living. In the absence of the traditional gentry to set before their eyes the standard of privileged status, these peasants were awakened from a sense of *non*privilege to one of *under*privilege and worked hard to do something about it. They discovered poverty; and they worked hard to buy out, in bits and pieces, the land holdings of the urbanizing gentry (Fei, 1944:56, 62).

The work of the land reform cadres in the villages was probably aided by the prior introduction of the idea of poverty, in the example of the kulaks who strove for incremental gains; the cadres could then appeal to a sense of injustice and *under*privilege among a class of poor peasants newly receptive to this self-conception. At the same time, the fatalistic morality associated with a sense of *non*privilege must have persisted so long as the population/land ratio worsened. According to the Communist cadres, the landlords and kulaks put on trial stood for the evils of land concentration and tenancy, befitting a theory of class warfare between exploiters and exploited. But for most peasants who participated in the trials, their whipped-up crys of "Kill! Kill!" must have stemmed rather more from a sometimes embittered sense of competition among themselves. The hardships engendered by land hunger did not, as one might expect, draw villagers together into a community of suffering but rather aroused what one observer called "mutual suspicion" (Smith, 1894:ch. 24); another has called attention to the absence of any "corporate character" belonging to Chinese village life (Johnston, 1910:157). On the basis of his cross-cultural experience with peasant societies, Foster concluded that, "The quality of interpersonal relations appears to be bad, and true cooperation is largely limited to certain types of labor exchange in agriculture and housebuilding." (Foster, 1962:50) It may well be that the success of the landlord trials owed to the land reform cadres' exploitation of the spirit of mutual suspicion long endemic to Chinese village life. This possibility is heightened by the fact that economically the accused were often only marginally differentiated from their accusers.

Historically the "socialist transformation of agriculture" in China took place in six steps as illustrated in Figure 10.

Phase One: Land Reform. Land reform began in areas of Chinese Communist control even before the establishment of the PRC in 1949. When completed nationwide, this program had redistributed millions of acres of land to millions of poor farmers. However, as noted above, the amount per capita was so small that its significance was much more political than economic. Land ownership and work tasks still rested with individual families.

Phase Two: Mutual Aid Teams. With the completion of land reform in 1953, the CCP organized several farm households into "mutual aid teams" for a season to plant or harvest a specific crop. This was patterned

FIGURE 10. Development of Socialist Agriculture in the People's Republic of China, 1950–72. Adapted from Crook and Bernstein, 1974: 8.

Year	Phase One: Seasonal Mutual Aid Teams	Phase Two: Permanent Mutual Aid Teams	Phase Three: Semisocialist APCs (number)	Phase Four: Collective Farms	Phase Five: Rural People's Communes	Phase Six: State Farms	Percentage of Peasant Households in Socialist Agricultural Units
1950	2,097,000	627,000	18	1	—	?	10.7
1951	3,600,000	1,075,000	129	1	—	?	19.2
1952	6,270,000	1,756,000	3,634	10	—	404	40.0
1953	5,634,000	1,816,000	15,053	15	—	?	39.5
1954	6,130,000	3,801,000	114,165	201	—	?	60.3
1955	3,975,000	3,172,000	633,213	529	—	?	64.9
1956	—	—	682,000	312,000	—	?	96.3
1957	—	—	72,022	680,081	—	710	97.0
1958	—	—	—	—	26,578	1,442	99.1
1959	—	—	—	—	24,000	?	?
1960	—	—	—	—	?	2,490	?
1961	—	—	—	—	26,000	2,500	?
1962	—	—	—	—	?	?	?
1963	—	—	—	—	?	?	?
1964	—	—	—	—	74,000	?	?
1965	—	—	—	—	?	2,000	?
1972	—	—	—	—	50,000	?	?

after the traditional custom of labor exchange, to which was added the exchange of tools and draft animals. Later, farmers in several seasonal teams, from three to ten households, were organized into year-round ("permanent mutual aid") teams. Individual families still retained their own means of production, but some economic decisions were made on a collective basis with the aid of a leader and an accountant, and some units accumulated capital equipment.

Phase Three. Agricultural Producers Cooperative (APCs). In this phase, from thirty to forty mutual aid teams were organized into semisocialist, or lower-stage, APCs for the purpose of farming their land in common. Decisions were centralized for each cooperative in the hands of its chairman, committees, and accountants. Member households were, in effect, paid rent for land shares contributed. The collective farms of the next phase are sometimes called higher-stage APCs.

Phase Four: Collective Farms. At this point, several semisocialist APCs were organized into collective farms consisting of a hundred or more households. The labor force was divided into production brigades, which were further divided into production teams. As farmers worked, they were credited with labor days according to the amount and quality of work accomplished. At the end of the agricultural year, the gross income of the collective was totaled, deductions were made for production costs, taxes, and capital accumulation, and the net income was divided by the total number of labor days credited to all farmers and staff members to determine the monetary value of a single labor day. This income was then distributed to the member families according to the number of labor days credited to each family in the collective accounts. In addition to paying the government a ten percent tax on the total agricultural output, collectives were also obliged to sell to the state almost all of their surplus in excess of rather tight consumption requirements in seed and fodder. A small portion of the output left the collectives through black markets and the state-controlled markets.

Phase Five: Rural People's Communes. By the fall of 1958, more than 26,000 communes had been amalgamated from about 680,000 collectives, consisting of over 123 million households, or ninety-nine percent of all peasant households in China. Depending on the nutrition density of the area, each commune consisted of from 1,000 to 5,000 households. The production brigade, corresponding in size to the former collective farm, became the middle level of management. Unlike the collectives, communes undertook industrial and commercial projects and assumed governmental, educational, and military functions as well. A series of reforms from 1959 through 1961 altered the scale of communes as established in 1958, reducing them in size and increasing their number, and placing the full responsibility for making decisions about production and distribution at the production brigade level rather than at the commune level. Today, communes number about 50,000, and their production teams are estimated to range from 4 million to 8 million. The average team in 1971 consisted of about 20 or 30 member households and was responsible for cultivating from 30 to 60 acres.

Phase Six: State Farms. This was to be the final phase in the socialist transformation of Chinese agriculture—the organization of communes into state farms. Through these large-scale entities, the various ministries of central government would be able to control production and distribution decisions directly. Making this an easier administrative task was the fact that all state farmworkers were to be wage earners, that is, true agricultural proletarians in contrast to collective members, who were technically part-owners. Finally, farming techniques were to be modernized. But there is no evidence that the present authorities plan to enlarge the number of state farms beyond the number organized by 1965 —approximately 2,000. At that time, they cultivated less than four percent of the total cultivated land, producing one percent of the total grain output, with something less than two percent of the rural population (Crook and Bernstein, 1974:4–7).

The aim of collectivization has been to end the "foundation for exploitation." In the bad old days, the neogentry mediated between the capitalized firms of the protected treaty ports and the household economies of peasant producers, extending credit and managing strings of commodity buyers. But for peasant producers, cash crops proved to be only an expensive and round-about way of earning subsistence, not a way to make profits. All their earnings were spent in repaying the indebtedness incurred, for example, from purchasing tobacco seed, bean cake fertilizer, charcoal for drying the tobacco leaf, and food, while their tobacco crop was maturing. Peasant economic impotence when confronted with dealers, middlemen, and usurers merely continued and magnified the traditional impotence experienced by peasant folk when confronted with tax rates set by government and rents set by landlords. This inability to muster enough productive and purchasing power to exercise a measure of control over their own economic destiny is the characteristic that sets peasants apart from the true farmers of industrialized nations. Farmers, in this technical meaning, unlike peasants, possess the power as members of rural pressure groups to adjust the price and market regime to their own advantage (Loomis and Beegle, 1950:622–28).

We have been speaking of peasants of the umland, who undoubtedly paid a disproportionate share of the costs of factory industrialism centered in the cities around which they lived. They paid directly in the form of confiscatory taxes exacted by the urban-based nationalist government and also as rent monies collected by the urbanized neogentry, who invested this money under the protection of that government; they paid indirectly by providing a cheap, self-maintaining pool of labor that raised food as well as industrial crops, and by remaining a subadministrative sector of society beyond the scope of payments for education, public health, transportation, and other social services. Peasants of the hinterland, of course, were isolated from the modernization process except as they served as migrant factory labor, who often returned to the village to buy land with their earnings. Otherwise, local taxes went to support local government, with its enlarged body of officials drawn from former landlords who had deserted their old rural homes, once having been resident agents of informal government. Nonetheless, peasants of the hinterland shared with those of the umland a subadministrative, self-maintaining existence.

A similar situation still seems to obtain under the PRC, except for the fact that the farming population is everywhere administered by the government in communes. (The so-called urban communes are simply residential areas organized in streets or around a factory.) Collectivization transformed the peasant into a rural proletarian but not yet into a true farmer. Economically he is still as impotent as ever. In the umland communes he is still exploited for the support of urban industry through the provision of food, industrial crops, and taxes, although this is necessarily redefined as a sacrificial contribution to nation-building, because these exactions are made wholly at government command. In the hinterland communes, the peasant is still living in a maintenance economy, albeit under the administration of a government that provides all the social services necessary for communal autonomy and insulation from urban influence. In other words, the hinterland—where the traditional agrarian economy coexisted and competed on its own merits with the modern sector—is still disarticulated, but now as a matter of policy. The weight of the past is heavy, indeed.

Policy has been added to the momentum of the past because the economic growth of the hinterland through its traditional means of areal expansion has slowed almost to a stop, without any parallel slowdown of population expansion. The amount of land under cultivation grew from 1,468,220 thousands of *mou* (a *mou* being one-third of an acre) in 1949 to only 1,616,800 thousands of *mou* by 1958, or from 10.20 percent of the total land area to only 11.23 percent (Kuo, 1972:37), and this with a population (as of 1970) that will double with a net increase of almost 500 million in 20 years (Aird, 1972:329). The policy of isolating the traditional sector of the economy, now governed by communes of the hinterland, works to protect the modern sector from being swamped by rural-urban migration.

This policy has been dubbed "the great leap farmward" (Lelyveld, 1974), but Chinese authorities refer to it as *hsia-fang*, or the "down-to-the-countryside" movement. Its purpose is not only to prevent rural-urban migration but also to reverse it in large numbers. This is not a pleasant prospect for the new generation because industry is favorved in wage earnings over agriculture, and besides, the traditional contempt for farm labor still runs strong. For that reason, the present generation of middle-school students, thirty-five million of them, would prefer to work in factories or even in coal mines than be "sent down" to "the great socialist countryside." As many as twenty-five million youths have been sent down since 1968 in the largest movement of population organized by any government since Stalin's notorious deportations. But the hard fact is that the urban opportunities for employment are very limited, and the deportations serve to get surplus, restless youths out of the cities, where they might create social or political difficulties. It is not surprising, therefore, that the government attempts through its propaganda to idealize farm labor as a patriotic occupation in support of the revolution, for it is desirable to persuade not only those who must be sent down but also those in the rural communes who must absorb them—inexperienced as these youths are in farm work—as extra mouths to feed.

Despite plans for development, the communes of the hinterland are now designed to accomplish what the Neolithic countryside did as a matter of course: absorb labor. The first Five-Year Plan (1953–57) was calculated to transfer the existing surplus from agriculture to industry with the least capitalization of the former. The Second Five Year Plan projected a "Great Leap Forward" for agriculture, in the expectation that it would continue to be productive with a minimum of state investment, even to

provide for its own industrialization with the notorious backyard smelting
furnaces. The years of the Great Leap lasted only from 1958 to 1960 before
these expectations were disappointed. The recognition that industry must
sooner or later serve agriculture, as in providing chemical fertilizers and
machinery, set in during the recovery period from 1961 to 1965; Chinese
planners then attempted to develop an economy that "walked on both
legs," that is, one that would simultaneously develop agriculture and industry as two interconnected parts of a problem. This was still the theme
of the Third-Year Plan (1966–70) before the *hsia-fang* movement began.

It is easy enough to say that the priorities of investment should not be
one-sided in favor of heavy industry. Yet to balance things with the
capitalization of agriculture presupposes the absence of a huge surplus of
agricultural labor (Chang, 1949:205). Chinese Communist planners hoped
that the broad, open fields of collective farms would accommodate extensive farming methods, but where tractors were introduced they were used
in the labor-absorptive manner of intensive farming—four men to a
machine that called for only one operator (Spencer, 1957:21). In any event,
tractor operations were obviated by the increasing dissection of the landscape in the planned expansion of irrigation ditches (Kuo, 1972:234).

Communes are big organizations from an administrative point of
view, representing a political achievement of great magnitude. But in the
end, they have come to serve as large-scale organizations for managing
those small-scale routines carried over from the ancient horticulture of the
Neolithic economy. Communes control land use, production planning,
labor use, and they act as units of local government, encompassing one or
more former townships *(hsiang)* or even a whole county *(hsien)*. Within
the commune are a number of production brigades, former collectives,
which in turn were former villages. Within the production brigades are the
agricultural teams, former village neighborhoods. At the bottom level are
the work teams, of eight to ten households, within the agricultural teams.
This is where the basic hand operations of horticulture are actually carried
out. They are the labor-absorptive manual tasks of constructing paddy
fields, maintaining embankments, digging wells, plowing, transplanting,
cultivating, harvesting, threshing, and applying night soil, dipperful by
dipperful. The only significant difference between current methods and
the Neolithic regimen is that self-responsibility for the intensive application of labor is carried out within a framework of collective planning and
supervision, and the reward of accrued work points is indirect (Pelzel,
1972:408).

Scholars in the late Ch'ing dynasty saw that the technology of extensive farming is incompatible with high nutrition density:

> In Western countries the territory is large, the population is thin,
> therefore they use machines even for agriculture. If China em-
> ploys them, one person's agricultural work may take away the
> livelihood of ten others. These ten others, if they do not want to
> sit down and wait by death and starvation would choose a risky
> road [for example, become bandits or rebels] (in Teng and Fair-
> bank, 1954:186)

A Western-trained sociologist of the present regime, Wu Ching-ch'ao, has
come to the same conclusion—that mechanization is bound to displace
troublesome surplus labor—a problem for which he foresees no solution.

He follows the Malthusian view of China's population problem now taken by Mao, the first and thus far the only head of state to advocate zero population growth (Aird, 1972:239–40).

In the meantime, a labor-absorptive technology under communal management serves the ends of social control. The hinterland communes are actually reservations for surplus labor that cannot be integrated with the national economy. By contrast, the industry-related sector has been given so much investment priority that in 1970, the urban population representing industry (fifteen percent) had produced six times as much of the gross national product (GNP) as their country brethren. In absolute terms, however, that fifteen percent of the labor force in the industrialized umlands produced its disproportionate share of a GNP in the amount of only $145. per capita. It is instructive to compare the Chinese data with figures for some other countries, from the least to the most developed (Ashbrook, 1972:43).

Per-Capita Gross National Product in 1970 (U.S. Dollars)

United States	4,800
West Germany	3,000
U.S.S.R.	2,200
Japan	1,900
Taiwan	350
China	145
India	100

This listing places China with less than half the per-capita GNP of a prosperous Taiwan and underscores its inferior economic position relative to Japan, although China has a somewhat better showing than the exceedingly backward economy of India.

In 1957, two-thirds of China's GNP originated in agriculture, but since then industry has come abreast and now surpasses it; and the prospects are for continuing divergence with increased opportunities for higher incomes in the urban areas, where the industrial system continues to grow in size and technical complexity. The increased differential between rural and urban incomes will probably lead to the government's decreasing ability to keep the rural communes in ignorance of the difference, despite propaganda about equality, and thus to prevent rural people from engaging in private activities (Ashbrook, 1972:41).

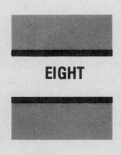

EIGHT

POLITICS

RULERS

Today's heads of state make enhancement of the economy their goal; the emperors of traditional China presided over a maintenance economy. Before factory industrialism made economic growth, as measured by increased output per capita, possible for national entities, the collective goal was economic enhancement by conquest and territorial expansion across frontiers, as in the Roman empire. Some of the ancient polities, such as the Mongol empire, were built on sweeping plunder alone. But older than Rome and the secondary civilizations is the primary civilization of China, whose military conquests were cyclical and carried out by competing royal families for the same territories. China's border expansions were aimed at protecting trade routes and the agricultural population from raiding nomads. The Chinese imperial military machine was used chiefly to guard against the external barbarians of the inner Asian steppelands and to protect the security of the Grand Canal—the court's economic lifeline to its rice basket in the Yangtze delta. The political goal sought by the emperor, in company with the nonhereditary elite of the realm, was limited to the quasi-religious objective of maintaining the sanctity of the great tradition among the politically relevant members of the Han collectivity. Political authority in traditional China was by default reduced to an administrative arm of moral authority, stressing the rightfulness of the stratification system embracing one great hierarchy from royalty, nobility, scholar-official-gentry, scholar-landlord-gentry, and all the ranks within the elite, down to the majority of commoners and its even lower class of expendables and outcasts (*see* Eisenstadt, 1963: ch. 9). Stable inequality was the business of government, first and last.

The unsubstantial politics of culturalism no less than the substantive politics of nationalism may comprise the natural aims of a ruling elite ambitious to maintain itself in power. The difference rests with the amount of political resources available to the ambitious. Culturalism implies low political resources—that is, a small influential sector and a large immobilized sector (Scalapino, 1972:29–31). The political resources belonging to the organic sovereignty of the modern nation-state include a population whose high levels of occupational differentiation, literacy, and exposure to radio and television combine to create articulate interest groups whose demand for a say in government cannot be ignored. In the jargon of political science, these demands from outside government consti- tute "inputs" that enlarge government's functions. By contrast, the only pressure on the Chinese pseudomorph came from the "withinputs" of an official body of government critics, the censorate (see Whitney, 1970:12).

The traditional Chinese ruling class had no need to appeal to peasant votes; it appealed rather to its own intrinsic moral superiority as sym- bolized by literacy in the classics of moral instruction. Indeed, the elite claimed to rule by the force of moral instruction alone, drawing their in- spiration from the emperor who, designated as a sage-king, served as a fountainhead of the state-idea that held moral supervision to be the very purpose of government.

Nothing better illustrates the influence on the majority by the elite, as self-conceived by members of the ruling class in both formal and informal government, than the following quotation from Confucius, well known to all of them: "The *chun-tze* [superior men] are like the wind, the *hsiao-jen* [little people] like the grass. When the wind blows, the grass bends" (*Lun Yu*, XII:19). The image is pacification by moral suasion, a harmless conceit that did not conflict with the reality principle for the sufficient reason that the illusion of government by morality accorded with the absence of gov- ernment by enforceable statutes. This lack of administrative controls over the population at large in turn reflected the people's low productive and purchasing power; commoners were in no position to make any "inputs." Hence the elite could afford to picture the noncoercive deference of the peasantry as the outcome of moral education from above—"the wind on the grass."

The corollary of a population of subjects is a governmental apparatus modest in its needs for manpower. The collection costs of confiscatory taxation are cheap because there is neither great economic diversity nor great measure of productivity to be taxed in a Neolithic peasantry and besides, no services need be given in return.

In accordance with the low level of occupational differentiation in a government of modest political resources, the few men who did hold bureaucratic posts were not employed as service personnel trained for a professional career in administration. Rather they invited themselves in as amateur worthies who took office as an emolument of privilege. This ex- plains the civilian psychology of the traditional Chinese bureaucracy—any official could take up military duties when the occasion demanded, as he took up all other duties of the most varied sort. Military officers on per- manent watch on the frontiers and in selected garrisons were viewed as specialists and thus accorded less esteem than civilian generalists, who were in a position to do everything or to hire any lowly experts in any field they needed.

Positions in formal government offered guaranteed opportunities for self-aggrandizement, competition for which was restricted to the literate minority whose moral training in the classics presupposed the leisure for study that only a birth elite could provide. The bureaucracy had, from the beginnings of empire, sided with the emperor in helping him eliminate all hereditary elites other than those of the royal house, but the bureaucrats had, in the course of this struggle, made education substitute for aristoc- racy as a basis for perpetuating class privilege. Because profiteering in the name of imperial taxation was acknowledged by the emperor, the right of appointed officials to confiscate the peasants' economic surplus made government the very cause of social inequality, from whose favored few bureaucrats were recruited. It could not be otherwise—the emperor lacked the fiscal base to pay his officials enough salary to professionalize their duties for anything *other* than profiteering.

It follows that a bureaucratic career in imperial China was not highly politicized. An official's deference to his superior was displayed not in passing down administrative orders like an obedient tool but in passing up some of the fruits of aggrandizement in the form of bribes. Of course, conventional limits were placed on the amount of profiteering allowed in any office. An incumbent who did not squeeze more than the conventional twenty percent of all transactions handled by his office was an honest official *(ch'ing kuan)* practicing honest graft *(lo kwei)*. Only one who exceeded this limit was stigmatized as a corrupt official *(tsang kuan)* (Sun, 1961:45).

Put another way, the bureaucratic system was not strong enough to make incumbents care for their official standing more than for their private interests. The system had no other administrative function than to administer the appointments of the officials themselves; it was not accountable for the discharge of their duties, only for the details of their paperwork. Indeed, a bureaucracy filled with careerists would have threatened an emperor whose only political resource was manipulation of the iconography of state for the sake of eliciting obedience in rituals upholding inequality. Knowledge of imperial arcana, by definition, reached the pinnacle of wisdom in the person of the sage-king, the emperor.

Despite talk about centralizing revenues collected through a bureaucracy, the emperor provided for the material needs of his court and those of the entire metropolitan center with tribute rice from the Shanghai district (Morse, 1910–18: vol. II, p. 362) through his monopoly on the realm's biggest transport system, the Grand Canal, and additionally through his monopolies on the salt tax and (after 1858) on foreign trade. The monetary, grain, and manpower needs of the provinces were supplied locally, and although these resources were said to be granted for local use by the emperor, they were in fact beyond his reach. His financial department drew up a nominal budget allocating these resources, ritual conformity to which constituted "serving the imperial will." The fiscal policies of the provinces were actually autonomous, except for deference to the emperor's ritual budget. The emperor stood at the apex of the governmental hierarchy in Peking, but this implied liturgical rather than operational powers. A nineteenth-century observer of Chinese imperial government wrote:

> The central government of China, so far as a system of this nature is recognized in the existing institutions, is arranged with the object rather of registering and checking the action of various provincial administrations, than with assuming a direct initiative in the conduct of affairs . . . Regulations, indeed, of the most minute and comprehensive character, are on record for the guidance of every conceivable act of administration; and the pricipal function of the Central Government consists in watching over the execution of this system of rules. (Mayers, 1897:12)

That the emperor's role was limited to the criticism of, and not control over, provincial administration was evident in the fact that no centralized treasury existed; revenue was collected in no common fiscus. The financial department merely recorded transactions in detail and specified categories of expenditure (Morse, 1908–10: vol. I, p. 28; Brinkley, 1902: vol. X, p. 94).

The remaining attributes reserved for central government were to distribute literary degrees as rewards for proficiency in the moral classics on which the polity of the empire was based, and to bestow higher appointments in the civil and military services. The emperor was empowered at all times to remove from his post any official whose conduct was found irregular or dangerous to the state. The grounds for dismissal, significantly, were chiefly those of ritual insubordination. It was disrespectful, for example, to take an imperial order as the starting point for a dialogue of information and reply. Any feedback by an official had to be couched in the apologetic language of confession to misdeeds. Loyal subordinates received imperial messages in uncritical silence; even to discuss them with colleagues was regarded as conspiratorial as was membership in a secret society. Loyalty was measured by fidelity to ritual forms because inconography, not money and manpower, was the only thing the emperor could control at a distance; it was his only political resource.

From this dependency on ritual forms derives the importance of the calendar—as a measured parade of civil and religious observances in the politics of culturalism. The court calendar, or Red Book, was published in four large volumes every three months (Barrow, 1805:272). Court ritual dictated official ritual. Out in the provinces, officials received each imperial dispatch by placing it on an altar in a special room decorated in imperial yellow, burnt incense before it, and kowtowed as if in the presence of the emperor himself. The kowtow *(k'ou-t'ou)* was a form of abasement in which the subordinate fell to his knees three times and at each bow touched his forehead to the floor three times, for a total of "three bows and nine knockings." Every official would have done this in the throne room at least once when he received his appointment to office, in tune with the solemn music of the court musicians playing *lung ping,* "A Splendid Humiliation" (Kidd, 1841:237). Ritual deference as highlighted by prostration is the corollary of low political commitment on the part of the official; likewise, symbolic deference exacted by the emperor is the corollary of low political resources available to him, which makes him unable to command power over substantive things.

From an economic viewpoint, central government was but a unit of local administration for the metropolitan area of the capital city, with its own source of supply derived from the grain tribute, the salt tax, and the monopoly on foreign trade. These resources financed Peking as a cultural center, which is what made it a political center. One fact that made the center the most glorious spot on earth was the location there of fully ninety percent of all officials in the imperial bureaucracy, all those attached to central government. The Red Book for 1852 shows that out of a total of 20,327 names listed in it, fewer than 2,000 in office above the rank of assistant district magistrate were posted in the eighteen provinces of China proper (Williams, 1895: vol. I, p. 438). Significantly, as many as 1,500 of the total were educational officials associated with the civil service examination system. This concentration of scholar-officials at the *axis mundi*, more than anything else, gave the Center its sanctity, in addition to all the other cultural splendors of the court, with its adepts in astronomy, historiography, ritual, gastronomy, the fine arts, and so on. This concentrated cultural power of the Center enabled it to radiate influence far beyond the few officials sent out to the provinces, for this was merely paradigmatic for a wider range of influence exerted by the 1.5 million educated gentlemen who constituted informal government, the real power in the countryside.

Yet Western observers have insisted on seeing in the Chinese imperial polity some version of substantive administration familiar to them in their own national governments, not believing that power persons could shape a political realm of continental scope out of materials as unpromising as religion and high culture. This picture, abetted by Confucian double-talk about governmental accountability, may be diagrammed as follows:

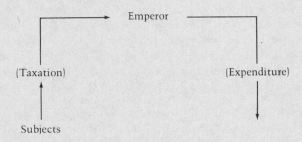

This fictional flowchart of empire suggests that services are rendered by public officials in exchange for tax monies collected in the name of the public good. The actual benefits received by the subjects were moral instruction in return for profiteering. A realistic flowchart of the Chinese pseudomorph would look more like the following, in which the solid lines represent substantive benefits and the broken lines represent unsubstantial gains.

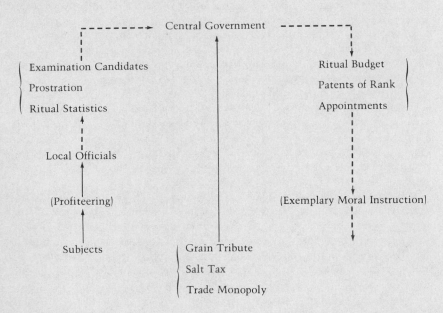

In exchange for the opportunity to get rich in the name of collecting imperial taxes, local officials had to satisfy Peking with only three things, none of them economically significant: (1) prostrating themselves before all messages received from the emperor, (2) keeping ritual statistics in conformity with the emperor's ritual budget, and (3) forwarding candidates to the metropolitan and palace examinations held every three years in the capital. This last obligation was vital to securing loyal recruits to the ongoing values of a cosmological empire. It was important that candidates for the highest degree awarded in the examination system, and thus the most worthy exemplars of the morality transmitted by the classics, should, like all official appointees, pass through the Center and there come in personal touch with imperial splendor—the imposing palace architecture and monumental art, the bustle of official life at its busiest, and the universal attendance on the court.

Scholars who competed in the district and provincial examinations nonetheless received their degrees from literary chancellors deputed from Peking. In the 1880s, 1.5 million men educated in the Confucian classics held imperial patents of rank of one degree or another. Only a few of these were appointed to office; the remainder, scholars of the realm living at home, constituted the local gentry who did the work of informal government in the countryside and in the towns. The patents of rank held by these Confucian gentlemen licensed them to conduct affairs in their home communities by giving official recognition to their self-educated qualifications: their literacy and managerial experience. Because local officials were transient outsiders, they had to rely on the local gentry if they were to bring in the tax revenues to support their own posts and for their own profit (Chang, 1955). The district magistrate had at his disposal a number of bailiffs drawn from the local garrison (Barrow, 1805:274), but in the end he was dependent on the cooperation of certain local gentry, with whom he split the proceeds (Fairbank *et al.*, 1965:110). The gentry, as permanent fixtures of dignity in the countryside, possessed both the necessary knowledge about real estate holdings and the power of noncoercive influence. This latter fact stemmed from an equation of interests with the peasantry, insofar as gentlemen patronized tenants, sheltered others from taxation for a smaller fee, settled disputes without punishment away from the magistrate's court, supervised the digging of irrigation ditches for peasant clients, and organized defense against bandits and rebels.

But again, the interests of the local gentry also equated with those of local officials, and this was preordained in the desire of both parties to glamorize their exploitative activities with the glories associated with a royal mission. Both scholar-officials and scholar-landlords were legalized members of the ruling class by virtue of their academic degrees. They thus voluntarily shared in the collective goals of culturalism, by which they found honor and dignity within an empire-wide system of ranking and stratification sanctified by the Dragon Throne.

The Chinese pseudomorph, however, was destroyed by contact with the West. A superficially centralized state held together only by the insubstantial psychology of culturalism was broken apart by the weight of substantial economic consequences attending the import of foreign technology. During the T'ai-p'ing Rebellion, regional forces in the effected areas met the threat by building up a modernized military industry paid for out of *likin*, local transit taxes instituted in 1838 on the increased shipment of goods flowing out the treaty ports. In the postrebellion era, *likin* spread farther, province by province. Peking's economic power had been strengthened by revenues for the maritime customs, instituted in 1858; but this was more than counterbalanced by the new arsenals and industries developed in provincial centers (Fairbank *et al.*, 1965:326, 352). The weighty pull of these regional projects of modernization carried out by leading officials and gentry finally broke the frail threads of cultural ties to the Center of a cosmological empire, whose unity by way of sacred geography no longer prevailed over the disunities of economic geography. The topocosmic Center could no longer dominate an imperium whose Neolithic landscape was beginning to offer the enlarged profit of diversified material opportunities. And in 1911, the monarchy fell.

The mystique of the Center lost even more influence in the postimperial era. Local appointments to government were no longer subject to the rule of avoidance, which forbad a man to hold office in his native province. The old law had the effect of congregating aspirants for office at Peking, where they came seeking posts as well as success in the examinations for the two highest literary degrees (Williams, 1895: vol. I, p. 448). For this privilege of touching ground at the *axis mundi* they paid heavy bribes to a whole series of gatekeepers (as noted earlier), from which the Center derived not a little income.

SUBJECTS

Feng Yu-hsiang, one of the great warlords and later a nationalist general, recalled in his autobiography what government meant in his childhood:

> The people, except for paying their taxes, had nothing to do with government. The government never paid any attention to the conditons under which people lived, and the people never bothered themselves about what the government was doing. One party collected the taxes; the other paid them. . . . No discussions of politics were heard. . . . All the big changes seem to have taken place in another world, and very seldom affected this place.
>
> When the government was about to collect taxes, the Li Chang [a village headman] would ring a gong from one end of the village to the other, shouting: "Pay your taxes! Four hundred and sixty coins to the mou [about one-third of an acre] for the first harvest!"
>
> When the people heard the gong, they did not go and pay their taxes immediately. . . . They would wait until the very last minute, until they could not put it off any more, and then go, group by group, to the city to hand in money they had earned by sweat and blood. (in Linebarger, 1943:104)

Government in dynastic China meant confiscatory taxation. It had the same meaning in the postimperial era, too, but with the difference that the founders and leaders of Republican China redefined the spoils system as corruption, in view of the Enlightenment ideals of public service, which they accepted from the West. Toward the end of the dynasty, the court had already employed Western administrators to supervise the Maritime Customs Service and the salt monopoly to police the collection of royalties for repaying foreign loans. The alternative to professionalism was foreign receivership in finance. Accordingly, the framers of the republican constitution redefined subjects as citizens and repudiated the formula by which officials squeezed the people to provide for themselves and contribute toward the expenses of their superiors. The formula was: "Big fish eat little fish, little fish eat shrimps, and shrimps eat mud" (Cornaby, 1895:18). It is no criticism of republican idealists to say that the formula persisted in practice and that former commoners remained subjects in fact. The heritage of the past, although acknowledged by Western-educated intellectuals and politicans as a source of weakness, was not to be swept away overnight by adopting a flag and a constitution.

Actually, the Ta Ch'ing, or Celestial Empire, as an archaic state-idea officially came to an end on 24 July 1901, with the creation of the Wai Wu Pu, or Ministry of Foreign Affairs. After the failure of the Boxer Rebellion to drive foreigners from the land, the conception of the Chinese state as coextensive with the civilized universe gave place to an idea of China as one of the many countries of the world. Foreign nations were thus put on a level of political equality without any hope of assimilating them (T'ang, 1928:67), although a strong sense of Chinese moral superiority remained.

However, the final collapse of the monarchy was in no way a response to the cries of an oppressed peasantry. Sun Yat-sen, the father of the Chinese revolution, coined the slogan "Land to the tiller," but in truth this was merely a sentimental idea he picked up from foreign books and had absolutely nothing to do with the actual making of the revolution. Real trouble for the peasantry began *after* the revolution, when gentry desertions had proceeded far enough to create a power vacuum in the countryside, which was filled by warlords and later by an expansion of formal government. At the same time, increased opportunities for banditry and Communist insurgents caused even more dislocations of the rural gentry.

The revolution was an antidynastic movement comprising the grievances of intellectuals, officials, and professional military men. In brief, this led to the following sequence of events. Sun Yat-sen, the man with the new political ideas, became president of the provisional republican government in January of 1912, drawing support from central and southern China. He was followed in that office after one month by the man holding military power in the north, Yuan Shih-k'ai. As one of the shapers of China's modern military establishment, the *Hsin-chun*, or New Army, Yuan was able to establish centralized controls with military support. Upon his death in 1916, however, his lieutenants founded independent provincial governments that lasted until 1928, the period of warlordism. The whole period between the revolution and 1928 is known as the First Republic. In 1928, Chiang K'ai-shek united the warlords under the Nationalist government seated at Nanking, whose ruling party was the KMT, founded by Sun Yat-sen. It was this government, the Second Republic, that the Communist insurgents warred upon from 1928 until 1936, at which time the Japanese invaded from their colony in Manchuria, held since 1932. The Japanese invasion eventually merged with World War II. When World War II ended in 1945, the civil war resumed and the Communists defeated the nationalist government in 1949, which then removed to the island of Formosa, where it still rules under the KMT flag as the Republic of China (for a history of this time, *see* Fairbank, 1971).

But in prerevolutionary China, a new state-idea was already brewing among the elite for some time before the monarchy's fall. This evolved in response to the failure of the Ch'ing court to cope with Westerners and with modernized Japan. Chinese scholars and officials had always resented the Manchu conquest of their country. That the top posts had gone to Manchu nobles still rankled; but only when the dynasty exposed China's weakness to the outside world did the Han Chinese begin to develop a national consciousness that called for national regeneration and a new form of government—without Manchus.

To begin with, it was clear to everybody that the Manchu dynasty, far from being able to protect itself from the forceful intrusion of Western colonists, was unable to defend itself against even a native rebellion without the help of these same Westerners. At the start of the T'ai-p'ing Rebellion (1850–64), the Manchu throne had in its pay 300,000 bannermen armed with pike, bow, and sword. Half these troops were stationed in Chihli province to guard the metropolitan capital. A part remained in the Manchurian homeland. The remainder were divided among small garrisons in the provincial capitals. All these troops (not to mention unposted Manchu noblemen living off taxes collected by Chinese officials) held their positions and drew their pay by right of conquest. In addition to the bannermen were the native armies of the Green Standard, which numbered 600,000 Chinese soldiers on paper, half that in reality, the difference in pay pocketed by their commanders.

To meet the rebels, the Manchu court was reduced to the humiliation of securing drill instruction and field leadership from Westerners, who also supplied modern arms. The foreign powers extended this help with the idea of protecting a government deeply in debt to them for loans of money required to pay the growing costs of administration incurred by culture contact in the first place. This help was given, however, not to the traditional armies but to new regional armies compounded from militiamen raised by the local gentry. These were the regional armies of Hunan and Anhwei provinces, organized, supplied, and commanded by Tseng Kuo-fan and Li Hung-chang, respectively, who had been called to this task by the two provincial governors on orders from the court. In customary fashion, Tseng and Li, who at the time had been officials employed in the Han-lin academy of learning in Peking, played the traditional role of amateur worthies who could turn from scholarly to military pursuits. And it was they who defeated the rebels.

But in their victory they enlarged the industrial base of their armies to such an extent that the court perceived a threat to the Center in regional autonomy united with material strength greater than its own. Accordingly, in 1904, the Ch'ing house proceeded to provide itself with a modern army under the Commission for Army Reorganization, which established military schools in almost all provinces. But students were drawn from the same families of rural gentry and rich merchants who had entered the examination system and become officials. On this basis they represented the outlook of the literate Chinese minority, which increasingly diverged from that of their Manchu rulers.

After the first China–Japanese War (1894–95), the Manchu rulers realized that the throne was too weak to refuse any concessions whatsoever to foreigners. This was the nadir of a downward trend started by the Opium War (1839–42), provoked by Great Britain as a means of forcing

China to grant commercial concessions and to recognize the principle of extrality. The Treaty of Shimonoseki of 1895, which concluded the war with Japan over control of Korea, ended with Korea neutralized, Formosa, the Liaotung Peninsula, and the Pescadores ceded to Japan, and the payment of a large indemnity (Morse, 1910–18: vol. III, p. 45).

Before 1895, only 15 newspapers existed in China. After the damaging treaty of that year, the number grew to 170, an upsurge reflecting the growing interest of the literati in political affairs as seen from a nationalistic perspective (Hatano, 1968:367, n. 3), or rather, from the viewpoint of Chinese subjects as against their dynastic rulers. Nationalism amounted to the racism of Han versus Manchu. The feelings were mutual. It was Prince Ch'un who said, at about the time he placed his infant son on the throne in 1875, that he would rather give away territory to foreigners than to Chinese. In fact, by 1894, the Ch'ing house had already given the colonial powers its claims over the vassal states of Liuchiu, Siam, Burma, Annam, and part of Sinkiang. The Manchus, after all, were indebted to Westerners for administrative loans. Thus, anti-Manchuism combined among the Han Chinese with an antiforeignism that broke out violently with the Boxer Rebellion (1898–1900) in those provinces where foreigners were most prominent: Chihli, Shanshi, Shantung, and Manchuria. The siege of the Peking legations at that time was secretly encouraged by the court in the vain hope of getting rid of its debts by getting rid of the foreigners, and thus reducing Chinese hostility to itself. The result was the occupation of Peking by foreign troops.

By this time, the court finally realized that it had to reform and adopt a policy of modernization or be overthrown by the Han Chinese, who had insisted on this alternative as a consequence of the China–Japanese War. Japan had absorbed Western learning, had adopted a constitution, had remodelled her army on modern lines; and China had only to do the same (Morse, 1910–18: vol. III, p. 434).

The manner in which modernization was undertaken by the court would have destroyed the power of Chinese officials and the local gentry, but in fact they made the changes their own and destroyed the dynasty. This struggle took place completely above the heads of peasant subjects, although the cost of modernization was theirs to bear. For example, new taxes were collected to support schools they were not disposed to attend.

In 1905, the court abolished the examination system, thus nullifying at a stroke the legal basis for privilege among the Han elite. To increase the effectiveness of central government in carrying out constitutional reforms, the Board of Revenue in the previous year had demanded strict fiscal accountability at the provincial level. Ritual statistics were to become real statistics and embezzlement prohibited. This would have put an end to the autonomy of local government and its equation of interests with local gentry. The resulting contest between Chinese vested interests in decentralization and the Manchu push for centralization was finally resolved in 1911 by revolution. This occurred in the capital city of Hupei province, Wuchang, on the tenth day of the tenth month, when the army attacked the yamen of the Manchu governor general, who fled with his commander, followed by a declaration of independence by other central and southern provinces. Thereafter, the "double tenth" was celebrated as a national holiday under the republic.

The army had revolted, but this was not the army of old—neither that of the bannermen nor of the Green Standard. It was the *Hsin-chun*, the New Army that came into being after 1906, with modern arms and German training. And because it was officered in great measure by the Han elite, the revolution in effect belonged to the Chinese gentry. Furthermore, it was supported by Chinese civilians who had argued the case for local self-government in the provincial assemblies that the Manchu throne had constituted for debating its proposed reforms.

The revolution was quick and bloodless because it attracted both conservative and progressive elements among the elite. The progressives, who believed in modernity, could take at face value the patriotic rhetoric about a corruption-free government with elected civil servants putting public monies to the public good, and the conservatives could find in the expanded service departments new opportunities for the old profiteering. In fact, both elements existed in the *Hsin-chun*.

Before the advent of the New Army, it had been said that good men were no more used for soldiers than good iron for nails. This did not apply after military service was put on a professional basis and when its career officers were drawn from the same class of men who formerly had entered officialdom as generalists to play civil or military roles, as the occasion demanded. Following the abolition of the examination system in 1905, a good many official-gentry, scholar-gentry, and merchant-gentry enrolled their sons in military schools in China or in Japan, looking to their offspring for a new route to family fame and fortune. Some gentlemen themselves enlisted in the *Hsin-chun* as soldiers, correctly anticipating that their literacy would bring them quick promotion to officer status (Hatano, 1968; Ichiko, 1968).

The postrevolutionary government of the First Republic was national in name only. Actually it was a mélange of regional military governments, its nominal center located in Peking to represent China as a political entity on the international scene. The Peking government was headed first by Yuan Shih-k'ai, followed by four other men in succession, all titled president of China.

The fact of warlordism behind this façade of republicanism is often viewed by facile humanists as a regression from the nationalistic ideals proclaimed by the revolution. We believe this to be a false conclusion because it reflexively dismisses from importance the role of the military in the modernizing process. The New Armies behind the regional governments of the warlord period were professionalized, politically indoctrinated, and led or advised by men who, in another guise, would have been recognized as the book-memorizing, newspaper-reading literati of old. As such they contributed to the nation-building process so far as it was possible, given the weak political resources of a country whose new state-idea of nationhood raced ahead of its means of realization in transportation, communications, and an informed citizenry. "Our native province governed by ourselves" was the slogan that fired the revolution; and the regional scope of the loyalties proclaimed thereby was surely in advance of those loyalties held by local officials—by Manchus in the higher ranks —once appointed as strangers from the outside and then quickly rotated out before they could establish vested interests.

Even the façade of the Peking government stood for something, however superficial. It collected revenues in the name of central government, although these were actually restricted to salt royalties, maritime duties, and the Peking octroi (taxes on commodities brought into a town), not to mention foreign loans (Arnold, 1926:280–99). But central government under the empire was supported in the same way. The difference is that the men who spoke for the republic dropped the double-talk of imperial government along with its nominal assertion over distant men and materials; instead, the new Peking officials spoke for centralization in plain language—as modern men disbelieving in the archaic game of culturalism—but discovered that the heritage of weak political resources did not allow them to carry it out in practice. Indeed, the Nanking government of the Second Republic made a virtue of its inability to exploit the interior and renounced the provincial land tax altogether. It then openly lived off the modern sector of the economy in the urban areas under its direct control, fifty percent of its revenue being derived from the maritime customs (Fairbank et al., 1965:700).

At the local level, however, things were materially different. The revolutionary slogans about self-government had taken effect from the start: The rule of avoidance no longer applied and the organs of local government were staffed by local men. In addition, many new service posts were established—in public education, military affairs, industry, agriculture, labor, and justice—with the provision that even men who were not heads of departments were counted as salaried members of government (T'ang, 1928:172). The image of the mandarin and his crew of unpaid underlings was as repulsive to the postrevolutionary leadership as to Western critics. Progressive officials would have accepted this unsympathetic picture of the district magistrate drawn by a missionary from central China toward the end of the dynasty:

> He must have his gorgeous chair with its four or more bearers, his red umbrellas of state, the bearers thereof, and his inevitable retinue of grown-up ragamuffins, hardly one of them paid by him. These too must live, partly from hush-money paid by their bosom friends, the burglars and blacklegs; principally upon their extortions in the autumn tax collecting. (Cornaby, 1895:17)

Not only did confiscatory taxation continue in modern dress; it increased rapaciously. Clothed no more in the costume of a royal mission to extend the glories of the empire, the traditional self-interest of the local officials now stood exposed as naked aggrandizement. Unrestrained by the polite rules of embezzlement that operated under culturalism, they took not twenty percent in squeeze but one hundred percent (Hanwell, 1937:48, 56).

The brakes of culturalism had slipped, not yet replaced by those of professionalism, although the concept was well advertised by 1935 with publication of a quarterly journal, *The Chinese Administrator* (T'ang, 1935:18). Causing this slippage were gentry desertions. These had already begun at the time of the revolution, leaving peasants in the countryside vulnerable to the expanded organs of formal government, whence some of the local gentry had in the first instance repaired. Traditionally, gentlemen landlords looked two ways—toward officialdom for privilege and toward the peasantry for their own constituency. For these squires, the psychology of culturalism rested with accepting as honorable the academic distinctions awarded them by the court in recognition of their local authority. This honor they reflected upward by preparing local gazetteers drawn from by court scholars in compiling dynastic history. Members of the rural gentry realized their elite status in performing before two audiences: their peers and "betters" in the world of letters and power, and their "inferiors," the unlettered, disadvantaged peasantry.

Under dynastic government, the rural elite enjoyed the extralegal privilege of paying only seventy to eighty percent of the legal tax rate on land; deserving households were marked in the magistrate's tax register as *kuan* (officials) or *ju* (scholars). Peasant owners suffered the negative privilege of paying two or three times the legal rate, owing to the squeeze system of the tax collectors (Ichiko, 1968:298; Hsiao, 1960:10). It is precisely that system against which gentlemen used their exemptions to protect their peasant clients. Some of the statistics on landlordism for late Ch'ing times are fictional, therefore, stemming from the fact that peasant owners in many instances would have their land registered for a private fee under the name of some landlord, who would then pay the reduced tax and pocket the difference (Jacobs, 1958: ch. 3). Even genuine tenants, like pretended ones, enjoyed immunity to the extortions of the magistrate's unpaid runners.

Because the increased cost of modernizing government away from the imperial pseudomorph toward professional administration was paid for by peasants in magnified taxes (legal and illegal), the revolution hurt peasants more than it did the gentry. In this respect, Chinese society remained as dichotomized as ever, open at the top by all the alternatives to manual labor and physical toil, closed by disadvantages at the bottom. The legal basis for this distinction no longer obtained, but a de facto elite continued to exist in the neogentry, who were able to draw on their heritage to claim fresh opportunities for expressing their influence under conditions of change; and a de facto body of commoners remained, as ever, a political resource unmobilized by the changing leadership (Chow, 1966; Jacobs, 1958: ch. 6).

Provincial government was staffed by men who were formerly classed as the upper gentry, possessors of higher degrees and government experience under the empire. Some of these evinced political concerns of national scope and economic affiliations with industry, commerce, and finance, not to mention the professions, the military, and education; all these opportunities lay open to them in Peking and in the treaty ports, many of which coincided with the great provincial centers. The gentlemen who took office at the prefectural, district, subdistrict, and village levels usually belonged to the lower gentry, men with the lowest academic degrees authenticating elite status under the old regime. They looked to local government in their capacities as town mayors and village headmen. For even the post of village headman was now an official one under the republican roster of local self-government. Under dynastic government, village headmen were appointed from among peasants by rural gentlemen to act as their runners in communication with the district magistrate, the lowest post in the prebendal hierarchy. Because gentlemen often outranked the magistrate, they did not wish to bow to a lesser man. They, too, were members of the ruling class, conducting the affairs of informal government. The new organs of republican government professionalized these affairs, including the post of village headman, to which both well-to-do peasants and lower gentry were attracted.

But in moving from informal government to formal government with an urban office, the local gentry for the first time appeared as agents of extortion; they were no longer interposed between officialdom and the peasantry but had become part of the apparatus. For the first time, peasants discontented with paying the excess cost of modernizing government, thrust on them by gentry desertions, were available as a political resource to be propagandized and mobilized as potential citizens of a nation-state. These were the discontents of transitional China on whom the communists capitalized, but in a "completely irresponsible fashion" (Scalapino, 1972:20), by acting on the claim that the problem was one of land concentration. In fact, Mao made no secret of his real intentions; as early as December 1947 he announced that land reform was no end itself but a means to collectivization and rural control (U.S. Department of State, 1948:31).

PEOPLE

Traditional China lacked both a professional bureaucracy and a professional military. Officials worked in the name of the emperor but not for him, and the imperium itself flew no flag; the little provincial armies of the realm flew banners inscribed with the names and titles of their officers. In 1836, the metropolitan government was forced to adopt a national flag for diplomatic purposes in dealing with the Western powers, but had not yet adopted a written constitution to be represented by that flag (Williams, 1895: vol. II, p. 752). A constitution on the Western model was drawn up for the government of the First Republic, but this underwrote no national sovereignty. Provincial autonomy still obtained, but at least the New Armies behind it were professional. It remained for the Communist regime to professionalize the bureaucracy as well. The flag of the PRC flys over a national entity that is centralized in name as well as in fact.

Only the literati of traditional China, in or out of office, were privileged to bear the transprovincial identity of being Chinese. The ruling class was unified in carrying the high culture of China's great tradition, the secret of its success in ruling with small numbers over the farmers, artisans, and petty merchants of the little tradition, who were divided by their parochial loyalties to village, marketing area, county, or province. After the revolution of 1911, the idea of nationality occurred among the political leadership groups of transitional China; but because these groups did not mobilize the mass of citizens to support this new state-idea, government remained regional in its claims.

The present-day regime calls on "the people" as a whole to participate in a political culture whose state-idea combines populism with totalitarianism. The breadth of participation is reflected in the makeup of the CCP. In 1957, the party numbered 12.7 million members, of which 66.8 percent were classed as peasants, 13.7 percent as workers, and 14.8 percent as intellectuals. This last category includes all educated persons from junior middle-school graduates through "higher intellectuals" comprised of college graduates, university faculty, doctors, engineers, editors, and the like (Wu, 1973:210). The political leadership must be counted among the intellectuals, deriving from the neogentry of republican times, although they are self-effacing about this (North, 1952). Their style of dressing at one with the people, in a plain national uniform, goes back to the regime's formative period, when it rose to power as an insurgent movement against the Japanese in occupied China. The leadership learned in the field that power and comfort were incompatible under conditions of guerrilla warfare and that the new road to power lay with adopting a false class-consciousness. Chou En-lai, premier of the PRC, recently said as much when he told a recent visitor that "we Communists are there to make everybody equal; and since we dress and live like the masses (almost) and have power, not wealth, we are not really a ruling class." (cited by Adie, 1975:11) The new political idea is founded on the mythos of equality, which asserts that material differences tend toward inequality, but that police powers used to *make* everybody equal economically do not. The substitution of political injustice for economic injustice is the fraudulent exchange at the heart of the equality mythos and the communist state-idea.

The mass of peasants' and workers' awareness of the new state-idea is enhanced by the appearance everywhere of personal images of national leaders such as Mao, and is sustained by means of propaganda communicated through a massive system of radio-listening groups, newspaper-reading groups, wall posters, comic books, films, and visiting cultural teams (Liu, 1971). But initially, the presence of the government made itself felt locally by means of terror. The political concept of "the people" was first driven home by the enactment of dramatic violence against its opposite, "enemies of the people." In a systematic sweep from north to south, people classified as landlords and counterrevolutionaries were put on public trial and often executed. Conservative estimates of the number killed during the first four years of land reform and counterrevolutionary campaigns run from fifteen to thirty million, not counting the eighteen to twenty-four million sent to forced-labor camps (Michael and Taylor, 1964:459; Walker, 1955: ch. 9).

To assert a political presence by staging accusation meetings and mass killings required a number of governmental agents far in excess of those in the service of the traditional pseudomorph. The agents in this case were millions of men and women styled *kan-pu*, or cadres, a type of political worker originating with the combat leaders of guerrilla warfare during the party's formative days. After some years as masters of China, the *kan-pu* came to occupy all formal leadership positions as state, military, medical, educational, administrative, commercial, agricultural, and industrial cadres (Wu, 1973:674–75). Not surprisingly, this swollen bureaucracy has tended to settle down into a neat hierarchy, each rank with its prerogatives in food, goods, and housing. Mao has watched with displeasure the old egalitarian spirit of his early revolutionary comrades fade away in the lives of these entrenched cadres. So, with the help of the army, he directed the Cultural Revolution (1966–69) against them, aiming to rerevolutionize the bureaucracy even if it meant creating conflict within the party itself (Barnett, 1967).

In 1958, the last year in which statistics about state employees were released, the number of party members in bureaucratic positions was given as 7.9 million. This figure accounted for state cadres only—those paid a salary by central government—excluding local cadres paid by a factory or some other local organization (Whitaker and Shinn, 1972:127; *see also* Schurmann, 1968:165). Even so, measured against a population of 600 million, the number of civil officials represents 1.3 percent of the total. Contrast this with the 1880s, when the official population numbered only 1/16,000 of the total population. The difference is a measure of the increase in political resources gained by the modern totalitarian state, compared with the traditional pseudomorph. Another difference is the percentage increase in state officers drawn from the available elite. In 1958, state cadres represented 60 percent of party membership, numbering 12 or 13 million. In the 1880s, the bureaucratic reservoir under imperial China consisted of 1.5 million degree-holding literati, of whom only 25,000, or 1.66 percent, held civil office (Sprenkel, 1962:75, n. 3). The summary below clearly shows a pyramiding of political resources. Modernization means more government and more to govern.

	1880s	*1958*
Population	400 Million	600 Million
Elite	1.5 Million (gentry de jure)	12–13 Million (CCP members)
Civil Officials	25,000	7.9 million (state cadres)
Official/Elite Ratio	1.66%	60%
Official/Population Ratio	0.000062%	1.3%

The increased ratio of officials to elites also means a change in the direction of job professionalization. The small number of imperial officials relative to the gentry as a whole reflected a high turnover of incumbents, except for the few old partriarchs who had direct access to the emperor. Dynastic officials were expected to use their short term to win prestige and wealth for their families, an arrangement favored by Confucian ideology. A bureaucratic career was embedded within the wider social and economic considerations of the official's kin group.

The career of the Communist official is not so embedded. He is at once the obedient tool of his superiors and also accountable to the public interest. In a selection of Mao's writings reprinted in his "little red book," the cadre is one who can: "Resolutely carry out the Party line, submit to Party discipline, be in close contact with the masses, have the ability to work independently, be willing to act 'positively,' and who does not seek private advantage" (tr. by Schurmann, 1968:164; *see* Mao, 1966:281). Unlike the traditional civil servant, the state cadre can be punished if he does not pay more attention to his duties than to his private interests. Communist ideology stresses not bureaucratic autonomy but commitment. It sets principles above privilege.

In this respect, however, the bureaucracy in Communist China is rather more politicized than professionalized. In fact, the state's political goals are more expensive than were those of imperial culturalism to achieve, and therefore the state must budget its tasks closely and deny to officeseekers an open field for graft. But the criteria for recruitment are far from professional, from the viewpoint of the Western administrator; they are strictly political.

Formerly a sponsor of social inequality, Chinese government is now the champion of equality—equality insofar as groups once excluded are now included. The present leadership speaks of democracy. By that it rightly adverts to wider participation. But this necessarily means that nonprofessional considerations must be applied in selecting cadres from a society still deficient in the educational means to bring technical competence to all possible recruits. In dynastic China, the scholar-official was nonprofessional in that he was a free agent of high culture, an amateur who depreciated specialization. Confucius said, "A gentleman is not a tool," one of the key sayings upholding prebendalism and the ideology of bureaucratic autonomy. Paradoxically, the cadre is nonprofessional though not antivocational, because he *is* a tool; he is hired for his selfless service and political loyalty. Like the scholar-officials of old, however, cadres require not administrative competence—a technical skill—but the quality of a personal virtue. Under Confucianism the virtue was one of the antivocational amateur; under communism it is the virtue of reliability. The difference is that the bureaucracy is now politicized, a necessary and revolutionary consequence of expanding it rapidly in a society of restricted literacy and limited managerial talent.

The ideological need to recruit men of political virtue as against the administrative need to recruit men of technical ability is phrased in the language of "Red versus expert." The phrase summarizes the problems that arise as the Chinese seek to bring into government persons of safe class origins despite the weakness of their professional and technical training and consequently of their poor administrative performance. By contrast, those who have expertise or the disposition for learning it are not "Red enough," because they come from educated or "bourgeois" families classed as enemies of the people (*see* Vogel, 1970). In an underdeveloped country such as China, job loyalty in government is a political resource in scarce supply because the masses, until this time, have been treated as distant subjects, not useful citizens. But job loyalty is a resource that can be supplied faster by way of indoctrination, coupled with the rewards of upward mobility, than can literacy and administrative skills be supplied by way of education.

The cadre holds an elevated position commanding more than noncoercive deference from politically irrelevant subjects, although the prestige of mental over manual labor that once dignified the gentlemen of the premodern ruling class has not yet been eliminated, despite efforts to downgrade it. The traditional basis for superiority of elite over majority—a pose of personal aloofness—persists as a subversive factor among a new elite obliged to exhibit concern for the people and accountability to the state. "If the badge of the old Chinese bureaucratic elite was a leisurely and cultivated air, the badge of the new is a full briefcase and an air of purposeful, energetic energy" (Human Relations Area Files, 1956: East China, vol. I, p. 229).

NINE

KINSHIP

CLAN

We have seen that the weak political goals of the Chinese pseudomorph, correlated with the absence of bureaucratic professionalization, which in turn meant no strict separation between public and private income. Consequently, office was taken as an emolument of privilege to be numbered among other resources held by wealthy and influential families. To fulfill the duties of office presupposed the environmental advantages of a private education undertaken by a birth elite; given the low importance of the free professions, there existed no public school system whose responsibility was vocational or professional training. As the nature of official duties was generalist rather than specialist, education for office was marked by the same Confucian training in moral culture that was suitable for sustaining the ethics of family life. Confucian learning thus provided an ideology at once upholding the career morality of bureaucratic autonomy and the domestic morality of self-help by a body of kinsmen who absorbed the benefits of government service as another of their corporate assets. In none of the sacred books of Confucianism are the politics of government coupled with the politics of kinship more expressly than in the *Hsiao Ching*, or the *Classic of Filial Piety*.

The *Hsiao Ching* was composed during the first century B.C. by Han mythologers who ascribed it to Tseng Shen, a pupil of Confucius. These were the opening years of the second aristocracy, following the failure of the Ch'in dynasty to defeat finally the feudal aristocracy that comprised the multistate system of the Chou dynasty. As a result, great families reasserted themselves in manorial estates if not in political states, a difference of definition imposed by the throne. Beginning with the Han dynasty, the emperor presided over a realm that was only partly under the control of appointed officials; the remainder was in the hands of landed magnates. As had the feudal states of preimperial times, the great families kept genealogical registers, a recognized historical genre that had long placed royalty in a supervisory position by way of guarding its own superior lineage. This is an aspect of culturalism that may go all the way back to Shang times (*see* Wheatley, 1971:52–61). The Han emperor maintained a genealogical bureau at court, which evaluated the pedigrees of the great families from which officials were drawn. Its archives were also a source of reference material, including the biographies of eminent clansmen, useful for writing dynastic history (Meskill, 1970:144–45).

From the start, the Han emperors were patrons of Confucianism. They appreciated its stress on the importance of a hereditary sovereign served by a nonhereditary class of disinterested officials unconnected with the ruler's clan court. Confucius named members of this class *chun-tze*, descendants of the ruler, although this meant gentlemen educated to nobility, not born to it. The emperor himself used the vocabulary of pre-Confucian politics to describe himself as a family head presiding over his nation-family, or *kwo-chia*, a designation for the realm once used by the Chou kings. The Chou kings used this designation in recognition of the historical fact that the founders of their line had fathered the Chou feudatories. Each of the feudatories conducted the business of state in his *kwo* as a family business, the place of business being the ruling clan's ancestral hall. The ancestral ceremonies of the Chou regent were carried out with the implication that the royal court stood over clan courts of the ducal states as the family of families.

In the end, the kinship ties that originally bound the local courts to the Center were no bar to interstate conflict, which came to a climax with the conquest of empire by Ch'in. The First Emperor then put into motion the basic rule of imperial politics—a monopoly by the royal house on hereditary privilege, all other aristocratic houses not to be tolerated without a struggle to diminish them to nothing. They were not finally abolished, however, until after Sung times, although the Chinese emperor continued to designate the realm as a *kwo-chia* and himself its family head. By the Sung dynasty, the size of the great estates had been reduced by centuries of patrimonial subdivision, territorial expansion into southern China notwithstanding.

Similarly, the aristocracy of education that had replaced the aristocracy of birth continued to keep genealogical records, complete with biographical and honorific material, family and clan traditions, and local news. Furthermore, selections from these records still contributed to the writing of dynastic history. The educated elite could therefore enjoy a sense of continuity with the pedigreed estates of the second aristocracy and even with the *kwo* existing at the time of Confucius. The families of the elite, after all, were asset-holding bodies organized like miniature states to obtain, hold, and exercise political influence in formal or informal government. Therefore, they continued to find relevance in the *Hsiao Ching*, which gave ideological force to the compact made by the great families of the Han dynasty with the throne: We will use our family resources above all to educate our men to political influence, not breed them to it by way of competing with the royal house. The stress is on educated merit, whatever the family advantages that contribute to its cultivation.

In this way, the *Classic of Filial Piety* underscored the job morality propounded by Confucius for officials in preimperial times, even though it was written a little over 400 years after his death and to fit the needs of empire. In training men to serve the ducal powers of the day, but doing so without becoming personally involved in the clan politics of the ducal court, Confucius anticipated the basic premise of imperial politics. Officials down until the Ch'ing dynasty served the emperor in the same way; they worked in his name, not for him as would his kinsmen. Only the emperor's clansmen, the hereditary nobility, shared his concern for the court and its function, which was to provide cultural illumination for the nonhereditary elite, including patronage of the doctrine that supported this arrangement.

Until the abolition of the examination system in 1905 A.D., the Chinese official could still find relevance in these words of the *Hsiao Ching*, written in about 50 B.C., almost two thousand years earlier: "To acquire for oneself a station in the world and be made famous, one should regulate one's conduct by correct principles, thereby glorifying one's father and mother and transmitting their name to future generations: this is the last word in filial piety." (*Hsiao Ching*, I) The official could interpret this to mean that a position with the imperial bureaucracy would win him "a station in the world" because all elite persons of the realm accepted the emperor's patents of rank and title as honorable. Elite status was by definition validated by academic degrees and enhanced by appointments. Therein lay the legal basis of culturalism. To "regulate one's conduct by right principles" can be taken to mean that the official must limit his participation in the royal cause to the glories of being "made famous" and must not trespass on the prerogative of the royal house. In other words, he may enjoy the privileges that obtain from the mystique of rank as conferred by the emperor but he may not compete with the emperor's harem-produced swarm of princes for the ultimate privilege of generating that mystique. That would mean setting up a rival court or, equally threatening, a professionalized bureaucracy that would reduce the emperor to a first among equals. Officials may participate in the imperial *cause*—the emperor's China-wide system of ranks and titles—but they may not trespass on the imperial *court*.

Officials were to find their distinction in office, not in a vocation. Hence the emperor supported an ideology that limited the professionalism of an official career by stressing, with the *Hsiao Ching*, the propriety of its being embedded in the wider social and economic context of the man's family. Self-aggrandizement in office, so long as it did not exceed the conventional limit on "squeeze," was a sign that officials kept a healthy distance from the prerogatives of the royal house.

The emperor's cultural leadership was well served if politically active men of the realm were content to redirect homeward the ambition that had caused them to compete for the distinctions of academic rank that were the emperor's to bestow, the wealth to be gained from an official hunting license that was his to distribute, and the courtly ritual that was his everlasting glory to be imitated in domestic ritual.

The most important pattern of court ritual reproduced at home was ancestor worship. The emperor not only worshipped Heaven in the name of the realm, he also worshipped his agnatic ancestors (paternal kinsmen) in the name of the royal clan. The ritual refinements of these proceedings set the cultural standards for the nonhereditary elite. But the objects of worship were mutually exclusive. Just as it would have been a treasonable offense for anyone other than the emperor to worship Heaven, so it was not fitting for anyone to usurp another's family rites (see Chapter Two). The emperor's cultural leadership reached its supreme expression in ancestor worship; it was the basis for designating his government as a government of filial piety and his realm as a great *kwo-chia,* or nation-family. Indeed, the success of the emperor's liturgical leadership depended on his encouragement of kin groups as interest groups.

Thus gentlemen of the realm shared in the translocal culture of the great tradition as this was highlighted in the royal cause, yet they stood apart from the royal court just as men of the little tradition stood apart in their parochial folk culture from both cause *and* court. As the *Li Chi* says in another early Han compilation attributed to Confucius:

> *People imitate the ruler, and they have their self-government. They nourish the ruler and so find their security; they serve the ruler and so find their distinction. Thus it is by the universal application of propriety and the rules of right behavior that the lots of different classes are fixed. (Li Yun, II:15)*

For the "lots of different classes" any Confucian scholar could specify at least four strata within the overarching dichotomy of elite and majority: (1) the hereditary elite of royalty and nobility at court, the source of all "distinctions," (2) the nonhereditary elite, embracing officials who found appointments honorable, (3) local gentry who, finding their academic degrees honorable, either aspired to office or to leadership in the informal government of their home communities, and (4) the nonelite, commoners excluded from high culture and the honors of the imperial cause altogether. Note, however, that to make certain that officials would not form a professional interest group with the potential for combining against the emperor, he practiced the tactic of divide and rule by admitting a certain number of commoners to the examinations and deliberately appointing some of them as supervisors over men of gentry birth (Chang, 1955).

The suspicion that gentlemen could form an interest group on the basis of their privilege was voiced in words of warning issued by the founding emperor of the Ch'ing dynasty against the *sheng-yuan,* members of the lower gentry who held the lowest academic degree legalizing elite status:

> *A* Sheng-yuan *should not present written discourses on the welfare or ills of military or civil affairs . . .* [nor should he] *. . . collect groups of people to establish alliances or form societies. . . .* [In addition,] *. . . a* Sheng-yuan *should not seek advancement through entreating officials or by making friends with powerful personages. If he has truly a good heart and flawless virtue, Heaven will recognize him and reward him with blessing.* (Chang, 1955:199)

The virtue in question, of course, is filial piety, which the emperor stressed by example in his own ritual of ancestor worship in order to refocus the political significance of literary attainments on the family as a localized interest group.

An edict of the K'ang Hsi emperor in 1729, to be read to all successful graduates of the palace examination (and thus men assured of receiving appointments), again stressed the point of ancestor worship: "Good conduct counts first, and literary attainment comes next. . . . Through these triennial examinations held by the government are accorded distinctions of 'robes of silk' and 'bows and flags,' by which not only you yourselves are honored but also your grandfathers and fathers share in the glory" (in Chang, 1955:200).

Congruent with the familistic policy of the emperor's government by filial piety was the fact that the family was actually an important institution by default: In the absence of other helping institutions, it functioned rather as a bastion of self-help. Chinese familism thus was rooted in economic and political necessity and was not merely the product of a sentimental regard for kinship per se, as alienated Westerners homesick for sodality often suppose. Thus, when the emperor sent officials home for long periods of mourning upon the death of a parent, or when he recommended that retired officials wear their official robes at family weddings, funerals, and ancestral sacrifices, he merely encouraged a preexisting reliance on familistic self-help. Without the added increment of ambition to do otherwise, power persons were inclined to rally their imperial distinctions around the family and to make their kinship group the basis for local influence by acting as territorial magnates. This was possible because, in a cosmological empire in which ninety percent of all officials were concentrated at the *axis mundi*, the immense countryside making up the rest of the realm was only thinly posted with agents of formal government. It was this concentration at the Center, however, that gave the politics of culturalism its force. Territorial magnates in de facto control of the countryside were so impressed with imperial distinctions that they were persuaded to take on a surcharge of dignity from a distant court rather than establish regional courts or baronies of their own.

The life cycle of the traditional magnates began with the wealth of a retired official invested in land and headquartered in a county seat with the usual sign of local rank and influence: big-family organization. On the decease of the founders or heads of such families, it was considered dignified for the sons to live together, sharing rents, profits, and political contacts in common. This was sometimes continued for several generations if the family was able to hold together against temptations to divide its property among member units, until the country seat became an agglomeration of households constituting an extended family or even a *tzu*, or localized lineage. A family or lineage of this sort, with literary traditions and political experience and the wealth and leisure to educate the young men with private tutors, was constantly sending its scions through the examination system. Those who won appointments returned their earnings to swell the common fund, while their distinctions enhanced the importance and standing of the group as a whole.

The family's property in land and other business assets, its political influence in the form of men in office or retired officials, and its local role in the affairs of informal government together acted as a magnet pulling the agglomeration of whatever size together. The opposite force was generated if the diplomatic workings of domestic ritual failed to prevent divisive quarrels.

The Chinese word for family is *chia*, but this may refer to a nuclear family or to an extended family. The component units of an extended family are designated as *fang*, or branches. Each *fang* of the large-family estate dwelt in its own quarters as a separate household with its own kitchen and kitchen god. The quarters may have consisted of an apartment within a larger building or a separate house within a walled compound. The estate

as a whole shared a common purse controlled by the *chia-chang,* or family
head, in consultation with the older sons. Large and wealthy families required so much managerial expertise that the titular head sometimes
assigned the real task to another who was more competent. This arrangement resembled a business corporation guided by its chairman of
the board.

The symbol of managerial unity for the extended family was its ancestral shrine, which was handed down in the charge of the eldest son and
may have occupied a separate temple building. Here the tablets of the deceased males and their wives for four generations were ranked on the ancestral altar by generation and age, and were worshipped collectively on
the major annual festivals and individually on their death dates. Routine
tendance was accorded them with daily incense and food offerings the first
and the fifteenth day of every lunar month. The same unit whose symbolic
locus of unity was the shrine also kept a *chia-p'u,* or genealogical record,
listing birth and death dates, spouses' names, academic degrees, offices if
any, with additional sections for biographies and honorific materials such
as poems and calligraphy by eminent members. Academic degrees and
other imperial honors hung in the ancestral shrine at home or in the ancestral hall belonging to a lineage or even a clan (Freedman, 1970).

The lineage brought a number of single or multifamily units together
into a single organization, but it held no common purse. It did, however,
possess temple lands whose proceeds were used to build and support a
lineage temple, defray the expenses of ancestral rituals, pay for court litigations involving members, assist young members in attaining an education, help orphaned, indigent, and elderly members, and provide burial
space for the dead. Duplicated in the hall of the lineage temple (and in the
branch halls of the big lineages) was a set of the ancestral tablets located
in shrines of the domestic cult. The duplicate sets were worshipped
collectively, never individually, and they did not include the tablets of
deceased wives.

Whereas the domestic shrine stood for the welfare of the *chia* and its
complete household, the hall stood for the economic and political ends
pursued by its male membership alone. The genealogical records, or
tsu-p'u, of lineages were often adjusted to accommodate men who wished
to share in the advantages of the lineage although they could not in fact
demonstrate descent in the lineage of their choice. Genealogical manipulation was a legitimate strategy when only the emperor himself was permitted to head up a political organization, that of the empire itself. As elites
of the realm drew their legal status from him, they voluntarily observed
the rules of the game that required all other political activity to seek the
cover of a kinship organization. Even secret societies given to antigovern-
mental activity were ostensibly kinship groupings, although the "brotherhood" that bound the members was patently fictitious.

Lineages were most common in the more productive rice region of
South China and in the commercially active region of the southeastern
coast, as well as in the area around Canton. It took more economic resources to build viable lineages than were available in the less productive
wheat region of the north. Lineage organization thus coincided with areas
of high rates of tenancy, and sometimes poor-relative tenants were the
preferred clients of landlord members—but not as frequently as one might

suppose. It was precisely in areas of high tenancy, caused by imbalance in the man/land ratio, that lineages did not have to rely on poor members because the population pressure supplied more than enough willing hands; moreover, the leadership was spared the nuisance of having to cope with claims for favored treatment based on kinship (Moore, 1966:168). Poor members, however, were enlisted nominally to swell the genealogical registers, a matter of competitive pride among lineages. Ordinary lineage members were made visible when they were invited to attend outdoor feasts held at the ancestral tombs, but never to sit with the grandees in the ancestral hall. Voting members who worshipped and deliberated in the hall had to be propertied owners who contributed plots to the fund of temple land (Hu, 1948). Poor members were taken on as tenants only where manpower was scarce, as in frontier areas, or in areas endangered by hostile aborigines where fighting men were needed for a private militia, or in areas where lineages were in contention with each other (Potter, 1970).

In other cases, lineages cut across class lines only if the grandees found it profitable to set up a school for all members, supported by temple land, for the purpose of casting as wide a net as possible to seek scholastic talent. Bright, young peasant lads could then be identified and groomed for the civil service examinations, to the benefit of the lineage as a whole, but especially to its leadership in repayment of a debt incurred. Ordinarily, though, lineage membership did not extend across class lines (Potter, 1970:128). We must not be misled by the multivolumed works of genealogy compiled by very wealthy families, in which everybody for miles around having the same family surname was included in what amounted to the register of a nonlocalized clan. These genealogies were not charters for large groups embarked on joint action but merely ornamental works of filial piety, published by the scholastic member of some influential family for historical prestige (Meskill, 1970:158).

These registers were simply large editions of the smaller records kept by each extended family, which were just as inegalitarian. An individual's standing was determined by his genealogical status relative to the principal person from whom his descent was traced (Fried, 1957). Grandfather stood highest, granddaughter the lowest, in a highly formalistic institution in which each member had his place graded by age, sex, and generation. "This was not a family circle; it was a family pyramid" (Davies, 1972:46). As such it was organized to secure economic and political advantages for a select group defined by kinship (as were the feudal states of old), in which the privileged standing of the *chun-tze*—the ranked male descendants of the ducal ruler—was so defined. From the classical Confucian interpretation of the word *chun-tze*, "superior men" of the realm applied it to themselves as educated worthies privileged to seek office, write history, and keep genealogies.

FAMILY

The Legislative Yuan of the nationalist government at Nanking embodied a number of radical reforms in the family system with its Kinship Relations Law of 1930. Probably the most important feature of the law was its provision that men and women were equal with regard to property rights and inheritance. In accordance with this curtailment of patrilineality, no mention of ancestor worship was included. Neither did the new legislation mention concubinage—a practice of the elite for ensuring male heirs —since both sexes could inherit from the family estate, claiming their share as their own personal property on attaining majority at the age of twenty. In addition, the law made the consent of the parties concerned a requirement for marriage, shifting marriage from a contract between families to one between individuals (Valk, 1956).

These provisions grew out of a changing intellectual climate known as the "New Culture Movement." Although the overthrow of the monarchy in 1911 had been a political and not a social revolution, China's leading scholars, engaged in educating a new generation in Western subjects, promoted Western values and goals including a university education for women. A modern intelligentsia, inheriting the influence of the traditional literati, called for the ideological reconstruction of the new republic.

The New Culture Movement came to a climax in 1919 with the onset of a new current of modernity, the May Fourth Movement, swept along by an outpouring of anti-Japanese feeling that deepened xenophobia into patriotic outrage. Japan, during the latter half of the nineteenth century, officially committed herself to modernization and had succeeded in making herself over by the end of that century, at which time she joined the competition among Western nations to obtain extrality from China. In fact, she went further than their quest for trade and imposed the right to *produce*. With textile mills in Shanghai, Japan was the first nation to introduce factory industrialism in China (Hauser, 1940:89). When the Europeans began fighting among themselves at the outset of World War I in 1915, Japan pressed home her advantage with an ultimatum whose "twenty-one demands" would have turned China into a Japanese protectorate. The weak Peking government largely acceded to these demands, one of which permitted the Japanese takeover of, and enlargement upon, German rights in Shantung province. Four years later, on the anniversary of that May fourth "day of shame," Chinese students launched a storm of violent protest that eventuated in a boycott of Japanese merchants and, more important, in a clarification of Chinese national goals.

National goals, as perceived by the new intelligentsia, went far beyond the xenophobia of the old literati. There was still antiforeignism, but not the vain policy that aimed at driving foreigners out of their extraterritorial enclaves without learning from them, as in the Boxer Rebellion. Nationhood meant standing up to foreign nationals on their own terms. It meant learning not only the secrets of their technology, which were put to good effect in routing the T'ai-p'ing rebels, but also learning the secrets of their social arrangements in administering that technology. This implied a retreat from the position of borrowing the technology of shipyards and arsenals without giving up the intrinsic superiority of China's moral culture. The old slogan directed at barbarians on the immediate periphery had been, "Come see, be converted." But these Western barbarians, from farther away and yet more powerful, had come, had seen, and were not converted. The self-evident "superiority" of the famous teachings of Confucius was not evident to them. Such was the realization behind the New Culture Movement.

In short, modernization called for conversion to a foreign morality. Otherwise, Westerners would continue to hold administrative positions within the Chinese government, policing its collection of salt royalties and customs duties against the repayment of foreign loans endangered by native nepotism and corruption. It was a matter of learning the Enlightenment ethics of Westerners or being swallowed by enlightened Westerners and their keen disciples, the Japanese. The lesson to be learned was well stated by Oliver Lockart, an American financial advisor to the salt administration. "The realization that taxes are in fact a contribution to collective purposes, not a mere 'one-sided' compulsory exaction of wealth by the government (or, it may be, by officials, largely for their private personal benefit), must be gradually build up through the devotion of public funds to useful public purposes" (in his *Report on Revenue Policy* to the Kemmerer Commission, 1929, quoted by Young, 1971:64). But a public educated to the idea of public service was not yet available as a political resource to leaders of the early republic, which is why the central government of old, based on culturalism, had relapsed after the revolution into the regional politics of warlordism.

Nonetheless, hopes were high in postrevolutionary China. One of its most forceful spokesman, Ch'en Tu-hsiu of Peking University, proposed in 1915 that the rising generation should be cosmopolitan, not isolationist:

> *Any change in the economic or political life of one nation will usually have repercussions over the whole world, just as the whole body is affected if one hair is pulled. The prosperity or decline, rise or fall of a nation of today depends half on domestic administration, and half on influences from outside the country. Take the recent events of our country as evidence: Japan suddenly rose in power, and stimulated our revolutionary and reform movements; the European War broke out, and then Japan presented her demands to us; is this not clear proof? When a nation is thrown into the currents of the world, traditionalists will certainly hasten the day of its fall, but those capable of change will take this opportunity to compete and progress.* (in Teng and Fairbank, 1954:243)

The feelings expressed here are ambivalent, but they could not be otherwise. If China was to become a nation with a modern polity and modern economy strong enough to expel foreigners from their hated enclaves, the virtues that enabled them to obtain extrality would first have to be imitated.

And what were these virtues? They were fairly well summed up in Chinese newspapers after the success of foreign generals in defending the city of Shanghai against T'ai-p'ing armies, before Chinese armies using foreign technical aid had finally quelled the rebellion. Chinese praise went to foreigners especially for the wealth of their banks and firms, the bravery and firepower of their soldiers, and the efficiency of their mandarins, who somehow or other collected the most abundant revenue without appropriating a cent for themselves; in short, foreigners were honest, rich and strong (reported in Hauser, 1940:63). Yet contempt for them returned soon enough, but without losing hold of the realization that Chinese had to become modern persons like the foreigners in order to be rid of them.

Modernization meant externalizing some of the functions of the traditional family, making for professional careers unembedded in the kinship group. Foreign methods of becoming rich and strong put aside kinship obligations to the family purse as so much baggage impeding the individual's freedom to contract the obligations of his choice in marriage and business—a freedom that contrasted nepotism with honesty, the family with the individual. Among the most expressive attacks on the traditional family system was Pa Chin's 1931 novel, *Chia* (*The Family*). It moved a whole generation of postrevolutionary intellectuals to perceive the big family as a self-help institution that victimized those it helped, notably women and the young, with oppressive protection.

The 1930 Kinship Relations Law, however, had little effect beyond the class of intellectuals that legislated it and read novels like *Chia*. A society in which the individual could live on his own merits outside the defensive structure of the family did not yet exist, except for a few members of the commercial bourgeoisie and their university-educated offspring living in the ordered environment of the treaty ports. Private homes in the treaty ports could rely on the helping institutions of police, hospital, public health, school, bank, and court of law—all made accountable to the public by the peculiar ethical culture of the Westerners, who had transplanted their institutions in their colonial enclaves. It was left to the Communist regime to implement the provisions of the Kinship Relations Law among the peasant masses and thereby mobilize them, in its Marriage Law of 1950. Before that, Chinese students and other movers of the New Culture Movement looked with disdain, in Marx's words, on "the idiocy of rural life." For them the countryside was politically meaningless, "a sodden mound of embarrassment to the feverish young modernizers of China" (Davies, 1972:125). The republic might institute the solar calendar, but village people could go on using the old lunar calendar (Lindquist, 1972:195).

Nothing in the arrangements of family life was changed among the peasantry during republican times, and very little among the elite, except for those self-conscious devotees of "new-style wedding[s] for new-style people" (*see* Chao, 1947: ch. 36). When the big change came for everybody under communism, however, it had different effects for the two forms of family life obtaining between peasant and gentry.

There is disagreement about the existence in Chinese society of class differences that could be expressed as differences of family type. One anthropologist has offered the fact that the average family size in Republican China was about five persons, and concluded that the large, extended family is a mythic concept because it was never typical (Hsu, 1943). Never typical for China as a whole, no doubt; but typical for the elite, surely. We must not fall victim to the illusion that one cannot speak of class differences simply because they do not emerge clearly from a statistical point of view. It is true that on a scale measured by wealth, family size increases with the expansion of land holdings (Tauber, 1970), but most observers concur that this economic continuum may be divided along subcultural lines corresponding in general to Redfield's little and great traditions and in particular to Fei Hsiao-t'ung's peasant and gentry (Fei, 1946; Fried, 1952; Chow, 1966; Yang, 1959b). These same differences were the basis for the legal distinction under the empire between elite and commoners.

With the fall of the monarchy, of course, the legal distinction was dropped, but the social differences continued to exist. As before, the peasant family remained an economic unit merely, its members drawn together by the possession of land for the purpose of cooperative toil, whereas the elite added to the magetism of land all other economic and political resources alternative to physical toil and retained its property as a managerial, not a working, unit. The families of the elite in traditional times tended to be large in number and organized as multigenerational extended families, with the exception of some of the lower gentry whose resources were too limited to hold together an extended kinship unit. Nonetheless, their intellectual orientation toward the great tradition placed them among the elite in the leisure/labor dichotomy, and they would rather sacrifice their standard of living than work with their hands. In republican times, some of the urbanized neogentry modernized away from the extended family and under the influence of the New Culture Movement, adopted the Western-style nuclear family.

Otherwise, the nuclear family typified the kinship organization of the peasantry. Extended families existed among those peasants who owned enough land to encourage married sons to stay home and work it, whereas in other cases enough land for only one son was available and the others had to leave home and seek work as hired laborers or as apprentices in some trade (Tauber, 1970). But only men dignified with a traditional or a modern education had the poise to face their local community without working the land themselves, be their holdings large or small. Rich peasants, or kulaks, by contrast, lacked this cultural background and almost invariably continued to work some part of their land, even though they had risen high enough on the economic scale to live on rents if they so chose. They did not. Of 235 headmen and their assistants surveyed in 1933 in six districts of the county of Wu-hsi, in Kiangsu province, 78.3 percent rented out the greater part of their land but cultivated the remainder themselves. The few genuine landlords of the old school also owned holdings larger than the average but worked none of it (Hanwell, 1937:52).

It is safe to say that in the minds of traditional gentlemen, the extended family was associated with their own class and the nuclear family with peasants and barbarians. It took the New Culture Movement to make the nuclear family respectable for the neogentry of republican times. Otherwise, the elite may have continued to find the Western type of family in which husband and wife lived in companionship as offensive as did Ch'i-ying when he first encountered it. Ch'i-ying, the imperial commissioner deputed to treat with the foreigners in resolving the Opium War, wrote the following to the emperor:

> These barbarians are very fond of their wives. So much so, in fact, that the American barbarian Parker and the French barbarian Lagrené have brought theirs along. When I went to their homes on an official call, suddenly these women appeared and greeted me. I was greatly embarrassed, but they were highly pleased. This shows plainly that it is impossible to obtain anything from these barbarians with regard to ceremonial, and that it would be useless to enlighten their stupidity. (quoted by Pelissier, 1967:86–87)

From Ch'i-ying's viewpoint, the Western barbarians lived like peasants. In the family life of the Chinese elite, managerial power descended through the generations in the male line, placing the son's loyalty to his parents, and especially to his father, in conflict with the son's loyalty to,

and affection for, his wife. The Western diplomats who gave preference to
the sentiments of the husband/wife axis over the formalities of the
father/son axis, as symbolized in Chinese ancestor worship—the rites of
"incense and fire"—looked very low-class indeed. Intimacy between husband and wife was expected in peasant families, whose cooperative labor
in the fields took precedence over "incense and fire" because they lacked
the resources of power and property deserving of managerial authority and
ceremonial regulation (see Smith, 1894:177–78; Hsu, 1949).

For the peasant, death of the father normally meant division of the
property among the sons. Based on population data collected about forty
years ago for the households of farm operators in diverse regions of China,
the demographer Irene Taeuber concluded that 60 percent of all peasant
families could be classified as nuclear (Taeuber, 1970:81). Few could be
classified as extended families. The majority of families that were not
nuclear could be classified as stem families—that is, their households included an elderly parent or two in addition to husband, wife, and unmar-
ried children. Incidentally, the same data suggest that about 70 percent of
all the men were illiterate, the remainder semiliterate after a little schooling; all the women were illiterate and had had no schooling (Taeuber,
1970:69). This confirms the native Chinese model of stratification, which
divided society between a literate elite and a nonliterate majority, and
which associated these classes (or subcultures) with differences in family
structure. The imperial elite and unmodernized members of the neogentry
in Republican China had the cultural resources of literacy and ceremony
to maintain the organizational unity of the extended family as a means of
perpetuating their economic advantages; the peasantry did not (Lindquist,
1968:198–99).

The limited family resources of the peasantry were inherited according to the rule of homoyogeniture, or equal division among all legitimate
heirs. This customary norm was the law of imperial China, originating in
the Sung dynasty as a means by which the government aimed to break at
last the power of the second aristocracy. But it had already run its course,
and the law of homoyogeniture merely enacted what had become a fact
—the increasing subdivision of patrimonial estates. Law continued to follow custom. The gentry of late imperial China cannot be said to have
violated the law, however, because their joint holdings in the extended
family were legal unless complaints were brought to the district magistrate on behalf of sons who desired subdivision. They did not usually press
to divide because they realized that the loss of managerial unity on a large
scale invariably meant slipping into the peasant condition for each independent nuclear family split off from the extended family. Awareness of
this fate was not always sufficient to forestall it among brothers who could
not maintain the diplomatic strain of keeping their families living together
in ritual harmony, if their proximity caused too much mutual enmity (see
Lamson, 1935:500–501). For peasants with fewer resources at stake and
no training in the cultivated manners of the great tradition, the ritual etiquette of big-family living, rehearsed with even more formal rigor at
periodic ceremonies of ancestor worship, was beyond their organizational
abilities.

As the population/land ratio grew worse, more and more peasant
families had smaller and smaller estates to divide among the sons. Thus if
the rule of homoyogeniture were followed, each son would be left with

less than enough to support his own *chia*. As a result, one son would work the bulk of the land himself, meanwhile holding all shares in trust for the others while they went abroad in the land or beyond (Cohen, 1970:33). In searching for employment, these men could pursue possibilities as defined by an economic network beyond the village, starting with the local market town, to more comprehensive locations of exchange, and finally to provincial capitals and the great entrepots enlarged by Western contact (*see* Fried, 1973:378; Skinner, 1971). Beyond that, some migrated to Southeast Asia or to America, sending home remittances as a claim on their holdings worked by the stay-at-home brother. The strong desire to be returned home for burial must be seen in the light of maintaining these claims to the death, despite the frequent failure to find abroad the success denied them at home.

OCCUPATION

The Marriage Law of 1950 was the first civil code produced by the Communist regime. Some of its provisions had been introduced originally in the Kinship Relationships Law of 1930, but whereas acceptance of the provisions of the earlier law was left to individuals who elected to go modern, adherence to the new law was compulsory. Pressures of various sorts, including well-organized mass movements, were used to achieve conformity.

First to benefit from the new marriage law were those most oppressed under the traditional family system—women and the young—especially those from extended families belonging to conservative elements among the neogentry and commercial bourgeoisie. The young men and women from these families had, through knowledge of Western custom, compared themselves with modern people and found themselves wanting in freedom. Like the unhappy heroes and heroines of Pa Chin's *Chia*, their educational opportunities had enabled them to learn about behavioral options not available in the society before its exposure to Western customs; they chafed against autocratic fathers, aloof managers of the family estate, and arranged marriages. Their liberation under the new law won them over as cadres for its enforcement in the countryside among millions of peasant families, whose response stemmed from dissatisfactions of another sort. Ignorant of peasant life, these cadres drawn from the urban intelligentsia pictured themselves as bringing to others the same liberation from the "feudalistic" family arrangements they had escaped, identifying rural ills with their own. One sociologist who saw the Communist revolution come to a little village near Canton described the land reform cadres who entered there as high-school graduates and college students of both sexes, clearly indicating an urban bourgeois background. Under the guise of false class-consciousness and dressed in dirty gray uniforms, they imitated the life of their peasant hosts—living in their houses, eating their poor food, and helping with farm chores—in order to talk with them and learn about village conflicts that might be resolved under communist law (Yang, 1959a:134).

In these opening years of the Communist regime, the marriage law was enforced in close support of the Agrarian Reform Law, also promulgated in 1950. The former accorded both marriage partners equal rights to own and manage land redistributed not to families but to individuals. By the end of 1952, 300 million peasants had received 110 million acres, amounting to 45 percent of the total land under cultivation. The amount of land acquired per capita through redistribution was necessarily small —from 0.15 to 0.45 of an acre (Whitaker and Shinn, 1972:417). But the political impact was immense. Mao had won his constituency of "vagrants"—the poor peasants and farm laborers who, by his account, made up 70 percent of the population.

The political possibilities of an imbalanced man/land ratio had been exploited, although officially the problem was stated as land concentration and the solution, confiscation from landlords. But owing to gentry desertions, most land was confiscated from kulaks. In short, rich and middle peasants were robbed to buy the support of the more numerous poor peasants and landless laborers. How was this accomplished? The terrorist method of pitting peasant against peasant in public trials, followed by executions, could have succeeded only if it exploited some deep-seated grievances endemic to village society.

In Chapter Seven we suggested that these grievances, stemming from the inherent disadvantages of the peasant condition, could be summarized under the phrase "mutual suspicion." Let us now refine that concept by adding that the conduits of mutual suspicion were village women; the currents of envy, suspicion, and jealousy that flowed between neighboring households and were reified in demon possession were generated by peasant wives. Husbands were at least temporarily absent from the grievous atmosphere of mutual suspicion during their trips to market, where they enjoyed each other's hospitality in the town teahouses. Far from being oppressed parties to a "feudalistic" marriage arrangement, peasant wives were partners in toil with their husbands and, cut off from all ties with their parental home, often dominated their conjugal home as mistress of the household, its "inside boss." Reginald Johnston, who served as a district magistrate in Weihaiwei, in Shantung, toward the end of the Ch'ing dynasty, reports that almost all cases of litigation brought before him were by women, protesting with shrewish agitation the transfer of landed property in their home village or the building of a new house in their neighborhood (Johnston, 1910:195–209). Here is a classic example of the peasant fear that with visibly limited resources, the gain of one is felt as a loss by all (described cross-culturally by Foster, 1965; in Potter et al., 1967). For the same period, files of district magistrates show that rent collectors were often the wives of tenants (Muramatsu, cited in Rawski, 1972:234, n. 25).

Mao has written that he never could have carried out his revolution without the help of peasant women, a newly exploited political resource. They played a key role in land reform as members of the Women's Association by identifying targets for "struggle meetings" carried out in the tribunals of the Farmers' Association, in which enemies of the people were forced to confess and were then publicly executed. By early 1955, women had become managers or deputy managers of 5,200 out of 6,000 APCs (Agricultural Producers Cooperatives) organized in Shansi province (Human Relations Area Files, 1956: North China, vol. II, pp. 512–13).

A vivid portrayal of how the forces of mutual suspicion were harnessed for the purposes of carrying out land reform in a northern village is given in Eileen Chang's novel of Communist tyranny, *Naked Earth* (1956). Student cadres from Peking first entered the village to identify potential activists and set up the Women's Association and the Farmers' Association. No landlords of the gentry type lived in the village, only kulaks and other peasants. Unfamiliar with the specific personal grievances native to the village, the cadres could only encourage the activists to bring their grievances out in the open, relying in the first instance on the most shrewish personality for their candidate as chairwoman of the Women's Association, a choice that was virtually self-selecting. The chairwoman then happily volunteered all the names of family heads whose wives' consumption habits she resented. These families were identified by the cadres according to their guidelines of class analysis as being middle peasants.

The names were brought forward by the chairwoman with the observation on one of these, a young man recently married, that he should be indicted for the following reason: "The wife's got a new padded jacket, too. Some real fancy cotton print" (Chang, 1956:41). The cadres wrote the man's name down on a list of "class enemies." Afterward the cadres would mobilize and direct resentment and the discontents of envy against these persons on behalf of a claimant group, "the people," represented by poor peasants and farm laborers brought into the Farmers' Association.

The result in the novel, as in real life, was parceling out to the claimants land shares too small to be of any economic value. The importance of redistribution lay rather with the fact that the CCP supported the claim of individuals to these shares, as against that of families. This followed from enforcement of the new marriage law that accorded both marriage partners equal rights to own and manage property as well as equal rights to participate in occupations or social activities outside the home, including the Women's and Farmers' Associations through which claims to land were exercised. The very act of mobilizing a sense of injustice created a sense of solidarity within organizations composed of individuals apart from the family. With the advent of the APCs and the People's Communes, the nuclear family ceased to function as an effective unit and lost some of its economic importance as each member was drawn into enterprises over which the family had no control, but on which its economic security depended (see Lindbeck, 1951; Yang 1959b).

The human cost of liberating the individual from kinship controls only to set him free for employment in an occupation under state control is perhaps unacceptably high. In Western industrial societies, the individual was freed from strong family ties only after he contracted other ones with powerful interest groups such as labor unions and professional associations. No such countervailing forces exist to protect the citizen of Communist China against the arbitrariness of the state. His vulnerability is complete (see Hu, 1960:180; but for a qualification see Parish, 1975).

Without underestimating the human cost of revolution, it is still fair to ask what the institutionalized results of voluntary or enforced participation in Communist-sponsored occupations have been. One thing is clear: To the degree that individuals depend on nonfamily organizations and the state for support and protection by claiming the legal rights extended to them in the new marriage law and other laws, the family declines in significance as a self-help institution. This has had important consequences for the leadership as well as for the led. To the extent that the Communists have been efficient in policing the new job structure, state and local cadres have become professional officials relatively freed of the nepotism and corruption that formerly embedded bureaucratic careers in the nexus of family interests.

Professionalism, untouched by family influence or personal interests, is idealized repeatedly in the works of Mao Tse-tung: "It is necessary to maintain the system of cadre participation in collective productive labor. The cadres of our Party and state are ordinary workers and not overlords sitting on the backs of the people. By taking part in collective labor, the cadres maintain extensive, constant and close ties with the working people" (Mao, 1966:281–82). By "cadre participation," Mao means that the administrative officers of socialized agriculture must be working managers who somehow are expected to cultivate opposites of habit and attitude (see Schurmann, 1968:162–67). On the one hand, the kan-pu, or cadre, is expected to keep alive the "Red" spirit of the revolutionary who overthrew the leisure/labor dichotomy set up by the old bureaucratic overlord, and on the other is expected to achieve "expert" competence in handling an administrative position in a two-way chain of command. The kan-pu is expected to be one with the masses in physical labor at the same time that he moves them to action as a middleman for directives from above. If this extreme combination of leadership qualities is not possible to find in one person, the Red activist is favored over the expert.

Such bias in selecting candidates for cadre training has been the subject of fierce debate in China; the leader of the opposing school of thought favoring expertise and all the self-cultivation that goes with it, President Liu-shao-ch'i, has been deposed. In open criticism of Mao, Liu said, "Personal interests must be looked after, for without personal interests there can be no group interests. . . . Therefore, instead of caring for the public and not for one's self, one should care for both." (Liu, 1968:62)

This Red versus expert debate, however, serves only to highlight the extent to which the ideals of selfless government service have prevailed over the embedded careers of old. Mao's victory in the debate has meant that officials can be made to care for their professional standing because, recruited from poor peasants and workers and not from the more literate children of the neogentry and bourgeoisie, officials are dependent on their superiors for upward mobility. This dependency operates as a political resource for the top leadership in recruiting an army of millions of selfless cadres willing to set an example in devaluating the prestige that used to go with the avoidance of physical toil and in eliminating the traditional gap between urban and rural life. Article 16 of the Constitution of 1954 says: "Work is a matter of honor for every citizen of the People's Republic of China who is able to work. The state encourages citizens to take an active and creative part in their work" (in Wu, 1973:802). The cadre is assigned to show the way.

The need for millions of state employees to carry out the enlarged tasks of government has raised more expectations of upward mobility than can be fulfilled. One unpromoted peasant cadre was encouraged to repent publicly his ambition to rise to become the chief of a ch'u. In a newspaper letter he said that he had brooded over the injustice of the Party's not recommending him, but soon realized that his worry about a career was selfish because it put his individual interest above the Party's general interest, and this was not compatible with Party membership. Henceforth he would be able to work free from worry (letter quoted in Lewis, ed., 1970:248, n. 2).

Time will tell if Mao's strategy has raised a "revolution of rising frustrations" (Lerner, 1963) more threatening to socialism than Liu's strategy for recruiting experts to administer a relatively unpoliticized peasantry. As it turns out, Mao's strategy has not worked as intended. He had originally planned on rural activists' electing their Reddist colleagues to the privilege of attending secondary schools in the cities with the view to their voluntary return as trained administrators. But they did not wish to return after their brief emancipation from toil in the urban classroom. That old refrain from the World War I song put it nicely: "How you gonna keep 'em down on the farm, after they've seen Paree?" And so, in the "great leap farmward," they were sent back involuntarily, and not to their home communities.

So far as the peasantry has been politicized in response to a politicized bureaucracy, the roles of the politician and the civil servant are no longer divergent; cadres at all levels work toward a convergence of interests between office and officeholder, a radical change from the past. The cadre, no longer autonomous, is the willing tool of his superiors. The official can no longer look to his post for graft; he is held accountable to his duties, and to that extent he is a professional.

Yet for all this convergence of interests, there remains something ineradicably Chinese and unchanged in the role of the cadre. Paradoxically, the cadre is just as Chinese in being a professional as the Ch'ing official was in being a noncareer-oriented amateur. In both instances the tension between virtue and ability is resolved in favor of virtue, and in both instances that virtue is one of imitability. By enjoining cadre participation, Mao enjoins state employees to present themselves as educative models to be imitated. Government by education is one of the oldest and most persistent ideas of Chinese civilization. Mao could just as well have quoted Confucius in saying that, "To rule is to be correct. If you lead along a correct way, who will not dare follow in correctness?" (*Lun Yu*, XII:17).

The difference between then and now is that the imperial official was a model for imitation only within the hierarchy of his own kind. Aloofness of the officials from nonleaders was not held to be bad. Under the culturalism of the emperors, social distance could induce a mystique of social rank, which in turn could induce a noncoercive deference for the august "lords of the soil," be they officials or gentlemen-landlords. In fact, landlords had to depend more on this mystique to collect rents than on the coercive powers of a thinly spread and ineffective military establishment. Gentlemen who couldn't carry the weight of dignity were left in arrears by their tenants. The rates of tenancy cited for late Ch'ing China must thus be balanced against a substantial rate of rent defaults and a large percentage of substantial discounts offered tenants as an inducement for payment (*see* Muramatsu, 1966). The ruling authorities of Communist China, by contrast, are trained to eliminate social distance; but on the other hand, their active participation in the work they are charged to administer sets them up as models to be imitated by the masses. In this sense, the imitability of the cadre is more intensely Chinese than was that of the imperial official, who acted as a model only for gentleman landlords and lower-ranking officials.

In the language of Confucianism, the imperial official acted as a model of government by filial piety. That is, he was expected to behave in office as he would as an elder in his family. As an elder, he received respect from his juniors; ancestor worship was paradigmatic for this relationship, the living paying respect to the dead just as subordinates were expected to defer to superiors along the father-son axis. So it was in office: The senior official received bribes and gifts from his juniors. Profiteering in office was not all profit; in the absence of a meaningful salary from above, the official had to pass on a substantial amount of his profits upward to his superiors, in effect paying their salary from below. Hence, this was government by filial piety, or what Norman Jacobs calls "rule by model" (1966:25–29). The model official took his cues for impressing rectitude on his inferiors from the very nexus of family interests he was obliged to benefit in the course of his bureaucratic career: He translated respect for family elders into support of superiors. The Communist official, paid a salary from above and obliged to do his duty, is more professional. Nonetheless, his duties include acting as a model for the peasantry to imitate, which is more politicized than acting as a model of aloofness calling for deference and avoidance. The cadre who, in Mao's ideal, is at once Red and expert, serves as a model of high involvement with the regime's national policies and with its practical means of carrying them out.

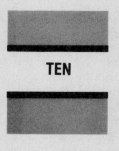

TEN

STRATIFICATION

POWER

The native model of stratification is derived from another of the early Han works in which the mythology of Confucian China was cast for all time, the *Kuan Tze*, whose source material dates back to the late Chou (Ho, 1962:18). The *Kuan Tze* describes the *ssu-min*, "the four classes of the people," ranked and grouped in the following order:

Elite *(kwei)* { 1. Scholars *(shih)*
{ 2. Farmers *(nung)* } The Fundamental Occupation
Commoners *(liang)* { 3. Merchants *(shang)* }
{ 4. Artisans *(kung)* } Accessory Occupations

In this list, farmers ranked above everybody else except scholars because the state regarded agriculture, not trade or a market economy, as its source of power. Nor was military conquest glorified—soldiers were merely farmers in another role and their officers merely scholar-officials in another role. Above the *ssu-min* were the emperor and the nobility. By the end of the Ch'ing dynasty, the nobility included about 700 imperial clansmen, 1.5 million bannermen (counting dependents), and all Manchu officials, who made up one-third of all officials. At the start of the dynasty, the ratio of Manchu to Chinese officials was 1:1.5, the difference being the measure of the earlier trespass by Chinese officials on the prerogatives of the court, asserting the right of merit over the right of birth *(see* Marsh, 1961:48). This factor contributed to the abolition of the examination system.

Below the *ssu-min* were the outcasts of the pariah occupations, notably prostitutes, actors, and boatmen. In other words, outside the ranks of the "four classes of people" there was a class of nonpeople as well as a hereditary elite. The *ssu-min* was divided into a nonhereditary elite *(shih)* including all Chinese officials and holders of academic degrees, and three classes of honorable occupations for commoners *(nung, kung,* and *shang)*.

The basis for the distinction between elite and commoners—rulers and ruled—was the leisure/labor dichotomy set forth by Mencius: "Inequalities are in the nature of things. There is the business of superior men and there is the business of little men. Hence the saying, 'Some work with their head; they govern others. Those who are governed feed the others; those who govern are the fed.' This is a just arrangement" *(Meng Tze,* IIIA:iv:6). In the original text, the distinction is between *lao-hsin* (mental labor and *lao-li* (manual labor). Manual labor has been interpreted to mean handling any implement other than the writing brush, be it the farmer's hoe, the merchant's steelyard, or the artisan's tool kit.

The *ssu-min* model of stratification, however, deviated from reality in one important respect. Wealthy members of the class *shang,* if they were not petty merchants, belonged to the ruling elite as degree-holders and agents of government monopolies. Nonetheless, the concept of the four classes served a definite purpose. On the general principle that native models are not meant to explain social phenomena but to perpetuate them (Lévi-Strauss, 1953:527), we can say that the phenomenon perpetuated by the *ssu-min* was the privilege of the scholar-elite to act as arbiters of social values (Jacobs, 1958:126–29). The literati thus defined big merchants as commoners, even though legally they were not, to assert their own power to decide the cultural definition of elite status as well as to decide who would be allowed to buy title to it. To the literati, even the merchant-gentry belonged to what we would call (after Redfield) the little tradition, because their use of local weights and measures and regional currencies made mercantile culture as divided by parochial interests as was peasant culture, whereas the scholar-gentry belonged to a translocal aristocracy of learning, sharing in the common literature, language, and educational ideals of the great tradition.

A more realistic model excluding royalty and nobility is represented in Figure 11: relative income is measured vertically; realtive numbers are measured horizontally. The heavy line separates a privileged minority holding legal title to elite status (gentry) from a legally defined order of commoners (peasantry).

Turning now to the internal stratification of the elite, officials were divided into eight ranks, civil and military, keyed to the hierarchy of the bureaus and offices to which they were assigned. Each rank was symbolized with a distinctive jewel set atop the summer or winter hat, ornamental belt, and mandarin square sewn on the front and back of the official dress. All officials, whatever their rank, were classified as either *liu kwan* (appointed within the metropolitan center) or *liu-wai kuan* (outside the metropolitan center).

Gentlemen holding academic degrees but not office were *shih,* scholars. With office they were *shen-shih,* scholar-officials. Only a small percentage of the gentry ever held office at one time. In the 1880s, the number of men legally entitled to privileged status, or *kwei,* was 1.5 million, of which 1.6 percent held office. The de facto elite, some 6 million kinsmen closely related to the elite de jure, brought the gentry minority to 7.5 million, or close to 2 percent of the total population.

All officials held academic degrees, but not all degree holders were eligible for office. At the bottom was the holder of the *hsiu-ts'ai* degree (also called the *sheng-yuan)* earned through triennial examinations held in the capital of the candidate's home district. It licensed the holder to pursue higher degrees, the *chu-jen* and then the *chin-shih,* examinations for which were conducted every three years at the provincial and metropolitan levels, respectively. A special palace examination could be taken for

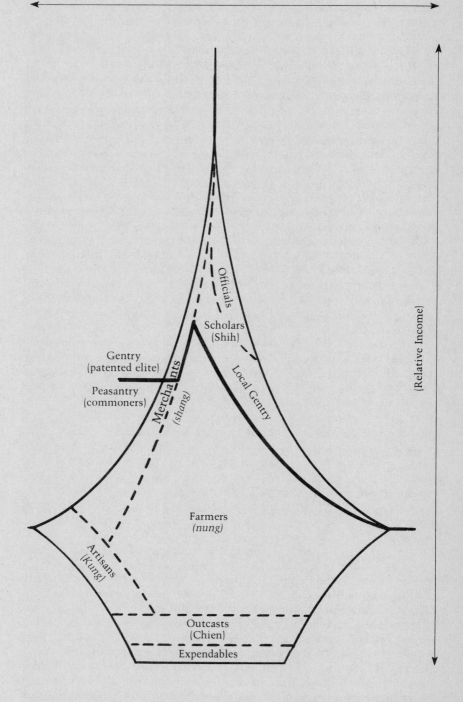

(Relative Numbers)

(Relative Income)

Officials

Scholars
(Shih)

Gentry
(patented elite)

Peasantry
(commoners)

Merchants
(shang)

Local Gentry

Farmers
(nung)

Artisans
(Kung)

Outcasts
(Chien)

Expendables

FIGURE 11.   The *ssu-min:* The Native Model of Stratification, Adjusted.

the added distinction of winning the *tien-shih* degree, for which an appointment was immediately guaranteed, but the *chin-shih* was sufficient to place one on the waiting list. About 500,000 candidates entered the examinations each year, of whom only 1 in 300 passed (Hsieh, 1925:156).

All holders of the *chu-jen* degree and above were classed as upper gentry. The licentiate holding a *hsiu-ts'ai*, or *sheng-yuan*, actually occupied a transitional status between commoners and the upper gentry. Licentiates were often portrayed in Chinese fiction as figures of shabby gentility, who had a hard time maintaining life without resorting to toil, often serving as ill-paid teachers in lineage schools or as tutors in private homes. Their number constituted about 86 percent of the total elite in late nineteenth-century China: the upper gentry constituted 14 percent. The upper gentry collected not only all income from office, they collected also 75 percent of all land rents going to the elite. Some 36 percent of all academic degrees were purchased at that time, a significant source of revenue for central government, whose fiscal needs displaced merit ratings. But this purchase of degrees was also a calculated effort on the emperor's part to introduce wealthy but unscholarly commoners into the bureaucratic system in order to divide the gentry who might possibly combine as an interest group against him (Chang, 1955). To the same end, offices were distributed by lot when not as promotional gifts (Hsieh, 1925:139).

The effectiveness of the emperor's divide-and-rule tactics may be estimated from the depth of contempt for which the holder of a purchased degree was held by scholars of merit: "To be fully fed and warmly clothed, and dwell at ease without learning, is little better than a bestial state" (Williams, 1885: vol. I, p. 722). Patron of scholarship though he was, the emperor nonetheless forfended himself from any approach to his preeminence by scholars (who might professionalize their careers in office) by heading them toward the safer scramble for power based on family influence and personal competition. Better for him "palace politics" than interest-group politics:

> The whole class [officials] form a body of men mutually jealous of each other's advance, where every incumbent endeavors to supplant his associate; they all agree in regarding the people as the source of their profits, the sponge which all must squeeze, but differ in degree to which they should carry on the same plan with each other. . . . Their life is spent in ambitious efforts to rise upon the fall of others, though they do not lose all sense of character or become reckless of the means of advance, for this would destroy their chance of success. (Williams, 1885: vol. I, p. 451).

Most readers will no doubt feel that the above description damns traditional Chinese officials with faint praise: They were too cultivated to use assassination and political murder as a means of rising on the fall of others. Yet the unflattering portrait has in it the truth of the emperor's own design, who saw to it that his government by filial piety was thereby enforced. The turnover of incumbents was in fact high. Yet the rewards brought home by the official to his kin group were great, so long as he kept on the right side of those above him. In the words of the *Hsiao Ching*, which implicitly likens the benefits gained by the deferential passage of bribes upward to the blessings gained for the family by its worship of dead ancestors: "Few are revered and many are made happy" (*Hsiao Ching*, XII).

The same slogan applied to commoners, who were said to acquire virtue by respecting it in their betters. In theory, gentlemen set themselves up as models of virtue to be imitated, and commoners did in practice defer to all members of the ruling class as "Your Excellency," and to officials as "Stars in Heaven." Actually, the elite had no intention of being imitated; instead, they sought to be avoided. Confucian talk about the happiness of the many in revering the few was aimed at persuading commoners to keep their distance and accept inequality with contentment; therein lay the *real* virtue to be obtained. The official Confucian handbook of the Ch'ing dynasty, the *Sacred Edict*, cautions that "persons must on no account abandon the Fundamental Occupation" because agriculture is the "Source of Power" (IV:5). It is wrong for "those now in humble circumstances to seek wealth and honor in some future day" (VII:15). The peasant is asked to "seek no happiness that does not pertain to your lot in life" (VII:15).

The virtue of peasant contentment, of course, was largely self-acquired. Divided by mutual suspicion and the parochialism of the little tradition, village folk were predisposed to react to gentlemen as models to avoid. Gentlemanly aloofness did no more than complement peasant denials of the possibility of upward mobility, lest the appearance of gain call forth the wrathful envy of fellow villagers. Men of the great tradition were the wise men of their civilization, who merely applied Confucian doctrine to the job of rationalizing the class structure that conferred on them their privileged position in it. Their education qualified them not only as literati but also as *illuminati*, whose very conduct exemplified the rightness of hierarchy over individualism. They were a living justification of the gap between elite and nonelite, and they carried it off with impressive dignity.

Not that all gentlemen were wealthy. They did constitute a birth elite, however, insofar as their families possessed traditions of education, good breeding, and a devotion to public achievement, from which their scions derived a decided advantage in the examination stalls. The deciding criterion was legal title to elite status, which itself was internally stratified by a wide range of wealth and power differences obtaining between the array of academic degrees and official ranks, not to mention differences in the range of family influence and personally cultivated power connections. Fundamental was an intellectual orientation to the great tradition, authenticated by academic degrees, with its accompanying literacy, cultivated manners, skepticism toward folk beliefs, and disdain for manual labor.

The leisure/labor dichotomy with the little tradition did not, however, make for leisure among the elite. It was rather that freedom from physical toil was needed to prepare for the examinations. Studying and memorizing the Confucian classics—immense volumes of poetry, history, and philosophy—did not permit the scholar to engage in any other activity. In addition, academic and/or official status once achieved, absolutely forbad physical labor or manual toil (Lindquist, 1968:202–3). Not that the Chinese official governed his immense territories nor the landlord his tenants with poetry and philosophy, but only that his self-assured aloofness from the masses—his charisma—was proved through the canonical correctness of his literary forms (*see* Weber, 1951:132).

Gentlemen of any station were the cosmopolitan agents of empire, illuminating the basic fact of imperial society—stabilized inequality—wherever they lived or officiated. Receiving their patents of rank and office from the emperor, they may have been assigned to preside over towns too obscure to appear on any map, yet they were men who, in any assemblage in New York or Paris, would be called "men of the world" (Nichols, 1902:151). This achievement was simply beyond emulation by commoners. The peasant knew that gentlemen knew not just books, but remote places and different kinds of people: "The Chinese think no gentleman's education is complete without travelling to visit the most remarkable regions, lakes, and mountains, in their own empire, to which allusions are constantly made in their lighter compositions" (Kidd, 1841:344). The translocal orientation of even the local gentry at home inspired awe for its domination over the parochial.

This unambiguous cultural authority gave the local elite the power to win noncoercive deference, unaided directly by the coercive backing of imperial armies or by a gendarmerie. Not all gentlemen could carry it off equally well; the peasant tenants' frequent defaulting on rents testifies to personality differences in the gentry's ability to project the mystery of aloofness and the charismatic appeal of social distance. For the most part, the local gentlemen were the embodiment of police power, especially evident in their mustering of the militia when organized defense was needed. Their homes were public offices where everyday disputes were settled. They named infants and were called on to direct wedding and funeral ceremonies, at which time they wore their official or academic robes. They organized labor on irrigation projects for peasant clients too riven by the mutual suspicions of village life to do so themselves (see Chow, 1966:87). In all this, of course, they had the complete backing of local government and were sustained by its imperial magnificence.

Traditional Chinese civilization was profoundly inegalitarian. The politics of culturalism took as its collective goal upholding hierarchy. The chief business of state was regulating good manners and customs, all those details of li—etiquette, ceremony, and formality—that maintained the stratification system (de Groot, 1903–4:264). For the late nineteenth century, the stratification system may be outlined as follows:

Emperor
Nobility
  Imperial Clansmen (about 700)
  Manchu Officials
  Bannermen (1.5 million, with dependents)
Gentry (5.5 million, with dependents)
  Upper (120,000 chin-shih and chu-jen)
  Lower (980,000 licentiates, or sheng-yuan)
Peasantry (400 million commoners, or shu-jen)
Outcasts (number unknown)
Expendables (5–10 percent of the population)

Above all was the concern for maintaining the distinction between elite and majority. The regulations of li applied only to the internal stratification of the elite; commoners were by definition not so regulated, subject only to penal law (fa) and kept apart by the elite's aloofness informed by high culture. The *Sacred Edict* reminds peasant subjects that they are unreflective and ignorant of high culture: "The rituals of *li* are exceedingly numerous. If we were to mention them, you people would necessarily be unable to learn them" (IX:3). Elsewhere, the *Sacred Edict* describes peasants as "foolish people" (VII:6), "great imbeciles" (VII:14), "stupid ones" (XIV:5), "dull and empty-headed" (VIII:5), "doltish" (XVI:12), and "naturally perverse, not understanding reason" (VII:6) (tr. by Baller, 1907).

Confucian tradition provided the elite with the intellectual tools to justify class differences and illuminate them in personal behavior, setting an example to avoid. The men of high culture did not pretend class differences did not exist, in the democratic, self-effacing method of disarming envy from below. Instead they controlled the disruptive powers of envy by asserting social distance with such confidence that aspirations for raised status among commoners were made to look presumptuous.

It therefore comes as a surprise to find Chinese society described by sinologists as democratic and Confucius as the Chinese Jefferson (for example: Creel, 1949). What is the source of this misperception? We believe it is the influence of an internationalized Chinese elite who never ceased to assert the moral superiority of their culture, even in the face of Western technological superiority, and who did so by persuading Western intellectuals that China, after all, was more democratic than the Western democracies that had humiliated her. The logic of the argument is casuistic in the extreme, but the Chinese have been so indomitably ethnocentric even to this day that it is nearly impossible to find anything but conviction in their sophistry.

A perfect example of Chinese ethnocentricity is this statement from a military attaché to the Chinese legation at Paris, who found, after ten years' sojourn in Europe and numerous studies, nothing among the institutions of the Western world that could really be called democratic or liberal. The Chinese were more democratic, he concluded, because in his country an official career was embedded in family concerns, whereas in Europe the upwardly mobile man was an individualist, leaving his kinsmen behind as surplus baggage.

> It might possibly happen, as we see elsewhere, that the parvenue son would despise his parents remaining in the same humble position as that in which he himself was born. But our laws have been prudent, and this scandal does not exist in our society. The father and mother rise at the same time as their son; they receive the rank and honor of his degree, and all the family are happy on the day of his triumphant examination. Ah, our ancestors understood the human heart, and their institutions are truly wise! They deserve the admiration and gratitude of every friend of humanity. The more I know of modern civilization, the more my love for our old institutions increases: for they alone realize what they promise—peace and equality. (Tcheng, 1885:71)

In 1904, some years after Col. Tcheng returned home from Paris, his favorite native institution was suspended, a root cause of the revolution. Thereafter, the ambitious continued to seek office in Peking, dressed now in frock coats and top hats; but the high school certificate required by the Peking government was not considered as dignified as the old academic degrees, although office remained under the early republic the most honorable highroad to wealth and power (Bland, 1912:82–83). Small wonder that some gentlemen turned to dress their ambitions in the authority of a Sam Browne belt and entered the politics of warlordism.

PROPERTY

The at-home gentry of traditional China formed a rather attractive ruling class. When they took up office away from home, of course, they were not so attractive, although one must admit that profiteering took place by default in the absence of interest-group politics. As gentlemen living on their country estates, they dwelled among their own constituents and were expected to live off their rents, but only to the extent that their properties provided enough leisure for study and public affairs, not luxury.

As the holder of a state-awarded title to privilege, the rural gentleman extended his influence in the countryside under the cultural umbrella of the imperial cause, which in essence reduced to the moral responsibility for upholding the hierarchy of things. This placed the gentry in a social order founded on something more than mere economic privilege. The material benefits of elite status were in theory a just reward for moral superiority (as evidenced by literacy and knowledge of the classics), which was said to have the effect on little people of wind on grass. Exploitation was cast into the language of government, and government meant maintaining the power gap between elite and majority. In the words of Mencius, "Without the gentry there would be none to control the country-folk. Without country-folk there would be none to feed the gentry" (*Meng Tze*, IIIA:iii:14; tr. by Dobson, 1963:37). Confucian theory thus gave rural gentry the confidence and self-respect, backed by the whole enterprise of imperial culturalism, to win noncoercive deference from tenants and clients alike.

But the virtue of superiority does not exist in the abstract. Just as a brave man must do brave things, so the superior man of Confucian persuasion acted out his superior morality in thrift and puritanical self-control. Acceptable as an important set of guidelines was a section in the *Li Chi* called "Behavior of a Confucian." The best-known lines from this text say that, "In his dwelling he will not be extravagant, in his eating and drinking he will not be luxurious" (*Ju Hsing*, 8). The basic formula was: Restrict material wants and thereby obtain an equitable distribution of land for others. The gentleman may take commoners for his meat and fish, but he should do so with the conservationist principles of a game warden. Historically, the reality corresponded fairly well with the ideal. Most peasants did indeed occupy their own small holdings and the elite, in their role as landlords, generally did not expand their estates beyond the size needed to satisfy their household consumption requirements, which rarely exceeded 500 *mou* (*see* Myers, 1972:28).

Even officials gave lip service to material restraints on material comfort, insofar as they allowed the exteriors and grounds of their official buildings to go untended. Their motto was: *Kuan pu hsiu ya-men*, "Officials do not waste money on the upkeep of the yamen." Upkeep was an offense to Confucian benevolence because the people would have to pay the cost in added taxes. Dilapidation was the outward sign of virtue, behind which the real profiteering of office took place (Stover, 1974b:10).

A genuinely high-living elite did arise, however, in the treaty ports, where Confucian morality was destroyed by the import of foreign luxuries (Feuerwerker, 1968:28). But this did not take place until after gentry desertions had shifted rural leadership from country to city.

In a study by Fei Hsiao-t'ung of 915 degree holders from 1644 to 1911 (the time span of the Ch'ing dynasty), he found that 52.50 percent came from cities, 41.16 percent from rural villages, and 6.34 percent from towns—an almost equal distribution between cities and rural areas. The ratio between degree holders whose fathers also held degrees and those who did not was 68:32 in the cities and 64:36 in the villages, showing that getting an education in those days did not cause the gentry to leave their rural homesteads (Fei, 1947).

Things changed radically after the abolition of the examination system and the passing away of classical education at the hands of private tutors. In a migration unprecedented in history, thousands of Chinese students went abroad to study in foreign schools, including military institutes in Japan. In China itself, Western-type schools appeared in the treaty ports and all the provincial capitals, founded by Christian missionaries, Chinese citizens, or the government. Diplomas from high schools and universities in these places were required by the postrevolutionary Peking government for entry into its service. By 1922, the number of students enrolled in the new educational system was 6,601,802 in the elementary schools, 182,804 in secondary schools, and 34,800 in universities (Latourette, 1926:621). Urban based, these schools exerted a positive force attracting elite families from their rural estates.

A negative factor driving out the rural elite was civil war and unrest in the countryside, a condition to which gentry desertions contributed at first, followed by new gentry careers in the military administrations of the warlords who filled the vacuum. By 1936, the size of regional armies in China was estimated at about 2,379,000 men. This figure does not include Communist rebels, brigands, or Manchurian troops in the service of the Japanese (the Manchukwo army), which would bring the total to 2.5 million men or more.

The chief significance of military regionalism was the professional quality of the warlord armies, which were westernized in every respect except for a political sense of national unity. Ordinary soldiers were given a taste of twentieth-century material standards of living—men with modern weapons must be cared for if they are to care for their sophisticated equipment—and their civilian kin, who lived under less favorable conditions, saw in the military establishment a mass demonstration of China's potential for modernization and development. But these modern armies were so expensive to maintain, and government was so enlarged to administer them, that the increase in taxation caused famine conditions in places rivalling the effects of murrains, floods, and droughts (Linebarger, 1938:103–11. See also Pye, 1971).

Under the nationalist government, the military remained the foremost product of the modern sector of the economy. But world commerce and industry did no more than support a central government superficially modern in appearance and confined in range of influence to the treaty ports, totally insulated from the country as a whole. By 1933, the modern sector of the economy accounted for only 2.2 percent of the net domestic product and had no direct influence on the traditional sector. Apart from an expansion of formal government, there had been no fundamental change in the occupational structure of China since the Ch'ing dynasty, down until the last days of the nationalist regime on the mainland, nor any change in the proportion of the net domestic product represented by agriculture or of the proportion of the labor force engaged in it (Feuerwerker, 1968:6, 17, 25).

The neogentry found new careers in Republican China. In a way this was made possible by the abolition of the examination system, which destroyed the basis in imperial culturalism for demarcating the moral and the economic life. For gentlemen, the division of mankind into two classes on the basis of spiritual values, as attested to by knowledge or ignorance of the classics, made for a fair and equitable arrangement since the exploitation of the ignorant by the superior was carried out in accordance with a compact agreed to by both parties. The meat and fish agreed to be eaten, as implied by the response of deference and avoidance on the part of peasants to the mysteries of aloofness and ritualized dignity on the part of gentlemen. But with the decay of self-respect in the moral sphere, the gentry of postrevolutionary China was freed as a class to seek privilege exclusively in the economic sphere, wherever opportunity beckoned. The old two-class system persisted, however, albeit reduced to an amoral distinction between consumption and productive work.

Under the monarchy, the gentry as a social group judged the standing of its own members not by wealth alone but more importantly by political power as measured by some combination of academic degree, official rank, influence as a retired official, activity in public affairs and informal government, and range of personal contacts cultivated with other power persons. The peasant majority was reduced to judging the standing of its own members on economic differences alone, a basis for internal stratification that fell to them by default because they shared in common a total lack of power. The peasantry was powerless in the absence of helping groups organized to defend its interests in the market place, in the homes of the gentry who set the terms of rent on land, interest on money loaned, or on justice arbitrated; the peasantry was similarly undefended in the offices of government that determined taxes and labor drafts. To the great men possessed of authoritative culture, the response of the folk was limited to supplication in a relationship cultivated under the name of *kan-ch'ing*, a technique for ameliorating exploitation by speaking of it as a quasi-friendly relationship (Folsom, 1968:28–29, Fried, 1953:224, 103–4; Sprenkel, 1962:100). To fellow villagers, the response was suspicion concerning differences in property ownership. By and large, the peasant condition persisted into republican times, even if we take into account the kulaks who bought parcels of land deserted by the gentry. Economic betterment, unless concealed behind a public show of conspicuous underconsumption (Fei, 1939:119–20), remained a threat to neighbors who, as ever, felt that one family's gain was everybody else's loss.

If 98 percent of the population were classified as commoners under the Ch'ing dynasty, the social facts determining their situation did not vanish with a legal reclassification as citizens under the republic. Relative to the neogentry, the peasantry was still disadvantaged by its lack of economic alternatives to physical toil, all of which were still monopolized by a corporate elite undivided by any struggle of vested interests. A privileged class still retained a multiplicity of controls in all fields relative to a nonprivileged class. Rents, interest, retail profits, investments, and peculations all belonged to the multifarious powers of the neogentry engaged in absentee landlordism in the umlands; in usury, trade, commerce, and industry; and in the expanded organs of local government, including military administration (Hanwell, 1937). Chinese society was still divided by a two-class system of stratification: the elite internally stratified by power differences as measured by degrees of access to economic privilege, the nonelite by property differences alone (see Jacobs, 1958:140–41; Wittfogel, 1957:303–5).

These were the inequalities of Chinese society that the Communist revolution set about to destroy with a program in land reform. However, Chinese Communist perception of this inequality was shaped by a Western formula about property relations borrowed from Marxist theory, in which owner-operators, part-owners, and tenants were arranged in a descending scale of economic stratification. This is not the basis on which Chinese peasants judged each other (Feuerwerker, 1968:35).

In any case, the following schedule of property relations was used by Communist land reform cadres. It is taken from a document drawn up in 1933 called "How to Analyze Class Status in the Countryside" (Foreign Languages Press, 1951:17–61).

1. *Landlord:* A person shall be classified as a landlord who owns land but does not engage in labor. . . . Exploitation by the landlords is chiefly in the form of land rent, plus money-lending, hiring of labor, or the simultaneous carrying on of industrial or commercial enterprises. But the major form of exploitation of the peasants by the landlords is the exacting of land rent from the peasants. . . .

   Warlords, bureaucrats, local despots, and villainous gentry are the political representatives of the landlord class and are exceptionally cruel and wicked elements among the landlords. (Among the rich peasants there are also small local despots and villainous gentry.)

   Any person who collects rent and manages the landed property for landlords and depends on the exploitation of peasants by the landlords as his main means of livelihood, and whose living conditions are better than those of an ordinary middle peasant shall be treated in the same manner as a landlord. . . .

2. *Rich Peasant:* A rich peasant generally owns land. But there are also rich peasants who own part of the land they cultivate and rent the rest from others. There are others who own no land but rent all their land from others. Generally speaking, they own better means of production and some floating capital and take part in labor themselves but are as a rule dependent on exploitation for a part or the major part of their means of livelihood. Exploitation by rich peasants is chiefly in the form of exploiting wage labor (hiring long-term laborers). In addition, they may also let out part of their land for rents, or lend money, or operate industrial or commercial enterprises. . . .

3. *Middle Peasant:* Many middle peasants own land. Some possess only a portion of the land . . . they cultivate, while the remainder is rented. Some of them are landless and rent all their land from others. The mid-

dle peasants own a certain number of farm implements. The middle peasants depend wholly or mainly upon their own labor for a living. In general, they do not exploit others. Many of them are themselves exploited on a small scale by others in the form of land rent and loan interest. But generally they do not sell their labor power. . . .

4. *Poor Peasant:* Some poor peasants own inadequate farm implements and a part of the land they cultivate. Some have no land at all and own only some inadequate farm implements. In general they have to rent land for cultivation and are exploited by others in the form of land rent, loan interest, or hired labor in a limited degree. These people shall be classified as poor peasants.

In general, the middle peasants need not sell their labor power, but the poor peasants have to sell their labor power for limited periods. This is the basic criterion for differentiating middle peasants from poor peasants.

5. *Worker:* Workers (including farm laborers) generally have neither land nor farm implements. Some of them have a very small amount of land and very few implements. They depend wholly or mainly upon the sale of their labor power for their living. These people shall be classified as workers. . . .

Apart from landlords of the old gentry, this class analysis is highly ambiguous. It was formulated by intellectuals on the basis of Western learning and with little knowledge of folk culture. Villagers did indeed react to economic differences among themselves, often with deep feelings of hatred and envy, but the basis for the judgment was not as described above. For example, the class "poor peasants" actually included not only tenants pushed out of land ownership by population pressure but also those who rented land as a business strategy, investing their capital in farm implements, not land. Some workers likewise hired out their labor as a business practice, not as a last resort. As for part-owners among "middle peasants," this class subsumes every case from a farmer who rents only 1 percent of his land (which would make him a "rich peasant") to one who rents 99 percent of it (which would make him a "poor peasant") (Feuerwerker, 1968:35, *see also* Wong, 1973:170–73). In practice, however, land reform cadres were guided by one overriding directive—to exploit resentments where they found them as a means of terrorizing any opposition to *chieh-fang,* or "Liberation," as the Communist takeover is officially designated.

In theory, the Liberation was supposed to liberate a massive outburst of productive agricultural forces held back by the oppressive forces of landlordism, rural usury, and inequitable taxation. But these were symptoms, not causes, of rural poverty. The problem of underdevelopment was the problem of one-sided Neolithic agriculture, not of social inequities. All Chinese farmers, whether classified as rich, middle, or poor peasants, belonged to the same class of undercapitalized Neolithic farmers working with a primitive technology and a primitive social reliance on self-help. The fact that an elite representing 2 percent of the total population lived off the rest without doing any manual toil did nothing to depress Neolithic productive forces beneath their natural state. The truth of the matter is that the destruction of the old social order, while it may have satisfied the morality of a new leadership imbued with egalitarian ideals, released no extra productive forces whatsoever. The taxes of the PRC, replacing the taxes and rents of the nationalist regime, have not been able to draw on an increase of output even sufficient to meet the demands of a growing population, much less the parallel and competing demands of industrial development. The statistics released by the PRC do show a growing disparity between food production and population growth:

> *Assessing the Chinese population in 1958 at about 650 million and at about 725 million in 1970, then the* per capita *grain production and production of other crops decreased—according to official and semi-official data from the Peking leadership—in twelve years from 385 to 330 kilograms* [250 to 240 million tons]. *If we use the average date of foreign estimates then there is a decrease from 315 to 290 kilograms. As population growth rates have been relatively low this retrogressive development may be traced back to the extraordinarily small expansion in agricultural production, especially if longer periods of time are compared.* (Domes, 1971:240–41)

The lesson for other underdeveloped countries would seem to be that ideological hostility to the old social order might be better translated into an intellectual understanding of Neolithic culture as the key to underdevelopment.

MASS SOCIETY

In essence, mass society means a "participant society," the enlargement of political participation and the spread of grass-roots organization (Lerner, 1958:60). It means "the loss of insulation of nonelites and the rise of elites bent on total mobilization of the population" (Kornhauser, 1960:22). The People's Republic of China is clearly a species of mass society. The leadership refers to it as a form of democratic society. That follows. Democracy is equated with participation. The leadership has brought peasants, not to say workers, into the ruling party. At the same time the CCP never became a party *of* peasants, although it brought peasants *into* the party until they swelled the vast majority of its membership. The party leadership was thus able to harness peasant energies, but for political ends never dreamed of by the peasantry (*see* Wolf, 1969:154).

In 1953–54, 323,809,684 voters elected 5,665,000 representatives to the people's congresses of villages and counties. These elected deputies at the provincial and municipal levels in turn elected 1,226 deputies to the First National People's Congress in time to sit in Peking's newly constructed Great Hall of the People. So huge was this task that it took a full year to carry out, following a long series of public meetings to discuss the candidates. With a picked slate of single candidates, screened voters, and rehearsals beforehand, it would be fanciful to judge this election even a perversion of Western democratic procedure, much less a costly deception designed to gull foreigners into believing Chinese democracy was an imitation of their countries' own. The actual voting took place in public by show of hands, under the eyes of local cadres (Hu, 1960:203–5).

This election was not designed to elicit a free expression of popular will, but to create opinion among vast numbers of people heretofore excluded from audience to political communications of any kind. It was but one of many mass campaigns organized by the government, for which trained agitators instructed the common people in the particulars of national life and attempted to arouse enthusiasm for national goals.

In the traditional society, ignorance and apathy were sources of convenience to a small ruling class unconcerned with economic growth and development; the elite simply lived off the small economic surplus produced by a vast and inefficient but self-policing Neolithic peasantry. In the new mass society, it takes more communication to get more productive work done, if only to support the enlarged organs of government required to carry out its social campaigns.

In principle, however, nothing has changed. The old Chinese politics of government by instruction is still in effect. The proverbial words of the *Shu Ching*, the *Book of History*, are still apt: "Heaven to protect the inferior people made for them rulers, and made for them instructors." It is true that the ruling elite of traditional China were aloof gentlemen whose educational value as a model for commoners served as a model for avoidance. All the same, officials and local gentry were defined as moral and cultural paragons, gentlemen rather than tools. Their unprofessionalized careers in office and their amateur ideals in private life communicated the values of generalism to the rest of society. If they had been specialized administrators in office or merely landlords at home, they would have been less imitable by other people and less able to communicate the widely relevant values of the civilization by personally enacting them. Their very imitability came from the time-tested generalness of their superiority, which allowed them to make their own standards of the all-purpose man all-pervasive. *

The self-sufficient peasant, wary of others, was nothing if he was not an all-purpose man—cultivating his own rice, building his own house, doing his own marketing, manufacturing his own handicrafts. And what is Mao's vision of the commune if not as a setting for the all-purpose man?

---

* It is easy to appreciate that Confucian generalists evolved by a process of orthogenesis from the all-purpose village folk of Neolithic times. Here again, gentlemen acted as illuminators of cultural forms raised up from the folk origins of civilization into the light of high culture for all to recognize and perpetuate unchanged. Not so obvious is the fact that even writing is an orthogenetic product in China, a rationalization of oral folk culture. All oral cultures depend on proverbs, clichés, and other formulaic expressions for the control of thought. In the absence of writing, the transmission of knowledge would become erratic unless managed within rigid formulas. But written compositions in China were just as cliché-ridden as the epithets of folk speech. Gentlemen were as fond as peasants of quoting pat phrases. The source of all literary clichés was the Confucian classics, which actually served as a back-up storage system for an oral culture based on their memorization. Indeed, after the Ch'in dynasty fell, the classics burnt by its first emperor were reconstituted from the memories of Confucian scholars. This Bronze Age style of writing was not altered until a literary reform movement began in 1917, in response to heterogenetic changes impinging on China from the West, a movement that favored the use of writing as a tool for breaking with tradition, communicating novelty, and stimulating curiosity. Dependence on the formulaic sayings of Chairman Mao in present-day China returns writing to its former status as a Bronze Age tool for the perpetuation of a two-class system divided, as of old, between moral proctors and their pupils.

The commune ideally abolishes rural/urban differences by assuming responsibility for the "seven guarantees" covering food, clothing, housing, education, medical care and childbirth, marriages and funerals; and abolishing the old leisure/labor dichotomy by absorbing hundreds of thousands of students while they learn the practical problems of farming (see Coates, 1972:252–53). The twenty million government cadres who work to enforce these ideals while stationed in the commune brigades and work teams do so, however, as both an example and a means of supervision (Donnithorne, 1967:65)—in short, as paragons of participation.

If government by education has enjoyed continuity in principle, its practice has surely changed radically. Communist exemplars are meant to be followed, not avoided. The appeal of mystery by which the imperial ruling class governed is now exchanged for the appeal of involvement. If the old elite restricted literacy, discouraged mobility, and fostered peasant contentment through ignorance, the new elite invites ambitious persons sensitive to political nuances to participate in social campaigns. Especially for junior personnel, the periods of mobilization provide opportunities for advancement up from the ranks of the local cadres at the same time that they carry high risk for senior personnel in the government, party, and state cadres.

Included in today's mass society are the ethnic minorities, as indicated by the iconography of the national flag: five yellow stars against a red field—one big star signifying the numerically and culturally dominant Han people and four little stars for the Mongol, Manchu, Uighur, and Tibetan minorities. This recognition of ethnic status does not stem from mere sentimental regard for exotic cultures but from an economic appreciation that these four peoples, small in numbers though they may be, occupy the big spaces of outer China, in which lie buried the nation's significant mineral resources. The horizontal stripes of red, yellow, blue, white, and black on the flag of the First Republic symbolized the same five groups, but the government had only the intellectual sense to appreciate, not the material power to exploit, the resources of outer China. The empire, of course, flew no national flag at all, only the emperor's personal flag—a red dragon on a yellow field—over the palace grounds.

Another group given political recognition in today's mass society is the military. In imperial times, the military officer was assimilated to the ranks of the civil service grades, and the status of common soldier to that of the peasantry from which he was recruited (Jacobs, 1958:138). The civil bureaucracy and the informal government of the local gentry provided all the organization required by the political pseudomorph of the old agrarian state. But culture contact with the West elicited the need for more organization, and the only effective source lay with the military administrations of the warlord period, coincident with the First Republic, whose leaders were extracted mainly from the traditional gentry. They stepped forward into politics as permanent military men, not temporary leaders of the militia, as in the old days. This change in self-identification established the fact that in modern China political power cannot be divorced from military power (Pye, 1971). Although the warlord troops formed on the basis of mercenary motives in the absence of ethical ones, they were a living demonstration of the only effective organization known in China at that time.

Out of this competitive warlordism emerged two military groups, the Communists and the Nationalists, which fought a civil war (interrupted by the Japanese invasion) for the right to implement national goals. The Communist insurgent group enlarged its field armies from 1945 (at the end of World War II) to 1949 (at the start of the Liberation) from 1.3 to 5 million troops (Barnett 1974:69–70). Today, the People's Liberation Army (PLA) is represented in the Chinese Communist Party with a membership of six percent. This overrepresents the "revolutionary armymen" as a percentage of the total population but does represent an access of political power following the Cultural Revolution, during which the PLA held regional control of the country while factions of the party in the government literally fought each other in the streets. Now more than ever, the army is a professional group, an autonomous community in arms with its own factories, farms, communications, transportation, and its own party organization dedicated to keeping it less politicized than the civil bureaucracy.

As in imperial China, the stratification system in Communist China consists of an elite, a nonelite, and outcasts, which in Communist China are named "party," "people," and "enemies of the people." The people are divided by family background into three class categories: peasants, workers, and intellectuals. The peasants constitute approximately eighty percent of the nation's total population, and in 1961 made up about two-thirds of the party membership. The working class consists chiefly of industrial laborers, who in 1962 made up fifteen percent of the CCP membership, as they did of the nation at large. The intellectuals are a small group of only 3.84 million, consisting of anyone having a better-than-average education. This includes technically but not politically many more millions of rural cadres and factory workers selected by their colleagues on the basis of activism for schooling up to the junior or senior middle-school levels; they are still designated on their party cards, however, as peasants or workers.

Intellectuals designated as such represent well under one percent of the total population, yet they figure very large as a potentially subversive element, especially the higher intellectuals. But of course, apart from those exempt from politics in order to pursue vital scientific research, intellectuals belong to the top leadership, responsible for the state-idea and its ruling doctrine. Above all, they must maintain doctrinal purity by subjecting themselves to group criticism and self-criticism meetings to earn the moral authority to impose party discipline on the cadres, who in turn carry out the party's organizational tasks. The old Confucian formula still obtains: doctrinal purity at the top, behavioral conformity at the bottom. Canonical correctness still takes the place of organizational positions of official and impersonal public trust. The character of the ruling elite is still moral and intellectual (Carr, 1974:17; but *see especially* Schwartz, 1973:366).

Not classified as peasants, workers, or intellectuals are those in a residual category, "others." This includes soldiers and a surviving class of national bourgeoisie—former owners of private enterprises who have been kept on as managers when their companies were converted into joint state-private enterprises. Beginning in the 1960s there developed a tendency for official PRC pronouncements to refer to "workers-peasants-soldiers" as a social category of politically reliable people, as distinguished from "intellectuals." The introduction of "revolutionary armymen" as a new and separate category in the CCP Constitution of 1969 is indicative of the new significance gained by the military during and after the Cultural Revolution (Whitaker and Shinn, 1972:122–24).

Unlike the class categories of imperial China, those of Communist China are not officially ranked; equality is one of its foremost points of doctrine, in contrast to the ethics of inequality that were the chief business of the traditional state to maintain through its policy of culturalism. Behind today's egalitarian ethic, however, lie the social facts of stratification. The actual system of ranking, based on income and job prestige, has been drawn up in the following tentative scheme by the American sociologist William Liu (1973:672).

(1) Intelligentsia
    (a) High Communist Party ruling elites
    (b) High-ranking non-Party intelligentsia, including governmental, economic, military and cultural bureaucrats
    (c) The middle-ranking professional and technical personnel, the middle-ranking bureaucrats, managers of smaller enterprises, junior military officers and diplomats, and artists
    (d) The white-collar workers, including accountants, clerks, bookkeepers, technical aids
(2) Working class
    (a) The skilled workers and workers in special national industries
    (b) The rank-and-file workers with lesser skill grades or those who are not politically active
(3) Peasants
    (a) The well-to-do peasants who profit at different times through the accumulation of greater private profit or through black marketeering. In the majority of cases, advantages are gained because of the geographical location or the nature of the crop raised, or because of some particular function they perform in the rural communes. This group may constitute about five percent of the rural population.
    (b) The average peasant with several shadings of productivity and political involvement. This includes poor peasants (about seventy-five percent of the rural population) and what might be called middle peasants (ten to fifteen percent of the rural population).

An explicit category of outcasts—enemies of the people—is a fluid category that changes over time with the different targets chosen during various social campaigns. Within ten years of coming to power, the regime had come to classify as enemies the "five bad elements": landlords, rich peasants, counterrevolutionaries, bad elements (thieves, murderers, and vandals), and rightists. In urban areas a series of class-struggle campaigns in 1952 succeeded in eliminating "bureaucratic capitalists," most private businessmen and traders of the commercial bourgeoisie, and many professional people and intellectuals taken over as government staff from the nationalist regime. Another movement against counterrevolutionary intellectuals followed the Hundred Flowers Campaign in the antirightest campaign of 1957. During the Cultural Revolution, factions of the CCP attacked each other as enemy elements, one side deploying students organized as the so-called Red Guards, who later fell out among themselves.

When a wave of killings brought about at least a million deaths, the PLA stepped in to restore order; all schools and universities were closed for four years and twenty-five million young people were "sent down" to the countryside to work in communes (Walker, 1971:16, 24). Afterward, those designated as "enemies" for killing were relabeled as "people." Special reception stations throughout the country were set up to take charge of "reversals" of labels.

Before the Cultural Revolution, however, the "enemy" label was not so reversible. In the land reform campaigns prior to the Liberation, one million "feudal bullies" were publicly executed in North China in 1949, according to official estimates. In the political liquidation campaigns of 1949–58, the estimate is thirty million executed. The Great Leap Forward and the establishment of communes resulted in about two million casualties. Struggles with minority nationalities, notably the Tibetans, have resulted in genocide figures of one million. Deaths in forced-labor camps over the twenty years of their formal existence is estimated conservatively at a ten-percent annual death rate amounting to a total of twenty-five million deaths (Walker, 1971:16).

As Mao wrote in 1927, "A revolution is not a dinner party. . . . To put it bluntly, it is necessary to create terror for a while in every rural area" (Mao, 1965: vol. 1, pp. 28–29). On the educational principle of "killing one to warn a hundred," the mass executions of the early period were held in public, and in 1969, public trials and executions of dissident intellectuals in Peking were given television coverage (Walker, 1971:25).

In spite of these tactics, the regime has succeeded in winning many admirers to the romanticized view of Mao as humanist revolutionary concerned with the fate of mankind. But Mao himself has explicitly rejected "humanism" as a motive or goal for his policies (see Walker, 1971:4, n. 1a). Yet the romantic view prevails. This can be explained on historical grounds. Successful revolutions have always been paradigmatic for all levels of protest—from dedicated revolutionaries in search of an effective strategy to students challenging the authority of parent and school. During the French Revolution it was the Parisian paradigm, evoking visions of the Bastille, the guillotine, and barricades. During the Bolshevik Revolution it was the Comintern paradigm of workers' organizations; and with the Chinese Communist Revolution of 1948 it was the guerrilla paradigm, copied by Ho Chi-minh in Vietnam, Fidel Castro in Cuba, and Che Guevara (unsuccessfully) in Bolivia. That we are still living in the age of the guerrilla paradigm, so far as it influences styles of dress and thought, can be confirmed by a visit to any American college campus (see Johnson, 1973:111). It seems strange, however, that American intellectuals should find anything romantic in the attitudes Mao is actually attempting to inculcate in his subjects: "Contempt for a qualitative grading system in middle schools and universities; contempt for the independence of scientific researchers; acceptance of political orthodoxy as the standard of excellence of all specialists; and acceptance of increased regimentation and even less remuneration for more work" (Cohen, 1967:98).

The system of stratification outlined above can be reindexed as a two-class system. The traditional dichotomy of an elite with privileged access to political protection and control, and a majority lacking it, still obtains. As always, the elite sector may be identified as the element in

Chinese society that names itself the most ethically and intellectually advanced, be it the Confucian literati, the Nationalist party elite, or the Communist party elite. The essential difference between the traditional ruling class and the new is that the CCP elite is a leader class that shows the way for its followers by direct participation and persuasion, whereas Confucian leadership was exercised by creating social distance from the led. In the last analysis, there is but one corporate class category for all privileged interests, and control of this category is monopolized by its members (Jacobs, 1958:138–39).

In functional terms, China's ruling class under communism consists of the organizational network of cadres, that is, party members in any responsible position in any organization of party, government, collective agriculture, industry, cultural life, or army (Lewis, 1963:186–89). There are no coexisting or competitive elites based on wealth, birth, tradition, or education. This is not to say no conflicting interests exist within the ruling elite, but only that all members of the elite belong to a single hierarchical organization whose apex is the Central Committee, within which is the inner elite of the Political Bureau, within which is the Standing Committee. The enlargement of the elite as a whole has made for more differentiation, to be sure. Rival groups may compete for control of the Politburo—nonparty agents, the Red Guards, were used during the Cultural Revolution by one party faction against another—but only recognition by the CCP authenticates career goals for ambitious and able individuals (Weiss, 1973:241–42).

Party membership and status as a party cadre is open from the viewpoint of individual mobility but is as closed as the Indian caste system from the viewpoint of group or class mobility. If workers or peasants belong to the CCP, their status and privilege derives not from their occupational membership in the proletariat but from belonging to the CCP as a corporate class. Mobility for the individual means renouncing one status position for another (Jacobs, 1958:139–43).

As all paths of ambition lead to one source of privilege in the leader class, so among the people in the follower class there is no escape from enemy status except in fulfilling the honorable role of compliance. Trade unions exist in China, but not to protect the rights of industrial workers. Rather the unions are instruments of a command economy designed to indoctrinate their members to appreciate the honorable role they are to play in working productively under Chairman Mao to make China a rich and strong socialist country (Jacobs, 1958:128–29). Similarly, the communes exist not only to direct peasant production but also to control peasant consumption, ensuring the transfer of an agricultural surplus for investment in industry or the absorption of labor not so productive.

For the romantic follower of the guerrilla paradigm in America, the People's Commune in China is grist for the counterculture, a model for an alternative life-style whose group living is at odds with the conventional single-family dwelling. Yet how thoroughly American is the option, given the wealth of alternatives in a highly developed country, to indulge the choice of life-styles—as in the choice of any other consumer product—for the sake of self-identity, rebellion, convenience, economy, or humanistic idealism. For the Chinese leadership, however, the commune is a strategy for rural control.

Not only primitive working conditions but also Spartan living conditions distinguish China from the modern industrial nations. In order to support a powerful military establishment and a massive investment program, Peking must treat the population as an input into the production process—to be fueled, maintained, and repaired, not catered to. (Ashbrook, 1972:6)

It is true that the Communist leadership attempts to elicit mass enthusiasm as well as regimentation. But in doing so, it reveals yet another similarity with the old Confucian elite. The one universal means of mass mobilization and social control is effected through small groups, called *hsiao tsu*, of from three to fifteen members for political study and mutual criticism (Whyte, 1974). Significantly, small-group activity is much higher among party members than among nonmembers; so many study meetings would interfere with the productive work of peasants and workers. Party members are subject to more ideological controls because of their power and responsibility; greater loyalty and discipline is expected of them than of ordinary citizens (Vogel, 1965:56).

In fact, the leadership claims to earn the right to carry out its own mandates, pleasing or not to its recipients, by virtue of its moral superiority not alone in doctrinal perfection but also in ethical perfection, so far as cadres are disciplined to set an example of Spartan living. Opposed to this are the organizational requirements of a large bureaucracy, with its differences in social position, political power, residential location, and security of tenure, make for differing personal interests (apart from class interests) that inevitably undermine the egalitarian ideals of a socialist state. Not yet ready to accept the inevitable, Mao launched the Cultural Revolution in part because the bureaucrats were losing the spirit of egalitarianism they had formed as guerrilla fighters leading to the Liberation. Moreover, the communes have not been effective in insulating peasants from the fact that industrial workers have been earning at least two or three times the income of the average peasant and have been entitled to various pension, health, and other social services that, unlike those of rural people, have been paid by the state.

Nonetheless, propaganda to the effect that China's national resurgence is built on self-sacrifice goes a long way, but only insofar as the leadership makes low standards of living easier to accept by setting an example of restraint. The political class is still as it was in traditional times a leader class by virtue of being closer to the cosmic Center of moral perfectability than are any followers of its authority (see Jacobs, 1971:249).

ELEVEN

RELIGION

CONFUCIANISM

Confucianism was the official religion of the Chinese pseudomorph—that is, it was a state religion without a state. It was also a religion without a priesthood set apart from secular life devoted to performing religious duties. The secular officials were hierophants in a political order so under-governed by Western standards that it bears closer comparison with the Catholic Church than with the government of the Roman empire, of which the Church was a vestige after the fall. The Chinese emperor is comparable to the pope, the metropolitan center to the Vatican. The district magistrate's post is comparable to the parish, the provincial governor to the bishop, and the viceroy to the cardinal. Like the wealth of the Chinese empire, that of the Church is embodied in its localized places and for the most part is not collectable by the center. The district magistrate, like the parish priest, holds a prebendal office with a revenue-producing territory, used for its own upkeep, attached to it. Like the Chinese empire, the Church is organized to propagate a moral-ethical doctrine by men educated in its intellectual tradition, who set a personal example. Local gentry act as laymen active in the same cause. Of course, the difference between the Catholic Church and the imperial hierarchy is that the Church coexists, within the context of the nation-state, with civil government, whereas the imperial hierarchy exists as the only bureaucracy on the Chinese scene. In both cases, however, incumbents defend an orthodoxy, whether theological in one case or sociological in the other, against all rival doctrines, declaring them heterodox. (On the development of the state cult of Confucius, *see* Shryock, 1932; on the sectarian intolerance of Confucianism, *see* de Groot, 1903–4).

As the Church has its books of the Bible and a tradition of interpreting them, so Confucianism has its sacred books and its exegetical tradition. The sacred books of Confucianism are the Thirteen Classics, listed below. In the following notes on their origin, *Han* always refers to the Former Han dynasty. References are to the most notable translations.

1. *I Ching (Book of Change)*
   A fortune teller's manual attributed to King Wen (1150 B.C.) and based on an oracular tradition at least 3,000 years old. Used in its present form, minus the "ten wings" added in Han times, by Confucius. (Wilhelm, 1967)

2. *Shih Ching (Book of Songs)*
   A collection of 305 court and folk songs collected from various city-states from the ninth to the fifth centuries B.C. (Legge, 1960: vol. IV; Waley, 1960)

3. *Shu Ching (Book of History)*
   A collection of speeches and prayers given on various historical occasions. Parts from tenth, eighth, and fifth centuries B.C. Mainly Eastern Chou with some Western Chou and possibly Shang pieces. (Legge, 1960: vol. III)

4. *Li Chi (Book of Rites)*
   Earliest pieces from fifth century B.C., with Han redactions about 50 B.C. Probably inspired by the *I Li*. (Legge, 1967)

5. *I Li (Book of Ceremonials)*
   Rituals of the Chou court; in existence in some form before the time of Confucius. Recovered and named by Han scholars. Probably antedated the *Li Chi*. (Steele, 1917)

6. *Chou Li (The Rites of Chou)*
   Han, with late Chou materials. (Biot, 1851)

7. *Ch'un-ch'iu (The Spring and Autumn Annals)*
   Chou chronicles from the state of Lu, kept between 722 and 479 B.C. (Legge, 1960: vol. V)

8. *Tso Chuan (Commentaries of Tso)*
   Said to be a commentary by Master Tso on the *Ch'un-ch'iu*, but actually an independent set of annals compiled between the fifth and fourth centuries B.C., with additions by Han editors. (Legge, 1960: vol. V)

9. *Kung-yang Chuan* and *Ku-liang Chuan*
   Commentaries on the *Ch'un-ch'iu* by Masters Kung-yang and Ku-liang; third and second centuries B.C., with Han redactions. (For selections, *see* Legge, 1960: vol. V)

10. *Lun Yu (Analects of Confucius)*
    Compiled by disciples of Confucius in the mid-fifth century B.C., with later interpolations. (Legge, 1960: vol. I; Ware, 1955; Waley, 1938)

11. *Hsiao Ching (Classic of Filial Piety)*
    Attributed to a disciple of Confucius in a composition of early Han date. (Makra, 1961)

12. *Erh Ya (Literary Expositor)*
    A topical collection of glosses on ancient terms in the classics; Chou material arranged by Han editors.

13. *Meng Tze (Mencius)*
    Eastern Chou, about 290 B.C. Last of the classics to be canonized in about A.D. 1100. (Legge, 1960: vol. II; Dobson, 1963)

The Thirteen Classics comprise the entire canon of Confucian literature, but the Chinese almost always refer to selected items known as the Five Classics and the Four Books, as grouped below. In the latter, arranged by Chu Hsi in A.D. 1200, the *Ta Hsueh (Great Learning)* and *Chung Yung (Doctrine of the Mean)* are choice books of the *Li Chi.*

FIVE CLASSICS	FOUR BOOKS
I Ching	*Lun Yu*
Shu Ching	*Meng Tze*
Shih Ching	*Ta Hsueh*
I Li and/or *Li Chi*	*Chung Yung*
Ch'un-ch'iu	

Apart from any meaning the philosophy of Confucianism may have for personal rectification, here we are concerned with its political significance for governing an empire. Because the empire drew its collective goals from an agreement among the Chinese elite to share in the conventions of the Confucian state-idea (and in little else), the main business of imperial politics was narrowed to upholding the orthodoxy. The Chinese pseudomorph thus made politics out of something insubstantial—what we have been calling culturalism—but the organizational and material consequences were real.

If political life, as Harold Laswell explains it, is a question of "who gets what?" (1963:345) the "what" in this case was the privilege of wielding a cultural tradition that had the material benefit of awing a Neolithic peasantry into paying rents and taxes without the coercive exercise of *force majeure.* The "who" were those "availing themselves of religious or traditional feelings of subordination" (to use John Stuart Mill's phrase). One gained access to this useful device by competing in the state examination system, in which the cultural majesty of elite status was conferred by the emperor. Thus were "lords of the soil" authenticated to serve in both formal and informal government. Because the royal house left almost all functions of social control to the local gentry, they as lay leaders were confirmed in the same Confucian orthodoxy as were officials. By seeking such confirmation, the local gentry joined with officials and the court in pursuing the one collective goal underwriting the political charter of the Chinese pseudomorph—doctrinal adherence to a sociological theory of inequality based on patriarchal imagery.

If Neolithic peasants were dominated by the "lords of the soil," the doctrinal content of the great tradition that established their dominance was, at the same time, continuous with the little tradition, in the patriarchal imagery associated with ancestor worship. Ancestor worship antedates Confucius, but its rationalization by men of the great tradition after him made it the orthodoxy of empire. The cultural force of ancestor worship derived from the fact that the Chinese have conceived of every one of their premodern organizations as a patriarchy with its internal stratification based on kinship distance and its origins traceable to some "ancestor" or initial progenitor. Confucius himself was a cult figure in state temples dedicated to his name, "the teacher of ten thousand generations." All human arts and social institutions, not just kinship organizations, were identified with an ancestor.

The preeminence of ancestor worship in traditional China, then, was not simply the religious expression of familism, if by *familism* is meant a preference shown to a kinsman in economic or political matters on the grounds that he was a friendly relative. Rather, given the tendency to rely on people with whom there is some preceding tie dictated by kinship, a man's circle of relatives is the most likely to contain an apt selection of individuals for help in whatever enterprise is to be undertaken (*see* Freedman, 1961–62:326). In the absence of helping institutions and without a legal system to protect capital and professional associations, the family created the pattern for self-help in all organizations, the patriarchy creating a model for their hierarchical structures.

District magistrates called themselves *fu-mu kuan*, father-and-mother officials, not for their accountability to the people, but because they were closest to the people in the business of profiteering; it was on their authority that taxes were collected in the last outposts of empire. Magistrates in turn had to nourish *their* elders on the model of filial piety by directing some of the profits of office upward to their superiors. On the same patriarchal principle, the empire itself was a great *kwo-chia*, a family-nation, whose metropolitan center was a complete polity unto itself. At the same time, the Center radiated its cultural influence outward: "The Master used the pronunciation of the capital in reciting the *Shih Ching* and the *Shu Ching*, and also when practicing the rites" *(Lun Yu,* VII:18). The emperor was the realm's family head in exercising this influence; and Shang Ti, synonymous with Heaven, was the emperor's paternal ancestor and worshipped by him at a round altar in the southern suburbs of Peking.

In the state cult of Confucius, then, functioned an ideology upholding a religious hierarchy of patriarchies, uniting the court and domestic rituals of ancestor worship into one system of stratification. (For a detailed description of the rites of Confucianism in the home and at court, *see* Williams 1932, chs. 12 and 13). As it says in the *Li Chi:* "The highest expression of worship is shown in the suburban sacrifices to Shang Ti, and in the offerings in the ancestral temple is the utmost expression of human affection" (*Li Chi*, II:18).

Both court and domestic ritual were informed by *li*, the dominant cultural policy of the great tradition. To follow voluntarily the gentleman's code of conduct regulated by *li* was to participate in the culture of the elite (the majority were subject to penal law, or *fa)*. *Li* refers to two aspects of behavior. First, it refers to the behavioral reserve called for in containing the free expression of sentiment—that is, in observing the formal boundaries that marked one's status, which it was improper to cross. Second, *li* refers to the actual formal ceremonies that defined and maintained the various gradations of human society. In the *Li Chi*, Confucius is made to say:

> *According to what I have heard, of all things by which people live, the rites* (li) *are the greatest. Without them they would have no means of regulating the services paid to the spirits of Heaven and Earth; without them they would have no means of distinguishing the positions proper to father and son, to high and low, to old and young; without them they would have no means of maintaining the separate character of the intimate relations between male and female, father and son, elder brother and younger, and conducting the relations between the contracting families in a marriage, and regulating the frequency of friendship.* (Ai Kung Wen, I. tr. by Legge, 1967, vol. 2, p. 261)

In this quotation, "the services paid to the spirits of Heaven and Earth" refer to the emperor's religious duties. He not only worshipped Heaven as his cosmic father but also Earth as his cosmic mother. Heaven worship took place during the winter solstice in the southern suburbs of Peking (the bright, yang side of the city) at a round altar of white marble. On this were placed for additional worship the ancestral tablets of his mortal agnates. As a man covers a women in sexual intercourse, so Heaven covers Earth below, t'ien-hsia (all-beneath-heaven). In respect of this hierarchy, the emperor comprehended the worship of Earth as well. This took place during the summer solstice in the northern suburbs of Peking (the dark, yin side of the city) at a square altar of dark yellow marble.

The cosmic idiom of the emperor's cultural supremacy as the "ruler of time" (of the calendar) was expressed by other ceremonies held at the temples of the sun and moon on the eastern and western suburbs, respectively, during which he was accompanied by high officials and ministers. But only the emperor and the nobility wore celestial insignia: the emperor, a round dragon motif on his costume (repeating the shape of the altar to Heaven), and his nobility, a striped cloud motif on their dress. His officials were definitely terrestrial creatures—mere snakes compared to the mighty dragon, who, like a water spout, occupies all regions high and low. Officials were identified by rank with embroidered mandarin squares on their official costumes, repeating the shape of the nether altar to Earth. In this distinction, the emperor was accorded cosmic majesty while his officials assumed substantive powers out in the provinces. As the proverb has it, Chiang lung nan ya ti tou sheh, "The mighty dragon is no match for the local snake, who knows the ins and outs of the place" (see Smith, 1914:14).

The state cult of Confucius, of which the emperor was the fountainhead, actually supported the thrust of this irreverent proverb. To the emperor and his nobility went celestial matters, that is, hereditary privileges; to officials and local gentry went terrestrial matters, that is, the nonhereditary privileges of collecting taxes and rents for self-aggrandizement in the emperor's name. The emperor endorsed bureaucratic autonomy (prebendalism) and the embedment of government careers within localized family interests to defend his royal prerogative against trespass by any combination of professional interests. Emperor and official both agreed that the royal prerogative consisted in hereditary cultural leadership as sanctioned by Heaven. In other words, while an official has only his local services to discharge, the emperor has a heavenly trust to maintain. That trust is the translocal business of the emperor alone. When the dynasty falls, the emperor is obliged to die for the sacrificial altars of state, whereas the services of the official are terminated, and he may leave them and save himself and return home. (For the canonical text supporting this idea, see Li Yun, II:18 in the Li Chi.)

As for the local gentry, they conducted the business of informal government within the same theoretical framework of inequality and with the same reinforcement from imperial culturalism. Any educated landlord was aware of the psychological strength given him by the mystique of cultural authority in winning the noncoercive deference of his tenants. This was illustrated in passages from Confucius such as, "If one is sedate in their presence, they [the little people] will be respectful" (Lun Yu, II:20).

Schoolboys learned about the cosmic mystification of hierarchy from children's books based on the classics. In one of these is a precocious lad named Hsiang T'ou ("Fragrant Head") in conversation with Confucius. For all living Chinese elite of traditional upbringing, the story of Hsiang T'ou is as familiar as the story of George Washington and the cherry tree is for American adults, recalling their days in primary school. One day while he is out rambling with his disciples in a carriage, Confucius questions the boy:

> "I wish to have you go with me, and fully equalize the Empire; what do you think of that?"
> The lad replied, "The Empire cannot be equalized. Here are high hills, there lakes and rivers. Either there are princes and nobles, or there are slaves and servants. If the hills be leveled, the birds and beasts will have no resort; if the rivers and lakes be filled up, the fishes and turtles will have nowhere to go. Do away with kings and nobles, and the common people will have much dispute about right and wrong; obliterate slaves and servants, and who will there be to serve the prince! If the Empire be so vast and unsettled, how can it be equalized?" (quoted in Williams, 1895, vol. I, pp. 534–35)

Needless to say, the Master expressed delight with this answer. Nature itself provided a model for the power gap between peasants and elite.

SUPERSTITION

One of the founding works in the scientific study of religion is a book written early this century by the French sociologist Émile Durkheim, *The Elementary Forms of the Religious Life* (1960; orig. 1912). This work explains religion functionally as the means whereby society maintains its collective identity. Durkheim broke new ground after Edward Tylor, the late nineteenth-century English anthropologist, introduced the doctrinal viewpoint in *Primitive Culture* (1874). Tylor emphasized the intellectual content of religion, its system of ideas and beliefs about the supernatural. Durkheim added that religious ideas, whatever their content, may be understood as "collective representations" of society. In other words, religious worship takes as its object the society itself, in a symbolic representation. Religious behavior thus keeps what is important to the organization of society at the center of human attention, thereby validating the basis for solidarity. Both traditions of analysis are essential to modern anthropology. What religion *does* and what its practitioners *believe* are complementary aspects.

The collective representation for high culture in traditional China was expressed in the ceremonies of ancestor worship, uniting court and domestic ritual in a single hierarchy. Herein lay the religious basis for the supremacy of authoritative culture over folk culture. With the fall of the monarchy, however, the moral distinction decayed. Exploitation carried out in the name of moral tutelage lost its name and degenerated into the sheerest kind of gangsterism—for example, military taxation paid years in advance in the hinterland under the warlords or commercialized agriculture in the umlands under absentee landlords, with monetized rent paid in advance and collected by agents backed by police powers (see Ch'en, 1928).

The Confucian benevolence of old, harsh and authoritarian and not very benevolent by Western standards, nonetheless owed to voluntary restraints on profiteering. These were lost when the ruling class was deprived of its collective representation in the symbols of empire.

At the same time, Chinese folk religion was unaffected. It lost none of its moral force in representing the parochial culture of the little tradition because it had never been a party to the horizontal ramifications of the great tradition. Before discussing this subject, however, it is necessary to distinguish between Durkheim's functional approach and Tylor's doctrinal approach because, oddly enough, activities associated with folk religion and ideas about it were divided between the little and great traditions.

Peasants practiced their religion and the elite reflected upon it. This transfer of doctrinal formulation to the literati follows from the fact that peasant societies are defined as "part-societies with part-cultures" (Kroeber, 1948:284. *See also* Fleure, 1937; and Foster, 1953). Peasant societies ordinarily lack sufficient cultural autonomy to project any collective representation of themselves. Thus they default their mythological charter as a whole people to an educated elite, which combines these different beliefs and practices (called "syncritizing") for the entire civilization, in which peasants reside as a relatively isolated subcultural unit.

As a small culture within the matrix of a civilized society, the peasantry keeps its subcultural distance and local plurality at the same time that it recognizes its relevance to the larger, or horizontal, context and the unchallenged cultural superiority therein.

> *A peasantry, by definition, is not autonomous and, therefore, it has a functional basis, within itself, for its degree of identification with the elite, great tradition. But this relationship takes, usually, a characteristic form, in which the peasantry, as a part-culture only, relegates most of its functions of formulation about its own behaviors and patterns, except for the unsystematic attempts, to the esoteric, syncretising elite. Its dependence upon the national cultural segments seems, along with its usual political dependence, to be peculiarly passive and supplicatory: It lets someone else tell it what it is doing. It is "popular" vs. "authoritative" culture. Whether in this respect, peasant cultures abrogate a portion of the explanatory function for their own culture—the function of myth as a charter justifying behavior —which is found even in primitive cultures, is an open question, but the possibility certainly suggests itself. (Lehman, 1959: 153–54. Author's references omitted)*

The possibility has indeed been realized in the Chinese case. Fei Hsiao-t'ung has described doctrinal abrogation to the literati on the part of peasants in the Yangtze valley. In that region, Lui-wan was a popular god. But Fei's informants told him that they honestly did not know who Lui-wan was although they had worshipped him for years, holding feasts in his honor the first and eighth months. The purpose of the feasts was said to be related to the harvest, but the link was unclear in the minds of the informants. Fei himself knew all about the god. Born into an educated family, he was told in childhood the elaborate mythology associated with Lui-wan's mission as a supernatural protector against locust plagues. Fei explains that the village he studied was not a self-sufficient religious unit, and that religious and magical performances on feast days connected with annual fairs or in case of locusts, flood, or drought took place in the market town, where a committee of leading shopkeepers and members of the landed gentry served (Fei, 1939:103. *See also* Skinner, 1964–65:38). It is significant, "that the lack of independent religious activity in the village on the occasion of agricultural crises is correlated with vagueness and ignorance about the myth connected with the god" (Fei, 1939:103). Far from a sodality of any kind, the village was broken up into eleven neighborhoods, each with its own idol of the god and its own meeting groups for feasting (Fei, 1939:102). But above all, the cult of Lui-wan had a different meaning at the popular and the authoritative levels (*see* Hsu, 1967:31). Peasants worshipped the god; educated men rationalized folk practice.

As another example, take the kitchen god, Tsao-shen, the supernatural inspector and policeman of each family: "the eyes and ears of Heaven above." This god held a much more important place in peasant households than did ancestor tablets (which were sometimes farmed out to Buddhist monasteries for care). The principles of descent—the "continuity of incense and fire" (Fei, 1939:29)—were important only to gentry families who had enough economic and political resources to merit the defensive activity of a protective organization. Wherever ancestor worship occurred among commoners, it did so out of affection for dead relatives on grounds of sentiment alone, not additionally as a managerial strategy to rally the larger kinship groups of joint family or lineage around a common symbolic center. Tsao-shen appeared in the kitchens of all nuclear families, belonging alike to small peasant households and to the joint families of the elite, but only for the former was it at the center of religious attention. The god received sacrifices twice a month, the first fruits of the harvest, and a birthday celebration at his altar above the kitchen stove. At the end of the year, his image was taken down and burned; through the fire he returned to Heaven to hold audience with the Jade Emperor (a heterodox Taoist conception), reporting on the particular family in his charge. Based on this report, the family fortunes for the new year were to be decided.

The mythological charter of the god and his mission to the world, Fei discovered, was almost totally unknown to the peasantry, the subculture having the greater stake in the god's surveillance (1939:100). Yet the god's myth is as much a part of the total religious complex as are the sacrificial acts. The myth was known only to educated persons, in a work known as *The Sacred Book of the Original Vows of the Kitchen God* (Graham, 1961:185). In deferring this doctrinal content upward to the elite, the peasant was left with only "the observance or nonobservance of certain taboos," such as never wasting rice and eating all that is cooked even if it turns sour (Fei, 1939:100).

The men of the great tradition recognized garbled fragments of their syncretism in folk beliefs and naturally took this as a sign of peasant stupidity. Unreflective superstition would be more accurate. Superstitions are by definition cognitive relics of systematic doctrine.

The following episode taken from Evan King's novel, *Children of the Black-Haired People* (1955), illustrates that such a stratification of truth served the power difference between elite and majority. This novel, in addition, is a reliable source on Chinese life in the 1920s in an area where the old patriarchal relationship between local gentry and villagers still obtained, untouched by warlordism and commercial agriculture. In the account, a couple try out the freedom-of-marriage reform advocated by the new revolutionary government, arranging their own marriage without a go-between—an act unheard of except among a wholly destitute class of expendables, the "grass-and-ashes" peasantry, among whom the woman simply "follows the man into the house" without ceremony. What is more, the bride attended the wedding feast in person, instead of sequestering herself. The villagers were outraged by this violation of custom. They faulted the woman, who came from another village, and accused her before the local gentry of being an incarnation of the fox demon. The head of the leading family concurred and ordered the woman banished from the village, after having her feet cut off.

The gentlemen, of course, were enlightened in matters of demonology. For them, the Fox Woman was merely a literary cliché (see Giles, 1925), whereas peasants accepted the idea of wereanimalism at face value. Enlightenment, however, was the coign of vantage from which the gentry were able to manipulate peasant superstition for their own ends. If reform were allowed in the sacred marriage rites, a train of unwanted social changes would follow to challenge local authority. But demonology kept peasant conservatism self-regulating, an advantage to the elite who thereby dominated informal government without incurring the costs of administration or coercion. Demonology had a continuous value across the two cultural traditions, but it was the elite who commanded the value of values. They could explicate one set of ideas in the religious sphere in terms of another, the political.

The premodern ruling class thus had a vested interest in malevolent supernaturalism as a form of cheap social control signified by peasant deference to the elite's global knowledge of the spirit world. Belief in demons was symptomatic of a village society divided against itself by mutual envy. If peasants kept their distance from the elite, they did so as individual families, not as a cohesive group sharing disadvantages with a spirit of common hardship. On the contrary, the village community was merely a setting for family life, a residential agglomeration of households, as reflected in its lack of religious coherence.

Envy is a special problem of peasant societies insofar as its overt manifestation in malevolent supernaturalism is concerned, precisely because exploitation is not sufficient to create village sodality. The exploiters, after all, are not the ones envied but the ones avoided. Envy is thus reserved for neighbors who share power at the zero point, and therefore small differences in socioeconomic status are unduly exaggerated. Fear of envy in peasant societies reduces the potential for cooperation. Decisions in the agricultural cycle are made as far as possible by the individual household (Foster, 1972). This policy was encouraged in China by the high population/land ratio, which allowed even poor peasants to hire landless labor during the busy season rather than to exchange labor on the basis of agreements to stagger planting dates. Thus the political needs of the gentry combined with surplus labor and the amoral striving of families to create in China that atomistic peasant society (Moore, 1966:208–11) Sun Yat-sen criticized in his famous indictment as *i pien san shah,* a "sheet of loose sand" (Sharman, 1968:361).

The collective representation of Chinese folk culture, then, is the absence of horizontal integration at the village level; the worship of Tsao-shen endorses what Edward Banfield (1958) has called "amoral familism." However, amoral familism was counterbalanced in China by those ceremonial expenditures that have served in all peasant societies to reduce envy by drawing off well-being from some people and redistributing it to others less well off (*see* Foster, 1972:185). In Chinese villages these were expenditures on temples, weddings, and funerals.

Peasants everywhere desire to appear poorer than they really are; the best defense of the "haves" against the resentment of the "have-nots" is to appear unenviable, however minute the differences in economic status. Since any advantage achieved by one family is perceived as a loss to the others, the differences are concealed by asserting a kind of egalitarian poverty reflected in underconsumption and thrift, a defensive ritual Wolf (1955) calls the "cult of poverty." Not to conceal unseemly prosperity can lead to acts of aggressive resentment, which Smith (1899) described for late nineteenth-century China as kidnapping, the planting of a dead relative on a neighbor's doorstep as a supposed suicide who took his life in anger, or the planting of a bag of salt for the salt inspector to find (once notified) in violation of the state monopoly. In China, fear of demons and evil spirits was a fear of envy, which in European peasant cultures has taken the form of the evil eye.

Essential to the cult of poverty is concealment, but this defense can be penetrated because privacy is hard to maintain when everybody in the village tries to know everything about everybody else; so differences in wealth are actually forced into channels of redistribution by way of ceremonial expenditures on public displays of merit and in fulfilling social obligations.

But the effect of meritorious redistribution can be achieved by symbolic sharing in the form of empty displays. Arthur Smith observed this at the turn of the century in North China:

> *Lists of contributions are kept in the larger temples, and the donors are expected to receive the worth of their money, through seeing their names posted in a conspicuous place, as subscribers of a certain sum. In some regions it is customary to set down the amount given as much larger than it really is, by a fiction equally agreeable to all concerned. Thus the donor of 250 cash sees his name paraded as the subscriber of 1,000 cash, and so throughout.* (Smith, 1899:136–37).

Still, the levelling effect was real enough. The number of temples in the villages—given to T'u-ti, the paired Earth-soil gods of any locality in one neighborhood and to Hua-kuang, the god of fire in another—reached as high as one to every ten families. Smith adds that, "It is a common saying among the Chinese that the more temples a village has, the poorer it is" (Ibid:139). The "encapsulation" (Foster, 1972:185) of temple neighborhoods made for smaller and smaller social units in which mutual envy could be contained.

Weddings were another occasion for ceremonial extravagance, one of the few times Fei (1939:128) says thrift was frowned on. Indeed, the costs of a wedding ceremony could amount to the annual expenses of one family (Ibid:53). While the wedding feast served to reinforce kinship ties (Ibid:45), it was also directed outward toward nonkin with a show of conspicuous public expenditure (Fried, 1953:92). Funerals for parents were taken as especially notable occasions for extravagant display of virtue. In connection with the mourning feast, Smith (1899:192) quotes the proverb, "When old folks die, the rest feed high."

But whereas the cult of Tsao-shen sanctioned the "loose sands" of amoral familism at the village level, the religious life (as well as the economic, political, and social lives) of the village was completed in a wider community centered on the market town. The true culture-bearing unit of the little tradition was the marketing area, comprising eighteen to twenty villages. If folk culture was pluralized and not translocal as was the culture of the great tradition, the boundaries of its parochialism in costume and custom were defined by the marketing area. This was the unit of endogamy for the peasantry, in which matchmakers from the market town drew their clients, and within which the bonds of affinal kinship ties were contained. For tradesmen, the market town was the unit of their local weights and measures. It was also the basic business unit for the local gentry in their role as landlords. They kept offices in town for meeting with their tenants on market days.

In the market town, gentry acted in their managerial roles as leaders of guilds in association with wealthy merchants, as officials of secret-society lodges, and as officers of local descent groups, whose lineage temples were located not in villages but in the market town. Economic decisions affected peasant welfare within the area when gentlemen invested their capital in pawnbroking, usury, artisan manufacture, and commerce. The ramifications upward of this commerce could extend from the local town throughout the higher centers of marketing, in a network covering China and its great entrepots opening on world trade. The same local marketing area was the essential unit of informal government, in which long-robed gentlemen served as mediators of peasant disputes. From their business dealings and leisurely strolls throughout the town, rural gentlemen collected a mental dossier on every adult in the area, and out of this impressive social wisdom held court in the teahouses of the market town or in their own townhouses (Skinner, 1964–65, part I; see also Yang, 1945:196).

The local political authority and extralocal business dealings of the elite persisted even after the fall of the formal religious hierarchy represented by the imperial state. For that reason, peasant life went on much as before. Villagers continued to visit the towns on market days, and if they no longer dealt directly with landlords but with their agents, they still met with each other under the cover of hospitality extended by the teahouses. There, every male adult spent at least an hour or two chatting with fellow peasants from all over the marketing area (Skinner, 1964–65:35). This wider hospitality extended to males from every village in the area, in contrast to the mutual envy of village life, which was generated by their wives (expressed in the way Communist cadres exploited jealousy and suspicion during land reform, as described in Chapter

the village level did not extend to the marketing area, which is the
administrative area for the present-day communes of the PRC.

COMMUNISM

Lionel Giles in his translation of the *Lun Yu* remarks that, "If we assent to
Comte's law of the Three States [of human consciousness], Confucianism
represents a more advanced civilization than biblical Christianity" (Giles,
1961:19. Orig. 1907). Quite apart from the notion of moral progress advanced by Comte, there is enough truth in the observation to remark that
communism in China also belongs to his third state, as well as Confucianism. This is one way of stating the ideological continuity between
the doctrinal orthodoxies of traditional and modern China.

Auguste Comte (1798–1857), the father of sociology, has been treated
with little respect in the wake of historical materialism; the influence of
Marx has been all-pervasive insofar as the social sciences now stress the
importance of material factors, such as the division of labor around a given
technology for a given economic output, in stimulating mental development. Social scientists now hold that the first stimulus is the
socioeconomic reality, then afterward society's explanation of itself.
Comte fancied it was rather the other way around, that mental factors
stimulated material ones. He aimed to demonstrate that, "Material development, as a whole, must follow a course, not only analogous, but perfectly correspondent, with that of intellectual development, which, as we
have seen, governs every other" (Comte, 1961:1339).

According to Comte, the course of history has been determined by a
succession of three states of human consciousness, three explanations of
man and nature that lie behind the three stages of social evolution. Consciousness I is "theological," in which political events, for example, are
explained religiously as the will of the gods, and political authority is derived from divine right. Consciousness II is "metaphysical," in which
political authority is based on the sovereignty of the people and social
facts are explained by the figment of a falling away from a state of nature.
Consciousness III is "positive," in which men explain social facts empiri-
cally. This is Comte's "positive method" of subordinating concepts to
facts, a method that in his day applied to physical and chemical facts and
that he hoped would extend—under his influence—to cover social facts.

By Comte's criteria, Confucianism stands with Consciousness III.
Surely it is not theological, for "the Master never spoke of . . . spirits" (*Lun
Yu*, VII:20). Nor is it metaphysical; the problem of the origin and existence
of evil is not touched upon and free will is taken for granted. For Confucius, the social environment makes the man: "By nature men are born
nearly alike; by practice their habits get to be wide apart" (*Lun Yu*,
XVII:2). The whole thrust of the classics is positive. Mencius explains at
length that the state is the sum of human endeavors working together as a
united organization; and Confucius is made to say in the *Chung Yung* (VI),
"Government depends on men."

Even ancestor worship was never for the Confucianists a matter of
belief in the spirits of the dead so much as it was a matter of right ritual
performing a useful function in holding the clan or the domestic kin group
together. Had the patristic writers of the early Han dynasty spoken the

sociological language of Auguste Comte, they would have said their job consisted in rationalizing theological materials of Consciousness I in the positive terms of Consciousness III. Thus the *Li Chi* claims for the intelligent mourner of Confucian persuasion that religious ceremonies benefit not the dead, as once believed, but the living. As Confucius is made to express it, "To treat the dead as dead would show a lack of humanity and is not done; to treat the dead as living would show a lack of wisdom, and likewise is not done" (*T'an Kung*, I:3). Ritual exists, in short, solely "to make a tradition which is handed on" (*T'an Kung*, I:2). What could be more empirical and downright sociological in outlook?

Educated men of the Confucian faith were well aware that they performed the rites of ancestor worship to focus the kin group on a symbolic center of attention, the better to integrate it for the purpose of harmony and continuity; they were able to supply for "incense and fire" an explanation as scientifically correct as any offered by Bronislaw Malinowski for the functions of any of the religions he studied. The native model closely approximates the anthropological model. Furthermore, Chinese gentlemen viewed folk religion as mere superstition; peasants, in making sacrifices to the kitchen god or even to their ancestors, did so to seek individual gain from blessings returned by appeased spirits. To this superstitious type of worship among peasants the literati gave the name *pai*; their own worship they named *chi*, with reference to ceremonies conducted for the kin group by the kin group on the basis of an enlightened theory of collective interests (*see* Chan, 1953:143). The elite could say, with the great Han scholar Hsun Tze, that religious ceremonies had a totally different meaning for the two classes: "To the gentlemen, they are a part of the way of man; to the common people they are something pertaining to the spirits (tr. Watson, 1963:110). Folk religion served only the interests of amoral familism and no wider integrative purpose. Had peasants made sacrifices in the name of a village collectivity, however, they no longer would have been peasants subordinated to exploitation by an enlightened elite, but an interest group with its own power base.

Under communism, a form of Consciousness III is promulgated among everyone. Herein lies the ideological continuity of Confucianism and communism, the chief difference resting with the fact that the former was restricted to an elite and that the latter is not. That is why Mao Tsetung can claim that communism is more Chinese than Confucianism —more Chinese are privy to it. Everybody participates in a nation-building ideology that urges peasants and factory laborers "to work hard for Chairman Mao and to make China a strong socialist country." But unlike Confucianism, communism by its nature as a participatory doctrine must conceal more in double-talk than it reveals in straight talk. The Confucianists were openly inegalitarian in their outlook: Society for them consisted of a moral/ethical/intellectual elite dominating a stupid majority. This native Chinese model of stratification accorded well with the actuality because the mass of Neolithic villagers had no alternative but to accept the cultural superiority of the great tradition, if only by default. That is, the traditional elite received deference as a by-product of the way peasants solved the envy problem within village society; they had to avoid paying attention to high culture as a way of avoiding the demons of mutual suspicion generated by their neighbors at the slightest show of material advantage.

This defensive ignorance within folk culture about the gentleman's life-style was complemented by the aloofness of the gentlemen themselves. The native model of stratification, with its morally superior elite on top and its laboring masses on the bottom, had behind it the reality of a great and little tradition divided by avoidance on the one side and aloofness on the other. But whereas the Confucian model of inequality was drawn close to the actuality, the communist model of equality is less accurate. It repudiates inequality in the face of a very real system of social stratification (See Chapter Ten). The ideals of a classless society take precedence over straight talk about reality.

Yet we must ask what social function this double-talk actually serves. There is a political purpose to it that works, so long as the leadership group is self-effacing. In other words, the stated ideals of equality may be widely accepted to apply in practice if government workers are careful enough, under orders from the highest councils of the regime, to display conspicuous economic equality in the course of exercising political inequality. The Spartan rule is: Power without comfort as a means of lowering the visibility of the actual power differences between rulers and ruled. Another symbol of equality is the commune system with its collectivization of land. Proletarians equal in nonownership must be at least somewhat relieved of the traditional envy problem that gave rise to demonology in the old folk community, and which kept the attention of villagers looking inward, away from the culture of the ruling class. Peasants who avoid political elites cannot be mobilized for a participant society. The Chinese Communists, therefore, made it possible for peasant attention to be directed outward to receive political messages, by undermining the basis for their inward-looking stance.

It is true that some production teams in areas where lineage organization used to be strong are in fact composed of the self-same lineages, with their leading families acting as the team cadres (see Donnithorne, 1967:66). All the same, such families are seen to be part of a uniform, translocal system of organization, whatever kinship roles still inhere in them. The abolition of private land has undoubtedly removed the biggest cause of mutual suspicion and thus has been effective in liberating the outlook of folk culture, allowing peasants to fasten at least some of their attention on the persons or images of state leaders and their policies, especially when this is encouraged by massive propaganda.

In one respect, nothing has changed. The Communist party elite remains, as was the Confucian chun-tze, an ethical elite endowed with the power to moralize on the basis of doctrinal perfection; likewise, it is still the fate of commoners to be the target of that moralizing, to accept government rule as fate. The right to transform the people below with the power of example still flows from some fountainhead of morality—be it the emperor or Mao—and not from the consent of those to be educated. But in another, more important, respect the change is profound. Whereas it was a matter of state policy among Confucian officials to remain aloof from all popular demands for governmental involvement, this policy is reversed for Communist cadres, whose mission it is to mobilize widespread participation in government-led plans. Imperial government demobilized demands on state resources with its wu-wei philosophy and by keeping the rate of bureaucratic officers down to as few as one for 100,000 to 250,000 population (Hsiao, 1960:5). The new Communist government by contrast mobilizes demands for official involvement and increases the number of governmental agencies accordingly (see Solomon, 1971:144). Passivity is no longer a virtue for the masses, any more than *wu-wei* or do-nothing is for officials; Mao's masses, as he wants them to be, are public spirited (see Lewis, ed., 1970:169).

Given the fact that political life is largely a question of "who gets what?" (as Harold Lasswell formulates the question), then it follows that a participant society is an expectant society: "When people get involved in politics, it is natural that they should expect to get more of whatever it is they want" (Lerner, 1936:345). In Communist China, however, with its heritage of a moralizing elite, it is government's job to decide just what the people, in their newly stimulated participation, want more of. As Mao explained to the editors of the *Shanshi-Suiyuan Daily* many years ago: "Your job is to educate the masses, to enable the masses to know their own interests, their own tasks and the party's general and specific policies" (quoted in Sulzberger, 1974:42). It cannot be more personal wealth people can be expected to want, because from the viewpoint of the political economy, the rural masses are at once "the main basis and the victims of the socialist version of primary capitalist accumulation" (Moore, 1966:481; see also Gamst, 1974:67).

But of course those who have been mobilized to reorder their lives for work in communes cannot be told with impartiality that they are the victims of the modernization process; rather they are its heroes. That the first order of business for the communes is forced savings for investment in the industrial sector is evident not only in the higher wages granted industrial workers but in the fact that provincial leaders in the politburo are drawn mainly from the most industrialized provinces. The same order of priorities occurred in the Soviet Union, the difference in China being that the collectivization of agriculture precedes its mechanization. This difference is Mao's chief claim to doctrinal innovation in the theory of communism (Cohen, 1964:189). One can readily appreciate the necessity for it, given the high dependency burden of the Chinese countryside—population pressure and underemployment.

Rural cadres work in the communes to serve as an example, as well as a means, of supervision. That the state should so define the aspirations of the people as well as mobilize them for increased effort is consistent with a tradition of leadership in which politics is viewed as education, but it is inconsistent with Marxism and its emphasis on the material determinants of history. Cadre involvement in making agricultural work patriotic, an act of participation in the business of nation-building, means inducing a change of mind about the traditional Chinese contempt for manual labor.

Thus, political consciousness is a precondition of economic development or, as Mao puts it, "a great spiritual force becomes a great material force." (Gray, 1973:116)

In the hands of Mao, communism as a modernizing ideology is thus the reverse of the Marxist orthodoxy he professes to follow with greater fidelity than do Russian leaders. In 1859, Marx wrote:

> *I was led by my studies to the conclusion that legal relations as well as forms of the state could neither be understood by them-*

selves, nor explained by the so-called general progress of the human mind, but that they are rooted in the material conditions of life. (quoted in Cohen, 1964:1)

This is Marx hitting at Comte. But Mao hits back at Marx with Comtian intellectual determinants when he studiously avoids economic planning on the basis of projecting trends and possibilities and creates instead new aspirations to work for (as in the Great Leap Forward).

Finally, we note the persistence in China not only of a moral elite but of a view of China itself as the moral Center of the universe. China is now "the People's Middle Kingdom" (Fairbank, 1966) so far as the rest of the Communist world is concerned, and the center at Peking is still closer to Heaven than the rest of *t'ien-hsia,* as quite consciously symbolized in the details of a poster entitled, "Advance under Mao Tse-tung's Victorious Banner" (illustrated in Chesneaux, 1973; 163, fig. 66). A great figure of Mao looms over smaller figures of peasants, workers, soldiers, sailors, air-men, and children, who throng the great square of Tien An Men in Peking. He sweeps his arm forward in the van of two red banners, one the flag of the People's Republic of China, the other that of the U.S.S.R. Naturally the flag of the PRC is the leading banner. But more, the finials of the two flags show a celestial and a terrestrial symbolism, respectively—a dichotomy as clearly divided between Heaven and Earth as the emperor's round insignia (the temple of Heaven) was superior to the square insignia of his mandarins (the temple of Earth). The finial on China's flag is a star, that of Russia's a spearpoint. By arranging these celestial and terrestrial symbols on an international scale, China's modern leaders have reasserted an ancient ideal of a political center at the *axis mundi* ruling by correct ideology over natives and neighbors alike.

TWELVE

WORLD VIEW

FACE

In "The Handler," a short story by Damon Knight, a short, ugly man operates a tall, handsome dummy from within. The dummy is the attractive center of admiring attention; but when his handler steps outside to join in the fun, everything comes to a stop. The little man is urged to get back inside the dummy so the party can start up again. He does. The contradiction between inside and outside is no longer visible, "and everything was all right, far into the night" (Knight, 1972:208). The author's purpose is to moralize about hypocrisy. But the morality is definitely American if not altogether Western. The Western theory of sincerity—a homunculus theory—requires that the actor within us correspond with the exterior action; that the authentic self not wear a false face. We should not be like the people who are insincerely called upon, in T. S. Eliot's words, "to prepare a face to meet the faces that you will meet" (Eliot, 1930:12).

Chinese do not behave in accord with the same theory. For them there is no psychological guesswork about sincerity because the self is defined by the sum of one's social roles, not by an inner man who handles those social roles with fidelity to one's true feelings (*see* Carr, 1974:35). Westerners naturally misunderstand the de-emotionalized control by the Chinese of their interpersonal behavior and take this as evidence of insincerity —what feelings do they hide behind the mask of formal niceties? In a way, the Western judgment is based on fact: The Chinese follow a success policy and not a truth policy.

Among the ways cultures may differ, as William Graham Sumner was the first to point out, is their regard for falsehood and deceit as devices by which to attain success in relation to interests. Truth may or may not be taken as a virtue policy; if not, untruth is just as virtuous a means of success. In traditional China as in many other cultures, it was regarded as stupid to tell the truth to others not intimate enough to know the difference. A success policy based on deceit with outsiders was approved as a virtuous means of protecting the interests of self and family. On the other hand, polite untruths were called for among insiders if that, too, would advance the success of group living.

For the Chinese, truth is not the final arbiter of sincerity, as it is for Westerners. The Chinese possess their own standard of sincerity, which is different from ours in that it is not affection they are sincere about but the relationship itself. Truth-telling can introduce friction into the smooth working of polished surfaces; harmony and group accord are more important than revealing one's inner state of mind. One has social duties to perform with others, not vulgar confessions to make. A man is sincere for doing what he has to do in his relationships, not in honestly exposing his motives. It is the *what* of behavior that is important, not the *why*.

However, if the Chinese do not make a distinction between the inner, emotional self and the outer, social self, they do distinguish sharply between an inner world of social relationships in which the rules of sincerity apply and an outer world in which they do not. The inner world is any set of relationships in which the individual is relatively permanently involved, starting with the family. One's life is embedded in a social setting from which he derives his status and to which he owes the duty of interaction. Sincerity means discharging one's formal duties to maintain the system in which one acts. Not to do so is to lose face, which is more than embarrassment or the loss of social poise, but the loss of one's power position in a set of stratified relationships. As William Carr (1974:14) writes, "A loss of 'face' may be embarrassing, but embarrassment is not loss of 'face.' "

Face is the Chinese name for one's office in a formal structure of rights and duties. It reflects the sociological orientation of Chinese behavior and their concern with doing the right thing to the right person for the sake of harmony *(ho)*—the success of the on-going social system—as set against the Westerners's psychological interest in human motives and the honest display of feelings. The inner world is where these concerns for harmony apply; in the outer world of strangers they do not. In the inner world, one may tell a lie for the sake of harmony, and everybody in that world is sufficiently intimate with each other to understand if the words are meant to have any substantive content other than their use as soothing ritual. As one Chinese student explained to George Danton (1938:122), "Courtesy is telling a lie to save the feelings of others." Strangers, by definition, are not intimate enough to appreciate the courtesy behind a lie, and therefore are treated with rudeness. In other words, a sharp dichotomy exists between a world of complex, subtle, and enduring relationships and a world of no relationships at all.

The inner world is exemplified in what the Chinese have called the *chi chao*, the Seven Relationships or seven obligations—those between emperor and official, father and son, husband and wife, brother and brother, friend and friend, elder and junior, and host and guest. Two related facts of outstanding significance are implied in this native model of behavior. The first implication is that all relationships obtain between unequals and that the power differences between them are personalized, not contractual in the legal sense. The seven obligations typify the inegalitarian nature of all premodern Chinese relationships; everybody in the structure of every relationship holds an *individuated* position, unequal in rights and duties. The archetypical situation is the big family, in which every kinship position is unequal to every other one as calculated in kinship distance, that is, by age, sex, and generation, starting with the eldest male at the head of the hierarchy. No two persons are of equal status in this or in any other setting. Even in friendships of the most intimate kind, the relationship is phrased as a kinship model between elder and younger brother, the role of the elder brother being to guide and instruct the younger in the particulars of mutuality. One party to the friendship is in charge of policing the equality for which the relationship was voluntarily joined in the first place, often as an escape from the repressive controls exercised in all other relationships. The "heart-belly friend" is a prized companion in a relationship whose emotional gratifications are defined as something that everything else is not; but because this definition is one narrowed by exclusion, a power relationship must nonetheless be introduced in order to control adherence to its highly specific terms.

The other social implication follows from the first. If all relationships in the inner world are inegalitarian ones between superior and subordinate, they are *personal* ones of superiority and subordination. The seven obligations are governed by men, not laws. A subordinate complies without doing injury to his ego because no image of a free man equal to others lurks behind the discharge of his duty. This is totally at odds with the Western conception of human relationships, first spelled out by the ancient Greeks, in which actual power differences are masked behind laws that govern and subject superior and subordinate alike (*see* Gouldner, 1965:304).

Furthermore, personal submission among the elite to superiors is voluntary (just as superiors dominate on the basis of personal claims), because elites are guided by custom, not penal law *(fa)*; *fa* is for uncultured people who lack the self-discipline to be controlled by codified ethical norms *(li)* (*see* Sprenkel, 1962:125). Those subject to law are also personally subordinate to those who are above penal law, as a commoner to his scholar-landlord, although more by necessity than ritual nicety.

The concept of *li* that governed the behavior of Chinese elites until the fall of the monarchy is traceable to the feudal aristocrats *(kwei)* of the Chou dynasty, who placed themselves outside the law. All but the *kwei* were subject to the penal code, which was used by the hereditary elite against commoners. At the time of the Ch'in dynasty, the First Emperor attempted, on Legalist advice, to make all but himself subject to the penal code, so that it was no longer a monopoly of the nobility to use against the people but his alone (Marsh, 1961:50). This experiment failed; and even though the aristocracy in time disappeared as a hereditary elite, a Confucian elite of cultivated gentlemen replaced it—an educated elite who defined themselves as that body of men who voluntarily lived by the proprieties of *li* as distinct from *fa*. The relevance of the Confucian classics as a guideline for behavior among the imperial gentry, right down until the twentieth century, stems from the fact that ancient sources describe rules of liturgical government for small communities of formal government in the feudal states; and that these rules apply equally well to the small, face-to-face community of informal government dominated by the local gentry. The rules of noncoercive deference described in the *Chung Yung* apply as well to a feudal lord as to an educated landlord. Thus the local gentry could well take to heart, with practical effect, those ancient principles of princely government that call for the feudal lord: "to inspire awe without being severe, as when a wise and good man watches over every minute detail connected with his daily life, not only in conduct and bearing but even in minor details of dress, so as to produce upon the public mind an effect which otherwise could be produced by fear only" (*Chung Yung*, XX:14, tr. by Ku Hung-ming, quoted in Brinkley, 1902, vol. XI, p. 73).

The stress in the ritualized behavior of *li* is on self-discipline, as explained in the *Lun Yu*, where Confucius says that, "If the ruler cherishes the principle of self-control, the people will be docile to his commands" (tr. by Giles, 1961:36). The main lesson imbibed by the Confucian gentlemen from the classics is that the mystification of status through control of self pays off in the effective control of others, as expressed in this passage from the *Li Chi:* "The *chun-tze* watches over the manner in which he maintains his intercourse with other men" (*Li Chi*, II:14).

The behavioral niceties of *li* thus call for de-emotionalized relationships in which consciousness of *form* may take precedence over the exchange of feelings. One may imbue relationships with feelings, but this is an option that may or may not be introduced as the emotional *content* of the formalities. This lesson is well put in the *Li Chi*, in the passage where Tsu Kung, a disciple of Confucius, asks about the mourning rites for parents: "The Master said, 'To be reverent is most important. The feeling of grief is second to it' " (*Tsa Chi*, II:1). Never mind the sorrow, just do your ritual. You may or may not feel genuine sorrow for the death of your parents, but above all you must make a show of reverence. You must look good doing what you have to do (that is the essence of "face") for the sake of the organization, which at the same time may serve either as a cover for your lack of sorrow or as a vehicle for expressing it. But family life goes on, regardless, and the rituals of ancestor worship play an important functional role in focusing the group's attention on a symbolic center and in rehearsing individuated status positions. The Chinese have traditionally possessed a sociological awareness concerning the practical gain from just this sort of behavioral formality.

It is precisely this sophisticated awareness, this conscious ability to distinguish between form and content, that made the Chinese appear to Westerners as inscrutable, deceptive, and insincere. The daughter-in-law may hate her mother-in-law's guts, but she must nonetheless perform her ritual of personal subordination, the kowtow, perfectly, not leaking out any trace of bad feeling by a show of insubordination. The two women must live together in the same household, whose minimal conditions of coherence are ritual harmony; all the forms must be observed even if they lack sincere emotional content (in the Western sense). Ritual conformity itself is an expression of sincerity (in the Chinese sense), a sincere contribution to the on-going system of family life. Personal dislike of a kinsman, however, need not be repressed; bad feeling can be conveyed indirectly via servants' gossip.

In contrast, the American soldier who dislikes his commanding officer is likely to communicate his feelings directly by way of introducing some imperfection into his ritual obligation—for example, by saluting from too far away, or too slowly, or by misplacing the hand. He does not omit the ritual altogether, or perform badly enough to be gigged for an omission, but just badly enough to communicate a message of dislike. This is Western sincerity—the frontal display of affect undisguised by misleading outward signs. But if Americans in particular, and Westerners in general, test sincerity by the honest refusal to distinguish between affection for the person and respect for his status, the Chinese test is in always making the distinction. Western truth policy aims at self-expression, Chinese success policy at making systems work. If Westerners think the Chinese evil for their duplicity in separating affect from formal obligations, the Chinese think Westerners ignorant and low class for not appreciating the value of the intricate over the simple (Stover, 1962; Stover, 1974a:262).

The Chinese sense of cultural superiority in perceiving and acting upon two realities—form (status) and content (affect)—follows from an explicit theory of duality stated in Neo-Confucian works of Sung dynasty vintage, when the Four Books were canonized as a set. In this model of duality, principle or form *(ri*)* is contrasted with matter or content *(ch'i)* *(see* Kang, 1974:198). The greatest of the Neo-Confucianists, Chu Hsi, famed for reworking the Han synthesis of Confucian materials, explained that: "in the universe there has never been any material-force *(ch'i)* without principle *(ri)* or principle without material-force" (in de Bary et al., 1960:536).

This theory of duality underlines the Chinese concept of sincerity, *hsin*, the fifth of the Five Virtues, also formulated by the Sung Neo-Confucianists. *Hsin* is the sincerity of any transaction in which one has performed *li* correctly without the mistake of leaking out inappropriate feelings. *Li*—politesse or right conduct in maintaining one's place in a hierarchical structure—is the first of the Five Virtues. This formulation is based on such remarks in the older classics as, "The *li* arrange people in their ranks" *(Tso Chuan,* tr. by Ch'u, 1961:233). In both theory and practice, educated men of premodern China made a point of separating "passion from action" (Pye, 1968:149) and of giving priority of action over the actor for the sake of system stability. The Chinese thus distinguished between persons and personnel the whole man and what is organizationally relevant about him, stressing the latter even in private life. This is just the opposite of the American emphasis, which gives priority to the actor over the action for the sake of behavioral freedom and the spontaneous show of affect, the very hallmark of Western sincerity.

Whereas Americans and other Westerners give and take away love or affection, Chinese give or take away face; that is, they mobilize or demobilize power relations (Stover, 1962). A society emphasizing face necessarily operates on a success policy, as clearly conceded in the Chinese proverb: "It is better to be strong on the outside than strong on the inside: that is; it is better to be able to carry one's point than to be in the right" (in Smith, 1914:220). This is in fundamental contrast with Western truth policy, so well stated by Nietzsche in *de Wille zur Macht:* "It is more distinguished to own oneself wrong than to maintain one's cause, especially if one is right" (cited and tr. in Baker, 1974:45). Small wonder that Westerners visiting China found in face behavior nothing but deceit, especially when dealing with Chinese as strangers in the outside world and not as intimates privy to the inside world.

But even when involved with the Chinese inner world, Westerners sometimes learned with dismay that the Chinese used them for personal gain rather than embracing them as friends. In other words, they discovered that relationships could be personalized without being privatized.

---

* Actually *li,* but spelled *ri* to avoid confusion with the word for rites and ceremonial.

Once the polite formalities were seen not as signs of friendship in a relationship of personal concern, the Chinese were accused of hypocrisy.

But the fact of the matter is that Chinese were never able, in the absence of helping institutions other than the family, to afford the open-ended relationships that Westerners so easily strike up with strangers as a matter of course. If the Seven Relationships were not sufficient to provide the goods and services a man needed, he had to cultivate power relationships outside them, called *kuan-hsi*. Westerners invariably misunderstood *kuan-hsi* as friendship, but it was distinct from both kinship and friendship. Such relationships were made to supplement the supportive role of the family and the incidental help of friends. *Kuan-hsi* relationships are still openly visible among the Chinese of Taiwan. William Carr has observed:

> With the conviction that to deal with strangers is to ask for trouble, the Chinese have little choice, however, but to develop "friendships" that will insure access to goods and services. Chinese kuan-hsi *relationships begin not with a vague, undefined feeling of compatibility, but with purposeful estimates of each person's value to the other. Contrary to the American ideal, material benefits are expected in* kuan-hsi *agreements and any that are derived serve to indicate the sincerity and reliability of the giver. . . .*
> Chinese prepare for a rainy day by having people, not money, in the bank. Job situations provide excellent opportunities for expanding one's kuan-hsi. The more jobs one has, the more kuan-hsi opportunities there are. (Carr, 1974:24, 28)

Such power relationships are obviously an extension into a modern economic setting of what Chinese officials did under the traditional political order in the absence of the rule of law—what Fei Hsiao-t'ung has described as the "personal approach to the power hierarchy" (Fei, 1946:8). Officials did not hold office very long. In a short period of time, a man had not only to earn back the costs of running his office plus a profit for himself, he had also to establish a record of personal influence to draw on for the protection and advance of his private interests after his retirement from office (*see* Chow, 1966:53).

CONTENTMENT

The more *kuan-hsi* a person could cultivate, the more face he could accrue. In theory everyone had face (*see* Hu, 1944), but like the power potential behind it, peasants had it at the zero point. The local gentry, even in republican times, were said to possess both "land and face" (Fei, 1946:9). That is, landed property for them had political as well as economic significance; it was the base from which they mobilized power relationships to some degree as translocal as the cultural tradition that backed up their collection of rents. The same power difference was also described as the difference between the *chih-shih fen-tzu*, "they who know," and the *yu-min*, "stupid people." The *yu-min* had no power and therefore their face had no *chuen*, or "weight."

The "stupidity" of the *yu-min* has given rise to a number of illusions held by the native elite as well as by outside observers concerning peasant contentment. Chinese landlords and officials, having a vital interest in keeping the work force under their authority as ignorant and dependent as possible, for that reason have not developed a very good explanation to account for compliance. Chinese gentlemen have been accustomed to viewing themselves as the exclusive bearers of culture, or *wen-hwa*, and to maintaining that the stupid people lacked culture altogether. But just because the *yu-min* lacked high culture did not mean that they lacked their own folk culture with its own norms of behavior, nonliterate though this tradition may be. Gentlemen viewed themselves as exemplars of morality and justified their position of leadership on the grounds that they supplied an indispensable pattern of conduct to be followed, however slowly the virtues of the example were expected to filter down to the people. But in reality, as we continue to stress, commoners responded to the example not by imitating it but by avoiding it, and did so for reasons internal to their own folk culture as well as for external ones belonging to elite policy.

Anthropologists, as outside observers, have not always hit the mark, either. The classic example is Robert Redfield's cross-cultural model of the cheerful rustic who loves the soil for its own sake and who follows ancestral ways out of sheer reverence for tradition. To be fair, Redfield did bring the study of peasant culture to the attention of anthropology, and only in the light of its development as a subfield does the founder's work now appear unrealistic in its emphasis on the sanctification of rural life as such. In *Peasant Society and Culture,* Redfield wrote that the good life of peasants everywhere includes: "an involvement of agricultural labor with traditional, often reverential, sentiments about the land; the connection of that labor with ideals as to peasant worth; the inculcation in the young of endurance and hard work rather than a disposition to take risks and to perform personal exploits; the acceptance of arduous labor, yet with a great enjoyment of its surcease" (Redfield, 1956:123). This makes the lot of the peasant seem no more than a pastoral life-style, chosen for its attractiveness from some cafeteria of cultural alternatives—precisely the attitude of an American family who recently chose to live and work for a time in a Chinese commune (Galston and Savage, 1973). The only difference in the two viewpoints is that in the former, contentment is seen to have arisen from the soil spontaneously, whereas in the latter, it was designed by humanistic revolutionaries as a new and improved way of life. The reality is that the Chinese commune was designed by a new political leadership class to enable a more thorough taxation of the rural economy in order to pay for modernization and growth. If the new language of government accountability speaks of taxes spent on the people in the form of investment in nation-building, the old Confucian elite spoke of nothing less than an exchange of taxes for moral instruction.

Redfield notwithstanding, "love of soil" under premodern conditions is more sanctimonious than sacral. Fei Hsiao-t'ung expressed the reality by describing the peasant's feeling about his lot as highly ambivalent, because it is the product of his reaction not only to his own cultural setting in folk society but to the unattainable culture of the gentry in its urban centers.

> The mass of peasants do not live in the town. They look at the seat of the gentry with a mixed feeling of repulsion and admiration. They support the living of the minority by paying taxes,

rent, and interests. The annual tribute is their burden. In the Yangtze Valley, with the social conditions of which I am most familiar, I believe, it will not be exaggerating to say that half of the yield of the peasants goes to the town. If the economic reason is still not sufficient to arouse the ill will of the peasant toward the town, he will no longer remain undisturbed when he finds his unsatisfied wife run away from home to work as a maid in a gentleman's big house, which he dare not enter. However, the town remains the ideal, the dream, and the incentive of peasants. It seems they are not antagonistic toward the town, nor the gentry, as such. What they are against is their own inability to become one of those who exploit them. (Fei, 1946:7. emph. added)*

One of the factors preventing them from becoming one of those who exploit them is the suspicion that their neighbors intend to do just that. No increments of landed wealth or of moveable wealth (if not hidden) can be built up without being levelled down by the relentless pressure of mutual envy. Social mobility across the gap of subcultures, if and when it occurs on the basis of covertly accumulated wealth, occurs suddenly. One day a poor peasant is seen living in his hovel, a tatterdemalion eating mud mixed with his grain as a filler; the next day he is living behind walls in town (*see* Fried, 1952).

The same habits that made for a quantum jump in pre-Communist China still obtain in the Chinese communities of Southeast Asia, which C. Northcote Parkinson humorously describes for Singapore as "breaking the hound barrier."

The Chinese coolie lives in a palm-thatched hovel on a bowl of rice. When he has risen to a higher occupation—hawking peanuts, for example, from a barrow—he still lives on rice and still lives in a hovel. When he has risen farther—to the selling, say, of possibly stolen bicycle parts, he keeps his hovel and his rice. The result is that he has money to invest. Of ten coolies in this situation, nine will lose their money in unwise speculation. The tenth will be clever or lucky. He will live, nevertheless, in his hovel. He will eat, as before, his rice. . . .

When he moves it is primarily to evade the exactions of secret societies, blackmailers, and gangs. To conceal his growing wealth from the tax collector is a relatively easy matter; but to conceal it from his business associates is practically impossible. Once the word goes round that he is prospering, accurate guesses will be made as to the sum for which he can be "touched." All this is admittedly well known, but previous investigators have jumped too readily to the conclusion that there is only one sum involved. In point of fact there are three: the sum the victim would pay if kidnaped and held to ransom; the sum he would pay to keep a defamatory article out of a Chinese newspaper; the sum he would subscribe to charity rather than lose face.

* Fei, Hsiao-t'ung, "Peasantry and Gentry: An Interpretation of Chinese Social Structure and its Changes," *The American Journal of Sociology,* 52, 1 (1947):7. Reprinted with the permission of the University of Chicago Press.

Our task was to ascertain the figure the first sum will have reached (on an average) at the moment when migration takes place from the original hovel to a well-fenced house guarded by an Alsatian hound. It is this move that has been termed "Breaking the Hound Barrier." (Parkinson, 1957:93–94)

In addition to mutual suspicion, another factor that used to work against incremental mobility in China was the attitude of government, both formal and informal. Republican officials and gentry, like their imperial predecessors, continued to use their authority in an aloof manner designed to demobilize claims of the governed. The powerful had the face to seek *kuan-hsi* relations with the more powerful, but the peasant had no face to seek any special considerations from authority, except in supplication. The leaders kept their distance from the led as a matter of policy, inasmuch as the elite exploited the majority merely, never administered it. For that reason, legal statutes introduced by the legislative Yuan of the nationalist government, using Western statutes as a model, were absorbed into Chinese politics as moral guides, not enforceable regulations. In 1931, a high Chinese official was asked about a new labor law with its regulations for an eight-hour day, insistence on pensions and accident insurance, and the abolition of child labor. Were these laws enforced as in Japan? "No," was the reply. "We have not enforced them. It is our belief the government should hold up high ideals to the people and should set standards toward which they should work" (Burgess, 1933:407).

The traditional Chinese enactment of government as moral instruction rather than legal enforcement of statutes is, at bottom, a policy of demobilization. The men of the great tradition kept the men of the little tradition at arm's length and in no way allowed them to participate in high culture. This political attitude is in sharp contrast with Western governments, even in classical times. The rulers of ancient Rome never pursued as studiously a plan of alienation as did Chinese authorities in all past ages. What Edward Gibbon has described for the Romans would never have applied in premodern China. In the magnificent imperial baths of Antoninus Caracalla, ". . . the meanest Roman could purchase, with a small copper coin, the daily enjoyment of a scene of pomp and luxury which might excite the envy of the kings of Asia. From these stately palaces issued a swarm of dirty and ragged plebians, without shoes and without a mantle. . . ." (Gibbon, 1963:440–41; orig., 1776–88)

On the basis of this contrast alone we may observe that heterogenetic civilizations from early times were participant societies—to the extent that the elite catered in any way to the majority—and that orthogenetic civilizations were not. Only after its cultural isolation and autonomous development were brought to an end did China become a participant society.

The appearance of peasant contentment in premodern China, considered as an orthogenetic civilization, results partly from the governmental policy of demobilization. Peasants who did not accept the low ceiling put on their aspirations, imposed either by their fellows or by their betters, had to express achievement by moving geographically outward rather than socially upward. The attraction of the town, which Fei describes as creating in the peasant a feeling of ambivalence about his own folk culture, was thus a center for his hopes economically, if not politically. A discontinuity

existed between great and little traditions; but if upward mobility along
the rungs of the power ladder were limited to the literati, then another
parallel ladder of commercial wealth was accessible to the ambitious
commoner willing to venture outward from village, through the local
marketing system, to the great economic regions beyond. This commercial
wealth could later be converted into political status, with educated sons
put through the examination system (Skinner, 1971).

At this point, factors other than cultural may be seen at work. Culture
is sometimes visibly the product of human biology. For example, endogen-
ous body odors are absent or weak in almost all members of the Mongolid
subspecies of man, even in crowded rooms and after not washing for a
week or so (Baker, 1974:173). In contrast with the more smelly subspecies
of man, such as the Europids and Negrids, the Mongolids can tolerate greater population densities, as expressed in more crowded living conditions.
Similarly, the mental as well as the physical qualities of different sections
of a race may have been altered over the centuries by migration or other
selective processes. A temperamental selection for the migrant achievers
leaves behind a population of "sedentes," to use a word coined by two
physical anthropologists (Shapiro and Hulse, 1939). Therefore, some of the
apparent contentment of the rural countryside in China may be due to the
village sedentes, the stay-at-home relatives of the out-migrants, who found
an outlet for their urge for mobility in the marketing network.

The sedentes evidently outnumbered the migrants, because the
number of achievers in any human population seems to be a low constant,
from the Bushman of the Kalahari desert to the school populations of
middle-class Americans. "Only about one out of a hundred persons exhibits a strong urge to achieve, although perhaps twenty to thirty percent
can be rated as moderately ambitious" (Pfeiffer, 1969:352). Thus the layout
of town and countryside in China may be a spatial expression of temperamental selection, so far as it has been undisturbed by enforced population
movements. We may speculate that the augmented powers of government
after the Cultural Revolution, which enabled it to remove twenty-five
million teenagers from the cities into the rural communes, have created a
self-perpetuating need for such powers, inasmuch as more social control is
required for mixed than for homogeneous folk populations. The rate of
surplus urban youth "sent down" is now about two million a year.

But above all we must not underestimate the cultural controls relating
to peasant contentment. If the traditional peasant loved the soil, sedente
or not, somebody made him do it—his neighbors. The same goes for hard
work: the extravagant care with which each plant is manicured, weeded,
and manured. This really doesn't make the garden grow any better, but it
does disarm the curse of envy by demonstrating rightful possession of the
land. Hard work is thus less an expression of personal worth, as the ro-
mance of folk culture would have it, than it is a defense against claims
asserted by neighbors to possess the plot of a lazy worker by promising, in
their own example, to work it harder. Martin Yang (1945:18–19) said of his
native village in Shantung that "the more weeding the better the crop."
We would say, "good weeding makes good neighbors," or, "less weeds, less
gossip." Indeed, the very fragmentation of family land holdings into scattered parcels (interpreted by Yang as an inconvenience) made it all the easier
to keep an eye on everyone else's work. Now that the Communist govern-

ment has collectivized the private plots that once gave rise to this competitive work ethic, new incentives to replace mutual suspicion must be provided by the same powers of organization that destroyed it.

ACTIVISM

Nothing could be more discontinuous in the history of Chinese political culture, for leaders and led alike, than the preference of the new ruling elite for techniques of mobilization and direct control over those of demobilization, which were exerted by the old elite. Here the mark of permanent change has been made, in the direction of a worldwide trend toward the participant society.

Behind the Liberation of 1949 lay twenty-two years of civil war, during most of which the Chinese Communist party was identical with the Red Army. Not until the early 1940s, when the CCP gained secure guerrilla bases behind the Japanese lines, did it mobilize civilian cadres on a large scale, in addition to recruiting soldiers. At the start of the war, the CCP controlled 4 million inhabitants with 80,000 members and 100,000 troops in North China, where Mao had led a decimated party on the "Long March" after attacks on its soviets in South China by the Nationalist Army under the personal command of Generalissimo Chiang K'ai-shek. By 1945, the Party numbered more than a million members, with almost a million troops and over 2 million local militiamen at its disposal for the control of 95 million inhabitants in the rural parts of North China and the northeastern (Tungpei) region centered in Manchuria. It was in Tungpei, in the first months after the close of the Pacific war, that the Soviet Union provided the CCP with the means to equip a strong, conventional military force by ceding to it, in violation of its treaty with the nationalist government, the entire equipment of the Japanese army, whose 700,000 troops had surrendered there to the Russians. After that, the Nationalist Army could no longer hold North China, and the Red Army entered Tientsin (15 January 1949) and Peking (31 January). Called the People's Liberation Army after advanced units had crossed the Yangtze in 21 April 1949, the Red Army took Nanking (23 April), Wuhan (16 May), Shanghai (27 May), and Canton (3 December). Remnants of the government and of the Nationalist Army then fled to Taiwan (Domes, 1973: ch. 1).

Having gained control of the entire country, however, Mao Tse-tung was not content to accept his inheritance of China's traditional political culture—the passivity and avoidance of followers and the aloofness and insulation of leaders. He was determined to extend to his conquered domain the organizational techniques he had developed as a means of winning that conquest. In an article of 1945 entitled, "Some Questions Concerning Methods of Leadership," Mao writes that the masses in any given place "are generally composed of three parts, the relatively active, the intermediate and relatively backward. The leaders must therefore be skilled in uniting the small number of active elements around the leadership," and must rely on them to lead the other elements. In other words, agitation by trained cadres is followed by recruitment of activist personalities, who in turn serve as local leaders. This is followed by a selective process that purges out unreliable recruits. "In the process of a great struggle . . .

the activists who come forward . . . must constantly be promoted to replace those original members of the leading group who are inferior by
comparison or who have degenerated" (Mao, 1965: vol. III, p. 118). It was
this "organizational engine of agitation, recruitment, and control" (Solomon, 1969:89) that extended the leadership cadres of the CCP in the
wake of the PLA's military sweep and thenceforth instituted a new
mechanism of activist controls unprecedented in Chinese politics.

Unprecedented also is Mao's concern, in developing this novel political culture, with the psychology of motivation—a typical Western concern. No doubt Mao's untraditional political behavior is in some way related to culture contact in China which now, under communism, has
begun to transform an orthogenetic civilization into a heterogenetic one.
At all events, the CCP under Mao was able to mobilize agitator personalities throughout China and to bring them forward as a means of expanding cadre leadership. And he did so as a matter of policy operating
from a psychological theory explaining the liberation of local resentments.
The struggle meetings called by outside cadres were designed to elicit resentment and hostility from potentially activist personalities, often in a
violent display, if they could be encouraged to "speak bitterness."

In the countryside, those with bitterness to speak were those with
resentments toward town life and fellow villagers. The feelings of hatred
for the town, as a seat of the gentry, were ambivalent ones because this
hatred amounted to a resentment on the part of peasants at their "own
inability to become one of those who exploit them" (as Fei Hsiao-t'ung has
pointed out). But this would refer to peasant males almost exclusively,
because it was they, not their wives, who made the journeys to the market
town on market days, there to do shopping, pay rents to the landlord, and
sit in the teahouses and receive the informal justice of the gentry. As for
resentments confined to the village, we note again, these were mainly the
mutual suspicions generated by peasant women, the motivating force of
the "speak bitterness" meetings arranged by Party cadres. In this Mao
realized the potency of female discontent as earlier apprehended by the
Ch'ing government in its displeasure with Buddhism, because female wor-
shippers prayed to Buddha to be a man in the next life (Baller, 1907:78).
The women's grievance surely was not that of subordination to male authority, as in gentry households, because peasant women worked as equal
partners with their husbands in farm labor. Rather they felt more keenly
than their more widely travelled husbands the fear of neighbors as potential competitors for limited resources.

Women oppressed by the authority structure of family life were self-
selected activists from the neogentry, who joined the revolution out of an
awareness of their situation heightened by contrast with the "bourgeois"
alternative, as displayed by resident foreigners in the treaty ports. This
contrast was emphasized in pre-Communist literature, which described
the Chinese joint family as "feudalistic." In the language of the political
Left in China, even before the advent of the PRC, feudalism was a strongly
emotional word of anathema for anything inegalitarian, exploitative, or
traditional in the republican order. The Communists succeeded in fulfilling the ambitions of those knowledgeable about Western family life, even
while damning what they attacked in the joint family as "feudal" and in

the nuclear family of foreign inspiration as "bourgeois." The outcome for everybody was the nuclear family, a form belonging to the little tradition (Freedman, 1961–62:334).

The difference is that the nuclear household under communism is associated not with the amoral familism of old but instead with the collective values of the commune, the new setting for family life, while the new literature extols the virtues of "self-denial as regards property or personal freedom" (Wu, 1973:726). The kitchen god survives, the old representation of amoral familism, but he has been subordinated to community values and national patriotism. Tsao-shen is still in the kitchen, but Mao Tse-tung is in the living room (Geddes, 1963:49).

The new collective values have made a difference insofar as everybody may now relate to everyone else in an important new way, as "comrades," or national citizens. One may help strangers and otherwise address persons one has never met before without engaging in face behavior or building up *kuan-hsi*; a universalistic ethic has replaced a particularistic ethic (*see* Vogel, 1965). The urban communes would be unthinkable without this new public ethic; for the first time in Chinese history street cohesion is possible, albeit enforced (Coates, 1972:117). In the cities, amoral familism had its own expression in the proverbial saying, "Sweep the mud from your own doorstep, but do not mind the snow on your neighbor's roof."

Today, every city is under the direct management of the Street Revolutionary Committees. By means of these, neighbors who had never noticed each other before "were obliged to be present at street meetings, at which not only did they come to learn each other's names, but were required publicly to confess their error in not previously noticing each other" (Coates, 1972:117). The committees are organized on the basis of streets and lanes without reference to a ward or a precinct, and may embrace a compact population of up to 60,000 individuals living in from 10,000 to 12,000 families. The next higher level on the organizational pyramid is occupied by the City Revolutionary Committees, which in turn are under the control of the provincial governments, with the exception of Peking, Tientsin, and Shanghai, whose municipal status is the equal of provincial status (Hsu-Balzer et al., 1974:77; Tregear, 1973:114).

The legal basis for commune organization was laid down as early as 1950 in Article 9 of the marriage law: "Both husband and wife shall have the right to free choice of occupation and free participation in work or in other social activities." This legal defense of the individual's right to join nonfamily associations must be interpreted to mean, in actuality, a moral obligation to participate in social forms which do not at all represent diverse individual interests but uniformly state-instituted and state-controlled agencies of production and control. Article 100 of the Constitution of 1954 applies here:

> Article 100. *Citizens of the People's Republic of China must abide by the Constitution and the law, uphold the discipline of work, keep public order, and respect social ethics.* (in Wu, 1973:802, 809)

At the Sze Ping commune in Shanghai, for example, each street committee is organized around one of eight local factories. "There is no choice about working in this factory—if you live in this commune, are under forty-five years of age, and have no other work, you must work here" (Hsu-Balzer et al., 1974:77). Older people run nurseries or do finishing work for other factories.

The enforcement policy behind the obligation to work is mediated by "social ethics." This means, in effect, that "public opinion would be very harsh toward someone who did not want to work" (Hsu-Balzer et al., 1974:77). Yet the public ethic is phrased legally in the language of individual rights to join voluntary groups. There is at once a similarity and difference here with mass society in the West. One of the basic tenets of the theory of mass society is that, "People become available for mobilization by elites when they lack or lose an independent group life" (Kornhauser, 1960:33). The Marriage Law of 1950 provides for this in its weakening of the family as an all-inclusive interest group. So far there is nothing here that is not familiar to us from the Western experience of family life.

> For most of the inhabitants of an industrialized society the family is a small residential group from which many of the major activities of life are excluded. The factory, the office, and the school separate the members of one family for many hours of the day and provide them with different ranges of relationships and interests. What they unite for as a family is a restricted number of activities of consumption, child care, amusement, and emotional exchange. (Freedman, 1961–62:333)

The difference is that the public ethic of Chinese mass society, with its cautions against close personal relationships, is not complemented by a private ethic.

> What is unique about Communist China is not the presence of a universalistic ethic governing personal relations, but the absence of a private ethic to supplement the public ethic and support the commitment of the individual to his friend. In most Western countries, close personal relationships may exist outside of a work context giving personal support to the individual for the tensions which exist in his more formal work requirements. In Communist China, the universalistic ethic penetrates much more deeply into personal lives so that it is difficult to gain personal support from the tensions generated in the more formal relationships. (Vogel, 1965:59)*

As a result, there is a measure of double-talk in the new political culture: Moral obligations to society are phrased as individual rights.

At this juncture, the current political culture of China departs from that of the past. If in the past China had subjects without a state (the pseudomorph, again), today China is a state without citizens. The native model of the imperial pseudomorph advanced by the literati was fairly

---

* It can be argued, however, that nothing different in Chinese behavior is required, that mutual suspicion has merely been harnessed to the purpose of mutual surveillance. This is an old Legalist technique of police enforcement, updated and given the name of public spiritedness. Ch'ing Shih Hwang Ti, the Legalist emperor, is in fact Mao's biggest hero drawn from Chinese history.

accurate in reflecting the reality of social stratification. Now that China is no longer undergoverned, the native model advanced by Party theoreticians is much less accurate; the reality of stratification is concealed behind idealistic language about equality. When traditional leaders used their influence to demobilize the masses, they made straight talk about the social gap separating top from bottom. Now that there is more government, whose leaders are less insulated from the people in their mobilization of a participant society, there is more double-talk and hypocrisy.

All states must necessarily be founded on an untruth, what Plato called the well-intentioned, or beautiful, lie. For elites, who by definition know more about political reality than the majority they govern, a stratification of truth is unavoidable. Plato explained that the reality of hierarchy requires a beautiful lie to make it acceptable to all as a defense against envy from below. The beautiful lie of his ideal state asserted that, "The deity who created man put either gold, silver, or brass into his soul, thus predestining him for his position in the state" (Falke, 1958:17). The beautiful lie of the Confucian state asserted that the morally superior men at the top, who had knowledge of the wisdom books, and the morally inferior men at the bottom, who were ignorant of the books, formed a division of labor between mind and strength, working for the harmony of the common good (see Chapter Ten). The elite got fed in exchange for moral instruction, of which the lie was a part.

In Communist China, the beautiful lie denies stratification altogether. The state comprises only "the people" who share the ideal of equality, in collision with disbelievers, "enemies of the people." The ideal nonetheless reflects a certain amount of reality, so far as political geography is concerned, because more government means less regional exclusion. In the traditional society, a political common denominator for all parts of China was limited to the carriers of high culture; folk culture was parochial and divided by its local manifestations. The rulers of Communist China, in projecting their political culture downward, have provided a common denominator for the peasantry as well, changing it from a folk society into a mass society.

One contradiction, however, emerges from the fact that activism has achieved greater equality of organizational results among the Han population, represented by the big star on the national flag, than it has among the six percent of the population who make up the national minorities, represented by the four little stars. The state disavows any policy of "Great Hanism," but in fact it finds the cultural differences of the non-Han minorities difficult to assimilate. If the non-Chinese do not conform, they are liquidated either by outright genocide—as in the Tibetan case—or by slow pressures to reduce population—as in the case of the Mongols (see Liu, 1973:680–86; Sulzberger, 1974:61–67).

The chief contradiction is that the state exists for a common cause rather than for a common good. The leadership applies activism in a different manner to itself than to the led. For the Party elite, activism is a matter of doctrinal purity, strengthened in criticism meetings and study groups and informed by orthodox learning in history, economics, and class relations. For the less informed, activism is a matter of bending to the winds of doctrinal superiority, grass blown and bent through mass agitation into organizational forms serving a totalitarian species of mass society, whose common cause is building a strong defense economy, rather than anything else (Balogh, 1967:326). In the absence of a common good, measured by the participation of conflicting interests coming out of a pluralistic society, the new political culture results in a state without citizens, an inversion of the traditional order. The activated bend to the socialist ideology of the activators, as those subject to *fa* bent to moral superiors informed by *li*. But this power differential is masked by an idealistic model of society that denies stratification in place of justifying it. The gap between social reality and its homemade model may be too great for any beautiful lie to maintain for long.

In conclusion, we can only regret that so many of today's Chinese intellectuals are denied the opportunity to help rationalize social facts as did their forebears, the literati. A society cut off from knowledge about itself must grow anomic. We read with dismay the self-denouncing words of Fei Hsiao-t'ung as spoken in 1972 to a visiting team of Western anthropologists, who had gone so far as to praise Dr. Fei for speaking such words. He denounced all he had written in the past as the misguided effort of a "bourgeois scholar" whose works "did not serve the peasants, but those who ruled over them" (in Cooper, 1973). This is not a fair self-criticism, but Dr. Fei's interlocutors certainly believed so out of their own conviction that anthropologists everywhere should always serve "the broad masses" and never "those in power." We hope the following rebuttal is instructive.

> One cannot in earnest accept Fei's 1972 statement that his past works served the interests of those in power (except as a reminder to them to mend their ways). Today, however, Fei and his colleagues, by effacing themselves completely as independent scholars and by "reeducating themselves through the study of Marxism–Leninism, and the thoughts of Mao Tse-tung," utterly put themselves at the service of those in power now. Yet if there is one thing such a political system—and, in fact, any political system—needs, it is independent social scientists who, though loyal to the system, point out discrepancies between the beautiful ideology and the less-than-beautiful reality, even if this is not to the liking of some or all authorities. It is revealing that there is no serious independent study of any of present-day China's 800,000-odd villages. (Köbben, 1974:315)

ENVOY

All civilizations began as poor and underdeveloped agrarian states. They began with an authoritative culture at the top and a nonrecognition of popular culture at the bottom. Not wealthy enough to finance the assertion of differences in religion, ethnicity, or political opinion, the old agrarian states kept for the rulers what amounted to their only commanding possession: the idea of a deserving elite. Political status was necessarily held as an intellectual monopoly.

The same is true for the underdeveloped nations of today. The oldest political crime in the history of civilization is still the chiefest crime. It was described by Confucius for China over twenty-six centuries ago: "He who holds no rank in the state does not discuss its policies" (*Lun Yu*, VIII:14, tr. by Waley, 1938). The anthropologist Fei Hsiao-t'ung committed this crime in June of 1957, during the "bloom and contend" period, for which he spent a term in a labor camp until December of 1959. An impressive advocate of communism, Fei meant only to reassure his fellow intellectuals, in a speech before the Central Committee of the China Democratic League, that "speakers will not be charged with guilt." On this point, he said, the government's promise could be relied on. He was released from camp the same day as his fellow inmate, the last emperor of China, Henry Pu Yi, who had been reformed to serve the people as a gardener in the Peking Botanical Gardens. Fei lost his position as vice-director of the Central Institute for National Minorities in Peking, where he had been in charge of the research division. This position's not being a policy-making organ of government, Fei had spoken out of turn by repeating a policy statement that was neither his to make or affirm.

In rich countries, the police defend the property of its successful citizens; in poor countries that have not yet arrived at the "takeoff" point from their traditional economic base, the police defend the authoritative ideas monopolized by their rulers. Intellectuals who do not belong to the government or to its ruling party pose a threat because, by originating and spreading alternative ideas, they may deny the rulers their sole claim to power. No writer could be as important, least of all as dangerous, in the United States as Aleksandr Solzhenitsyn is to the Soviet Union. Such writers are in effect rival politicians who undermine political power in a way they could never hurt money power. In rich countries, political status is so extended by economic status, with its prestige for all who earn high incomes, that politicians find no competition in the ideas of writers, however much these writers may disagree with governmental policy. All ideas may be heard because they do not speak as loudly as money. Ideas speak only for parochial interests—for Catholics or Quakers, oilmen or the poor, blacks or chicanos, homosexuals or women, masons or labor unions —whereas money is the universal coinage of a popular national culture.

In poor countries, ideas are the one and only currency of power, and these must be defended as the exclusive privilege of politicians who are in charge of implementing them for the majority; otherwise the politicians must yield to rivals who seek the same career.

To the Western eye, Communist Chinese politicians appear to be self-effacing because they live plainly and dress in a kind of national uniform. Unlike Western politicians, however, they can afford to trade off comfort for power. One is privileged to deal in ideas or one is not. There is no mistaking the political elite because there is no other kind.

In traditional times, the political ideology was cheap to defend because Chinese rulers made no effort to mobilize the people to uplift their maintenance economy. The poverty of the economic base insulated politicians from attack because few others were literate enough to command the ideas whose monopoly was the basis for their privilege. Now the ruling elite has undertaken to mobilize the whole population to create wealth in accordance with the extreme socialist idea that the nation should be run as a single business concern. It is more costly to protect an ideology of development, however, because the pursuit of economic growth militates against political stability. In the past, the safety of elites was secured by the very fact of their noninvestment in nation-building. Investment brings about development in the economy by extending not only its material capital but also its human capital through training and organization. To mobilize and educate the masses is to stimulate a counter elite critical of the regime in light of the education that the regime itself has provided. Rivals may debate the question of how much or how little income from would-be consumers, working harder under the commanding idea, should be channeled away in taxes to create capital. Investment in development, then, must be limited more or less by security costs in the form of propaganda and repression.

By propaganda is meant an information program designed to assure the masses that the past was worse than the future will be, and that present hardships will pay off under a leadership pictured as superhuman in its vision. The image projected is irrational, but the rational posting of statistics alone can do little to ratify a government that restricts political ideas to itself at the same time that it stimulates the public to show approval. The techniques of propaganda include the orchestration by the Communist party of activists for "revolutionary mass criticism" of particular officials and their aides. That this is carried out in the streets by factions within the Party does not lessen the factual existence of a political elite unambiguously defined by its power to mobilize organized groups in the name of the state (phrased in the name of the people).

By repression is meant that whole range of police activities aimed at surveillance and imprisonment, intimidation by mass trials and displays of force, and the prevention of rival ideas by controlling the communications media and forbidding public discussion. In China today, the Ministry of Public Security, with direct control over the People's Police at all levels, is incorporated under the command of the People's Liberation Army. One of the world's largest military forces, the PLA numbers over five percent of a population in which seven million reach the draft age of eighteen annually. Its mission is to implement domestic Party policies in addition to its military duties, not surprising in view of the fact that its predecessor, the Red Army, was coextensive with the Party until a few years before the Liberation of 1949. In the cities, one public security station is usually established for every ten streets. Its chief officer is assisted by one or more deputies, a security secretary, administrative staff, a force of plain clothesmen, and from seven to eighteen patrolmen on the beat. The dispersal of such stations is naturally much thinner in the less dense populations of the countryside. But common to all public security stations regardless of size or area is a section of the staff known as the "household office," whose task is to compile a dossier on the members of every household under its surveillance. For politically relevant persons, this includes detailed information on source of income, education, class category, family background for three generations, personal history from childhood, and number of relatives inside and outside China (*see* Whitaker and Shinn, 1972: sec. IV).

A concern for political liberty is a luxury only the developed countries can afford. One expression of this concern is Freedom House, a private organization in the United States that in its annual report ranks political rights and civil rights in all nations on a scale from one (free) to seven (totalitarian). In 1974 it again ranked Communist China in seventh place, together with Albania, Bulgaria, Burundi, Central African Republic, Cuba, Czechoslovakia, East Germany, Guinea, Iraq, North Korea, Libya, Mongolia, Syria, Uganda, North Vietnam, and Yemen.

The rise of liberalism in the West is clearly related to the emergence of individual differences and economic abundance out of a restrictive class society and low productivity per capita. When in this book we describe Chinese society as one in which individual freedom is circumscribed by placement in a class structure divided in the past between elite and majority, and now between mobilizers and mobilized, we do not make a value judgment but merely contrast China with the West. In an affluent society, civil rights defend the power of money to talk for everybody (even for those who claim their rights to more of it); but in a poor society, only politicians can talk. The high expenditures on the military and on the police and propaganda machine in China today amount to a defense economy. This is related, however, to the security problems of the ruling elite during a time of dangerous transition, while it is still necessary to supervise economic change under the conservative influence of cultural lag in a government defined as a monopoly of ideas. Indeed, productive work done by enemies of the regime in forced labor camps is an integral part of the state's plan of economic construction. But in time, we may expect efficient repression and extensive propaganda to recombine with enough economic development to create new elites committed to the regime in new ways.

APPENDIX

THE GREAT CHINESE MUSEUM OF 1849[*]

The most extensive and systematic ethnographic collection ever assembled in the formative or prescientific period of museum history in the United States was brought together by Caleb Cushing, the American lawyer, diplomat, and amateur ethnologist, during his mission to China in 1844, when with the Imperial Commissioner Keying (Ch'i-ying) he signed the Treaty of Wanghia. Sinologists have remarked that Article 18 of this treaty "emphasized for the first time, in the mutual relations of Westerners and Chinese, that they may have something to do with each other outside the boundaries of trade" (Danton, 1931:111).

In view of such an appraisal, it is more than a little surprising that virtually nothing is known of the advantage Cushing himself took of his own unique provision. Article 18 reads:

> *It shall be lawful for the officers or citizens of the United States to employ scholars and people of any part of China without distinction of persons, to teach any of the languages of the empire, and to assist in literary labors; and the persons so employed shall not, for that cause, be subject to any injury on the part of the government or of individuals; and it shall in like manner be lawful for citizens of the United States to purchase all manner of books on China.* (Miller, 1939:565)

That Cushing took advantage of this provision to purchase a large collection of books for the Library of Congress, providing it with the nucleus of its now extensive Oriental holdings, already has been brought to light by Arthur W. Hummel. But that Cushing also collected a vast number of ethnological specimens for a museum in New York, then the financial center of the China trade, has remained completely unknown both by local historians of New York City and by historians of early Sino-American culture contact.

The museum in New York no longer exists. But its contents and their

[*] A retitled reprint of Stover, 1971. For detailed notes, *see* Stover, 1961.

method of exhibition are recorded in a descriptive handbook sold on the museum premises, a few copies of which survive today (one of them in my own possession, together with other memorabilia of the times). The guidebook was written by the "principal" (or what we now call "curator") of the Chinese Museum, John R. Peters, Jr. Peters was one of Cushing's unpaid diplomatic attachés on the mission to China. It was Cushing, however, who financed and organized the museum project. Peters took charge of the museum while Cushing toured the Eastern Seaboard, delivering a series of public lectures on Chinese civilization.

Cushing intended to establish a permanent museum dedicated to educating the public about the country his diplomatic negotiations promised to bring closer to the United States in the years to follow. It is difficult to understand why such a meritorious, and scientifically sound, undertaking at the hands of one of the most exhaustively treated figures in American history should drop into oblivion for over a century.

For one thing, Cushing was too far ahead of his time in the field of museology. The museum, of whatever kind, was not then characteristically the object of public endowment that it is today, but instead was a business enterprise dependent on the entertainment market for support. When paying customers declined in volume, museum collections usually were broken up and sold piecemeal. Cushing's Chinese Museum lasted not five years before suffering a financial crisis.

The odd circumstances surrounding the sale of the Chinese Museum help to explain its historical oblivion. It was sold to none other than P. T. Barnum, the famous American showman and mountebank, yet there is nothing in the voluminous literature on Barnum to indicate this transaction. Newspapers of the day describe a bitter struggle between the museum staff and Barnum, during the early stages of which Barnum was worsted, and there is reason to believe he kept silent about the transaction in his autobiography on that account. That Cushing's official biographer, Claude M. Fuess, has nothing whatsoever to say about the Chinese Museum might be explained on the hypothesis that the papers and letters from which Fuess worked, and which now are deposited at Yale University, were screened beforehand by Cushing's family; they may have wished to suppress any reference to the museum out of embarrassment over its ignominious fate, falling as it did into the hands of such a charlatan as Barnum.

In any case, it is still possible to reconstruct in outline the career of the Chinese Museum before its demise, and more importantly, to evaluate its anthropological significance.

The museum specimens were collected in and around Canton sometime during the six-month stay of the American Embassy in Portuguese Macao, from February 24 until August 27 of 1844. Assistance was given by Cushing's joint Chinese secretaries, Dr. Peter Parker and the Rev. Elijah Bridgman, who already had been residing in China. These two men were unusually educated for Americans in knowledge of Chinese culture at that time. Bridgman, the first American to acquire a Chinese language, and the first one to carry the Christian mission to China, dating from 1830, served Cushing not only as his interpreter and bilingual scribe, as did Parker, but also as his close advisor in the negotiations with Keying. Parker was the first American missionary physician to China, dating from 1834. Both men were important to the success of Cushing's official mission as well as to the integrity of his personal museum project.

The Chinese Museum first opened in Boston on September 8, 1845, in the Marlboro' Chapel on Washington Street. The single admission price of fifty cents was rather high for those days. But the museum encouraged repeated visits and reflective study by selling seasonal tickets good for three months at only two dollars. The Chinese Museum survived in Boston as a commercially successful public attraction for almost two years, before moving to Philadelphia in 1847, and then on to New York in 1849.

The descriptive handbook was sold by the Chinese Museum at each of its three locations, printed locally from a single set of plates. Peters gave it the prolix title, *Miscellaneous Remarks upon the Government, History, Religions, Literature, Agriculture, Arts, Trade, Manners, and Customs of the Chinese, As Suggested by an Examination of the Articles Comprising the Chinese Museum*. In it he cites Medhurst, Davis, Barrow, Staunton, Timkowski, Kidd, Gutzlaff, and the *Chinese Repository*. The first American classic of sinology, *The Middle Kingdom*, by S. Wells Williams, did not appear until 1848. On the whole, Peters is freer of ethnocentrism than his sources, reflecting no doubt the wisdom of his mentor, Caleb Cushing.

This guidebook is far in advance of the patronizing string of anecdotes written by William Langdon under the title, *Ten Thousand Things Relating to China and the Chinese*, for Nathan Dunn's collection, which exhibited in Philadelphia from 1839 before its removal to England in 1842. When Cushing brought his museum to Philadelphia, critics did not fail to compare its authenticity to the Dunn collection, which they said was manufactured at least in part in Philadelphia itself. Even so, the collection put together by Nathan Dunn, an American merchant in the China trade, was regarded as such an important novelty in England that it was accorded a private viewing by Queen Victoria.

For its permanent headquarters in New York, the Chinese Museum was moved into a palatial mansion at 539-541 Broadway. Henceforth this edifice, formerly one of the most notable private homes in Manhattan, came to be known as the "Chinese Building," from the title so inscribed across its granite face. The upper stories were known as "The Chinese Assembly Rooms," which were leased by the museum to various civic and private groups as an extra means of earning self-support in addition to paid admissions. It would seem that Cushing had found a way to make his educational project pay for itself. In fact, the admission fee was reduced to twenty-five cents in New York, now that the museum had intended to settle down for an indefinite stay there.

The Chinese Museum opened in New York on January 1, 1849. By then it was billed as "The Great Chinese Museum." On that day, almost every newspaper in the city carried the following notice in its amusement columns:

THE GREAT CHINESE MUSEUM, Chinese Buildings, 539 Broadway now open. This large and splendid collection consists of upward of sixty figures of the full size of life, likenesses of individual Chinese, dressed in the costumes appropriate to the situation and employment in which they are represented, and shows the Costumes of the Chinese, from the Emperor, in his *court dress, to the beggar soliciting alms; with Barbers, Brokers, Carpenters, Blacksmiths, Shoemakers, Doctors, Husbandmen, Soldiers, Fortune-Tellers; each surrounded by the implements of his trade or profession. An exact representation of a Chinese Silk Store, with Merchant, Purchaser, Clerk, Coolie, &c. Two complete Chinese rooms, one showing Opium Smoking, and the other the "Inner Apartments" of a gentleman's residence. A court of Justice, the different sects of Priests. A real "Tanka Boat," with its crew, &c—with models of Temples, Stores, Summer Houses, Theatres, Bridges, Junks and Boats, specimens of manufacture of Cotton, Silk, Porcelain, Marble, Ivory, Silver and Wood. Upwards of 400 Paintings in oil and water colors, among which are portraits of the High Imperial Commissioner Keying and his assistant, Wang; of the Hong merchants, Hougua, Samgua and Linehong, and the great ship Comprador, Boston Jack. A view of Canton, seven feet by three, and of Honan, of the same size; representations of the growth and manufacture of Tea, Silk, Cotton and Porcelain; also of scenery throughout the empire, Processions, Furniture, Flowers, Boats, Fish, Shells, &c. From the upper part of the hall is suspended a great number of Lanterns of the most curious shape and description. Admittance 25 cents; children, under twelve years of age, half price.*

This advertisement hardly overstates the extent and diversity of the collection. A study of the handbook will show that perhaps only two ethnological collections from China now deposited in the United States can begin to match those of the Great Chinese Museum. The one is the Berthold Laufer collection, divided between the Field Museum of Natural History in Chicago and the American Museum of Natural History in New York. The other is the Chinese collection exhibited in Weld Hall of the Peabody Museum at Salem, Massachusetts. The number of different items in the Great Chinese Museum probably was greater than that in either of these—it occupied floor space measuring seventy-five by two hundred feet. And it was at least as extensive in scope as the Laufer collection, and certainly more so than the collection at Salem, which is weighted almost entirely in favor of elite products belonging to the old upper class in China.

The material culture of both the peasant and gentry sectors of traditional Chinese society was adequately represented in the Great Chinese Museum. It did not confine itself to objects d'art nor exclude the most common utensils of everyday life even among the rural population.

Everything was arranged with an intelligent sense of classification. An obvious example is the grouped display of mannequins dressed in the official costumes of both the civil and military mandarins for each of the seven ranks. More subtle is the grouping together of all specialized forms of blank paper, such as account books, invitation forms, stationery, children's copybooks, and theme paper used in the civil service examinations. This is set off from brushes, ink sticks, ink stones, and samples of calligraphy.

All of the tools, raw materials, and typical finished products belonging to a wide variety of craftsmen are represented. Chinese ethnobotany forms the basis for a series of displays, with exhaustive samples of the seeds of tillage, food plants, and medicinal herbs. Bamboo is given special attention for its uses in the making of paper and rope, as a textile in basketry and matting, in furniture making, coopery and joinery, and as a garden ornamental.

Agricultural technology is well represented by a series of life-sized figures portrayed at work ploughing with water buffalo, at threshing, winnowing and whitening rice, as well as by a large variety of other implements and machines, such as chainpump, fanning mill, wheelbarrow, rakes, hoes, and numerous types of containers.

A special exhibit devoted to the art of cartography is especially convincing evidence of thoroughness.

Unfortunately, financial difficulties caused the museum to close its doors by October of 1849. The museum staff then attempted to revive interest by sending to China for some native personnel. In April of 1850, a company of six Chinese arrived from Canton, led by an aristocratic lady named Pwan Ye-koo, who appears on circumstantial evidence to have been a close relative of Keying's chief advisor at Wanghia.

At this point, P. T. Barnum somehow managed to purchase the Great Chinese Museum so as to have the advantage of displaying Pwan Ye-koo to the public himself. His purchase included plates to the museum's guidebook. He struck the name of John R. Peters from the title page and rewrote its heading to read, echoing the more theatrical rendering of Langdon's earlier work, *Barnum's Chinese Museum: Ten Thousand Things on China and the Chinese.*

The Chinese entourage departed after two weeks. Barnum then dismantled the museum to make way for a menagerie show, which he advertised by pillaging the mandarin costumes for use in a publicity stunt.

Barnum was handed the opportunity to despoil the Great Chinese Museum because no public institution then existed in mid-nineteenth-century America for the deposition of ethnological specimens. The Library of Congress was equipped only to receive the books Cushing brought back from China.

It will be noted that Cushing is the contemporary of Lewis Henry Morgan, also a lawyer by profession and amateur ethnologist. If Morgan provided the foundations of scientific ethnology in America through his publications, Cushing must rank as his equal in marking the beginnings of scientific museology.

Arriving on the scene during the prescientific period of museum history in America, Cushing's achievement must be rated as the forerunner of modern ethnographic museology on the following counts:

1. The Chinese Museum was established for the purpose of stimulating reflective study, not merely of amusing with a show of curiosities.
2. In representing a complex civilization through the medium of its material culture, Cushing did not confine his attention to elite products, but collected from both the two main subcultures of Chinese society, peasantry and gentry alike.
3. Orderly principles of exhibition brought functionally related materials together in discrete units of display.
4. The museum published a guide to its collections, whose descriptive content is free of ethnocentric bias.

226

BIBLIOGRAPHY

Adie, W. A. C.
 1975.   China and the "detente": theory and practice. *Lugano Review* 1:10–16.
Aird, John S.
 1972.   Population policy and demographic prospects in the People's Republic of China. In *U.S. Congress,* 1972, q.v.:220–331.
Allen, G. C. and Audrey G. Donnithorne.
 1954.   *Western enterprise in Far Eastern economic development: China and Japan.* London: George Allen and Unwin.
Andelman, David A.
 1973.   U.S. and Chinese libraries trade books. *New York Times,* 21 August:1, 9.
Anderson, J. G.
 1943.   Researches into the prehistory of the Chinese. Stockholm: *Bulletin of the Museum of Far Eastern Antiquities* 15.
Arnold, Julean.
 1926.   China: a commercial and industrial handbook. *Department of Commerce, Trade Promotion Series* 38. Washington, D.C.: U.S. Government Printing Office.
Ashbrook, Arthur G.
 1972.   China: economic policy and economic results, 1949–71. In *U.S. Congress,* 1972, q.v.:3–51.
Backhouse, E., and J. O. P. Bland.
 1914.   *Annals and memoirs of the court of Peking.* London: William Heinemann.
Baker, John R.
 1974.   *Race.* New York: Oxford Univ. Press.
Baker, O. E.
 1928.   Agriculture and the future of China. *Foreign Affairs* 6, 3:483–97.
Baller, F. W.
 1907.   *The sacred edict, with a translation of the colloquial rendering,* 2nd ed. Shanghai: American Presbyterian Mission Press.
Balogh, Thomas.
 1967.   *The economics of poverty.* New York: Macmillan.
Banfield, Edward C.
 1958.   *The moral basis of a backward society.* New York: Free Press.

Barnett, A. Doak.
   1967.   *Cadres, bureaucracy, and political power in Communist China*. New York: Columbia Univ. Press.
   1974.   *Uncertain passage: China's transition to the post-Mao era*. Washington, D.C.: Brookings Institution.

Barrow, John.
   1805.   *Travels in China*. Philadelphia: W. F. M'Laughlin.

Bessac, Francis Bagnall.
   1963.   *Culture types of northern and wesern China*. Ann Arbor, Mich.: Univ. Microfilms.

Biggerstaff, Knight.
   1966.   Modernization and early modern China. *Journal of Asian Studies* 25, 4:607–19.

Biot, Édouard.
   1851.   *Le Tcheou-Li ou rites des Tcheou*, 2 vols. Paris: Duprat.

Bishop, Carl Whiting.
   1922.   Geographical factors in the development of Chinese civilization. *Geographical Review* 12:19–41.

Black, Davidson (ed.).
   1933.   Fossil man in China. *Memoirs of the Geological Society of China* 11, series A.

Bland, J. O. P.
   1912.   *Recent events and present policies in China*. London: William Heinemann.
   1932.   *China: the pity of it*. Garden City, N.Y.: Doubleday, Doran.

Bodde, Derk.
   1938.   *China's first unifier*. Leiden: E. J. Brill.
   1956.   Feudalism in China. In *Feudalism in history*. Rushton Coulborn (ed.). Princeton, N.J.: Princeton Univ. Press.
   1961.   Myths of ancient China. In *Mythologies of the ancient world*. Samuel Noah Kramer (ed.). Garden City, N.Y.: Doubleday Anchor.

Boeke, J. H.
   1953.   *Economics and economic policy of dual societies*. New York: Institute of Pacific Relations.

Braidwood, Robert J.
   1952.   *The Near East and the foundations for civilization*. Eugene, Ore.: State System of Higher Education.

Brinkley, Captain F.
   1902.   China: its history, arts and literature. *Oriental Series* 9–12. Boston: J. B. Millet.

Buchanan, Keith.
   1970.   *The transformation of the Chinese earth*. London: G. Bell.

Buck, John Lossing.
   1937.   *Land utilization in China*, 3 vols. Shanghai: Commercial Press.

Buck, Pearl S.
   1931.   *The good earth*. New York: John Day.
   1937.   *All men are brothers* (trans. of *Shui hu chuan*), 2 vols. New York: John Day. Reprinted 1957. New York: Grove Press.

Bullock, Alan.
   1962.   *Hitler, a study in tyranny*. Harmondsworth, England: Penguin.

Burgess, J. S.
   1933.   Chinese village life. *Social Forces* 11, 3:402–9.

Burki, Shahid Javed.
  1969. A study of Chinese communes, 1965. *Harvard East Asian Monographs* 29. Cambridge, Mass.: Harvard Univ. Press.

Carr, William K.
  1974. *Introducing metalinguistic instructional material into language and area studies programs: a syllabus for American-Chinese intercultural training: final report.* (Xerox.) Washington, D.C.: Office of Education, Division of International Education, U.S. Department of Health, Education and Welfare.

Chan Wing-tsit.
  1953. *Religious trends in modern China.* New York: Columbia Univ. Press.

Chang Chung-li.
  1955. *The Chinese gentry: studies on their role in nineteenth-century Chinese society.* Seattle: Univ. of Washington Press.
  1962. *The income of the Chinese gentry.* Seattle: Univ. of Washington Press.

Chang, Eileen.
  1956. *Naked earth.* Trans. by the author. Hong Kong: Union Press.

Chang Kwang-chih.
  1968. *The archaeology of ancient China,* 2nd ed. New Haven, Conn.: Yale Univ. Press.
  1970. The beginnings of agriculture in the Far East. *Antiquity* 44:175–85.
  1973. Chinese archaeology. In John T. Meskill (ed.), 1973, q.v.:379–415.

Chang Pei-kang.
  1949. *Agriculture and industrialization.* Cambridge, Mass.: Harvard Univ. Press.

Chao Buwei Yang.
  1947. *Autobiography of a Chinese woman.* New York: John Day.

Chapple, Eliot D., and Carleton S. Coon.
  1942. *Principles of anthropology.* New York: Henry Holt.

Ch'en Han-seng.
  1928. The burdens of the Chinese peasantry. *Pacific Affairs* 2, 10:644–58.
  1936. *Landlord and peasant in China.* New York: International Publishers.
  1939. *Industrial capital and Chinese peasants.* Shanghai: Kelly and Walsh.

Ch'en, Jerome.
  1972. *Yuan Shih-ka'i,* 2nd ed. Stanford, Calif.: Stanford Univ. Press.

Cheng Te-k'un.
  1959. Prehistoric China *Archaeology in China* 1. Cambridge, England: W. Heffer.
  1960. Shang China. *Archaeology in China* 2. Cambridge, England: W. Heffer.
  1963. Chou China. *Archaeology in China* 3. Cambridge, England: W. Heffer.
  1966. New light on prehistoric China. *Archaeology in China* (Supp. to 1). Cambridge, England: W. Heffer.
  1973. The beginning of Chinese civilization. *Antiquity* 47:197–209.

Chesneaux, Jean.
  1971. *Secret societies in China.* Ann Arbor, Mich.: Univ. of Michigan Press.
  1973. *Peasant revolts in China, 1840–1949.* New York: W. W. Norton.

Chi Ch'ao-ting.
  1936. *Key economic areas in Chinese history, as revealed in the development of public works for water control.* London: Allen and Unwin.

Chi, Hoang Van.
  1962. Collectivisation and rice production. *China Quarterly* 9:94–104.

Chow Yung-teh.
  1966. *Social mobility in China.* New York: Atherton Press.

Ch'u T'ung-tsu.

1961. *Law and society in traditional China.* The Hague: Mouton.

1962. *Local government in China under the Ch'ing.* Cambridge, Mass.: Harvard Univ. Press.

1972. *Han social structure.* Seattle: Univ. of Washington Press.

Coates, Austin.

1972. *China, India and the ruins of Washington.* New York: John Day.

Cohen, Arthur A.

1964. *The communism of Mao Tse-tung.* Chicago: Univ. of Chicago Press.

1967. Notes and views: discussion on the mind of a revolutionary, by Chou I-kua. *Problems of Communism* 16, 2:97–99.

Comte, Auguste.

1961. On the three states of social evolution. Orig. 1830–42. In *Theories and society,* vol. 2. Talcott Parsons et al. (eds.). New York: Free Press.

Coon, Carleton S.

1965. *The living races of man.* New York: Alfred A. Knopf.

1969. *The story of man,* 3rd ed. New York: Alfred A. Knopf.

Cooper, Gene.

1973. An interview with Chinese anthropologists. *Current Anthropology* 14, 4:480–81.

Cornaby, W. Arthur.

1895. *A string of Chinese peach-stones.* London: Charles H. Kelly.

Cottrell, Fred.

1955. *Energy and society: the relation between energy, social change, and economic development.* New York: McGraw-Hill.

Couling, Samuel.

1917. *The encyclopedia Sinica.* Shanghai: Kelly and Walsh.

Creel, Herrlee G.

1929. *Sinism: a study of the evolution of the Chinese world-view.* Chicago: Open Court.

1937. *The birth of China.* New York: Reynal and Hitchcock.

1949. *Confucius: the man and the myth.* New York: John Day.

1953. *Chinese thought from Confucius to Mao Tse-tung.* New York: New American Library.

1970. *The origins of statecraft in China,* vol. 1. Chicago: Univ. of Chicago Press.

Cressey, George B.

1930. The geographic regions of China. *The Annals of the American Academy of Political and Social Science* 152:1–9.

1934. *China's geographic foundations.* New York: McGraw-Hill.

Crook, Frederick W., and Linda A. Berstein.

1974. Agriculture in the United States and the People's Republic of China, 1967–71. *Foreign Agricultural Economic Report* 94, U.S. Department of Agriculture. Washington, D.C.: U.S. Government Printing Office.

Daniel, Glyn.

1963. *The idea of prehistory.* Cleveland and New York: World.

Danton, George H.

1931. *The culture contacts of the United States and China: the earliest Sino-American culture contacts, 1784–1844.* New York: Columbia Univ. Press.

1938. *The Chinese people.* Boston: Marshall Jones.

Davies, John Paton.

1972. *Dragon by the tail: American, British, Japanese, and Russian encounters with China and one another.* New York: W. W. Norton.

230   Davis, John Francis.

    1836. *The Chinese: a general description of the empire of China and its inhabitants*, 2 vols. New York: Harper and Brothers.

de Bary, William Theodore, Chang Wing-tsit, and Burton Watson.

    1960. *Sources of Chinese tradition.* New York: Columbia Univ. Press.

deGroot, J. J. M.

    1903–4. *Sectarianism and religious persecution in China*, 2 vols. Amsterdam: Johannes Muller. Reprinted 1970 in one vol. Taipei: Ch'eng Wen.

Diringer, David.

    1953. *The alphabet*, 2nd ed. New York: Philosophical Library.

Dittmer, C. G.

    1925. Density of population and the standards of living in north China. *Publications of the American Sociological Society* 19.

Dobson, W. A. C. H.

    1963. *Mencius.* Toronto: Univ. of Toronto Press.

Domes, Jürgen.

    1971. *The internal politics of China, 1949–1972.* New York: Praeger.

Donnithorne, Audrey.

    1967. *China's economic system.* New York: Praeger.

Drucker, Peter F.

    1967. Technology and society in the twentieth century. In *Technology and western civilization*, vol. 1. Melvin Kranzberg and Carroll W. Pursell, Jr. (eds.). New York: Oxford Univ. Press.

Durkheim, Emile.

    1960. *The elementary forms of the religious life.* Trans. from the original French of 1912 by Joseph W. Swain. New York: Collier.

Eberhard, Wolfram.

    1950. *A history of China.* London: Routledge and Kegan Paul.

    1956. Data on the structure of the Chinese city in the preindustrial period. *Economic Development and Cultural Change* 4, 3:253–68.

    1957. The political function of astronomy and astronomers in Han China. In *Chinese thought and institutions.* John K. Fairbank (ed.). Chicago: Univ. of Chicago Press.

    1965. *Conquerors and rulers: social forces in medieval China*, 2nd ed. Leiden: E. J. Brill.

    1966. Social mobility and stratification in China. In *Class, status, and power*, 2nd ed. Reinhard Bendix and Seymour Martin Lipset (eds.). New York: Free Press.

Eichhorn, Werner.

    1969. *Chinese civilization.* Trans. by Janet Seligman. New York and Washington, D.C.: Praeger.

Eisenstadt, S. N.

    1963. *The political systems of empires.* New York: Free Press.

Eliot, T. S.

    1930. The love song of J. Alfred Prufrock. *Collected poems.* New York: Harcourt, Brace.

Elisseeff, Vadime.

    1963. The middle empire, a distant empire without neighbors. *Diogenes* 42:44–59.

Elvin, Mark.

    1973. *The pattern of the Chinese past.* London: Eyre Methuen.

Etherton, P. T.

    1927. *The crisis in China.* Boston: Little, Brown.

Fairbank, John K.
   1966.   The people's middle kingdom. *Foreign Affairs* 44, 4:574–86.
   1971.   *The United States and China,* 3rd ed. Cambridge, Mass.: Harvard Univ.
            Press.

Fairbank, John K., Edwin O. Reischauer, and Albert M. Craig.
   1965.   East Asia, the modern transformation. *A history of East Asian civiliza-
            tion,* vol. 1. Boston: Houghton Mifflin.

Fairservice, Walter.
   1959.   The Origins of Oriental Civilization. New York: New American Library.

Falke, Rita.
   1958.   Problems of utopias. *Diogenes* 23:14–22.

Farnsworth, Clyde H.
   1975.   "Big rise in China oil output forseen." *New York Times,* 12 May.

Fei Hsiao-t'ung.
   1939.   *Peasant life in China.* London: Kegan Paul, Trench, Trubner.
   1944.   Some social problems of free China. In *Voices from unoccupied China.*
            Harley Farnsworth MacNair (ed.). Chicago: Univ. of Chicago Press.
   1946.   Peasantry and gentry: an interpretation of Chinese social structure and its
            changes. *American Journal of Sociology* 52, 1:1–17.
   1947.   Social erosion of Chinese villages. In *Ta Kung Pao,* cited by Shen, 1951,
            q.v.:128.
   1953.   *China's gentry: essays in rural-urban relations.* Chicago: Univ. of Chicago
            Press.

Fei Hsiao-t'ung, and Chang Chuh-i.
   1945.   *Earthbound China: a study of rural economy in Yunnan.* Chicago: Univ.
            of Chicago Press.

Feuerwerker, Albert.
   1968.   The Chinese economy, 1912–1949. *Michigan Papers on Chinese Studies*
            1. Ann Arbor, Mich.: Univ. of Michigan Center for Chinese Studies.
   1969.   The Chinese economy, ca. 1870–1911. *Michigan Papers on Chinese
            Studies* 5. Ann Arbor, Mich.: Univ. of Michigan Center for Chinese
            Studies.

Feuerwerker, Albert, Rhoads Murphey, and Mary C. Wright (eds.).
   1967.   *Approaches to modern Chinese history.* Berkeley and Los Angeles: Univ.
            of California Press.

Feuerwerker, Albert (ed.).
   1968.   *History in Communist China.* Cambridge, Mass.: M.I.T. Press.

Fitzgerald, C. P.
   1950.   *China, a short cultural history,* 2nd ed. London: Cresset Press.
   1968.   The Chinese middle ages in communist historiography. In Feuerwerker
            (ed.), 1968, q.v.: 124–39.
   1971.   China: an Asian model of revolutionary communism. In *The politics of
            new states.* Roger Scott (ed.). New York: Harper and Row.

Fleure, Herbert J.
   1937.   What is a peasantry? *Bulletin of the John Rylands Library* 21:387–405.

Folsom, Kenneth E.
   1968.   *Friends, guests, and colleagues: the* mu fu *system in the late Ch'ing
            period.* Berkeley and Los Angeles: Univ. of California Press.

Foreign Languages Press.
   1951.   *The agrarian reform law of the People's Republic of China.* Peking.
   1971.   *Red detachment of women.* A set of 16 picture postcards, with folder and
            descriptive blurb. Peking.

232

Foster, George M.
1953. What is a folk culture? *American Anthropologist* 55, 1:159–73.
1962. *Traditional cultures and the impact of technological change.* New York: Harper and Brothers.
1965. Peasant society and the image of limited good. *American Anthropologist* 67, 2:293–315.
1972. The anatomy of envy: a study in symbolic behavior. *Current Anthropology* 13, 2:165–202.

Freedman, Maurice.
1961–62. The family in China, past and present. *Pacific Affairs* 34, 4:323–36.
1970. Ritual aspects of Chinese kinship and marriage. In Freedman (ed.), 1970, q.v.:163–88.

Freedman, Maurice (ed.).
1970. *Family and kinship in Chinese society.* Stanford, Calif.: Stanford Univ. Press.

Fried, Morton H.
1952. Chinese society: class as subculture. *Transactions of the New York Academy of Sciences, Series II* 14, 8:331–36.
1953. *Fabric of Chinese society.* New York: Praeger.
1957. The classification of corporate unilineal descent groups. *Journal of the Royal Anthropological Institute* 87:1–29.
1966. Some political aspects of clanship in a modern Chinese city. In *Political anthropology.* Marc J. Swartz, Victor W. Turner, and Arthur Tuden (eds.). Chicago: Aldine.
1967. *The evolution of political society.* New York: Random House.
1973. China: anthropology. In John T. Meskill (ed.), 1973, q.v.:341–78.

Fung Yu-lan.
1952. *A history of Chinese philosophy,* vol. 1. Trans. by Derk Bodde. Princeton, N.J.: Princeton Univ. Press.

Gale, Esson M.
1931–34. Discourses on salt and iron: a debate on state control of commerce and industry in ancient China. Trans. from The Chinese of Huan K'uan. Leiden: E. J. Brill.

Galston, Arthur W., and Jean S. Savage.
1973. *Daily life in people's China.* New York: Crowell.

Gamst, Frederick C.
1974. Peasants in complex society. *Basic anthropology units.* New York: Holt, Rinehart and Winston.

Gardner, Brian.
1973. Perspective. *New Scientist,* October 18.

Geddes, W. R.
1963. Peasant life in Communist China. *Monographs of the Society for Applied Anthropology* 6.

Gernet, Jacques.
1968. *Ancient China: from the beginnings to the empire.* Berkeley and Los Angeles: Univ. of California Press.

Gibbon, Edward.
1963. *The decline and fall of the Roman empire.* Abridged by D. M. Low. Orig. 6 vols, 1776–88. Harmondsworth, England: Penguin.

Giles, Herbert A.
1911. *The civilization of China.* London: Williams and Norgate.
1925. *Strange stories from a Chinese studio.* New York: Boni and Liverright.

Giles, Lionel.
1961. *The sayings of Confucius.* Orig. 1907, London: John Murray. New York: Grove Press.

Goldschmidt, Walter.
  1959. *Man's way.* New York: Holt, Rinehart and Winston.

Goodnow, F. J.
  1927. *China: an analysis.* Baltimore, Md.: Johns Hopkins Press.

Goodrich, L. Carrington.
  1959. *A short history of the Chinese people,* 3rd ed. New York: Harper and Row.

Gouldner, Alvin W.
  1965. *Enter Plato: classical Greece and the origins of social theory.* New York: Basic Books.

Graham, David Crockett.
  1961. Folk religion in southwest China. *Smithsonian Miscellaneous Collections* 142, 2. Washington, D.C.: Smithsonian Institution.

Gray, Jack.
  1966. Some aspects of development of Chinese agrarian policies. In *Contemporary China.* Ruth Adams (ed.). New York: Vintage Books.
  1973. The two roads: alternative strategies of social change and economic growth in China. In *Authority, participation and cultural change in China.* Stuart R. Schram (ed.). Cambridge, England: Cambridge Univ. Press.

Hanwell, Norman.
  1937. The dragnet of local government in China. *Pacific Affairs* 10, 1:43–63.

Harrison, John A.
  1972. *The Chinese empire.* New York: Harcourt Brace Jovanovich.

Hatano, Yoshihiro.
  1968. The new armies. In *China in revolution: the first phase, 1900–1911.* Mary C. Wright (ed.). New Haven, Conn.: Yale Univ. Press.

Hauser, Ernest O.
  1940. *Shanghai: city for sale.* New York: Harcourt, Brace.

Hinton, Harold C.
  1956. The grain tribute system of China (1845–1911). *Harvard East Asian Monographs* 2. Cambridge, Mass.: Harvard Univ. Press.

Hirth, Friedrich.
  1908. *The ancient history of China.* New York: Columbia Univ. Press.

Ho Ping-ti.
  1959. *Studies on the population of China, 1368–1953.* Cambridge, Mass.: Harvard Univ. Press.
  1962. *The ladder of success in imperial China.* New York: Columbia Univ. Press.

Holden, Constance.
  1974. World population: U.N. on the move but grounds for optimism are scant. *Science* 183:833–36.

Hsiao Kung-chuan.
  1960. *Rural China: imperial control in the nineteenth century.* Seattle: Univ. of Washington Press.

Hsieh Pao-chao.
  1925. *The government of China (1644–1911).* Baltimore, Md.: Johns Hopkins Press.

Hsu Cho-yun.
  1965. *Ancient China in transition.* Stanford, Calif.: Stanford Univ. Press.

Hsu, Francis Lang-kwang.
  1943. The myth of Chinese family size. *American Journal of Sociology* 47, 5:555–62.
  1949. *Under the ancestors' shadow.* London: Routledge and Kegan Paul.

234

Hsu, Immanuel C. Y.
    1970. *The rise of modern China*. New York and London: Oxford Univ. Press.

Hsu Shin-yi.
    1967. *A multivariate approach to the analysis of the cultural-geographical factors of the Chinese folk religion*. Ann Arbor, Mich.: Univ. Microfilms.

Hsu-Balzer, Eileen, Richard J. Balzer, and Francis L. K. Hsu.
    1974. *China day by day*. New Haven, Conn.: Yale Univ. Press.

Hu Chang-tu et al.
    1960. *China: its people, its society, its culture*. New Haven, Conn.: Human Relations Area Files Press.

Hu Hsien-chin.
    1944. The Chinese concepts of face. *American Anthropologist* 46, 1:45–64.
    1948. The common descent group in China and its functions. *Viking Fund Publications in Anthropology* 10.

Huc, M.
    1855. *A journey through the Chinese empire*, 2 vols. New York: Harper and Brothers.

Hughes, E. R.
    1954. *Chinese philosophy in classical times*. London: J. M. Dent.

Human Relations Area Files.
    1956. *Subcontractor's monograph, China*, 10 vols. New Haven, Conn.

Huntington, Elsworth.
    1927. *The human habitat*. New York: D. Van Nostrand.

Ichiko, Chūzō.
    1968. The role of the gentry: an hypothesis. In *China in revolution: the first phase, 1900–1913*. Mary C. Wright (ed.). New Haven, Conn.: Yale Univ. Press.

Institute of Pacific Relations.
    1939. *Agrarian China: selected source materials from Chinese authors*. Comp. and trans. by the research staff of the Secretariat, Institute of Pacific Relations. Shanghai: Kelly and Walsh.

Ishida, Eiichirō.
    1964. Japan rediscovered. *Japan Quarterly* 11, 3:276–82.

Jacobs, Norman.
    1958. *The origin of modern capitalism and Eastern Asia*. Hong Kong: Hong Kong Univ. Press.
    1966. *Sociology of development: Iran as an Asian case study*. New York: Praeger.
    1971. *Modernization without development: Thailand as an Asian case study*. New York: Praeger.

Johnson, Chalmers A.
    1962. *Peasant nationalism and communist power*. Stanford, Calif.: Stanford Univ. Press.
    1973. *Autopsy on people's war*. Berkeley and Los Angeles: Univ. of California Press.

Johnson, E. A. J.
    1970. *The organization of space in developing countries*. Cambridge, Mass.: Harvard Univ. Press.

Johnston, R. F.
    1910. *Lion and dragon in northern China*. London: John Murray.

Kaizuka, Shigeki.
    1956. *Confucius*. Trans. by Geoffrey Bownas. London: George Allen and Unwin.

Kang Shin-pyo.   **235**
    1974.   The structural principle of the Chinese world view. In *The unconscious in culture: the structuralism of Claude Lévi-Strauss in perspective.* Ino Rossi (ed.). New York: Dutton.

Karlgren, Bernard.
    1946.   Legends and cults in ancient China. Stockholm: *Bulletin of the Museum of Far Eastern Antiquities* 18.

Kidd, Samuel.
    1841.   *China.* London: Taylor and Walton.

King, Evan.
    1955.   *Children of the black-haired people.* New York: Rinehart.

King, F. H.
    1911.   *Farmers of forty centuries.* Madison, Wis.: privately printed.

King, Frank H. H.
    1968.   *A concise economic history of modern China (1840–1961).* New York: Praeger.

Knight, Damon.
    1972.   The handler. Orig. 1960, reprinted in *Above the human landscape: an anthology of social science fiction.* Willis E. McNelly and Leon E. Stover (eds.). Pacific Palisades, Calif.: Goodyear.

Köbben, A. J. F.
    1974.   On former Chinese anthropologists. *Current Anthropology* 15, 3:315–16.

Kornhauser, William.
    1960.   *The politics of mass society.* London: Routledge and Kegan Paul.

Kroeber, A. L.
    1948.   *Anthropology.* New York: Harcourt, Brace.

Kuhn, Philip A.
    1970.   *Rebellion and its enemies in late imperial China.* Cambridge, Mass.: Harvard Univ. Press.

Kuo, Leslie T. C.
    1972.   *The technical transformation of agriculture in Communist China.* New York: Praeger.

Lamson, Herbert Day.
    1935.   *Social pathology in China.* Shanghai: Commercial Press.

Lasswell, Harold D.
    1936.   *Politics; who gets what, when, how.* New York: McGraw-Hill.

Latourette, Kenneth Scott.
    1926.   China. In *Encyclopedia Britannica,* 13th ed., new vol. 1:614–27.

Lattimore, Owen.
    1940.   Inner Asian frontiers of China. *American Geographic Society, Research Series* 21.

Legge, James.
    1960.   *The Chinese classics.* Copyright reissue in 5 vols. Orig. Oxford, 1893–95. Hong Kong: Hong Kong Univ. Press.
    1967.   *Li Chi: book of rites,* 2 vols. Orig. Oxford, 1885. New York: University Books.

Lehman, Frederic K.
    1959.   *Some anthropological parameters of a civilization: the ecology and evolution of India's high culture,* 2 vols. Ann Arbor, Mich.: Univ. Microfilms.

Lelyveld, Joseph.
    1974.   The great leap farmward. *The New York Times Magazine,* 28 July, 6, 56–63.

236 Lenski, Gerhard.
1966. *Power and privilege: a theory of social stratification.* New York: McGraw-Hill.

Lerner, Daniel.
1958. *The passing of traditional society.* Glencoe, Ill.: Free Press.
1963. Toward a communication theory of modernization. In *Communications and political development.* Lucian W. Pye (ed.). Princeton, N.J.: Princeton Univ. Press.
1964. Basic problems in the contemporary transformation of traditional societies. In *Approaches to Asian civilizations.* William Theodore de Bary and Ainslie T. Embree (eds.). New York: Columbia Univ. Press.

Levenson, Joseph R., and Franz Schurmann.
1969. *China: an interpretive history.* Berkeley and Los Angeles: Univ. of California Press.

Lévi-Strauss, Claude.
1953. Social structure. In *Anthropology today.* A. L. Kroeber (ed.). Chicago: Univ. of Chicago Press.

Lewis, John Wilson
1963. *Leadership in Communist China.* Ithaca, N.Y.: Cornell Univ. Press.

Lewis, John Wilson (ed.).
1970. *Party leadership and revolutionary power in China.* Cambridge, England: Cambridge Univ. Press.

Li Chi (ed.).
1956. Ch'eng-tzu-yai: the Black Pottery culture site at Lung-shan-chen in Li-ch'eng-hsien, Shantung province. *Yale Univ. Publications in Anthropology* 52.

Li Chi.
1957. *The beginnings of Chinese civilization.* Seattle: Univ. of Washington Press.

Li, Dun J.
1971. *The ageless Chinese: a history,* 2nd ed. New York: Scribner's.

Liao, W. K.
1959. *The complete works of Han Fei Tzu,* 2 vols. London: Arthur Probsthain.

Lindbeck, J. M. H.
1951. Communist policy and the Chinese family. *Far Eastern Survey* 20, 14:137–41.

Linebarger, Paul M. A.
1938. *Government in Republican China.* New York: McGraw-Hill.
1943. *The China of Chiang K'ai-shek.* Boston: World Peace Foundation.

Lindquist, Henry M.
1968. *North China villages: a comparative analysis of models in the published and unpublished writings of Arthur Henderson Smith, American missionary to China.* Ann Arbor, Mich.: Univ. Microfilms.

Liu, Alan P. L.
1971. *Communications and national integration in Communist China.* Berkeley and Los Angeles: Univ. of California Press.

Liu Shao-ch'i.
1968. *Quotations from President Liu.* Tokyo: John Weatherhill.

Liu, William.
1973. Chinese society: stratification, minorities, and the family. In Wu (ed.), 1973, q.v.:669–90.

Lockwood, William W.
1974. Asian triangle: China, India, Japan. *Foreign Affairs* 52, 4:818–38.

Loewe, Michael.
1965. *Imperial China.* New York: Praeger.

Loomis, Charles P., and J. Allan Beegle.
1950. *Rural social systems.* New York: Prentice-Hall.

MacIver, R. M.
1926. *The modern state.* London: Oxford Univ. Press.

McNeill, William H.
1963. *The rise of the West.* Chicago: Univ. of Chicago Press.

Makra, Mary Lelia.
1961. *The Hsiao Ching.* New York: St. John's Univ. Press.

Mao Tse-tung.
1965. *Selected works,* 4 vols. Peking: Foreign Languages Press.
1966. *Quotations from Chairman Mao.* Peking: Foreign Languages Press.

Marriott, McKim (ed.).
1955. *Village India.* Chicago: Univ. of Chicago Press.

Marsh, Robert M.
1961. *The mandarins: the circulation of elites in China.* Glencoe, Ill.: Free Press.

Maverick, Lewis.
1954. *Economic dialogues in ancient China: selections from the Kuan-tze.* Carbondale, Ill.: Southern Illinois Univ. Press.

Mayers, William F.
1897. *The Chinese government.* Shanghai: Kelly and Walsh.

Mead, Margaret.
1962. The underdeveloped and the overdeveloped. *Foreign Affairs* 41, 1:78–89.

Meskill, Johanna M.
1970. The Chinese genealogy as a research source. In Maurice Freedman (ed.), 1970, q.v.:139–62.

Meskill, John T.
1973. History of China. In John Meskill (ed.), 1973, q.v.:3–338.

Meskill, John T. (ed.).
1965. *The pattern of Chinese history: cycles, development, or stagnation?* Lexington, Mass.: D. C. Heath.
1973. *An introduction to Chinese civilization.* Lexington, Mass.: D. C. Heath.

Metzger, Thomas A.
1973. *The internal organization of Ch'ing bureaucracy.* Cambridge, Mass.: Harvard Univ. Press.

Michael, Franz H., and George E. Taylor.
1964. *The Far East in the modern world,* rev. ed. Seattle: Univ. of Washington Press.

Mill, John Stuart.
1901. *Principles of political economy,* 2 vols. From the 5th London ed. New York: D. Appleton.

Miller, Hunter (ed.).
1939. *Treaties and other international acts of the United States of America* 4. Washington, D.C.: U.S. Government Printing Office.

Moore, Barrington, Jr.
1966. *Social origins of dictatorship and democracy: lord and peasant in the making of the modern world.* Boston: Beacon Press.

Morse, Hosea Ballou.
1908. *The trade and administration of the Chinese empire.* London: Longmans, Green.
1910–18. *The international relations of the Chinese empire,* 3 vols. London: Longmans, Green.

238

Moseley, George.
    1966.   The party and the nation question in China. Cambridge, Mass.: M.I.T. Press.

Muramatsu, Yūji.
    1966.   A documentary study of Chinese landlordism in late Ch'ing and early Republican Kiangnan. *Bulletin of the School of Oriental and African Studies* 29, 3:566–99.

Murphey, Rhoads.
    1970.   The treaty ports and China's modernization: what went wrong? *Michigan Papers on Chinese Studies* 7. Ann Arbor, Mich.: Univ. of Michigan Center for Chinese Studies.

Myers, Ramon H.
    1970.   *The Chinese peasant economy.* Cambridge, Mass.: Harvard Univ. Press.
    1972.   Commercialization, agricultural development, and landlord behavior in Shantung province in the late Ch'ing. *Ch'ing-shih Wen-ti (Society for Ch'ing Studies)* 2, 8:31–55.

Needham, Joseph.
    1954.   *Science and civilization in China, vol. I: introductory orientations.* Cambridge, England: Cambridge Univ. Press.
    1956.   *Science and civilization in China, vol. II: history of scientific thought.* Cambridge, England: Cambridge Univ. Press.
    1971.   *Science and civilization in China, vol. IV, pt. 3: civil engineering and nautics.* Cambridge, England: Cambridge Univ. Press.

Newall, W. H.
    1957.   The sociology of ritual in early China. *Sociological Bulletin* 5, 6:1–13.

Newberry, John Strong.
    1934.   *The rainbow bridge.* Boston and New York: Houghton Mifflin.

New York Times.
    1954.   Stone-age "marimba" is discovered in Vietnam. 18 March, 3.

Nichols, Francis H.
    1902.   *Through hidden Shensi.* New York: Scribner's.

North, Robert C.
    1952.   *Kuomintang and Chinese communist elites.* Stanford, Calif.: Stanford Univ. Press.

Orleans, Leo A., and Richard P. Suttmeier.
    1970.   The Mao ethic and environmental quality. *Science* 170:1173–76.

Osgood, Cornelius.
    1963.   *Village life in old China.* New York: Ronald Press.

Pa Chin.
    1972.   *Family.* Introduction by Olga Lang. Orig. 1931. New York: Doubleday Anchor.

Parish, William L., Jr.
    1975.   Socialism and the Chinese family. *Journal of Asian Studies* 24, 3:613–630.

Parkinson, C. Northcote.
    1957.   *Parkinson's law and other studies in administration.* Boston: Houghton Mifflin.

Pearson, Richard.
    1973.   Radiocarbon dates from China. *Antiquity* 47:141–43.

Pelissier, Roger.
    1967.   *The awakening of China, 1793–1949.* New York: Capricorn.

Pelzel, John C.
    1972.   Economic management of a production brigade in post-Leap China. In *Economic organization in Chinese society.* W. E. Willmott (ed.). Stanford, Calif.: Stanford Univ. Press.

Perry, John Wein.
1966. *Lord of the four quarters: myths of the royal father.* New York: George Braziller.

Pfeiffer, John E.
1969. *The emergence of man.* New York: Harper and Row.

Phillips, Ralph, Roy G. Johnson, and Raymond T. Mayer.
1945. The livestock of China. *Far Eastern Series* 9, U.S. Department of State Publication no. 2249. Washington, D.C.: U.S. Government Printing Office.

Piggott, Stuart.
1974. Chariots in the Caucasus and in China. *Antiquity* 48:16–24.

Plumb, J. H.
1973. *The death of the past.* Harmondsworth, England: Penguin.

Potter, Jack M.
1968. *Capitalism and the Chinese peasant.* Berkeley and Los Angeles: Univ. of California Press.
1970. Land and lineage in traditional China. In Maurice Freedman (ed.), 1970, q.v.:121–38.

Potter, Jack M. et al.
1967. *Peasant Society: A Reader.* Boston: Little, Brown.

Price, Maurice T.
1946. Differentiating myth, legend, and history in ancient Chinese culture. *American Anthropologist* 48:31–42.

Pulleybank, Edwin G.
1954. China. In *Orientalism and history.* Denis Sinor (ed.). Cambridge, England: W. Heffer.
1966. Chinese and Indo-Europeans. *Journal of the Royal Asiatic Society* (April):9–39.

Pye, Lucian W.
1968. *The spirit of Chinese politics.* Cambridge, Mass.: M.I.T. Press.
1971. *Warlord politics.* New York: Praeger.

Rawski, Evelyn Sakakida.
1972. *Agricultural change and the peasant economy of south China.* Cambridge, Mass.: Harvard Univ. Press.

Redfield, Robert.
1947. The folk society. *American Journal of Sociology* 52:293–308.
1953. *The primitive world and transformations.* Ithaca, N.Y.: Cornell Univ. Press.
1955a. The social organization of tradition. *Far Eastern Quarterly* 15:13–21.
1955b. *The little community.* Chicago: Univ. of Chicago Press.
1956. *Peasant society and culture.* Chicago: Univ. of Chicago Press.

Redfield, Robert, and Milton B. Singer.
1954. The cultural role of cities. *Economic Development and Cultural Change* 3:53–73.

Reinsch, Paul S.
1922. *An American diplomat in China.* Garden City, N.Y.: Doubleday.

Riggs, Fred W. (ed.).
1970. *Frontiers of development administration.* Durham, N.C.: Duke Univ. Press.

Rockhill, W. W.
1905. *Diplomatic audiences at the court of China.* London: Luzoc.

Ross, E. A.
1911. *The changing Chinese.* London: Unwin.

240 Rozman, Gilbert.
  1973. *Urban networks in Ch'ing China and Tokugawa Japan.* Princeton, N.J.: Princeton Univ. Press.
Rudd, Herbert F.
  1928. *Chinese social origins.* Chicago: Univ. of Chicago Press.
Rudofsky, Bernard.
  1964. *Architecture without architects.* New York: Doubleday.
Sauer, Carl O.
  1969. *Agricultural origins and dispersals,* 2nd ed. Cambridge, Mass.: M.I.T. Press.
Scalapino, Robert A. (ed.).
  1972. *Elites in the People's Republic of China.* Seattle: Univ. of Washington Press.
Schram, Stuart R.
  1963. *The political thought of Mao Tse-tung.* New York: Praeger.
Schram, Stuart R. (ed.).
  1967. *Quotations from Chairman Mao Tse-tung.* New York: Bantam.
Schurmann, Franz.
  1968. *Ideology and organization in Communist China,* 2nd ed. Berkeley and Los Angeles: Univ. of California Press.
Schwartz, Benjamin I.
  1973. A personal view of some thoughts of Mao Tse-tung. In *Ideology and politics in contemporary China.* Chalmers Johnson (ed.). Seattle: Univ. of Washington Press.
Shabad, Theodore.
  1972. *China's changing map,* rev. ed. New York: Praeger.
Shapiro, H. L., with Frederick Hulse.
  1939. *Migration and environment.* New York: Oxford Univ. Press.
Sharman, Lyon.
  1968. *Sun Yat-sen, his life and meaning.* Orig. 1934, New York: John Day. Stanford, Calif.: Stanford Univ. Press.
Shen, T. H.
  1951. *Agricultural resources of China.* Ithaca, N.Y.: Cornell Univ. Press.
Shirokogoroff, S. M.
  1939–40. Review of Fei, 1939. *Monumenta Serica* 4:377–78.
Shryock, John K.
  1932. *The origins and development of the state cult of Confucius.* New York: Appleton-Century. Reprinted 1966. New York: Paragon.
Skinner, G. William.
  1964–65. Marketing and social structure in rural China. *Journal of Asian Studies* 24, 1:3–43; 24, 2:195–228; 24, 3:363–99.
  1971. Chinese peasants and the closed community: an open and shut case. *Comparative Studies in Society and History* 13, 3:270–81.
Smith, Arthur H.
  1894. *Chinese characteristics.* New York: Fleming H. Revell.
  1899. *Village life in China.* New York: Fleming H. Revell.
  1914. *Proverbs and common sayings from the Chinese,* rev. ed. Shanghai: American Presbyterian Mission Press. Reprinted 1965. New York: Dover.
Smith, D. Howard.
  1973. *Confucius.* London: Temple Smith.
Solomon, Richard H.
  1969. On activism and activists: Maoist conceptions of motivation and political role linking state to society. *China Quarterly* 39:76–114.
  1971. *Mao's revolution and the Chinese political culture.* Berkeley and Los Angeles: Univ. of California Press.

Soothill, W. E.
1952. *The hall of light: a study of early Chinese kingship.* New York: Philosophical Library.

Spencer, J. E., and William L. Thomas.
1971. *Asia, east by south: a cultural geography.* New York: John Wiley.

Spencer, Paul A. V.
1957. Impressions of Chinese agriculture. *Royal Central Asian Journal* 44, 1:17–27.

Spraque, G. F.
1975. Agriculture in China. *Science* 188:549–555.

Steele, John.
1917. *The I Li, or book of etiquette and ceremonial.* London: Probsthain. Reprinted 1966. Taipei: Ch'eng-wen.

Steinhart, John S., and Carol E. Steinhart.
1974. Energy use in the U.S. food system. *Science* 184.

Steward, Julian H.
1950. Area research: theory and practice. *Social Science Research Council, Bulletin 63.*
1955. *Theory of culture change.* Urbana, Ill.: Univ. of Illinois Press.

Steward, Julian H. et al.
1955. The irrigation civilizations: a comparative study. *Pan American Union, Social Sciences Monographs* 1.

Stover, Leon E.
1961. Cushing's mission and the Great Chinese Museum of New York City, 1849. Paper read before the 13th Association for Asian Studies, Chicago. Ms. with photographs and 12 p. of notes.
1962. *"Face" and verbal analogs of interaction in Chinese culture: a theory of formalized social behavior based upon participant-observation of an upper-class Chinese household, together with a biography of the primary informant.* Ann Arbor, Mich.: Univ. Microfilms.
1971. An early ethnographic museum from mid-nineteenth-century America: forerunner of modern collection and exhibition techniques. Moscow: [*Proceedings*], VII Congrès International des Sciences Anthropologiques et Ethnologiques 11:653–57.
1974a. *The cultural ecology of Chinese civilization: peasants and elites in the last of the agrarian states.* New York: Pica Press.
1974b. China—last of the agrarian states. *Technology and Human Affairs* 6, 1:10–13.

Sulzberger, C. L.
1974. *The coldest war: Russia's game in China.* New York: Harcourt Brace Jovanovich.

Sumner, William Graham.
1960. *Folkways.* Orig. 1934. New York: Mentor.

Sun, E-tu Zen.
1961. *Ch'ing administrative terms: a translation of the terminology of the Six Boards with explanatory notes.* Cambridge, Mass.: Harvard Univ. Press.

Taeuber, Irene B.
1970. The families of Chinese farmers. In Freedman (ed.), 1970, q.v.:63–86.

T'ang Leang-li.
1928. *The foundations of modern China.* London: Noel Douglass.
1935. *Reconstruction in China.* Shanghai: Chinese United Press.

Tawney, R. H.
1932. *Land and labour in China.* London: George Allen and Unwin.

242   Tcheng Ki-tong (Ch'en Chi-t'ung).
       [1885.] *The Chinese painted by themselves*. Trans. from the French by James
              Millington. London: Field and Tuer, Leadenhall Press.
     Teilhard de Chardin, P.
       1941. *Early man in China*. Peiping: Institut de Géo-Biologie.
     Teng Ssu-yu, and John K. Fairbank et al.
       1954. *China's response to the west: a documentary survey, 1839–1923*.
              Cambridge, Mass.: Harvard Univ. Press.
     Thomas, William L., Jr. (ed.).
       1956. *Man's role in changing the face of the earth*. Chicago: Univ. of Chicago
              Press.
     Tjan Tjoe Som.
       1949–52.. *Po Hu T'ung: the comprehensive discussions in the White Tiger Hall*,
              2 vols. Leiden: E. J. Brill.
     Tregear, T. R.
       1965. *A geography of China*. Chicago: Aldine.
       1973. *The Chinese: how they live and work*. Newton Abbott, England: David
              and Charles.
     Trewartha, Glenn T.
       1957. New maps of China's population. *The Geographical Review* 47, 2:234–39.
     Tylor, Edward B.
       1874. *Primitive culture*, 2 vols. London: John Murray.
     Ullmann, Morris B.
       1961. *Cities of mainland China: 1953 and 1958*. U.S. Department of Com-
              merce, Bureau of the Census. Washington, D.C.: U.S. Government Print-
              ing Office.
     United Nations.
       1951. *Land reform: defects in agrarian structure as obstacles to economic de-
              velopment*. New York: United Nations, Department of Economic Affairs.
     U.S. Central Intelligence Agency.
       1971. *People's Republic of China: atlas*. Washington, D.C.: U.S. Government
              Printing Office.
     U.S. Congress.
       1972. *People's Republic of China: an economic assessment*. A compendium of
              papers submitted to the Joint Economic Committee. Washington, D.C.:
              U.S. Government Printing Office.
     U.S. Department of Agriculture.
       1945. *Report of the China-United States agricultural mission, report no. 2*.
              Washington, D.C.: Office of Foreign Agricultural Relations.
     U.S. Department of State.
       1948. *Foreign relations of the United States, 1948, vol. 7, the Far East: China*.
              Washington, D.C.: U.S. Government Printing Office.
     van der Sprenkel, Sybille.
       1962. *Legal Institutions in Manchu China*. London: Athlone Press.
     van der Valk, M. H.
       1956. *Conservatism in modern Chinese family law*. Leiden: E. J. Brill.
     Vogel, Ezra F.
       1965. From friendship to comradeship: the change in personal relations in
              Communist China. *China Quarterly* 21:46–60.
       1970. Politicized bureaucracy: Communist China. In Fred W. Riggs (ed.), 1970,
              q.v.: 556–68.
     Wakeman, Frederic.
       1966. *Strangers at the gate: social disorders in south China, 1839–1861*.
              Berkeley and Los Angeles: Univ. of California Press.

Waley, Arthur.
  1934. *The way and its power: a study of the* Tao Te Ching *and its place in Chinese thought.* London: George Allen and Unwin.
  1938. *The analects of Confucius.* London: George Allen and Unwin.
  1939. *Three ways of thought in ancient China.* London: George Allen and Unwin.
  1958. *The Opium War through Chinese eyes.* New York: Macmillan.
  1960. *The book of songs.* New York: Grove Press.

Walker, Richard L.
  1955. *China under communism: the first five years.* New Haven, Conn.: Yale Univ. Press.
  1971. *The human cost of communism in China.* U.S. Congress, Committee on the Judiciary. Washington, D.C.: U.S. Government Printing Office.

Wang Gungwu.
  1963. *The structure of power in north China during the five dynasties.* Kuala Lumpur: Univ. of Malaya Press.

Wang Yeh-chien.
  1973. *Land taxation in imperial China, 1750–1911.* Cambridge, Mass.: Harvard Univ. Press.

Ware, James R.
  1955. *The sayings of Confucius.* New York: Mentor.

Watson, Burton.
  1961. *Records of the grand historian of China, translated from the* Shih-chi *of Ssu-ma Ch'ien,* 2 vols. New York: Columbia Univ. Press.
  1962. *Early Chinese literature.* New York: Columbia Univ. Press.
  1963. *Hsun Tzu: basic writings.* New York: Columbia Univ. Press.

Watson, William.
  1966. *Early civilization in China.* New York: McGraw-Hill.
  1971. *Cultural Frontiers in Ancient East Asia.* Edinburgh: Univ. of Edinburgh Press.

Weber, Max.
  1951. *The religion of China.* Trans. and ed. by Hans H. Gerth. Orig. 1922. New York: Free Press.

Weidenreich, Franz.
  1939. Six lectures on *Sinanthropus pekinensis* and related problems. *Bulletin of the Geological Society of China* 19, 1.

Weiss, Thomas J.
  1973. The ruling elite. In Wu (ed.), 1973, q.v.:241–59.

Werner, E. T. C.
  1919. *China of the Chinese.* New York: Scribner's.
  1941. *The origin of the Chinese priesthood.* Shanghai: Shanghai Times.

Wheatley, Paul.
  1971. *The pivot of the four quarters: a preliminary inquiry into the origins and character of the ancient Chinese city.* Chicago: Aldine.

Whitaker, Donald P., and Rinn-Sup Shinn et al.
  1972. *Area handbook for the People's Republic of China.* Washington, D.C.: U.S. Government Printing Office.

Whitney, Joseph B.
  1970. *China: area, administration, and nation-building.* Chicago: Department of Geography, Univ. of Chicago.

Whyte, Martin King.
  1974. *Small groups and political rituals in China.* Berkeley and Los Angeles: Univ. of California Press.

Wilbur, C. Martin.
  1943. *Slavery in China during the Former Han dynasty, 206 B.C.–A.D. 25.* Chicago: Field Museum of Natural History.

Wilhelm, Richard.
  1967. *The I Ching or book of changes,* 3rd ed. The German translation rendered into English by Cary F. Baynes. Princeton, N.J.: Princeton Univ. Press.

Williams, Edward Thomas.
  1932. *China yesterday and today,* 5th ed. New York: Thomas Y. Crowell.

Williams, S. Wells.
  1895. *The middle kingdom,* 2 vols. New York: Scribner's.

Winick, Charles.
  1958. *Dictionary of anthropology.* Ames, Iowa: Littlefield, Adams.

Wittfogel, Karl A.
  1956. The hydraulic civilizations. In Thomas (ed.), 1956, q.v.:152–64.
  1957. *Oriental despotism: a comparative study of total power.* New Haven, Conn.: Yale Univ. Press.

Wolf, Eric.
  1955. Types of Latin American peasantry. *American Anthropologist* 57, 3:452–71.
  1966. *Peasants.* Englewood Cliffs, N.J.: Prentice-Hall.
  1969. *Peasant wars of the twentieth century.* New York: Harper and Row.

Wong, John.
  1973. *Land reform in the People's Republic of China.* New York: Praeger.

Woo Ju-kang.
  1965. Preliminary report on a skull of *Sinanthropus-lantianensis* of Lantian, Shensi. *Scientia Sinica* 14, 7:1032–35.

Wren, Christopher S.
  1974. Soviet says China profits on drugs. *New York Times,* 18 November:15.

Wright, Arthur F.
  1963. On the uses of generalization in the study of Chinese history. In *Generalization in the writing of history.* Louis Gottschalk, (ed.). Chicago: Univ. of Chicago Press.

Wright, Arthur F. (ed.).
  1953. *Studies in Chinese thought.* Chicago: Univ. of Chicago Press.

Wu Kuo-cheng.
  1928. *Ancient Chinese political theories.* Shanghai: Commercial Press.

Wu Yuan-li.
  1967. *The spatial economy of Communist China.* New York: Praeger.

Wu Yuan-li (ed.).
  1973. *China: a handbook.* New York: Praeger.

Yang Ching-kun.
  1959a. *A Chinese village in early Communist transition.* Cambridge, Mass.: M.I.T. Press.
  1959b. *The Chinese family in the Communist revolution.* Cambridge, Mass.: M.I.T. Press.

Yang, Martin C.
  1945. *A Chinese village: Taitou, Shantung Province.* New York: Columbia University Press.

Young, Arthur W.
  1971. *China's nation-building effort, 1927–1937.* Stanford, Calif.: Stanford Univ. Press.